58-9

THE CALIFORNIA-MEXICO CONNECTION

This book is due on the last date stamped below.
Failure to return books on the date due may result in assessment of overdue fees.

DEC 0 9 REC'D
MAY 1 8 2006
MAY 1 6 REC'D

FINES .50 per day

AMERICAN RIVER COLLEGE
3 3204 01410009 R

AMERICAN RIVER COLLEGE LIBRARY
4700 College Oak Drive
Sacramento, California 95841

Contributors

HAROLD BRACKMAN
KATRINA BURGESS
JORGE G. CASTAÑEDA
DENISE DRESSER
STEVEN P. ERIE
AGUSTÍN ESCOBAR LATAPÍ
CARLOS GONZÁLEZ GUTIÉRREZ
DAVID E. HAYES-BAUTISTA
ABRAHAM F. LOWENTHAL
CARLOS RICO
JAMES N. ROSENAU
RICHARD ROTHSTEIN
LUIS RUBIO
GABRIEL SZÉKELY
FERNANDO TORRES-GIL
GUILLERMO TREJO
GEORGES VERNEZ

THE CALIFORNIA-MEXICO CONNECTION

EDITED BY ABRAHAM F. LOWENTHAL
AND KATRINA BURGESS

STANFORD UNIVERSITY PRESS
Stanford, California 1993

Stanford University Press, Stanford, California
© 1993 by the Board of Trustees of the
Leland Stanford Junior University
Printed in the United States of America

CIP data appear at the end of the book

Preface

THE WESTERN HEMISPHERE has long been sharply divided, at the Rio Grande, between North and South. Politically, economically, demographically, and culturally, Latin America and North America have been worlds apart, despite their geographic proximity. Fundamental differences have been obvious in language, religion, values, mores, and institutions. Latin America has looked, smelled, and sounded very different from Anglo America. Pan-American organizations and rhetoric have never bridged the gap.

Five hundred years after Christopher Columbus first brought the New World to Europe's attention, however, the line between North America and Latin America is eroding. A vast Latin American diaspora now lives on the mainland of the United States. Mexicans, Cubans, Salvadorans, Nicaraguans, Hondurans, Dominicans, Haitians, Puerto Ricans, Colombians, Peruvians, Ecuadorians, Brazilians, and others have been streaming into this country. They come no longer in isolated or temporary waves but in a sustained and growing flow. Some 10 percent of the total U.S. population are now Latin American immigrants and their descendants. The Latino population is the fastest growing group in the United States.

The most pervasive amalgam between the United States and Latin America is occurring in southern California. In California's "southland," it is not only that Mexicans and Central Americans have been immigrating in very large numbers; it is also that the production and marketing of goods is becoming ever more integrated. The barriers to the movement of people, goods, and money across the Mexico-California border are fast disappearing. Not since the early nineteenth century, when California was still part of Mexico itself, have there been such close ties between Mexico and its former northern territory. For many practical purposes, indeed, the frontier has become something of an abstraction.

To put it another way, the border between Mexico and the United States is becoming blurred. Millions of persons from southern California and northern Mexico engage each day in an intricate web of mundane transactions, most of them legal but some not, in which the border is much less significant than shared aims and interaction. What Stanford economist Clark Reynolds some years ago perspicaciously called the "silent integration" of Mexico and the United States has become progressively louder, especially in southern California.

California's Mexico connection has intensified remarkably during the past twenty years. One Californian in five today is of Mexican heritage, compared with fewer than one in ten in 1970. Latinos, mostly of Mexican origin, are expected to be about 30 percent of California's population by the end of the decade; already they make up 38 percent of the residents in Los Angeles County. Half of the babies born in Los Angeles County during the 1980s were Latinos, 80 percent of them Mexican or Mexican-American. Latinos accounted for nearly half of California's population growth during the 1980s, both through continuing immigration and through high rates of fertility.

Mexican and Central American migration to California, legal and illegal, continues apace. More than half the detentions of undocumented migrants entering the United States during the 1980s occurred at the San Diego–Tijuana border, and the number of detentions there has been rising since 1986. Authorized border crossings at that same spot doubled during the late 1980s, reaching 60 million per year entering the United States. And the migration of Mexicans to California has been changing in character, as Mexicans become settlers, ending the long-time illusion of impermanence. Of the 1.25 million undocumented Mexican immigrants whose status in the United States was regularized under the provisions of the Immigration Reform and Control Act of 1986 (IRCA), fully 43 percent reside in California, as do 53 percent of the more than one million "special agriculture workers" whose status was also protected by IRCA's provisions. Migration patterns in Mexico have changed, as increasing numbers of Mexicans think that living in California is an option.

Trade between California and Mexico has exploded since the mid-1980s, increasing by some 60 percent in value from 1988 to 1991, from $6 billion to more than $10 billion. Mexico is California's second largest foreign market (after Japan), and it is likewise the source of ever larger and more diverse numbers of imports, both agricultural and manufactured.

Mexico's *maquiladora* (assembly) industries near the border, many of them established with U.S. capital and tied into the production and distribution chains of U.S. firms, employ hundreds of thousands of workers, who consume on both sides of the frontier in a functionally integrated border economy. What used to be primarily a trading link between the economies of Mexico and California has increasingly become a production relationship because manufacturing takes place through intrafirm integration across the political frontier.

Financial ties between Mexico and California are equally strong, though more difficult to document. In addition to investing billions of dollars in the *maquiladora* sector, Californian and other firms are increasingly attracted to Mexico by its growth prospects and by its changing attitudes and regulations on foreign investment. An estimated $3 billion per year is remitted to Mexico, moreover, by workers in the United States; as much as $2 billion of that may come from Mexicans in California.

Although the flow of funds and goods is asymmetric, it is not all in one direction. Many billions of dollars of Mexican flight capital have been invested in California banks, real estate, and industries. Mexican beer and cement are winning increasing favor in California, as are Mexican fruits and vegetables. Mexican-produced television programs are being used by Spanish-language stations, and Mexican firms have been entering the U.S. print and electronic media aimed at Latino markets.

Mexico has been opening its economy to the outside world and integrating more fully into world markets, in which California firms are vital. California's economy has likewise been looking outward and has become more dependent on foreign trade, including that with Mexico.

California's growing Mexico connection shapes the state's life in many realms: from culture to cuisine, schools to board rooms, workplace to voting booths. Education is one sector of particularly high impact. Sixty-three percent of the students in the public schools of the Los Angeles Unified District—and 67 percent of those in elementary schools—are of Latin American (mostly Mexican) descent; more than half of them are from Spanish-speaking homes. Two of the central issues facing southern California's public schools—overcrowded facilities and the complexities of bilingual education—result directly from Mexican immigration.

The health delivery and broader social service systems of southern California are also strongly affected by Mexican and other Latin American immigrants. Contrary to broad popular perceptions, Mexican immigrants are by and large healthy, with low incidence of most communicable diseases, low rates of infant mortality or inadequate birthweight, few drug-affected infants, good hygienic habits, stable family structures, and a strong work ethic. But Latino immigrants, young and often economically disadvantaged, do impose special needs on California's public health system: for prenatal and maternal programs, the enforcement of sanitary regulations, mass immunization, and—in the second and third generations—for substance abuse counseling and related drug syndrome programs. Failure to address these special needs would badly damage California's general health and productivity.

Yet there is a profound gap between the needs of Latino immigrants and the services for which the older and politically more enfranchised Anglo population is willing to pay. The obstacles to health care and other essential services for Latino immigrants are exacerbated by regulations that withhold services from the undocumented, and by prejudice and discrimination.

Southern California's politics have not thus far been as substantially affected by Mexico, largely because Mexican immigrants have been slow to naturalize and slower yet to register, vote, and pursue group interests through politics. Despite the huge Latino population of southern California, fewer than 7 percent of voters in California's primary elections in 1990 were of Latino heritage. Whereas about two-thirds of European immigrants to the United States during the 1980s have become or are in the process of becoming U.S. citizens, only one-fifth of recent Latino immigrants have yet taken these steps. Even those Latinos who do become U.S. citizens have so far had little direct impact on public policy, mainly because they are residentially dispersed or victims of gerrymandering calculated to dilute their votes, but also because they lack strong interest groups.

But this, too, is beginning to change. Latino voter registration in California increased by about 25 percent during the second half of the 1980s, and implementation of the IRCA makes it more likely that the large and stable Latino noncitizen population will now move toward citizenship. Efforts by the Mexican American Legal Defense Fund (MALDEF) and other civic organizations, reinforced by partisan competition, are redrawing the electoral map of California, with the likely consequence of expanding Mexican-American and other Latino voting and political influence. In 1992 there were two Mexican-Americans on the Los Angeles City Council, one each on the school board and the powerful five-person County Board of Supervisors, four Latinos in the California legislature, and three Latino members of California's congressional delegation—representations almost twice as great as ten years ago. By the end of the decade, it would not be surprising if multiethnic and multiracial coalition building in southern California led to a Mexican-American mayor in Los Angeles, a Mexican-American majority on the Los Angeles City Council, ten to fifteen Latinos in the California legislature, and twice as many visible Latino leaders as at present. Such Latino empowerment should reshape public policy, not only on education and health questions but on family and child-oriented social policies and a whole range of other questions arising from Mexico's proximity to California.

The merging of southern California and northern Mexico is also beginning to affect the politics of Mexico itself. Since the late 1980s, California has increasingly become a major battleground of Mexican political competition. Opposition parties and the Mexican governing party have all recognized that California's Mexican-origin population is important as a source of support, funding, and legitimacy, and that the Mexican population in California can substantially affect politics south of the border.

Interest groups, parties, and governments in both Mexico and the United States, in short, are increasingly able to mobilize and affect people whose interests and ties are not defined by the national border. Fascinating issues of rights and representation are being raised. Some groups are calling for Mexicans in the United States to gain the right to vote in Mexico's elections through absentee ballots, while others campaign to give all Latin American immigrants, regardless of citizenship, the right to vote in California's school board and other local elections. Transnational alliances among workers, investors, environmentalists, human rights advocates, and others all contribute to a tangle of overlapping interests and incomplete sovereignties that is captured in the phrase we have coined, the "California-Mexico Connection."

This book is the first in any language to explore and begin to map the California-Mexico Connection. Despite the myriad ways in which California is affected by Mexico, no systematic effort has ever been made to examine the Connection's nature and scope, or to assess its main effects. By bringing together qualified experts on Mexico, California, and the issue areas where they intersect, we have tried not only to describe and analyze California's Mexico Connection but to consider how Mexicans and Californians can help assure that the Connection's effects are more consistently and mutually positive. All the essays in this book are original contributions, prepared especially for this volume, and discussed among the authors at a planning workshop and a conference held at the University of Southern California in April 1991.

The book is organized in four parts and two appendixes. In Part I, a conceptual introduction by James N. Rosenau situates the California-Mexico Connection in comparative and theoretical terms, and shows why and how interesting and innovative questions are posed by the interconnections this book explores. Jorge G. Castañeda then provides an overview comment from the Mexican perspective on the mutual impact of California and Mexico, full of surprises and unintended—even unperceived—consequences. Part II outlines demographic, economic, political, and social changes in Mexico and how they are affecting California. Part III focuses more sharply on Mexico's presence within California and its impact upon the economy, society, education, health, labor, and politics. Part IV analyzes what can be done—by Mexicans and by Californians—to strengthen the positive effects of the California-Mexico Connection. The appendixes, prepared by Dan Himelstein and Ignacio García Lascuraín, present in visual form salient data on Mexico and California.

A symposium volume always takes much more work than its editors anticipate, but in this case we were fortunate to have such good support and colleagueship as to make most of the chores seem pleasant. We express great appreciation to our fellow contributors to this volume; to others who participated in the project's workshops and conference, including Stephen Levy, Cathryn Thorup, Douglas Chalmers, Wayne Cornelius, David Ronfeldt, Geoffrey Bogart, Leo Estrada, Paul Ganster, Kevin Starr, Marilyn Snell, and David Rieff; to Muriel Bell and Ellen F. Smith of Stanford University Press; and to Dan Himelstein, Ignacio García Lascuraín, David Ayón, Clarissa Martínez de Castro, and Cristina Gallop of USC's California-Mexico project staff. Most of all, we thank the officers and trustees of the John Randolph Haynes and Dora Haynes Foundation of Los Angeles, whose generous support made this project possible, and our colleagues at the University of Southern California who encouraged this effort.

A.F.L.
K.B.

Contents

Tables and Figures

Tables

Figures

Contributors

HAROLD BRACKMAN consults on interethnic relations for the Simon Wiesenthal Center in Los Angeles. In 1990–91, he and Steven Erie completed a major project on ethnic politics in the Los Angeles metropolitan area for the California Policy Seminar.

KATRINA BURGESS is a Ph.D. candidate in the Politics Department at Princeton University. She served as assistant director of the U.S.-Mexico Project at the Overseas Development Council and as associate director of the California-Mexico Project at the University of Southern California.

JORGE G. CASTAÑEDA is a professor of political science at the National Autonomous University of Mexico (UNAM) and has been a visiting professor at the University of California, Berkeley (UCB) and Princeton University. A frequent commentator on Mexican and Latin American affairs, he is coauthor with Robert Pastor of *Limits to Friendship: The United States and Mexico* and author of *Beyond Revolution: The Latin American Left After the Cold War.*

DENISE DRESSER is a Ph.D. candidate at Princeton University and professor of political science at the Autonomous Technological Institute of Mexico (ITAM). As a research associate in the School of International Relations at the University of Southern California, she helped design the California-Mexico Project.

STEVEN P. ERIE is associate professor of political science at the University of California, San Diego (UCSD). In addition to publishing numerous articles on the politics of race, ethnicity, and gender, he is author of *Rainbow's End*, an award-winning study of urban ethnic politics.

AGUSTÍN ESCOBAR LATAPÍ is research professor at CIESAS Occidente in Guadalajara, Mexico. During the last ten years, he has studied changes in Mexican urban labor markets, the informal sector, and migration. Together with Mercedes González Gutiérrez de la Rocha, he edited *Social Responses to Mexico's Economic Crisis of the 80s.*

CARLOS GONZÁLEZ GUTIÉRREZ is consul for community affairs at the Mexican Consulate in Los Angeles. He received a master's degree in international relations from the University of Southern California and has been a member of the Mexican Foreign Service since 1987.

DAVID E. HAYES-BAUTISTA is professor of medicine at the University of California, Los Angeles (UCLA) and director of the Center for the Study of Latino Health at the UCLA School of Medicine. He is coauthor of *The Burden of Support: The Young Latino Population in an Aging American Society.*

ABRAHAM F. LOWENTHAL is professor of international relations and director of the Center for International Studies at the University of Southern California. He was the founding executive director of the Aspen Institute's Inter-American Dialogue, and of the Wilson Center's Latin American Program.

CARLOS RICO is Minister, Deputy Chief of Mission at the Mexican Embassy in Tokyo. He is on leave from his position as professor of international relations at the Center for International Studies, El Colegio de Mexico.

JAMES N. ROSENAU is university professor of international affairs at George Washington University and professor emeritus of the School of International Relations at the University of Southern California. Among his numerous works, his most recent is *Turbulence in World Politics: A Theory of Change and Continuity.*

RICHARD ROTHSTEIN is a Los Angeles–based research associate of the Economic Policy Institute in Washington, D.C. He writes regular columns on economic affairs for the *Sacramento Bee*, *L.A. Weekly*, and *La Opinion* newspapers.

LUIS RUBIO is director general of the Center of Research for Development in Mexico City. He is a member of the Board of Directors of Banamex and writes a weekly column for *La Jornada.* He is author or editor of sixteen books, including *Mexico's Dilemma: The Political Origins of Economic Crisis.*

GABRIEL SZÉKELY is senior fellow at the Center for U.S.-Mexico studies, University of California, San Diego (UCSD), and at El Colegio de Mexico in Mexico City. He is a consultant on international trade and investment for U.S., European, and Latin American firms.

FERNANDO TORRES-GIL is professor of social welfare at the University of California, Los Angeles (UCLA) and adjunct professor of gerontology at the University of Southern California. He has been special assistant to two Secretaries of Health and Human Services and staff director of the U.S. Health Select Committee on Aging.

GUILLERMO TREJO is an economist from the Autonomous Technological Institute of Mexico (ITAM) and a political scientist at the National Autonomous University of Mexico (UNAM). He is research assistant at the Center of Research for Development.

GEORGES VERNEZ is director of the Institute on Education and Training and director of the Program for Research on Immigration Policy at the RAND Corporation. He writes extensively on immigration, human resources, and urban and economic development.

PART I:

Introduction

CHAPTER 1

Coherent Connection or Commonplace Contiguity?

Theorizing About the California-Mexico Overlap

JAMES N. ROSENAU

SOCIAL SCIENTIFIC MAPS all depict communities that are sustained by a modicum of cohesion, that have at least a semblance of legitimacy, that are able to enact and implement policies, and that have members who are sufficiently linked to a shared history or a current plight to appreciate the symbiosis of mutual benefit. None of these cartographical features, however, obtains with respect to the links between California and Mexico. They subsume neither the shared values normally associated with a community nor the structures usually conceived to mark a system. More precisely, the overlap of California and Mexico encompasses communities, but it is not in itself a community. It occupies a specified territory, but it is not in itself bound together by the deep bonds normally associated with territoriality. It embraces a host of social, economic, and political structures, but it does not in itself appear to have a coherent structure.

Despite the absence of community and structured coherence, something about the proximity of Mexico and California captures our attention. Something tells us that their contiguity has substantial consequences, that the ways in which the people, communities, and structures of Mexico and California overlap, interact, or otherwise intersect along a number of dimensions are important. So we refer to them as forming a "Connection," a label that seems appropriate because the standard nomenclature does not fit.[1] The label suggests the presence of a meaningful whole, of diverse interdependencies, of unavoidable interactions, even as it also implies that the prevailing structures of California and Mexico are such that the interactions are endemic and likely to endure for the foreseeable future.

Beyond the intimation of systemic links, moreover, the label is usefully ambiguous. It justifies our search for patterns in an unfamiliar political terrain, in a geographic space that is not bounded by a sovereign state, that does not embrace an integrated economy, that does not partake of a common culture, that does not consist of a formal international relationship, and that lacks any kind of authority structure for making decisions on behalf of those who fall within its scope. Involved, rather, are numerous layers of authority (a sovereign state, a large state within a larger union, large communities within the large state, small border towns), overlapping economies, discrepant cultures, migrating populations, and a long, tension-filled border area.

One way to discern the unfamiliarity of this terrain is to note that it lacks officials or public institutions responsible for worrying about and improving the welfare and coherence of the California-Mexico Connection as a holistic entity. Where the problems and opportunities that arise out of the contiguity of West European or Southeast Asian communities are the concern of interstate institutions such as the European Community (EC) and Association of Southeast Asian Nations (ASEAN) or interlocal institutions such as the Conference on Local and Regional Authorities or the Outline Convention on Transfrontier Cooperation Between Territorial Communities and Authorities,[2] the problems of Mexico and California are not the preoccupation of bureaucracies that can negotiate differences and evolve institutions. There is no Tijuana–San Diego County Commission, or Baja California–Imperial Valley Organization, or any other entity comprised of associated governments charged with addressing challenges to the region. To be sure, local communities have reached out to counterparts across the Mexico-U.S. border to conclude agreements and form regulatory bodies that are marked by transborder preoccupations and a modicum of authority;[3] but these are institutional expressions with limited jurisdictions, and none of them has been extended on a regional scale that treats the California-Mexico Connection as a single entity.[4] Indeed, academics may be alone in positing a larger system that could benefit from recognition as a whole in need of coordination and management.[5] And even then, as the essays of this volume reveal, the boundaries and internal coherence of the whole entity do not readily come into focus for scholars who worry about its integrity and well-being.

How then to proceed? How to construct a map that will lead us out of the network of unfamiliar links and enable us to clarify the underlying dynamics of the California-Mexico Connection? How to fashion a theoretical perspective on which we can fall back in order to address particular policy problems in a larger context?

While answers to such questions are not easily developed, the process of searching for them has enormous theoretical implications that extend well beyond the particulars of the California-Mexico Connection. For the dynamics of global change are fostering ever more numerous, diverse, and salient Connections that ignore, negate, or otherwise span long-established cultural, economic, and political boundaries. Increasingly the world is witnessing "the decline of the great collective forms of identification and the emergence of fragmented and multiple collective actors."[6] That is, the evolution of new social movements, the growing impotence of governments, the advent of pervasive authority crises, the globalization of national economies, and the expanded repertoire of skills available to citizens everywhere in the world has intensified the decentralizing tendencies and transnational links that presently sustain public affairs. The map of the world's political wilderness has become an endless array of unfamiliar ties among disaggregated units that do not conform to established and historic boundaries and, accordingly, that do not lend themselves to treatment as mere variations on known forms of collective action.

Viewed in this way, the California-Mexico Connection is more typical than it is unique. Although perhaps less explosive, it bears more than a little resemblance to the Kashmir-Pakistan Connection, the Quebec-U.S. Connection, the French–North Africa Connection, and the Baltic-Russian Connection—to mention only some of the contiguities that have become more salient under the relentless press of the global tendencies toward decentralization. In short, if we can evolve a theoretical context in which to examine the California-Mexico Connection, we may have also taken important steps toward developing bases for probing characteristic situations that mark world politics today.

The Theoretical Challenge

Some might argue that theorizing about the California-Mexico Connection is a waste of time, that the very uniqueness of the Connection makes it impervious to theory, or that the thicket of theoretical challenges ought not be entered because the immediate task is to ameliorate specific situations that have made life more difficult for Chicanos and more discomforting for mainstream southern Californians. Such reasoning breaks down, however, when it is appreciated that no matter how unique the California-Mexico Connection may be, it cannot be grasped in its entirety. Analysts have neither the time nor the resources to identify, let alone probe, all the myriad details that comprise the Connection. Hence they have to select some of its aspects as important and dismiss others as trivial—which is to say that perforce they must engage in theorizing! They have no choice but to ask a profoundly theoretical question—"Of what is this an instance?"—about any detail they observe if they are to place it in a larger context that enriches understanding.

In order to develop appropriate theoretical contexts, it is obviously important to specify the kinds of questions that hopefully they will clarify. All-encompassing theories are not in themselves inherently valuable. Only when they highlight relationships that might otherwise be overlooked, or when they infuse meaning into causal processes that might otherwise be viewed as peripheral, are theoretical probes likely to sustain further inquiry. If it is concluded that the California-Mexico Connection is no more than a label for diverse, unrelated problems that happen to be located in the same geographic space, then the search for broad theory is best modified, and attention is best focused on the narrow contexts from which particular issue-based problems derive. If, that is, the education, language, labor, welfare, demographic, and other foci of the essays in this book are viewed as relatively self-contained, then the problems each poses are explicable in their own terms and can be probed through well-developed theories in each field. Put more precisely, if an overall theoretical context can only account for a small portion of the variance inherent in key questions that arise in each problem area, then analysts are justified in confining themselves to the immediate task of devising micro-management strategies for time- and place-bound situations.

So the challenge is clear: we need to determine at the outset whether the California-Mexico Connection is subject to an overall theoretical perspective. Is it a single topic or many? And, if it is many topics, are they essentially independent of or inextricably interdependent with each other? If there is no overall authority capable of infusing the Connection with institutional structures, do the various fields of activity nonetheless have common threads that warrant a larger context into which to locate them? Can it be said that the disparate actors and processes encompassed by the Connection cumulate to a modicum of structure, to recurrent practices that fuse together into recognizable and interactive patterns?

The relevance of these questions can usefully be demonstrated in diagrammatic form. Table 1.1 depicts, horizontally, the diverse realms of life encompassed by any community. Each row represents an issue area and the shared concerns that set apart the informal groups active within it. The arrows of the horizontal lines are used to highlight the presence of a variety of conflicting interests and functional consensuses. The vertical domains of Table 1.1, on the other hand, depict various types of territorial communities, ranging from the least to the most encompassing. Each column represents a political organization that has responsibility for the course of events and the quality of life within its jurisdiction. The arrows of the vertical lines are intended to call attention to the broad consensuses across issue areas that sustain the coherence of local, provincial, national, and international communities.

TABLE 1.1.
The Political Space Occupied by Twelve Types of Issue Areas and Six Types of Political Communities

	LEVELS OF POLITICAL ORGANIZATION					
ISSUE AREAS	Towns	Cities	Counties	Provinces	Nation-states	International agencies
Science and technology						
Commerce and trade						
Conservation vs. development						
Labor						
Agriculture						
Immigration						
Education						
Human rights						
Religion						
Environment						
Health and welfare						
Other						

By reading across the rows one discerns the high degree to which various types of communities are interdependent, just as reading down the columns conveys a picture of how any community is confronted with a diverse array of overlapping and inextricably linked challenges. But where does the California-Mexico Connection fit in the maze of 72 activities represented by the 72 cells of Table 1.1? It lacks a formal political organization and yet it embraces all the issue areas that arise within territorial communities. Does this mean that the Connection consists of 72 separate sets of problems that cry out for solution? Or are there common threads that tie all the problems inextricably together and infuse the Connection with structure, incoherent as it may be?[7] Does the diagonal space depicted in Table 1.2 adequately represent the Connection and the way it may cut across all issue areas and involve communities at every level of political

TABLE 1.2.
The Political Space Occupied by the California-Mexico Connection

	LEVELS OF POLITICAL ORGANIZATION					
ISSUE AREAS	Towns	Cities	Counties	Provinces	Nation-states	International agencies
Science and technology						
Commerce and trade						
Conservation vs. development						
Labor						
Agriculture						
Immigration						
Education						
Human rights						
Religion						
Environment						
Health and welfare						
Other						

CALIFORNIA-MEXICO CONNECTION

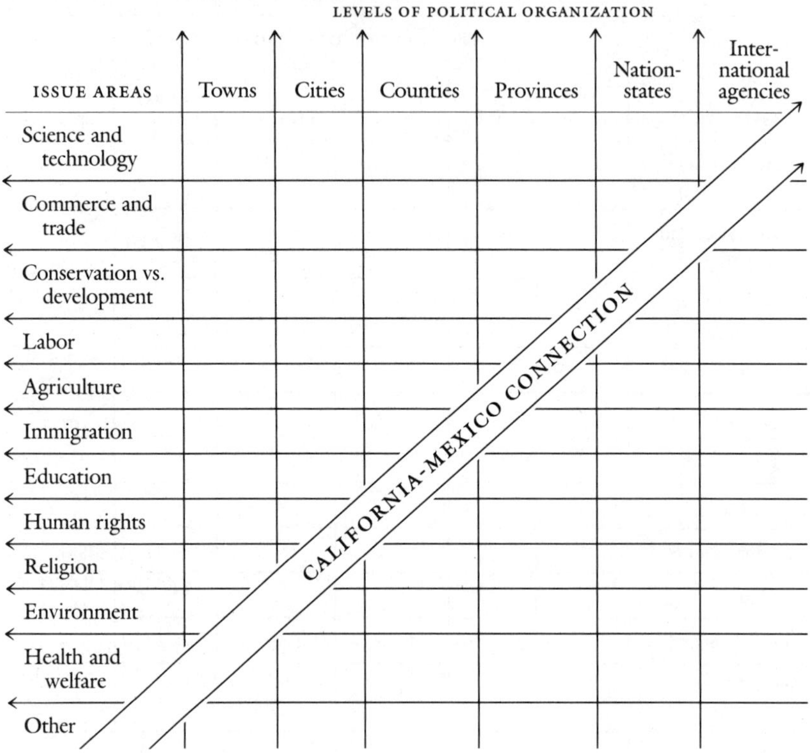

organization? Can the space bounded by the diagonal lines be viewed as suggestive of common threads? Is it appropriate to view these lines as arrows highlighting the Connection's potential for evolving consensual foundations?

Here the analysis proceeds from the premise that, indeed, the diagonal space is rooted in reality, that it represents the common threads that are sufficiently woven into the fabric of the Connection to justify an effort at theory building. My essential argument is that regional contiguities have become increasingly salient precisely because their numerous problems impact on each other with sufficient force to create processes that cannot be accounted for, much less managed by, standard perspectives and strategies. The enormous complexities and interdependencies that have been fostered by a multiplicity of postindustrial dynamics are simply too extensive for the diverse problems of communities in a contiguous region not to meld into a larger set of challenges, which, in turn, foster the evolution of overall structures.

Before assessing the theoretical perspectives that may facilitate clarification of the California-Mexico Connection, it is useful to note briefly why it matters whether or not the Connection is structured. What does the presence of an overall structure, regardless of how incoherent it may be, imply for the present and future state of affairs in the realm represented by the diagonal space of Table 1.2? Although it is highly unlikely that such a structure will ever evolve into a state or any other type of independent political entity, it does matter if the Connection is an instance of more than merely a congeries of disparate, unalike, autonomous, and conflictful actors compelled by geographic contiguity to cope with each other. A structural linking of these actors means that they have at least a dim recognition of their interdependence, that they may not be unmindful of the wider ramifications of their actions, and that they are unlikely to pursue their self-interested policies beyond the point where recurrent, predictable, and established patterns yield to disorder and chaos. Given these underlying predispositions, the presence of structural constraints opens up the possibility of the disparate and unalike actors engaging in trade-offs and other forms of coordination that, in turn, allow for the gathering of a Connection-wide momentum when crises arise. The dire circumstances from which crises spring can worsen in the absence of a capacity for mobilizing and focusing support, but the probability of crises exploding into sheer disarray is much less when the motives, attitudes, and habits that sustain structures are operative.

Some Empirical Premises

Whatever the Connection may be an instance of, four of its configuring characteristics need to be specified at the outset. In the present period, that is, certain presumptions need to be made if a proper theoretical context is to be developed.

Dynamism as Process

One such presumption concerns the concept of change. Theorizing about the Connection will not get very far if it proceeds from the premise that the people, groups, and situations encompassed by the overlap of California and Mexico are static and resistant to change—subject to incremental adjustments perhaps, but too ensconced in traditional patterns to undergo basic transformation. The Connection is presently in motion, restlessly shifting directions, explosively undergoing deep and profound alterations that are so dynamic as to feed on themselves and intensify the pace of change. From the proliferation of *maquiladoras* to the liberalizing economic policies of the Salinas government, from the southward movement of capital to the northward movement of people, from the influx of Japanese entrepreneurs to the outflow of Mexican culture, from the advent of effective opposition parties to the mushrooming of tourism, the California-Mexico Connection has entered into a dynamism that is self-perpetuating, rapid, and pervaded with repercussions. In 1989, to cite only one indicator of the dynamism, the traffic of legal northbound crossings at the San Diego–Tijuana border was recorded at 60,223,426, virtually doubling the volume of five years earlier.[8] In short, one must be continuously aware that any new patterns anticipated by one's theory may prove temporary and operate as sources of their own transformation.

The Implications of Interdependence

Furthermore, the dynamism of change is moving in a particular direction—toward ever greater interdependence among the individuals, families, groups, municipalities, economies, and cultures on either side of the border separating California and Mexico. The activities and actors comprising the Connection are not simply more numerous, but as they proliferate they also constrict, enlarge, or otherwise impact upon each other. Social, economic, and political networks are multiplying as the densities and complexities of the Connection deepen and expand.

It follows that the use of the concept of interdependence entails a sensitivity to unintended consequences of actions and latent repercussions of seemingly simple and self-contained interactions. Thus, in tracing the Connection's fault lines of conflict and its pillars of cooperation, the theorist must exercise care in not isolating the key variables from the context in which they operate.

The Concept of Integration

Neither the dynamism nor the interdependence that pervades the Connection, however, necessarily signifies an evolution in integrative directions. For this to occur in any social system, its underlying values must be increasingly shared, its members must become increasingly aware of themselves as a potentially coherent collectivity, and its leaders must increasingly give voice to aspirations for greater unity. None of these processes is inherent in the dynamics of ever greater interdependence; on the contrary, all of them are as susceptible to moving in disintegrative as in integrative directions. People can experience the proximity and density of expanding networks of interdependence as noxious, as undermining their traditional ways and imposing unwanted obligations.

It is not a foregone conclusion, therefore, that the Connection's proliferating economic interdependencies will supersede and transform its innumerable cultural and political disparities. Our theories must leave room for fragmenting as well as consensual values, for perceptions of disarray as well as coherence, for leaders espousing self-interests as well as collective needs. Detached observers may prefer integrative outcomes, but sound theory requires probing for them rather than presuming their likelihood.

Definitional Subtleties

Good definitions do not assure good theory, but ambiguous definitions can surely impair its development and accuracy. It makes a difference whether the entity we conceive to be undergoing dynamic transformation in interdependent and possibly integrative directions is all of California and Mexico, or just southern California and northern Mexico, or only those jurisdictions that are immediately adjacent to the border. Is Los Angeles part of the Connection, and, if so, why not San Francisco? Is Mexico City a component, and, if so, why not Washington, D.C.? Are we theorizing about a transboundary region, a borderland, or both?

The easiest course would be to use a precise geographic definition. One inquiry, for example, confines the analysis to the counties and municipalities adjacent to the border.[9] But the scope and concerns of the ensuing essays suggest that this is too narrow a focus, that the social, economic, and political processes of interest extend beyond the border region to those centers where both private citizens and public officials make decisions that initiate, sustain, or otherwise affect the activities, goods, services, and ideas that span the border between California and Mexico. Despite geographic incongruities, in short, the Connection is here conceived to consist of a primary zone that extends from the borderlands to Los Angeles and a secondary zone whose focal points are Washington, D.C., Mexico City, and Sacramento. To the extent that trends in the American and Mexican economies and polities, not to mention the activities of traders, producers, and governments elsewhere on the Pacific Rim, have consequences for the primary zone, these are treated as inputs into, rather than as integral parts of, the Connection.

Broad Theoretical Perspectives

This definitional formulation has important consequences for the approach to theory framed here. It means that we have to pursue several trails into the thicket and meld together bits and pieces from several theoretical literatures that help account for different dimensions of the Connection. None of these is mutually exclusive, but at the same time none is perfectly suited to the Connection's ungainly composition. In some cases their scope is limited to particular issue areas (as in the rows of Table 1.1), or their focus is on holistic entities that, unlike the Connection, have a legal standing and mechanisms of authority for implementing policies and maintaining order (as in the columns of Table 1.1). Despite these limitations, however, all the trails are lined with kernels of theory that can be put to good use. The challenge is to synthesize the relevant theoretical traces without losing sight of the complex and disparate entity that we seek to comprehend.

Integration Theories

A rich literature exists on the processes whereby separate social systems, knowingly or otherwise, do or do not overcome their historical, cultural, economic, and political boundaries and achieve a modicum of integration with each other.[10] Most of these studies empirically focus on geographic regions—particularly, though far from exclusively, western Europe—that are presumed to render their inhabitants so proximate to each other as to facilitate intended or unintended efforts to surmount their differences and converge around shared institutions. Such a focus has led to penetrating theories on whether economic integration can foster political union, or vice versa. One result is the "spill-over hypothesis," which proposes that the more economic convergence occurs in one issue area, the greater is the likelihood that synthesis will occur in other areas and thereby promote impulses toward political integration.

On the face of it, therefore, the empirical foci and theoretical perspectives of the integration literature appear to correspond closely to much of the writing about the Connection, which sometimes explicitly and often implicitly refers approvingly to "silent" processes at work that are drawing the people, cultures, industries, and communities on either side of the California-Mexico border into closer harmony with each other. The spill-over hypothesis, for example, may well be useful in clarifying the processes whereby synthesis can occur across either the rows or columns of Table 1.1.

Yet, although there is thus much that can be gained through analyses in which the insights, findings, and propositions generated by integration theories are applied to the circumstances and dynamics at work in the Connection, there is also one major dimension of the integration perspective that limits its applicability. Virtually all the studies of regional integration posit the convergence and synthesis of existing political entities, nation-states, in either a more encompassing entity (as in European Community) or a set of international institutions that preserve the existing states but more fully control their functioning in certain issue areas (as in the Organization of African Unity or the Organization of American States). Central to the integration literature, therefore, is a preoccupation with the sources, limits, and development of effective authority, with policy-making arrangements that allow for concerted efforts to address region-wide problems. Irrespective of the priorities they attach to the relative strength of economic and political dynamics, such studies all proceed from the premise that the integrating systems consist exclusively of coherent and sovereign states. But, obviously, such a premise is inappropriate as a basis for any theory designed to probe systems comprised of nonsovereign entities. Or at least I have not discovered any themes in the literature on the California-Mexico Connection that allude to the possible evolution of centralized or coordinated authority structures. The spill-over hypothesis may well be useful in clarifying the processes whereby synthesis can occur across either the rows or columns of Table 1.1, but its fit to the diagonal space of Table 1.2 would appear to have limited value.

State-Making Perspectives

Similar circumstances obtain with respect to theories of state making. Again one finds a concern with how more encompassing holistic entities evolve out of disparate communities and incoherent structures. While the early literature on state making focused on the successful formation processes of Europe,[11] increasingly the unsuccessful processes in the Third World are being subjected to close scrutiny.[12] Given the asymmetrical cultural, economic, and political differences between California and Mexico, the work on state formation in both Europe and the Third World can be usefully brought together and plumbed for hypotheses that can be modified for application to the Connection.

The problem of centralized authority, however, also arises with state-making theories. They also proceed from the presumption that the circumstances of the communities and structures in the nascent state are sufficiently pliable to allow for their supersession by more encompassing entities. Studies of Europe focus on how states did supersede previous authority structures, and those concerned with the Third World trace how the history of colonialism distorted the emergence of effective states, but neither set of theories strays from the premise that the prime outcome to be grasped is a centralized and sovereign government capable of governing. In the case of the California-Mexico Connection, on the other hand, the disparate communities and inchoate structures it embraces are too deeply embedded in long-standing historical systems to allow for their replacement. The Connection may well evolve into a more coherent entity, but it is extremely unlikely that its California component will break off from the United States and become part of an independent sovereign state.

Global Policy Studies

Conceived to include a focus on "trans-boundary problems like people, pollution, or goods literally going across international boundaries,"[13] global policy studies highlight multidisciplinary inquiries into societal problems that "can potentially be improved upon by purposeful action."[14] Since states have long been regarded as the predominant sources of meaningful purposeful action, policy studies have traditionally focused on the efforts of national governments or their subunits (the first four columns of Table 1.1) to bring about change in a variety of issue domains (all the rows that might be included in Table 1.1). Despite a recent recognition among a few policy study specialists that this focus has to be expanded to encompass a host of new transnational issues, many of those who specialize in policy studies "have been reluctant to apply their perspective and method beyond the domain of nation-states to the international and global levels of political organization. One apparent reason is the common conception of a policy as being the product of a type of governmental structure that does not exist in the anarchic international political order."[15]

Unfortunately, those analysts who are willing to venture into the anarchic order of world politics—by assuming that, despite the absence of an overarching government, "forms of international governance have evolved through which public policies are formulated and implemented to address global problems"[16]—have yet to develop a conception of the policy processes embraced by transnational entities such as the California-Mexico Connection. They do concentrate on "transborder problems" that "originate in one state but have ramifications for others,"[17] but their analyses nevertheless remain locked into state or international organizations (the last two columns of Table 1.1) as the originators and managers of policy efforts. Perhaps because they have labeled their enterprise "global policy studies," these analysts have been inclined to confine their inquiries to international organizations, such as the United Nations and its various agencies, that address large earth-spanning problems, which undermine the global commons. Hence they have not extended (they might say "narrowed") their scope to the constellation of public and private actors who undertake purposeful action in the communities that comprise contiguous connections.

This is not to imply, however, that the policy studies literature has no utility as a source of tools that can be applied to the California-Mexico Connection. It may be conspicuously lacking in systematic inquiries designed to probe the realms of activity identified in Table 1.2, but its insights into the processes and sequences whereby new policies can modify old patterns are not without value. If one ignores the requirement of a coherent authority structure as the source of policy programs and instead simply looks at the Connection through the eyes of any of its organizations seeking to change prevailing attitudes and practices, the global policy literature can provide some guidance through the thicket of interdependencies with which the essays of this volume are concerned. The task of designing programs that transgress national boundaries and ameliorate problems of education, welfare, and the environment, for example, are as of much concern to global policy analysts as they are to students of the California-Mexico Connection.

Regime Theory

Developed out of a recognition that world politics is undergoing vast changes, regime theory is perhaps an even more promising line of inquiry. It is especially relevant to probing the Connection inasmuch as its core premises do not presume the presence of an established and constitutional political authority. Instead, international regimes are conceived to promote cooperation and inhibit conflict through "sets of explicit or implicit principles, norms, rules, and decision-making procedures around which actors' expectations converge" to sustain the transnational activities that fall within their scope.[18] Like the Connection, in other words, international regimes subsume effective instruments of governance despite their lack of authoritative institutions. Like the Connection, they have structure even though they do not have a central decision-making body capable of implementing and enforcing regime-wide policies. And like the Connection, they embrace a congeries of public and private actors whose transnational interactions spring from contiguity rather than constitutional mandates.

On the other hand, regime theory has only limited applicability to the Connection. The definition of regimes has another clause that greatly narrows the scope of the concept. The principles, norms, rules, and procedures are conceived as converging "in a given area of international relations,"[19] that is, in an issue area. It turns out, therefore, that regimes are based on limited functional contiguities, on a narrow range of activities (only one row in Table 1.1) rather than a broad array of issues such as is encompassed by the Connection (and represented by all the rows of Table 1.1). Comprehending the overlap and trade-offs through which the diverse and unlike groups of the Connection might maintain its structure as they bargain across issues lies beyond the capacity of regime theory.

Despite its limits as an instrument for the study of holistic entities, however, regime theory could be put to good use in tracing and explaining some aspects of the Connection. One can readily imagine, for example, subjecting the problems and processes that surround the functioning of *maquiladoras* to regime analysis or, perhaps better, the complex arrangements that have evolved in the area of human migration. It could readily be argued, moreover, that a mature regime has already developed around the drug trade and the premise that the California-Mexico border is especially vulnerable to trafficking.

World Cities as an Organizing Concept

Although still very much in an early stage of development, the theoretical apparatus that urban political economists have evolved around the concept of "world cities" exhibits some of the dimensions inherent in Connections. Where local communities were once studied as autonomous entities essentially isolated from the world, today they are increasingly approached as both sources and products of larger dynamics, as nodes in systems of production, distribution, and exchange that can be global in scope, as the sites of social movements that sustain their momentum through local responses to worldwide socioeconomic processes, as the loci of conflicts between transnational elites who serve the interests of transnational capital and local residents whose concerns are much more limited in scope.[20] This conception of the growing centrality of local settings has, understandably, tended to converge around those communities whose activities have the most extensive consequences, namely, "world cities," those huge urban areas that are linked through computers, communication satellites, and wide-bodied jets, which, in turn, facilitate worldwide networks of finance, advertising, construction, real estate, hotels, entertainment, shopping, private police, domestic services, and labor recruitment, not to mention assembly operations dependent on unskilled labor. Some large urban cities, in other words, are seen as having been internationalized as part of a vast new international division of labor (NIDL) and, as such, to form a network unto themselves in which the vast proportion of local communities are not yet able to participate. Indeed, a hierarchy of cities based on participation in the NIDL has been conceived to evolve in which six (Tokyo, Los Angeles, Chicago, New York, London, and Paris) are considered "primary core cities," two (Singapore and Rio–São Paulo) as "primary semi-periphery cities," nine (Sydney, San Francisco, Houston, Miami, Toronto, Madrid, Milan, Vienna, and Johannesburg) as "secondary core cities," and eight (Bangkok, Hong Kong, Taipei, Seoul, Manila, Mexico City, Caracas, and Buenos Aires) as "secondary semi-periphery cities."[21]

While a foray into the world-cities literature does yield a discernible trail that can usefully be followed to bring the California-Mexico Connection into clearer focus, again the fit is not perfect. Even though the Connection encompasses a core primary city (Los Angeles), a core secondary city (San Francisco), and a secondary semi-periphery city (Mexico City), it also embraces rural areas and borderlands beset with dynamics and problems that the world-cities approach does not purport to address. That is, many of the economic, educational, and political problems of the Connection do lend themselves to explanation through properties derived from the NIDL and the hierarchical structures it has fostered, but this perspective does less well in probing the migratory labor, agricultural, and cultural challenges that are no less central to the functioning of the Connection. To be sure, the rural areas of the Connection are far from predominant—both the California counties and Mexican municipalities adjacent to the border, for example, are more than 90 percent urban[22]—but nevertheless their needs and demands cannot simply be ignored because world-cities theory focuses its conceptual equipment elsewhere.

Borderlands

To some extent the limitations of the world-cities approach are offset by a perspective that locates borderlands at the center of the analytic framework. Also referred to as "perforated sovereignties" and "transborder regionalism," borderlands include rural areas as well as any contiguous communities that are traversed by a national boundary. Stated differently, the borderlands perspective is organized around the dynamics of immediate proximity marking neighborhoods that happen to lie on either side of a boundary dividing sovereign states. Several features of this perspective seem particularly relevant to the California-Mexico Connection. One is that the Connection's very raison d'être, transborder flows, are a prime focus of borderland specialists. Two types of flows are conceived to be operative, both of which can foster conflict as well as cooperation:

> An *ingressive* flow represents a movement of ideas, persons, products, and pollutants across national boundaries from the inside out; an *egressive* stream of challenges and opportunities—economic, environmental, ideological, and cultural—flows from the outside in. Neither aims at tearing territorial boundaries down, only at piercing them, leaving them otherwise intact. Thus, while political authority everywhere remains solidly territory-bound, its spatial limits are being perforated by these two inbound and outbound flows, which intermingle, at times reinforcing each other, at times slowing one another down occasionally to a standstill. Both streams, battering at the territorial boundaries separating one national community from another, are only sometimes compatible and cumulative. Quite often, they are competitive or mutually intolerant.[23]

The second advantage of the borderlands perspective is that it is geared to identifying, emphasizing, and assessing the culture shared by the peoples on both sides of the national boundary that divides them. Whereas cultural norms and practices are usually linked to national experiences and histories, so can they derive from the geographic proximity that defines a borderland. This is not the place to explore the nature of the unique and distinguishable culture that has evolved along the California-Mexico boundary, but it should be noted that it is a culture that draws upon the linguistic affinities, common challenges, and shared fates of persons who have been thrown together by geographic proximity and who have thus developed norms, orientations, and practices that stand apart from the two national cultures of which they are also a product. That is, borderland culture has a momentum of its own that contributes to and, indeed, partially shapes the overall structure of the Connection. As one borderland scholar put it, "Along the more free-flowing Canadian border there is a weak or nonexistent border culture whereas a strong border culture extends across the entire length of our southwestern border with Mexico. . . . We depend on one another. To try to separate us [U.S.-Mexico borderlands] will kill both of the Siamese twins."[24]

Furthermore, borderland culture is not static. Its momentum is in the direction of expansion, both in terms of specific activities and the repercussions to which they give rise. For not only are "transboundary cultural events in fine arts, classical and contemporary music, and literature . . . ubiquitous," but "these cultural and social ties that link the two border communities seem to be increasing, creating what might be termed interdependency at the social and political levels. This sharing of many cultural features serves, in a modest way, to soften the impacts of political and economic asymmetries."[25]

Still another relevant feature of the borderlands approach concerns the high degree to which the problems that arise in the region are addressed by ad hoc agreements designed and accepted by actors on both sides of the border. Sometimes called "compacts" and sometimes referred to as "transborder regional cooperatives," these agreements involve

> the networks of communication channels, implicit and explicit rules, and informal and formal procedures that permit and regulate (within a transborder region) cooperative interaction between municipal and regional governments as well as individual citizens and private enterprises. Within such transborder regional cooperatives, the mode of common decision making is not—and cannot be—majoritarian; it is consociational. Agreements between territorial segments of neighboring sovereignties have to be necessarily reached by negotiation and consensus."[26]

I have not come upon a precise figure for the number of transborder regional cooperatives bounded by the California-Mexico Connection; but given the wide range of issues that it spans, presumably the figure is enormous if an outdated 1978 number (766) for the U.S.-Canada border is any indication.

Despite the attractive dimensions of the borderlands perspective, however, it too is somewhat flawed as a trail to theoretical clarity. In the first place, it lacks a thrust toward overarching theory. Analysts working in different disciplines do rely, of course, on theoretical underpinnings—such as multiplier models for the economies of border twin cities or frameworks for transborder familial structures—but none has undertaken to frame a multidisciplinary theory that could be applied to the diagonal area of Table 1.2.[27] Rather than providing a basis for anticipating future developments within the California-Mexico Connection, therefore, the borderlands perspective does not move beyond an analytic framework that highlights significant dimensions of the Connection. Nor can it be said to specify how the transborder flows, unique cultural norms, or transborder regional cooperatives may operate differently under different circumstances.

Secondly, and no less important, the borderlands astride the U.S.-Mexico boundary are not normally considered to include the large metropolises that lie only a few hundred miles away. As previously noted, borderlands are not conceived on a regional scale. They consist, rather, of mostly small communities, albeit the twin metropolises of Tijuana–San Diego and Calexico-Mexicali are surely part of the Connection. There has been some discussion in the borderlands literature of treating Los Angeles and San Antonio as border cities, but to my knowledge this theme has yet to result in a theoretical formulation that allows for such an extension of the perspective. In short, while the borderlands perspective calls attention to some central features of the Connection, it has yet to become broad enough to span all the phenomena of interest.

The Two Worlds of World Politics

An especially promising theoretical path has been cleared in the emergent field of transnational relations, which also focuses on structures and processes that are not bound by the prerogatives of sovereignty, the cohesion of shared cultural premises, or the functioning of an integrated economy. This path can be discerned in a "bifurcationist" perspective derived from an application of turbulence theory.[28] The core of the theory posits every region and country of the world as experiencing continual tensions between decentralizing and centralizing pressures, between con-

TABLE 1.3.
Transformation of the Three Basic Parameters of World Politics

	From	To
Macro parameter	Anarchic system of nation-states	Bifurcation into state-centric and multi-centric systems
Micro parameter	Individuals less analytically skillful and cathectically competent	Individuals more analytically skillful and cathectically competent
Macro-micro parameter	Authority structures in place as people rely on traditional and/or constitutional sources of legitimacy to comply with directives emanating from macro institutions	Authority structures in crisis as people evolve performance criteria for legitimacy and comply with directives viewed as associated with appropriate conduct by macro officials

flictful tendencies toward fragmentation within groups, states, and societies on the one hand and cooperative tendencies toward coherence among states and within regions on the other. Even as the separate republics of Yugoslavia and the Soviet Union were going their own way, for example, so was the former seeking membership in the European Community while the latter aspired to access to the General Agreement on Tariffs and Trade (GATT) and the International Monetary Fund. Or, to cite a more relevant example, even as the Institutional Revolutionary Party (PRI) in Mexico is splintering, so is Mexico seeking a free trade agreement with the United States.

This particular bifurcationist theory argues that as a consequence of decentralizing-centralizing tensions unfolding on a global scale, three basic parameters of world politics have entered a period of dynamism and complexity: the overall structures of world politics (the macro parameter) have undergone a bifurcation in which a multi-centric system of diverse types of actors has emerged to rival the anarchic world of nation-states; the authority structures of macro collectivities (the macro-micro parameter) have moved from being in place to being in crisis; and individual citizens (the micro parameter) have experienced a substantial expansion in their analytic skills. Table 1.3 summarizes the changes in the three core parameters, Table 1.4 suggests several dimensions along which the skills and orientations of citizens have undergone change, and Table 1.5 lists a variety of ways in which the two worlds of world politics differ from each other.

Much of the turbulence in world politics, moreover, stems from the intermeshing of the forces for change. The changes in all three parameters are conceived to be interactive, with the bifurcated macro structures fostering coherence within subgroups and authority crises for states that, in

TABLE 1.4.
Changes in Attributes of Individuals Resulting from Turbulence in World Politics

Attributes	From	Toward
Learning	Habitual	Adaptive
Analytic skills	Rudimentary	Developed
Cognitive maps	Simplistic	Complex
Role scenarios	Truncated	Elaborate
Cathectic capacities	Dormant or crude	Active and refined
Compliance orientations	Unthinking	Questioning
Legitimacy sentiments	Traditional criteria	Performance criteria
Political loyalties	Focused on nation-state	Variable foci
Locus of control	Distant	Close

SOURCE: James N. Rosenau, *Turbulence in World Politics: A Theory of Change and Continuity* (Princeton, N.J.: Princeton University Press, 1990), p. 211.

turn, sustain and deepen the skill revolution. The latter then feeds back to deepen the authority crises and the coherence and autonomy of collective actors in the multi-centric world. Similarly, the decentralizing-centralizing tensions and the several parametric transformations are also interactive: just as the latter have hastened fragmenting tendencies within social systems and heightened the interdependencies among them, so have these sources of dynamism and complexity in the global system intensified the transformation of its parameters.

The complexities and interdependencies that are the product of all these interactive processes establish for any issue a context in which events do not simply occur. Rather they cascade. In bifurcationist theory it is anticipated that any development in either the state- or multi-centric world can trigger reactions on the part of a multiplicity of actors whose interests are in some way affected, and, in turn, these initial reactions can trigger still other reactions by still other actors who are brought into the cascades through the secondary set of reactions, and so on through all the overlapping jurisdictions, economic linkages, and social networks that sustain the interdependencies of an ever shrinking, rapidly changing world. Put more simply, public affairs in a bifurcated world is comprised not of events, but of repercussions, not of action sequences, but of cascading processes.

Notwithstanding the dynamism of these processes of global turbulence, they are not seen as amounting to sheer chaos. They do have structure. As indicated in Table 1.5, actors in the multi-centric world are no less subject to structural constraints and regularized procedures than those which operate in the state-centric world. Indeed, elsewhere I have sought

TABLE 1.5
Differentiating the Two Worlds of World Politics

	State-Centric World	Multi-Centric World
Number of essential actors	Fewer than 200	Hundreds of thousands
Prime dilemma of actors	Security	Autonomy
Principal goals of actors	Preservation of territorial integrity, and physical security	Increase in world market shares, maintenance of integration of subsystems
Ultimate resort for realizing goals	Armed force	Withholding of cooperation or compliance
Normative priorities	Processes, especially those that preserve sovereignty and the rule of law	Outcomes, especially those that expand human rights, justice, and wealth
Modes of collaboration	Formal alliances whenever possible	Temporary coalitions
Scope of agenda	Limited	Unlimited
Rules governing interactions among actors	Diplomatic practices	Ad hoc, situational
Distribution of power among actors	Hierarchical by amount of power	Relative equality in initiating action
Interaction patterns among actors	Symmetrical	Asymmetrical
Locus of leadership	Great powers	Innovative actors with extensive resources
Institutionalization	Well established	Emergent
Susceptibility to change	Relatively low	Relatively high
Control over outcomes	Concentrated	Diffused
Bases of decisional structures	Formal authority, law	Various types of authority, effective leadership

SOURCE: Rosenau, *Turbulence in World Politics*, p. 250.

to demonstrate that the structures of the multi-centric world are sufficiently developed to allow for the derivation of shared decision rules through which its actors respond to counterparts in and challenges from the state-centric world.[29]

The relevance of this formulation for the California-Mexico Connection is so extensive that only a few of its more salient implications can be noted here. First, given the multiplicity of ways in which Americans and Mexicans converge upon each other, the bifurcation of world politics into two worlds is perhaps as clear-cut and thoroughgoing in this case as anywhere else today. On the one hand, the governments of the United States and Mexico are deeply involved in efforts to protect their separate and collective interests in the Connection, as are state and municipal governments as well as a wide range of local authorities on both sides of the border. On the other hand, the opening up of the Mexican economy, the arrival of the *maquiladoras*, the proliferation of cultural groups and social networks, the rapid growth of border cities, the expansion of Hispanic organizations, the explosion of tourism, the flow of immigrants, the fallout of the drug trade, and a host of other dynamics have resulted in a vibrant multi-centric world that is only partly responsive to the efforts of governments and that sustains the impetus toward decentralizing tendencies even as it also fosters expanding interdependencies.

The routines of this multi-centric world, moreover, conform closely to the characteristics set forth in the right-hand column of Table 1.5. In the case of pollutants and other environmental problems, for instance, efforts to cope with such issues involve a multitude of actors who share the goal of preserving the Connection's quality of life, who are ready to withhold cooperation and compliance to achieve this goal, who persevere through a combination of formal and informal alliances, organizations, and rules that are not highly institutionalized, who interact along asymmetrical lines shaped by power differentials, and who resort to diverse types of authority and leadership to exercise diffused control over the emission of pollutants, the distribution of toxic wastes, and the various other ways in which environmental degradation occurs along the California-Mexican border. And ranged against these actors are those who, using the same skills and means of implementing their goals, seek to expand existing levels of productivity or maintain habitual ways of disposing of wastes.[30] If one appreciates that comparable activities mark life in all the major issue areas set forth in Table 1.2 as comprising the Connection's public affairs, one is hard put to avoid being overawed by the enormity of its intricacies.

And if one then superimposes on the extensive bifurcation of the Connection the bewildering array of public agencies on both sides of the border responsible for some part of its affairs, one gets a picture of complexity that virtually defies description. Consider, for example, law-enforcement agencies involved in stemming the northward flow of illegal people, goods, and drugs. On the U.S. side some responsibility attaches to federal agencies such as the Department of State, the Justice Department, the Immigration and Naturalization Service (INS), the National Guard, the FBI, and customs officials as well as comparable agencies at the state and local levels. The Mexican side is no less diffuse: it includes municipal police, federal highway police, state judicial police, federal judicial police, customs officials, migration officials, the Federal Security Directorate, and various military units. The state-centric world, in other words, is hardly less decentralized than its multi-centric counterpart, an arrangement that makes it difficult for governments to coordinate their efforts and thus encourages, even necessitates, considerable innovation on the part of actors in the multi-centric world to circumvent the bureaucratic contradictions and paralysis they must endlessly confront.

Indeed, given the state-centric world's fragmented involvement in border issues, it can be readily hypothesized that, on balance, the Connection will witness its multi-centric actors becoming more independent of, if not more encroaching upon, state-centric officials. In the words of one study, "As border economic interdependence increases it seems likely that the ability of the U.S. federal government to undertake . . . actions in the face of increasing opposition at the state and local levels will diminish."[31] That this shifting balance has also been recognized in the state-centric world is readily evident in this recent observation by one of its representatives, a U.S. ambassador to Mexico: "The greatest challenge in U.S.-Mexican affairs for the future lies in responding positively to public interactions that far outweigh government-to-government relations."[32]

A second and closely related aspect of the bifurcationist perspective that bears directly on the California-Mexico Connection is its concern with the loci of authority and the crises they are undergoing. As implied by the foregoing account of widely distributed formal authorities and innovative informal authorities, the Connection's authority structures lack coherence and clear-cut hierarchical channels through which policy directives can be framed and issued. As a result, it can reasonably be hypothesized, challenges to formal authority will become more frequent as the dynamism of change unfolds throughout and within the communities of the primary zone. Some of the challenges, incidentally, may come from Mexican officials, who operate within a centralized policy-making system and thus have difficulty comprehending how different U.S. agencies can act independently of, if not in contradiction to, the Department of State. Other challenges may originate with local U.S. officials, who are, for example, "often at odds with federal officials on how border law enforcement problems should be dealt with. Many local law enforcement agencies along the border, under intense pressure from local Hispanic organizations, refuse to assist the Border Patrol in the apprehension of undocumented persons."[33] Still other challenges, of course, will derive from groups in the multi-centric world who, through seeking to enhance their autonomy, may ignore, dilute, or otherwise counter the directives issued by state-centric authorities at every governmental level.

In short, the bifurcationist perspective calls attention to the many ways in which the authority to solve problems inherent in the Connection lies elsewhere than in the governments of Mexico and the United States. Agreement between the two—say, on immigration or trade—may contribute to the context in which problems are addressed, just as their disagreements can have disastrous consequences for long-standing cooperative projects along their borders.[34] For the most part, however, the location of policy-making responsibilities for the situations embraced by the Connection are likely to be far removed from national agencies and to be, instead, dispersed among an unfamiliar array of interactive local subdivisions and nongovernmental actors.[35]

With authority dispersed widely, and with national governments performing as remote actors in the secondary zone of the Connection, the decentralizing tendencies that underlie the autonomy of its diverse multicentric actors and the centralizing tendencies that deepen their interdependence seem likely to render ever more difficult the tasks of coordinating policies designed to ameliorate tensions. Bifurcationist theory posits the decentralizing dynamics as unending, as exerting continual pressures for fragmentation and self-serving policies, as relentlessly challenging the structural constraints that encourage diverse groups to engage in cooperative projects. As one observer put it in 1989–90, the growing dispersion of authority fostered by the decentralizing dynamics at work in the multicentric world may be of such consequence that

> the flash points of tension in the bilateral relationship will not emanate so consistently from Washington and Mexico City, but rather from within the ranks of domestic interest groups in both countries. This rogue conflict will be *ad hoc* and resistant to quick policy fixes. By the same token, future cooperation *across* the border (transcending infighting among interest groups on each side of the border) also will frequently originate outside of government-to-government channels—reflecting a growing recognition of a commonality of interests among some groups.[36]

In short, the Connection's structures and processes can never be taken for granted. Their coherence is endlessly in flux and always susceptible to transformation. Thus, even though the interdependencies on which they rest may deepen and expand, the dispersed authority structures and fragmented processes of the Connection may be unable to exercise effective control over its burgeoning problems.

Part of the control problem, of course, lies in the cascading processes to which the complexities of a bifurcated world give rise. These are particularly conspicuous and pervasive in the Connection, where

> even relatively minor occurences on one side of the border can have important impacts on the other. Thus, decisions made in Mexico City regarding the value of the peso relative to the dollar can have positive effects on the U.S. side of the border in terms of increased Mexican retail purchases and export of capital to the United States or negative effects such as precipitous declines in retail purchases by Mexican shoppers. Economic declines in regions of Mexico can increase pressure for outmigration to the United States, the impact of which is strongly felt in the border region. Of course, economic cycles or economic policy decisions made in the United States can have significant reverberations on the Mexican side of the border.[37]

Nor are such cascades confined to economic realms. The outmigrations fostered by economic declines in Mexico can in time bring about significant shifts in the ethnic composition of California, which, in turn, can affect the politics of Los Angeles, the welfare problems of San Diego, and the educational practices of Californian schools.

The bifurcationist perspective, in other words, alerts us to the fact that the Connection's problems are not easy to contain, that their repercussions move quickly from issue area to issue area, up and down the diagonal region indicated in Table 1.2, thereby making it extremely difficult to design policies for one set of challenges without fostering new dilemmas elsewhere. It would not be far-fetched to hypothesize that the more suddenly a change occurs anywhere in the Connection, the greater will be the spread and depth of its repercussions.

Still another implication of bifurcationist theory concerns the skill revolution. It anticipates a heightened awareness of the Connection among the diverse groups it encompasses, a process that is likely, depending on the quality and direction of subgroup leadership, either to exacerbate or moderate racial, class, and ethnic conflicts. As implied in Table 1.4, a central feature of the skill revolution is that people are becoming increasingly able to discern how the course of events may impact upon their rights, pocketbooks, and general well-being, a capacity which in turn better enables them to appreciate how they can be served by participating in collective actions. In the case of the California-Mexico Connection, however, the impact of the skill revolution is complicated by the fact that it has occurred in two languages and the context of two different cultures. It may well be that the ability to analyze the dynamics and destinations of cascading processes is different depending upon whether one thinks and works in English or Spanish. If so, it seems reasonable to hypothesize that the more policies promoting bilingual education are successful, the greater is the likelihood that sizable publics can be mobilized in support of candidates or programs committed to improving or altering transnational circumstances. In any event, whatever language may be involved, it seems clear that the Connection's structures are exceedingly vulnerable to the ways in which its various elites define self and community interests and then call for cooperative or conflictful action on the part of subgroup members.[38]

Finally, and relatedly, the bifurcationist perspective calls attention to several dynamics within the Connection that are pervaded with potential for the mushrooming of cooperation and coherence. The fact that a preponderance of its key actors are located in the multi-centric world means that they are not bound by the obligations of sovereignty and are thus relatively free to cooperate in creative and innovative enterprises with each other to the extent that they recognize the need for such projects and have the political will to press for them. Viewed in this way, it is hardly surprising that "over the years, border residents have evolved a whole range of informal arrangements to deal with transborder aspects of their daily lives. Examples that come to mind are seen in the informal, but regular cooperation of fire departments, health authorities, and police to deal with emergencies without the intervention of either federal government."[39]

In other words, even though the Connection encompasses overlapping problems that require coordinated efforts across any two or more of the issue areas identified by the diagonal space in Table 1.2, it will not be legal boundaries that stand in the way of their implementation. Unlike conventional political jurisdictions, the Connection, by its very nature, allows for fluid and flexible attempts to synthesize conflicting needs and demands. As previously noted with respect to the right-hand column of Table 1.5, the multi-centric world is structured in such a way as to render all its actors susceptible to change and to permit them to join temporary coalitions, to initiate independent actions, and to participate in ad hoc arrangements. To be sure, they are also essentially free to withhold their cooperation and to avoid complying with others who seek to include them in innovative and synthesizing projects. Nevertheless, the incentives and bases for addressing and resolving complex challenges do accrue to the various actors whose interests are affected by the Connection. Whether they are Californians or Mexicans, they are proximate to each other, share certain characteristics, live with the same dilemmas, interact in a multiplicity of ways, and are ever aware that they are both producers and recipients of the wide repercussions that can flow from whatever happens in their limited but dynamic part of the world.

A cogent illustration of the multi-centric world's convergence and cooperation across the California-Mexico boundary is provided by what happened at a three-day meeting of diverse nongovernmental organizations

(NGOs) from Canada, Mexico, and the United States designed to strengthen their network of contacts. The fourth in a series of conferences labeled the "Trinational Exchange," the meeting focused on the fast-track approach to the proposed Free Trade Agreement between Mexico and the U.S. The results were as remarkable as they were unexpected, since they

> served as a catalyst to hasten the appearance of multisectoral, cross-border coalitions and working groups. The discussions that the debate provoked enabled the NGO participants to: view their specific issues within a broader framework; to come into contact; to identify areas of common concern and to explores areas of disagreement; to create public forums of high visibility at which to express their points of view; to explore alternative tactics and strategies for the pursuit of their objectives—both trade and non-trade related—with potential political allies; and to identify sources of intellectual and financial support for their efforts.[40]

Especially noteworthy, moreover, were the changes that occurred when the participants in this Trinational Exchange differed sharply on issues:

> As the meeting progressed and information was shared, stereotypes that had caricatured the position of some of the interest groups in the eyes of other such groups were removed and areas of overlapping interest emerged. Environmentalists and labor representatives coincided in their concern over workplace environmental standards in the border maquiladora plants, for example. Agricultural representatives and environmentalists began to explore measures that would promote sustainable rural development. Union representatives from all three countries agreed to meet in Mexico to further discuss a variety of common concerns. Finally, participants in the meeting emphasized that they should begin to regularly take into account the collateral impact of their activities on the interests of other NGOs. Environmentalists, for example, were encouraged to incorporate a concern for job creation into their thinking.[41]

In sum, the Connection's potential for innovative projects designed to meet challenges and resolve conflicts is especially propitious at the present time. The spirit of cooperation and problem solving is, so to speak, in the U.S.-Mexican air. Not only do the leaders of the two countries aspire to harmonizing their economies through a free trade agreement, but this is only the most conspicuous indicator of the extent to which the 1988 election of Carlos Salinas de Gortari to the Mexican presidency resulted in a new cooperative orientation toward relations with Washington. As one inquiry put it, the new Mexican leadership has

> set a tone of openness and frankness when dealing with the United States that has been reflected at even the lowest levels of government agencies. All along the border, observers report improved relations with officials in Mexican gov-

> ernment agencies and a much warmer climate for working together to solve many of the day-to-day problems of life on the border. At the state and municipal levels, this is also apparent. For example, the [1990] Border Governors' Conference . . . was characterized by lack of political rhetoric and cordial but direct discussion of border problems and opportunities. This stands in strong contrast to the formality and emphasis on protocol of earlier meetings of the group.[42]

Is this to imply that the underlying direction of the California-Mexico relationship is determined in distant national capitals? Bifurcationist theory would answer in the negative. Given the parametric transformations and dynamic interdependence fostered by the onset of global turbulence, the impetus for change can and does originate at all levels of aggregation in both the state- and multi-centric worlds. Indeed, one could argue that the Salinas government initiated a new approach to relations with the U.S. precisely because the conditions that prevail within the primary and secondary zones of all the connections linking the two countries propelled it to break with the past.

Some Theoretical Foundations

Like the other theoretical perspectives examined, bifurcationist theory is short on tight propositions that can be adapted to the specifics of California-Mexico relations. It identifies processes and structures that have undergone change but does not specify when and how they might change under particular circumstances. It clarifies what we should theorize about but has yet to be developed to the point where it elaborates on what the theory should look like.

Yet, an initial outline of the foundations of such a theory can be derived from the foregoing analysis. That is, having ventured down seven theoretical trails and found them all studded with both exciting possibilities and difficult obstacles, we can now return to the question that led us to be venturesome: of what is the California-Mexico Connection an instance? The answer is at once simple and difficult. Based on our exploration, it is a complex mix of state- and multi-centric dimensions that do not sum to a conventional socioeconomic and political entity. On the contrary, it exhibits some of the characteristics of international regimes, world cities, borderlands, and a bifurcated world, all of which subsume some of the characteristics of political entities undergoing formation and integration even as they also have sufficient degrees of concentrated authority to allow for policy studies. The Connection is, in other words, a composite, and, as such, it will require a composite of diverse theories to explain how it may develop and to anticipate the conditions under which it is likely to become increasingly integrated.

That is the simple answer. The difficult part lies in constructing a cogent theoretical composite that sorts out the complex mix of state- and multi-centric dimensions and identifies where the main points of conflict are likely to arise and specifies those points at which cooperation is possible. Difficult as this task may be, however, an outline of the steps it entails does seem possible. The question of whether the California-Mexico overlap is a coherent connection or a commonplace contiguity—and especially its potential for undergoing a silent integration susceptible to management—is so central to the ensuing essays that it is perhaps useful to exploit this foray into the unfamiliar thicket of California-Mexico relations with a view to synthesizing the insights offered by the several trails that have been traversed. It seems reasonable to hypothesize, for example, that the Connection is not on the verge of exploding and breaking apart. It may never achieve greater integration, but nothing in the foregoing exploration suggests that it will disintegrate. Why? Precisely because of its diffuse, uncoordinated, nonhierarchical structure. Theories of world cities, state making, and international regimes allow for deterioration and collapse, and history has surely demonstrated that cities, states, and regimes can in fact come apart, as Beirut, Yugoslavia, and the League of Nations so vividly illustrate. But it is difficult to imagine a comparable fate for the Connection. Its components—the diagonal in Table 1.2—are too numerous, too tenuously connected, and too linked into diverse decision centers for any dynamics to intrude permanent rifts that might irreparably splinter the Connection. There can be no authority crises in social systems that have no system-wide authorities.

To anticipate that the asymmetries, dislocations, and tensions that mark the Connection are unlikely to culminate in disintegration is not, however, to predict a future in which integrative processes transform a commonplace contiguity into a coherent Connection. Conceivably such processes are not operative. Or possibly they are too weak and fragmented, too lacking in power, to bring the parts of the Connection together into a larger whole. All the theories examined suggest otherwise. Integration theory points to spill-over processes as having occurred in international regions to foster shared perspectives. State-making theories call attention to situations where authority structures have been fashioned out of contiguous but conflicting groups. Regime theory highlights a variety of issue areas wherein self-interests intersect enough to shape common principles, rules, norms, and practices. Analyses of world cities are not lacking in success stories about large metropolitan areas that have enjoyed progress through extensive cooperation. The borderlands literature is filled with vignettes on how local needs fostered cross-boundary mechanisms designed to achieve a modicum of integration. And bifurcation theory specifies a number of ways in which multi-centric actors have converged around common interests, sometimes with the assistance of actors in the state-centric world and sometimes quite independently of that world.

If one focuses on the proximity and common needs of Californians and Mexicans, in short, there are good reasons to anticipate a future in which integrative processes will transform the Connection in the decades ahead. Some of the movement in this direction may be silent and only get recognized years later when a series of micro increments finally culminate in a macro outcome, while along other dimensions integration will be quite noisy as groups conflict and compete to have their view of the proper integrative processes prevail. Put differently, it can be hypothesized that increasingly discernible structures will emerge out of the informal interactions of multi-centric actors and the formal policies of governments. The hypothesis can be readily tested at any time. All one needs to do is determine whether it has become easier to draw a political map of the Connection, easier to know where the levers for coordinated action on a particular problem or crisis are located, and easier to trace the interdependencies across issues, communities, and jurisdictions.

To have identified trails that cut through the underbrush is not, of course, to traverse the trails and move beyond the thicket. To have concluded that integrative processes are likely to unfold is not to anticipate how, where, when, and why they will take particular forms under hypothesized circumstances. While the derivation of such hypotheses is best undertaken after pondering the data and insights of the ensuing chapters, here it is possible to extend the foregoing analysis by suggesting some of the underlying conditions that, if they prevail, are likely to render the California-Mexico Connection more coherent as well as those that may induce deleterious tendencies away from integration. Two broad sets of hypotheses seem especially relevant, one that specifies developments *external* to the Connection, which are likely to enhance (or corrode) its coherence, and a second set that focuses on *internal* dynamics, which may stimulate movement in integrative (or disintegrative) directions.

Five important dimensions of the Connection's external setting seem especially subject to variation and thus worthy of development in the context of a bifucationist framework. Initial versions of these hypotheses can be framed as follows: the California-Mexico Connection is likely to become more integrated and coherent, the more that (1) relations between the governments of the U.S. and Mexico are marked by cordiality; (2) the economies of the U.S. and Mexico become interdependent; (3) the global economy expands; (4) the mass media of the two countries avoid stereotypical characterizations and stress cooperative rather than competitive themes; and (5) elites and publics in all walks of life in the two countries comprehend that their futures are interlocking rather than disconnected.

In short, the larger national and global contexts in which the California-Mexico Connection is located can, through cascading and circuitous processes that unfold in both the state- and multi-centric worlds, improve (or undermine) the ways in which its individuals and groups relate to each other. But these larger contexts are not constants. The cascades to which they give rise can move in diverse directions, waxing and waning as political, economic, and social conditions change, thus precipitating a momentum that, given the complexities of the postindustrial era, seems bound to encompass and shape the attitudinal orientations and institutional processes at work within the Connection. In the present period both the national and global contexts and the momentum sustaining them conduce to greater coherence at the California-Mexico level, but it is worth reiterating that such circumstances are not necessarily permanent, that economic downturns, political paralysis, and isolationist sentiments can reverse the momentum and inhibit, even halt, both the silent and observable tendencies toward an integrated Connection.

Bifurcation theory calls attention to five internal dynamics that can also be explored as powerful sources of movement toward more structured links between California and Mexico. Posed as hypotheses, these can be identified as follows: the Connection is likely to become more integrated, the more that (1) cross-border coalitions cohere and proliferate; (2) the control of Washington, D.C., and Mexico City over the interactions that span the boundary dividing them weakens; (3) subgroupism intensifies, thereby undermining central authorities, strengthening tendencies toward decentralization, and allowing for the flourishing of cross-border coalitions; (4) authority crises lead to the relocation of legitimacy in decentralized units, thereby facilitating the growth and strengthening of local structures; and (5) the processes of bifurcation free up actors to join cross-border coalitions.

It follows that if the parametric changes posited by bifurcationist theory are accurate, and if the decentralizing tendencies forecast by these changes do occur, there are good reasons to anticipate that the California-Mexico Connection will become increasingly structured in the years ahead. Such structures may never be formalized into established and readily recognizable institutions, but the interplay of external conditions and internal dynamics seem bound to root the Connection ever more solidly into the life and routines of the people it encompasses. Ungainly and unfamiliar as they may be, the links between California and Mexico are increasingly likely to be the products of tendencies toward coherence rather than merely the by-products of commonplace contiguities.

Theory, of course, offers no automatic or simple answers. And it may be founded on faulty premises and thus prove erroneous. But the lines of theoretical development available for present purposes do point to the conclusion that the vast complexities of the California-Mexico Connection are more than sheer confusion, that they consist rather of a totality susceptible—through explorations like those this volume undertakes—to improved comprehension.

CHAPTER 2

Mexico and California

The Paradox of Tolerance and Dedemocratization

JORGE G. CASTAÑEDA

BROADWAY IN DOWNTOWN Los Angeles is a Mexico City shopping street, San Juan de Letrán in days gone by: crowded, noisy, boisterous, and overwhelming. Los Angeles is in a time warp; its Mexican neighborhoods resemble Mexico City's years ago, before they were either bulldozed for *ejes viales* (high-speed multilane avenues) or intolerably overpopulated by the explosion of the informal economy. It reminds any *chilango* of his home town. Or in any case of what it used to be. Long ago, the workers and women of the job-holding poor sectors of Mexican society would shop downtown on weekends, where shopping was dignified, in cheap but well-supplied stores, on the main streets but off the sidewalks: Broadway. Today, their choice is between a poor man's version of a California mall and the Lima-like *tianguis* sprawling over and across the streets of the inner city: a part of Mexico City's past has moved north.

Mexico's effect on California is of course much more than this, but it starts in the sights, sounds, fragrances, and memories evoked by two cities that have more in common than either appreciates. The influence Mexico is bringing to bear on the society of its northwestern neighbor lies here: urban and different, unassimilable and obtrusive. Mexico's presence is still felt in the orchards and fields of the Central Valley, but it is most prevalent in the parking lots, restaurants, and gardens of Los Angeles, and in the twenty-first-century manufacturing plants of Silicon Valley.

The Mexico-California Connection is at first sight a well-balanced exchange. California gets the best Mexico has to offer: color and culture, vitality, and joie de vivre. Mexico gets modernity and tolerance, but not before they have been processed by its emigrants abroad. But there is a basic difference between the two exchanges. California influences Mexican society through Mexicans, what writer and social critic Carlos Monsiváis has called "la chicanización de las comunidades."[1] To the extent that California's impact can be distinguished from overall U.S. influence, it is subtle, indirect, and convoluted, channeled through the customs, habits, and experience Mexicans pick up in California and take home on their seasonal, festive, or permanent return to native towns and barrios. It is by remote control and delayed, and in the final analysis is more cultural than political, at least for now.

Mexico acts on California society much more directly, through the millions of expatriates who bring their lives and families, language and food, music and mores to a foreign land that can scarcely handle the resulting cultural and political explosion. Its impact is immediate and apparently cultural; but below the surface it is political. Mexico helps establish what Mike Davis, in *City of Quartz*, has called the basic distinction between "those who work and those who vote." The massive numbers of Mexican (and Central American) undocumented immigrants who swell the bottom tier of an increasingly two-tier society are not only excluded socially and economically and disenfranchised politically; they are barred from even formal national belonging. Thus, immigration from Mexico in its undocumented, politically maimed form is directly linked to the "dedemocratization" of California society.

La Chicanización de las Comunidades

Mexican immigration to the United States differs from previous migratory waves by virtue of the twin phenomena of contiguity and continuity. Emigrating from next door has sharply different effects on the mind-set and lifestyle of the migrant than embarking on a long, often once-in-a-lifetime voyage with no return. Modern technology has enhanced this distinction: the modern-day "*mojado* red-eye" daily, nonstop flights from León, Guadalajara, or Zacatecas packed with migrants—some legal, some not—are a far cry from the ships that washed millions of Europeans ashore on Ellis Island.

Continuity also makes a difference. Previous waves of immigration were of fixed duration; they came to a halt after a certain period. Mexican emigration to the United States will soon enter its hundredth year, according to accounts from the sending communities of Guanajuato and Los Altos de Jalisco and the reports of Mexican immigrants used to break strikes at steel mills in Gary, Indiana, before the turn of the century. This emigration shows no signs of stopping; every demographic, economic, or social projection minimally rooted in reality foresees it lasting well beyond the year 2000.

Contiguity and continuity mean that the impact of Mexican immigration on the home country is very different from that of its precursors—or even of contemporary flows from Asia and Central and South America. In contrast to other eras, countries, and contexts, Mexican immigration to California has a "blowback" cultural effect on Mexico. It is not a one-shot deal, a once-and-for-all event with no return, halfway measures, or shades of consummation. On the contrary, study after study has shown how Mexicans, be they from rural communities or urban centers, come and go for a sustained period of time before—in many cases but not all—they finalize their departure from Mexico.

This process, as important as it has been for many years, was dramatically enhanced by the legalization provisions of the 1986 Immigration Reform and Control Act (IRCA). Well over two million Mexicans, and perhaps as many as three million if family reunification is included, suddenly saw their undocumented status in the United States transformed. Among the many consequences of this change was the opening up of new possibilities for frequent return trips by hundreds of thousands to their home towns. The Mexican government launched an entire federal initiative—the *paisano* program—to handle this flow. Some estimates point to as many as one million "returnees" at Christmas or Easter. Although Mexicans in California have always maintained close links to their communities—through money, family, and friends—they are doing so now more than ever, encouraged by the reduced danger and cost of traversing the California-Mexico border as a legalized immigrant.

This is the crux of California's influence on Mexico. Mexicans returning to Mexico bring back with them their exposure to California society, which involves a completely different social, existential, and economic experience. To what degree this affects their entire worldview is open to question and will only be determined by further research. But the visible, obvious impact of the California experience on myriad sending communities is already evident and has been for decades.

Studies and (as always in Latin America) novels, such as Agustín Yañez's *Al filo del agua*, show how small towns have been transformed by the return of the migrants, beginning years ago with a simple shift from the white, thick-cloth *calzones*, or one-piece garb worn ancestrally by Mexican peasants, to overalls and then to "pants with a waist."[2] Similar changes are taking place today. Throughout the small rural communities of the Bajío, at least half the scarce young men visible on the streets wear traditional Mexican boots; the other half wear American-style running shoes. Among the flocks of children still crowding the dusty streets and open-air schools, the U.S. influence is even greater: they all wear sneakers.

Much more important, of course, are the other transformations that immigration has wrought since its onset. One trend stands out in particular: the formation of the equivalent of a local middle class in the small towns, thanks to the money made abroad: "In Jaripo these migrants are more than simple agricultural workers; with their dollars they appear before the rest of the population as a middle class . . . they are the only ones with big cars or vans, they own the best houses, and they are the "main event" at all the parties held over the winter: weddings, baptisms, confirmations, *quinceaños*, etc."[3]

Other changes introduced by the migrants' return are more impressionistic and intangible, ranging from the "disrespect" for elders that many Mexicans detect in the young as they return from the North, to the "development of an idea of success," so foreign to Mexico as a whole and in particular to its rural communities.[4] Similarly, although the "cholo" movement was short-lived in both Mexico and the United States, the way in which "cholo" habits—dress, music, graffiti, and a certain degree of violence—spread from Mexican neighborhoods in Los Angeles to communities in Mexico is another well-studied example of the blowback effect. Gustavo López Castro has described this process well:

> In Gómez Farias (a small town in Michoacán), there is a migratory tradition to the United States that dates back to the first decade of the century. Upon their arrival in California, and specifically in Watsonville, these young emigrés are received with hostility by the "northern cholos," that is by young chicanos born and raised in the United States. Their only defense is to band together in "cholo gangs" of their own. On their return in "cholo groups," these young men bring back with them new ways of dressing, a new language, and new way of seeing the world and life itself.[5]

These kinds of exchanges have intensified since the end of the Bracero program in 1965, reflecting an ongoing process of modernization in Mexico. For half a century now, Mexico has been changing at a dizzying pace, evolving from a rural, peasant, illiterate society to a largely urban and literate one. This process has demolished many of the forms of traditional resistance used by rural communities to ward off influences from abroad. Invaded by the extension of telephones, radio, and television to most towns and villages; the partial alphabetization of millions of Mexicans; the integration of rural areas into the country's mainstream; and the general process of urbanization, where small towns of ten or fifteen thousand inhabitants take the place of remote, isolated villages of several hundred, the old culture is destroyed. The ensuing vacuum is frequently and rapidly filled by the only existing alternative, or at least the strongest one: what the migrants bring back with them from the North.

In the meantime, changes in work patterns, occupations, and even geographical location in California have exposed Mexican immigrants to different aspects of life north of the border. Rather than living, working, and suffering exclusively in the fields alongside other Mexicans, they are mostly employed in industrial and service jobs in large, urban centers. By coming into contact with a much more commonplace picture of American life, they receive a different good-bye gift for their trip home. They are endowed with a more "modern," movable, and universal piece of cultural baggage with which to travel.

Finally, changing demographics have made a qualitative difference in California's impact on Mexican society. There are simply far more Mexicans coming and going between Mexico and California than ever before. Although difficulties persist in establishing precisely how many Mexicans have journeyed north over the past decade, there is wide agreement that an astounding increase took place after 1982. Discrepancies between forecasts and the 1990 Mexican census point to approximately 4.5 people "missing"; they can probably be found in the United States. By some estimates, there are now up to eight million Mexican nationals living north of the border.[6] In each rural sending community, in every small urban center, the volume of immigration, and thus its impact, is staggering.

The chief effect of this migratory process—from which nearly all other effects are derived—is an awareness of "otherness": awakening to the existence of other peoples, customs, attitudes, political views, fashions, religions, music, movies, gender roles, labor relations, and drinking habits. Mexicans who go to California no longer perceive their own cultural environment as unique, but as just another part of a more complex whole: multifaceted, plural, and varied. Carlos Monsiváis has phrased this development more eloquently than anyone:

> This could be the migrant's prayer: I thank you, my Virgencita de Guadalupe, because you allow me to be the same as I have always been, even though you may have noticed, my Patron Saint, I am much more tolerant toward what I cannot understand or share, I can now be faithful to you—our nation—even though I am a pentecostalist, Jehovah's witness, adventist, baptist, or Mormon, bent on not changing although my aspect is so different, with my giant radio—this *rancho blaster*, I think it's called—from which burst forth melodies I never thought I would love. I swear, Virgencita, I am the same as always, although I cannot recognize myself in the mirror.[7]

A contemporary example of how California's influence on Mexico comes to bear is the tale of Los tigres del norte, a Mexican *norteño* band that has become immensely popular in California and throughout Mexico. The Tigres began as a typical Sinaloan *tambora* back in the early 1970s and started playing in small bars and moviehouses in California for *mojados* and nostalgic Chicanos. At the beginning, their songs reflected classical *corrido* motifs: love, treason, fights, and anguish. But little by little they began to incorporate border and migrant themes into their music, from Camelia la tejana's drug escapades in "Contrabando y traición" to "La jaula de oro," a melancholy complaint about a migrant's life in the United States. Not surprisingly, the popularity, sales, and movies of the Tigres soared everywhere in the United States and Mexico where migrants come and go.

As Jesús Martínez has shown in his work on the band, Los tigres del norte are a typical product of the immigration and return process: originating in Mexico, moving north and "making it," then coming back to Mexico.

> In Mexico and the United States, the social sectors associated with the international migration process are the consumers most likely to purchase the records, attend the dances and watch the movies of the *conjunto*. Thus it is in the best interest of the musicians to continue producing materials in accord with the experience and preferences of their principal market. . . . If the Tigres sang favorably about assimilation, acculturation or economic success in the United States, who would buy their songs? [8]

The explosion of local and regional radio stations throughout Mexico, their tight, almost incestous link with Mexican truckers and what Monsiváis has called "la ruta del trailer," and the almost perfect overlap of the land transport and migrant networks have made the Tigres a marvelous example of California's influence on Mexico: Mexicans north of the border affect Mexicans south of the border, through their music and laments, their obsessions, fears, and successes.

Another example of the impact of "otherness" on Mexican society can be found in changing attitudes toward gender relations. As an increasing number of women and entire families travel north, the type of interaction between men and women that tends to emerge in the United States is transferred back to Mexico. Women exposed to the way their husbands, fathers, brothers, or companions treated them in the United States—nothing out of this world, simply with decency—refuse to accept the behavior these same individuals often revert to on their return to Mexico. Just as in years gone by migrants brought pants back to their communities and banished the traditional women's dresses forever, today men and women are importing customs and attitudes that are transforming their native towns and villages.

A third important change sweeping down from the North through the migrants is exposure to "religious otherness." Obviously the expansion of Protestant sects in Mexico is not exclusively, or even chiefly, brought about by emigration to the United States and the sporadic trip home.[9] But for years scholars have stressed how undocumented Mexican workers in the United States seek the easily available, if not entirely altruistic, solace of Protestant sects and churches in the fields of California. This exposure to otherness contributes to a weakening of rejection mechanisms toward Protestantism in Mexican communities. Even in the small towns of Guanajuato one can now find posters on walls stating: "Protestants, stay away; we have already chosen our religion"—a sure sign of intolerance, but also of the growth of Protestantism in strongly devout Catholic areas. The more tolerant attitude toward different religious beliefs that appears to be emerging throughout Mexico is undoubtedly linked to the acceptance of "otherness" that myriad migrants bring back with them from California.

A similar situation may be developing with regard to political activity. Initially, the process appears to have worked the other way around: it was the emergence of mass electoral politics in Mexico in 1988 that sparked the growth of Mexican campaigning among California migrants, particularly by followers of Cuauhtémoc Cárdenas. But the type of political activity that is emerging among *cardenistas* in California—be it in Los Angeles, San Jose, or Fresno—will most likely be brought home to Mexico through the migrants themselves. And, inevitably, practices such as fund-raising, voter registration drives, access to the local media, freewheeling, often divisive debate—all forms of political endeavor largely absent from Mexico and unprecedented in the migrants' small towns and villages—will blossom in Mexico.

It would be naive, of course, to believe that tolerance and pluralism are all that Mexicans in California see and take home with them. Violence, racism, and "apple-pie" authoritarianism are also part of their American experience. They are discriminated against, excluded, sometimes beaten, and often cheated; their human, social, and labor rights are flagrantly disregarded. In a nutshell, there are aspects of their residence in California that resemble the worst features of their times in Mexico. Fortunately, the positive sides of California—otherness, openness, and tolerance—are likely to leave the strongest mark because they provide the sharpest contrasts to what the migrants leave behind.

It would also be wrong to attribute every change in Mexican society to the migrants. In most cases, the transformations to which they are contributing are already taking place and would occur with or without them. Profound modifications in government policies are affecting Mexico's economic and political realities; they may in time bring about a transformation of its mentalities, habits, and institutions. Mexico is also experiencing a deep alteration of its attitudes toward and relations with the United States. Immigration provides a backdrop to these changes, but it does not define them. Where the migrants make a fundamental difference is in breaking down obstacles and resistance to change in their native towns and villages.

At a time when so many detrimental influences are flowing from the United States to Mexico, California's democratizing impact is beneficial. Mexico should seek even greater access to this traditional, democratic, open, plural, and tolerant side of American life, which the migrants do not encounter often enough, but which they cannot help but contrast with the many closed, archaic, and narrow-minded facets of Mexican society. Ramón "Tianguis" Pérez sums up splendidly the returning migrant's ambivalent attitude toward his country:

> I hand the extra money to the officials, and one of them puts it in his pocket. Without so much as saying thank you for the thousands I have given them, they walk silently away, taking long paces with great dignity, as if instead of a robbery, they'd just carried out an act of justice. That's the way Mexico works. It had always been that way. Back in *bracero* days my father paid *mordidas* to bring clothing with him, and my townsmen pay today. Everybody comes back ready to pay bribes, and the only real differences between individuals are that some have more to pay than others, for no apparent reason. . . . Besides, getting home with my tools is worth more than I had to pay. The inconveniences of a wetback's life last only until he gets home again.[10]

Notwithstanding the bitterness, deceit, and even absurdity of some returning migrants' claims of success and glory "del otro lado," these expatriates bring back much of what the rest of the world admires in the United States and California. The flow of people to and from Mexico, despite the resistance in both countries to giving this part of the bilateral relationship its due importance, is contributing far more to Mexico's *aggiornamento* than massive microwave imports or free-trade hyperbole.

Those Who Work and Those Who Vote

Unfortunately, Mexico's influence on California is not so positive or beneficial. Through no fault of its own, undocumented Mexican immigration is contributing to the "dedemocratization" of California society. In an increasingly polarized environment, these illegal migratory flows are depoliticizing, denationalizing, and depriving of security and protection a significant sector of the so-called California underclass. Mexico's most lasting effect on California is thus political: by the end of the twentieth century, the richest state in the world will have a terribly skewed political system, with a foreign plurality that works, consumes, and pays taxes, but does not vote, run for office, organize, or carry much political clout.

This outcome is linked, not to the migrants themselves, but to the specific conditions of Mexican immigration to California, and to the evolving character of California society and politics. Together with other regions of the United States, California is becoming what many have called a two-tier society.[11] Structural change and adjustment have been accompanied by a dramatic growth in economic inequality and social polarization. Homelessness, unemployment, urban blight, drugs and delinquency, ostentatious (often insulting) disparities in wealth and living standards: the symptoms of underdevelopment in the United States and California are too striking to be ignored.

Mexican immigrants are particularly vulnerable to the negative effects of a two-tier society. In California today, the upward mobility achieved by previous migrants may no longer be possible. As Mike Davis writes in his book on Los Angeles:

> In the absence of any movement toward social justice, the most explosive social contradiction may become the blocked mobility of these children of the new imigrants. As a 1989 UCLA study revealed, poverty is increasing faster amongst Los Angeles Latinos, especially youth, than among any other urban group in the United States.[12]

According to Jackie Goldberg, president of the Los Angeles School Board, one-fourth of the children in Los Angeles, a large number of whom are Latino, live below the poverty line. One-seventh can be classified as being in "dire poverty," which Goldberg describes as those who "pay rent or have health care, but not both; choose between food, clothing or transportation, but not any two together; and whose only food is the free breakfast and lunch they receive in school."[13] Mexican immigrants are disproportionately represented in the bottom tier of society; and because their numbers are constantly replenished from abroad, even upward mobility does not reduce the size of the poor, Mexican-born share of California's population.

Economic and social polarization are exacerbated by the fact that the number of people actually voting in California represents a sharply decreasing percentage of the total population. Kevin Phillips documents this trend at the national level:

> Seventy-five percent of the citizenry voted in Pacific Palisades, 25 percent in the South Bronx. Election analysts could not be quite sure, but persons in the top quintile conceivably cast almost 30 percent of the total presidential vote

ballots in Ronald Reagan's 1984 landslide, and people in the two top quintiles together probably accounted for over 50 percent of turnout.[14]

California statistics convey a similar impression at the state level. Of California's 30 million residents, only 7.5 million vote; indeed, this figure has remained stable for several years despite substantial increases in the total population. Seventy-five percent of the electorate is white, compared to only 60 percent of the total population, and half of those who vote are over 50 years of age.[15] By contrast, the state's younger ethnic groups are seriously underrepresented. Asians, who account for 10 percent of the population, cast only 4 percent of the votes; Latinos, who make up 26 percent of the population, cast only 10 percent. Thus, only a minority participates in elections, and that minority is white, Anglo, middle or upper-middle class, and elderly. Most important, from the perspective of this essay, it is American: foreigners do not vote.

This dilemma cannot be reduced to the shortcomings of Mexican political culture. It is true that Mexicans have been far more reluctant to seek naturalization than previous immigrants to the United States: "Overall, fewer Mexican than other immigrants become citizens, and when they do, they take an average of four more years to do so (11 versus 7)."[16] Moreover, Mexicans who acquire U.S. citizenship continue to be informed by their own political traditions: elections and other political endeavors are viewed with a complete sense of futility. But apathy among immigrants eligible to participate politically is only part of a much larger problem. As long as undocumented immigration is a fixture of California life, "dedemocratization" will remain one of the central ways in which Mexico and other nations affect the state.

The emergence of what has been called "electoral apartheid" in California is related to the fact that a significant and growing portion of its population is of foreign nationality. According to the Current Population Survey, 55 percent of California's six million Latinos do not have citizenship; in Los Angeles, the figure rises to 62 percent.[17] This means that more than three million people, or one-tenth of the state's population, are politically disenfranchised. Mike Davis's distinction between those who vote and those who work is beginning to overlap with the distinction between Americans and foreigners, those with documents and those living outside legality.

These overlapping distinctions have dire implications for California society. In effect, a small, privileged minority is determining the fate of a largely poor, nonvoting majority. This minority uses fewer and fewer of the social programs its taxes are financing. According to Jackie Goldberg, 75 percent of registered voters and 88 percent of the people who actually go to the polls in California *have no children in school.*[18] In the meantime, as Richard Rothstein describes in his chapter, 63 percent of the student population in the Los Angeles school district is Latino; of these, 200,000 are not proficient in English. Faced with a choice between funding programs of little direct benefit to themselves and paying lower taxes, the response of the electorate should come as no surprise. California, which is the richest state in the union, ranks last both in class size and in the share of personal income spent on education.[19]

The bias in favor of the top tier, and against the bottom tier, is aggravated by a proliferation of user and impact fees to pay for schools, roads, mass transit, hospitals, and other "public facilities." In contrast to taxes, these fees are levied on those who consume (or are affected by) a given service or project. Only those projects funded by fees can be carried out, and only those projects that provide a service to a paying community of users can be funded. Because these fees severely dilute the redistributive effects of taxation and the democratic process, they are the fiscal equivalent of dedemocratization. Those who least need public services receive them, while those who need them the most do not, since they lack the means to pay for them. When coupled with the transfer of fiscal responsibilities from the federal level to local communities, these fees have the following effect:

> These voters (suburban, affluent, white, anglo) can satisfy their need for government services through increased local expenditures, guaranteeing the highest possible return to themselves on their tax dollars, while continuing to demand austerity at the federal level. Suburbanization has permitted whites to satisfy liberal ideas revolving around activist government while keeping to a minimum the number of blacks and poor people who share in government largesse.[20]

Under these circumstances, it is virtually impossible for a democratic system to function. What is being asked of California's "top-tier" electorate is to vote for higher taxes to finance public schools for blacks and Latinos in the bottom tier. A system based on universal suffrage should work the opposite way. Blacks and Latinos should vote for higher taxes levied progressively on everyone to finance public services. But, in California, universal suffrage is quickly becoming de facto restricted suffrage as the poor and the foreign do not vote. And since the large majority of California's foreign population is and will continue to be Mexican, part of the problem, and certainly part of the solution, is also Mexican.

Immigration from Mexico is likely to continue regardless of what enthusiasts of free trade, peace in Central America, or the closing of the border may say or do. The only realistic way to alter the negative effect of Mexican influence on California, then, is to change the nature of its origin by legalizing immigration and giving foreigners the right to vote in state and local elections.

Legalization is much less out of the question than many tend to believe. IRCA itself was a mass legalization venture, regularizing the status of over three million undocumented foreigners. Recent Justice Department rulings on asylum and refugee status for Central Americans also constitute the equivalent of generalized legalization, as do family reunification and semi–"green-card marriages." In Europe, following a long period when legal immigration was virtually halted and illegal migratory flows took its place, the trend is once again toward "regularization," as the consequences of maintaining large, highly concentrated, and illegal populations are deemed greater than the disadvantages of legalization.

There is no dispute that legalization poses costs and perils. The main danger lies in the incentive for future immigration and in the increased migratory flows that would undoubtedly result in the short term. But these costs are clearly no greater than the costs of the status quo, which threatens to tear California society apart. The real stumbling block is that the decision to legalize immigration will not be made by those who would benefit from it most—the bottom tier—but rather by a white, Anglo, middle-class, and elderly electorate. The only way to change the nature of California politics is through legalization, but the only way to achieve legalization is to change the nature of California politics. Not an easy circle to square.

Giving foreigners the right to vote is also a complex task, but it too represents a growing trend elsewhere in the world. As one study concludes: "The main reason Hispanics have not yet fully translated their increasing numbers into proportional increases in political representation and power is because most are not eligible to vote because of their age or lack of citizenship."[21] It would be naive to expect that simply by granting Mexicans in the United States the right to vote, they would immediately jettison the remnants of their political and cultural baggage and turn out like Scandinavians or Italians. But if they were placed on equal legal footing with their peers in the United States, the process of eliminating the vestiges of Mexican political culture would undoubtedly be swifter and less painful.

In 1975, Sweden became the first European nation to grant foreigners the right to vote in municipal and state legislative elections. Denmark, Norway, and Finland all followed suit in the early 1980s; the Netherlands, Ireland, and Switzerland proceeded in the same fashion later.[22] In France, the Socialist Party included granting the right to vote in municipal elections in its 1981 party platform, although President Francois Mitterand did not carry out his promise. This cross-national trend reflects the spectacular increase in the numbers of foreigners, either refugees or working immigrants, flocking to Scandinavia from Greece, Turkey, and Yugoslavia, and to other parts of Europe from West Asia, the Caribbean, the Maghreb, and sub-Saharan Africa.

In the United States, members of the Santa Monica and New York city councils have raised the possibility of granting foreigners the right to vote, but until now, the idea has met with indifference or outrage. The tradition in the United States has always been that foreigners should become U.S. citizens if they want to stay in the country and should not be granted political rights if they are only passing through. But qualitative and perhaps even quantitative changes in recent migratory flows to the United States show that this tradition is no longer appropriate to existing realities. Many people from Mexico and Central America have simply not made up their mind as to the length or nature of their stay. Moreover, since the flows are ongoing, there is always a large cohort of nonnaturalized foreigners in the United States. As this number grows, and the proportion of naturalized citizens relative to all foreign-born individuals in the United States diminishes, enfranchising foreigners only through naturalization becomes a less effective option.

The choice, then, lies between enfranchisement along European lines or continuing to deny foreigners political rights and relegating them to the bottom tier of California society. The fact that the problem is so strongly concentrated in California should serve as an incentive to finding a state or municipal solution. What happens in California or Los Angeles and San Jose need not be a federal policy applicable throughout the country. Although most Californians are likely to balk at the idea of giving foreigners the vote, regardless of what may be happening in other countries, the short-term feasibility of the idea should not detract from its instrinsic merits. Simply initiating a debate on this issue could push Californians to question long-held assumptions about political rights and responsibilities that no longer work in the face of new social and economic realities.

Legalization and foreigner-enfranchisement will not solve California's democratic crisis, nor will it automatically lead millions of Mexican and other Latin American immigrants to the polls. But without such changes in firmly entrenched American customs, the dedemocratization of California society will only get worse. Mexico's influence will become more pernicious, not because it is Mexican, but because any such mass, illegal, continuing migratory flow cannot but harm a society already as polarized and unequal as California's. There are no easy solutions to California's plight, which foreshadows that of the rest of the country. In the long term, however, all Californians will lose more from letting dedemocratization continue than from giving foreigners the right to vote. Enfranchising the bottom tier is not a panacea, nor is it a sufficient condition for rolling back the two-tier economy, but it is a necessary step in the right direction.

Conclusion

The complex, convoluted, and endlessly changing Mexico-California interface expresses itself today in a paradox. California's influence on Mexico has never been healthier, as mass migration and reflows bring change to Mexican communities that would otherwise remain fixed in time and custom. As Mexico ever so slowly and painfully is forced to reject its past, its new identity—if one is forged—will inevitably have California, Chicano features. The more the Chicano experience reaches Mexico, the stronger the country's refurbished nationalism will be, if it emerges intact from the ruins of the last decade and the havoc wrought by the headlong rush into economic integration with the United States.

Mexico, for its part, solves many of California's social and economic problems through the export of part of the country's labor force; but the undocumented, disenfranchised, and massive nature of this labor force aggravates the state's existing problems by denationalizing the poorer, excluded, and oppressed sector of California society. The intensifying rivalries between blacks, Mexicans, and Central Americans in areas where they coexist is nothing more than a violent, tragic, and foreseeable expression of this situation. In the very long run, these problems may simply fade away, as emigration from Mexico and Central America winds down and American society begins to tackle the disparities it has created and continues to ignore. The problem, however, is the meantime, as it generally tends to be in matters of human endeavor.

PART II

Trends in Mexico: Implications for California

CHAPTER 3

Reform, Globalization, and Structural Interdependence

New Economic Ties Between Mexico and California

LUIS RUBIO AND GUILLERMO TREJO

AS NEIGHBORS, Mexico and California are natural economic partners. Their relationship has historically been dominated by the exchange of goods, services, and labor. Trade has taken place for more than a century, and the *maquiladora* program along the border was first established in the 1960s. Generations of Mexican workers have journeyed to California in search of employment and better wages.

Since 1982, however, the nature of the economic interaction between Mexico and California has changed. As a result of crisis and reform in Mexico and expansion in California, the two regions are engaged in a new and intense process of structural interdependence. In addition to fulfilling its historical role as Mexico's second largest U.S. trading partner and the destination of half of its immigrants, California is becoming linked to Mexico through transnational production networks.[1]

This chapter analyzes the implications of economic restructuring in Mexico and California for the California-Mexico economic connection. The first two sections deal with crisis and reform in Mexico and the recent evolution of the California economy. The third section evaluates existing economic ties between the two regions. The conclusion examines the likely impact on California of the success or failure of the Mexican economic reform, particularly as it relates to the negotiation of a North American Free Trade Agreement.

Economic Crisis and Reform in Mexico

Economic change is the single most important feature of Mexico today and is likely to remain so into the twenty-first century. But economic change is a deeply political process with far-reaching political as well as economic consequences. The restructuring that began in Mexico in the 1980s is not only transforming the Mexican economy, but it is challenging existing political institutions and reshaping the norms, values, and behaviors that govern daily life.

Economic change is characterized by a shift in government priorities. From the 1940s to the early 1980s, the goal of the Mexican government was to develop a strong and independent domestic industrial base. Today's objective is to integrate Mexico into world markets. Although the government has pursued a policy of industrial development in both cases, the earlier strategy was based on inward-oriented production and government intervention in the economy, whereas the current approach favors international trade and investment, market mechanisms, and competitive standards of performance.

Mexico's economic reform stems from the collapse of the policy of import substitution industrialization (ISI) adopted in the 1940s. Until the mid-1980s, the government encouraged the domestic production of manufactured goods through import protection, subsidies, an overvalued exchange rate, and state-led investment. Imports were concentrated in raw materials and machinery, whereas exports consisted mostly of agricultural goods, minerals, and, after the mid-1970s, oil. Although the private sector was critical to Mexico's industrialization, the government played a central role in economic life. For the first thirty years of ISI, Mexico enjoyed annual average growth rates of 6 percent, relatively low levels of inflation, and impressive industrial expansion.

Even during the years of rapid growth, however, ISI sowed tensions in the Mexican economy. Excessive protection fostered an antiexport bias and supported an inefficient, uncompetitive, and oligopolistic industrial structure overly dependent on government largesse. Together with the internal bottlenecks caused by languishing agricultural production and a highly inequitable distribution of income, Mexico began to experience serious balance of payments problems. To finance a trade deficit of several billion dollars in the 1970s, Mexico relied increasingly on foreign loans and oil revenues.

When oil prices collapsed and foreign loans dried up in the early 1980s, Mexico could no longer sustain inward-oriented growth. For the first time in over 40 years, the country found itself in a severe economic crisis, with soaring levels of inflation, negative growth rates, and falling real wages and investment. In addition to discrediting ISI, the crisis revealed that the government's ubiquitous presence in the economy had become counterproductive: resources were not being used efficiently, innovation was stifled, and shoddy products filled Mexican stores and warehouses. As Mexico's leaders were soon to acknowledge, paying the country's import bill would require a redefinition of the state's role in the economy.

When President Miguel de la Madrid inherited Mexico's devastated economy in December 1982, he made reform a top priority of his administration. In an effort to close the fiscal and trade gaps, he slashed public spending, increased taxes, and presided over a dramatic reduction in imports. By the second year of his presidency, the trade deficit had been overturned, and the fiscal deficit had been cut in half. Because the adjustment came at the expense of investment and growth, however, the macroeconomic correction soon became paralyzed.

By 1985, it was obvious that stabilization alone would not revive the Mexican economy. Emboldened by the need for deeper changes, a group of reformers took control of Mexico's economic policymaking apparatus. Based on the belief that resolving the crisis required a restructuring of the government itself, they unleashed a series of reforms that would fundamentally alter the nature of the Mexican state and its responsibilities in the economy. This transformation of the state constitutes the single most important feature of Mexico's economic reform.

Since 1985, structural reform has been carried out through three general pieces of economic policy: trade liberalization, privatization, and deregulation. In 1986, Mexico entered the GATT and launched a unilateral program of import liberalization, becoming one of the most open economies in the world. By 1988, only 23.7 percent of the production of tradable goods was subject to nontariff barriers, down from 92 percent in 1985. Import quotas were replaced by tariffs, which, in turn, were drastically reduced: the average weighted tariff fell from 24 percent in 1982 to 11.8 percent in 1987 to 5.4 percent in 1991.[2]

The government also began to privatize state-controlled companies in the mid-1980s. By the end of the decade, 53 percent of the 1,155 enterprises owned by the government in 1982 had been sold. In May 1990, the Mexican Congress approved a constitutional amendment allowing for private ownership of the banks, reversing their nationalization in 1982. Other major enterprises released from governmental control have included Aeromexico, Teléfonos de Mexico, Cananea (a mining company), and Asemex (an insurance firm).

Finally, deregulation became an essential component of the reform by the end of de la Madrid's term and has since reached almost every corner of the Mexican economy. The most impressive changes have been in the transportation industry. In addition, the government has liberalized Mexico's foreign investment regulations, granting automatic approval to projects meeting certain criteria and opening most of the Mexican economy to 100-percent foreign ownership.

These structural reforms have altered the nature and dynamic of the Mexican economy. Import competition and deregulation are eliminating those businesses or products unable to compete while inducing an export-driven boom in sectors or firms that are competitive at world levels. Exports have become a critical phase of industrial production, and the manufacturing of components, rather than finished goods, is incorporating many of Mexico's most dynamic industries into a highly complementary manufacturing base for foreign firms. These changes have taken place with remarkably little economic dislocation. Historical employment patterns have remained relatively stable, with very low unemployment and still high levels of so-called underemployment, and there have been very few bankruptcies. Since the reform took hold, Mexico has experienced rapid industrial growth and a sustained rate of export expansion.

The consequences of the reform have not been limited to economics, however. By transforming the structure of power in society, the reform has eroded the traditional power base of the ruling Institutional Revolutionary Party (PRI). Each and every component of the reform has affected important interests within the PRI and has alienated traditional constituencies of the government. Mexico's ability respond to these pressures will have a determining impact on the future course of the reform.

The Political Impact of Economic Reform

Mexico's policy of ISI was matched by a semiauthoritarian political system. Since the 1930s, the Mexican government has exercised political control through a skillful combination of institutionalized bargaining, patronage, and the incorporation of key interest groups into the PRI. This system of corporatist control complemented the restrictive economic policies of ISI and enabled the economy to flourish in an environment of political stability.

With the shift away from ISI and the adoption of market criteria, however, corporatist one-party rule has become an anachronism. The old institutions and "rules of the game" do not fit the new circumstances and often hinder economic activity. In an open economy, the consumer—individual as well as industrial—becomes more important than organized groups of workers, peasants, or entrepreneurs. Traditional strongholds of the political system are weakened—if not destroyed—by the new economic logic. The privatization of government-owned corporations eliminates an important source of jobs and benefits for the highest echelons of the bureaucracy, liberalization of imports and the deregulation of economic activity strip the bureaucracy of many of its sources of power and corruption, and the reform of public finances reduces the discretionary spending available to government officials. Meanwhile, new stakeholders in the reform emerge, demanding accountability, participation, and electoral transparency.

The Mexican political system has already begun to reflect these pressures. In the last few years, Mexico has experienced the relatively new phenomenon of party competition. Although the three major parties are not modern structures capable of leading and channeling change, electoral competition is rapidly becoming the rule rather than the exception. As in all modern societies, economic adjustment and performance have proven to be critical factors in determining electoral outcomes. In the 1988 presidential election, both the recession and the lack of evidence of the potential benefits of the reform were central to the creation and impressive show of strength of the Frente Democrático Nacional (later the PRD) headed by Cuauhtémoc Cárdenas.

Economic crisis and reform have also led to a rapid decentralization of decision-making authority away from Mexico City. When the Mexican economy collapsed in 1982, the federal government lost its capacity to act as the engine of growth. In response, Mexican society at large had to take on the task of working, producing, importing, and exporting, regardless of the preferences of Mexico City bureaucrats. Faced with shrinking employment in the formal sector and drastic cuts in public investment, many Mexicans turned to the informal economy and the *maquiladora* industry to survive.

As a result of these changes, the northern border region became crucial for Mexico's development. In stark contrast to the rest of the country, the border states experienced an economic dynamism during the 1980s that brought jobs, new manufacturing plants, and a rapidly growing stream of dollars. The spark for this dynamism was the *maquiladora* industry. Attracted by an undervalued peso and the low Mexican wages that accompanied Mexico's financial crisis, foreign companies began investing in the *maquiladoras* in growing numbers, building more than 50 new plants every year after 1982. From 1982 to 1988, the *maquiladoras* provided 50 percent of all the new jobs created in Mexico as a whole.

As northern Mexico became the country's fastest-growing region, it gained economic and political clout. Mexico City now depended on border communities to generate foreign exchange and provide scarce jobs. The region's autonomy was deepened by the reform, which loosened the grip of the federal bureaucracy on northern entrepreneurs. Not surprisingly, border residents sought to match their new-found economic power with a more independent political voice. Beginning in the mid-1980s, the opposition Partido Acción Nacional (PAN) made consistently strong showings in northern state elections, finally winning the governorship of Baja California Norte in 1989.

Although Mexico's underlying political reality has changed drastically, many of the old structures remain in place. No new political system has emerged in the wake of overall institutional decay. A key question in Mexico today is how the government will act upon its shrinking power base—the PRI—while it has not yet begun to institutionalize the constituencies for reform that have emerged all over the country. The toughest challenge will be to manage a political system that has ceased to be based upon pyramidlike structures of power and is becoming increasingly diversified and pluralist in its sources of political influence. Whether the government can meet this challenge will have an critical impact on the future of the economic reform and, thus, on Mexico's relationship with California.

The Changing California Economy

The transformation of the California-Mexico economic connection reflects changes in California as well as in Mexico. Following several decades of rapid expansion, California has become the eighth largest economy in the world and home to 30 million inhabitants. In 1989, California contributed over 13 percent of the nation's gross domestic product, up from 11.8 percent in 1979. Disposable personal income in California grew from $83 billion in 1970 to $454 billion in 1989; the size of the state's economy was estimated to be over $777 billion in 1991. During the 1980s, nearly one in six new U.S. jobs was created in California.[3]

Much of California's dynamism can be attributed to its diverse economic base and growing integration into world markets, particularly in the Pacific Rim. These factors, together with the sheer size of the state's economy, help explain the deepening ties between California and Mexico. Economic diversity translates into vertical and horizontal linkages, particularly as Mexico expands opportunities for foreign participation in its economy. Global integration heightens California's dependence on foreign markets and suppliers, and places the state at the center of the Pacific Rim, of which Mexico is becoming an increasingly important part.

Economic Diversity

The California economy is characterized by remarkable diversity. In 1986, manufacturing, trade, finance, and services each accounted for at least

17 percent of California's gross state product. The only sectors of the economy to employ less than 5 percent of the state's work force are mining and agriculture; yet California is the nation's leading agricultural producer.[4]

Manufacturing is critical to California. Between 1970 and 1986, real manufacturing output increased from $45.4 billion to $96.3 billion in constant 1982 dollars. In 1989, the sector employed 2.2 million people, or 17.2 percent of California's nonagricultural labor force. Although this figure is five percentage points lower than in 1970, growth in manufacturing employment in California has outpaced that of the nation as a whole. Between 1979 and 1989, California increased its share of the nation's manufacturing jobs from 9.6 to 11 percent. During this period, the sector gained from import substitution as firms expanded or relocated to California to take advantage of relatively newer capital stock and rapidly growing markets.

One-third of the state's manufacturing employment is in high technology, which includes computers, communication equipment, electronic components, aircraft, missiles and space vehicles, and instruments. High technology jobs grew from 427,000 in 1970 to 754,00 in 1985 before declining as a result of defense cutbacks and foreign competition. Although this sector has been hard hit by the $6-billion decline in prime defense contracts to California between 1985 and 1989, industries such as computers, instruments, and communications equipment continue to register modest gains. In addition, California remains the nation's leading center for start-ups and new product development.

Another important sector for California is agriculture. Although farm-related goods and services account for less than 3 percent of the state's employment, earnings, or output, California is the leading U.S. producer of 39 agricultural commodities and the source of over 90 percent of the United States' broccoli, processed tomatoes, almonds, walnuts, pistachios, apricots, grapes, kiwifruit, nectarines, olives, pomegranates, and prunes. In 1988, the sector accounted for 360,600 jobs and generated $17.2 billion in income. Though production employment increased by only 12 percent between 1972 and 1989, jobs in agricultural services more than doubled. The state's top-ranking agricultural goods are milk and cream, grapes, and cattle.

Manufacturing and agriculture have long been central to California's economy, but the state's most impressive economic performance has been in service-producing industries, which include transportation and utilities; finance, insurance, and real estate; wholesale and retail trade; services; and government. The share of nonagricultural workers employed in these industries increased from 73.9 percent in 1972 to 77.3 percent in 1989. In December 1989, service-related employment surpassed ten million and accounted for more than four-fifths of all new jobs created in the state that year.

One of California's most dynamic service-producing industries is wholesale and retail trade. Between 1975 and 1986, jobs in trade increased by half, and real output in constant 1982 dollars expanded by 71.7 percent. In 1989, total sales reached $507 billion, and the sector employed three million people, or 23.7 percent of California's nonagricultural labor force. From 1982 to 1987, the most dynamic products in terms of sales were furniture and home furnishings, general merchandise, and family clothing. In addition to having the highest retail sales in the the country in 1988, California accounts for nearly 12 percent of the nation's jobs in wholesale and retail trade.

California also has a large and dynamic financial sector. With an average annual job growth rate of 3.4 percent in finance, insurance, and real estate, it outperformed the nation as a whole during the 1980s. Although these industries provide less than 7 percent of the state's employment or earnings, they were responsible for 17.6 percent of California's gross state product in 1986. Most of this output comes from real estate, but vast sums of money are represented by the assets, deposits, and loans of the state's commercial lending institutions. Between 1985 and 1989, the total assets of commercial banks and savings and loan institutions in California expanded by 10 percent and 35 percent, respectively, reaching a combined total of $693 billion in 1989. Although the savings and loan crisis and economic recession have hurt financial services in California, the sector continues to be important to the state and the nation.

The largest and fastest-growing sector of the California economy—both within service-producing industries and overall—is services. This sector covers a wide range of activities, including hotels and motels; motion pictures; recreation; private education; engineering and management consulting; and personal, business, and health services. In 1988, services accounted for 27.3 percent of the state's industrial earnings and 25.6 percent of its nonagricultural employment. Reflecting an average annual growth rate of 4.7 percent, service jobs expanded from 2.2 million in 1980 to 3.3 million in 1989. The largest activities in this sector are business and health services, which had combined receipts of $59.8 billion in 1987 and employed nearly 1.5 million people in 1989.

Integration into the World Economy

One of the reasons California has been able to maintain such economic diversity is its entrance into the global economy. In the last two decades, California has become a gateway to foreign markets. The value of traded goods flowing through the state's customs districts increased fourfold in constant dollars between 1973 and 1987. In 1989, California's ports and airports handled 19 percent of total U.S. trade, up from 12 percent in 1980. The total value of foreign trade passing through California in 1989 was $157.1 billion. More than $120 billion, or 77 percent, of this trade was with countries in the Pacific Rim.

Foreign trade has supported job growth in nearly every sector of the California economy. In 1988, the state's $4 billion in agricultural exports was equivalent to 24 percent of total farm receipts. California has the highest number of exported-related manufacturing jobs of any state in the country and ranks tenth in its export-related share of manufacturing employment. According to the U.S. Chamber of Commerce, one of every ten jobs in California was related to international trade in the mid-1980s; by 1995, the ratio is expected to be one in five.[5] The total volume of trade in high technology manufactures approached $50 billion in 1989, with office machine parts and computers among the state's leading exports and imports.

California has also become a magnet for foreign capital. Accumulated direct investment in the state has increased tenfold since 1977, reaching $42.6 billion in 1989. More than 100 foreign banks, with total combined assets of $126 billion in 1990, have offices and/or corporate subsidiaries in California. Japan is the state's leading supplier of foreign capital, with $8.1 billion in direct foreign investment and $104.4 billion in total combined bank assets.[6]

Mexico and California: The New Economic Connection

The combination of crisis and reform in Mexico and globally driven expansion in California has deeply affected the California-Mexico economic connection. What used to be primarily a trading relationship is evolving into a manufacturing relationship based on the de facto integration of the two economies. As Mexico modernizes and opens up its economy, it looks to California for markets, capital, and technology. California, meanwhile, relies on Mexico to purchase its goods and services, and to provide the complementary manfacturing processes necessary to consolidate its position in global marketing and production networks.

Flows of goods and services between Mexico and California have taken off since Mexico joined the GATT and launched its unilateral program of economic liberalization and stabilization in 1986. According to the California World Trade Commission, Mexico ranks third among California's trading partners and second as an export market for California commodities.[7] In 1990, trade between the two regions reached $9 billion, up from $7.4 billion in 1989. Although the state continues to run a trade deficit with Mexico, exports have risen by 25 percent each year since 1988, far above the average growth rate of 17 percent for imports.[8] These exports directly or indirectly account for approximately 100,000 California jobs.[9] Among the leading items traded in both directions are electronic equipment, fabricated metals, and computer products.

Increased trade with Mexico threatens some sectors in California, particularly agriculture. Because of differences in climate and a ten-to-one differential between U.S. and Mexican wages, producers in northwestern Mexico enjoy a comparative advantage in vegetables and fresh fruits, especially during the winter. Mexico produces one-quarter of all fruits and vegetables imported by the United States each year, and the value of its exports of fresh tomatoes, broccoli, and cauliflower to the United States is greater than that of all other foreign suppliers combined. In recent years, California has run a deficit with Mexico in fresh and chilled tomatoes, and in fresh fruits (excluding grapes and citrus).

The recent expansion of trade between Mexico and California is closely related to deepening production ties. The most dramatic example is the *maquiladora* industry, which is estimated to produce 80 percent of all California imports. Four out of ten *maquiladoras* are located along the California-Mexico border; at least 315 have their home base in San Diego.[10] Most of these California-based plants assemble or manufacture electronic equipment, textiles, or paper-related products. According to the U.S. International Trade Commission, the *maquiladora* payroll generates between $73 million and $95 million each year for southern California.[11]

The *maquiladora* program has demonstrated the tremendous potential for complementarity and production-sharing processes between Mexico and California. By providing access to low-cost labor, the program has enabled California industries to achieve the competitiveness and efficiency necessary to prosper in world markets. It has also allowed consumers to enjoy commodities at competitive prices. The "export" of California jobs to Mexico has been offset by the creation of *maquiladora*-related employment north of the border. In trade, such jobs range from low-skilled activities, such as cargo transportation, packaging, and handling, to high-skilled occupations, such as design, marketing, and finance. California workers also manufacture many of the *maquiladora* inputs. According to one estimate, some 200,000 new high-skilled jobs related to the *maquiladora* industry have been created in California in recent years.

Agriculture is another area in which production sharing is becoming increasingly common. Faced with Mexico's comparative advantage in fruits and vegetables, many large- and medium-sized California growers are opting for partnerships or contractual arrangements to carry out the production and processing of these goods in northern Mexico. Labor-intensive activities are moved to Mexico, leaving California operators to concentrate on capital-intensive activities. In the production of vine-ripened tomatoes, for example, peasants in Baja California specialize in hand-picked fresh tomatoes, while hardier varieties are harvested by machines in California. An estimated 90 percent of the funding for Baja California farming operations comes from the United States, and California is undoubtedly a major participant.[12]

Impact of Alternative Scenarios in Mexico

The future of the California-Mexico economic connection is closely related to the success or failure of the Mexican economic reform. This reform, in turn, is by its very nature inextricably linked to the management of Mexico's relationship with the United States. The most pivotal issue in U.S.-Mexican relations today is the negotiation of a North American Free Trade Agreement (NAFTA). The successful legislative ratification of these negotiations will consolidate Mexico's reform; otherwise, the reform will be vulnerable to the vagaries of economic and political cycles in both countries.

Success of the Mexican Reform

Mexico's economic reform might survive even without a free trade agreement. Favorable economic conditions on both sides of the border could sustain the reform despite a lack of signed guarantees. Given Mexico's heavy reliance on U.S. capital and markets, however, a failure to formalize free trade would entail high levels of economic and political uncertainty. Economic growth would most likely be modest, meaning further postponement of social demands already delayed for a decade. Moreover, the Salinas administration would experience a severe political blow, since a central item on its agenda would have been defeated. Although a unilateral continuation of Mexico's economic opening would deepen trade and investment ties with California, the pace of integration would be limited. Trade disputes would be harder to resolve and could become highly volatile in the event of increased U.S. protectionism. Investors, who would remain skeptical of the long-term permanence of the reform, would be less likely to engage in sophisticated production-sharing arrangements.

The most favorable scenario for the success of the Mexican reform would be the signing and ratification of a NAFTA. Such an agreement would be a natural extension of the reform, since it would extend liberal economic policies and accelerate the globalization of the Mexican economy.

Moreover, a NAFTA would secure for Mexico the foreign investment and U.S. market access upon which the reform's success depends. The ensuing economic growth would ease pressing social demands, broaden the reform's constituency, and provide a more favorable climate in which to modernize Mexico's anachronistic and unstable political institutions.

California stands to reap significant benefits from the completion of a NAFTA and the consequent success of the Mexican reform. Further liberalization and economic growth in Mexico could spur renewed dynamism in sectors that have suffered from defense cutbacks and recession. It would also offer a more stable environment to foreign investors and encourage greater California participation in the Mexican economy. Finally, it would foster competition and economies of scale, thereby providing an opportunity for specialization and higher levels of efficiency.

California's diverse and sophisticated economy is ideally suited to respond to Mexico's modernization. The deepening and consolidation of Mexico's reform would enable California firms to capitalize on their strengths in high technology manufacturing, agriculture, and services. A study by the California World Trade Commission finds that the greatest potential for California exports to Mexico is in high-tech products, particularly computers and telecommunications. Further opening of the Mexican economy would deepen production-sharing arrangements in manufacturing and agriculture and provide new investment opportunities in tourism, finance, and transportation. According to the California Department of Food and Agriculture, liberalization of Mexican agriculture would bring windfall gains to California exporters of beef, deciduous fruits, and wine.[13]

Ultimately, this scenario would lead to the consolidation of an important network of production-sharing arrangements in North America. As Japan has demonstrated through its complex set of sourcing relationships in the Pacific Basin, production-sharing heightens competitiveness by enabling firms to combine high technology with low-cost labor to produce a wide range of products for global consumption. In 1990, over 35 percent of all Japanese exports were the result of production-sharing arrangements. The collapse of the Berlin Wall offers the European community similar opportunities to develop complementary production processes. By providing access to low-cost Mexican labor and securer investment opportunities, the success of Mexico's reform would strengthen California firms relative to their Japanese and European competitors. In the process, the California-Mexico region would enhance its role as a key arena for trade and production in the Pacific Rim.

Although most sectors of the California economy stand to reap immediate benefits from the Mexican reform, the consolidation of production-sharing arrangements with Mexico would heighten labor market adjustment. As further specialization took place, and California experienced an accelerated shift toward a service and high technology economy, the state's labor force would be exposed to shifts in labor market requirements: firms would demand higher-skilled workers. Because of the deterioration of California's basic education, labor might not adjust rapidly to these changes, especially workers now employed in low-skilled, labor-intensive activities. For those workers unable to find jobs in the service sector, unemployment and poverty would increase, at least in the short term.

Eventually, however, even less-skilled workers in California would benefit from closer trade and investment ties with Mexico. The reduced Mexican immigration resulting from job creation in Mexico would increase demand (and presumably wages) in those sectors currently dependent on low-cost Mexican immigrant labor. More important, a prolonged shortage of high-skilled workers would encourage California firms to invest in the education and training necessary to prepare an adequate work force, leading to higher standards of living for all Californians.

The Demise of the Reform

If the free trade negotiations break down, Mexico's reform has a limited chance of attaining the expected results. Rather than abandoning the reform, Mexico's governing coalition would probably deepen and accelerate it in an attempt to consolidate the structural changes and prevent a serious economic downturn. But absent the guarantees offered by a free trade agreement, the reform would become fully dependent on the political will and capacity of the Mexican government and on the reaction of constituencies for and against the government's program.

Under this scenario, the reform would be highly vulnerable to two related factors. First, the evolution of the Mexican economy is closely tied to U.S. economic performance. A strong rate of growth in the United States, combined with proper domestic management in Mexico, might prove decisive in sustaining, and even deepening, the reform. A prolonged U.S. recession, on the other hand, would most likely have the opposite effect. Many of Mexico's exports are related to the most recession-prone sectors of the U.S. economy, particularly automobiles and construction, and would be seriously thwarted by economic crisis north of the border. Without a NAFTA, these negative economic effects would be compounded by growing pressures in the United States to raise protectionist barriers to Mexican goods and services. Confronted with these obstacles to export-led growth, Mexico's leaders might be tempted to abandon the reform.

Second, and relatedly, Mexico's government faces growing political tensions. The most obvious and influential source of opposition at present stems from those groups undermined by the reform: bureaucrats, politicians, union leaders, and some businessmen. As net losers in the process of liberalization, they were the first to challenge the political system. Some left the PRI, while others have become an internal opposition resisting the reform from within. The failure of a NAFTA would embolden these groups, enhancing their ability to place obstacles in the way of the reform. Weak export performance because of recession and protectionism in the United States would further strengthen their appeal. In the event of a severe economic downturn and increasing social unrest, they might even gain sufficient influence to roll back the reform in favor of a greater centralization of economic and political power.

The demise of the Mexican reform would entail deep negative consequences for California. Bilateral exchange and trade-related employment in California would decline as import substitution policies were imposed and Mexican production was reoriented to satisfy the domestic market. With greater regulation and government intervention in the economy, California investment would face strong incentives to flow elsewhere. Efforts to reverse the decentralization of economic power could dampen rapid growth along the California-Mexico border.

If these policies were accompanied by economic downturn and social unrest in Mexico, California could experience difficult adjustments. As in previous periods, the failure of the Mexican economy to generate sufficient employment would result in the mass migration of Mexicans to California. Likewise, economic downturn in Mexico would cause border communities to suffer a retail crisis similar to the one experienced in the early 1980s. But because of the structural interdependence that has emerged between the two regions in the last decade, California would feel the effects of a Mexican crisis more profoundly than ever before. California today is as dependent on manufacturing processes in Mexico as Mexico is on California investment. With the onset of crisis in Mexico, there could be serious problems in delivering products—parts and components made in Mexico—that have become critical to California firms. Thousands of supplier and service jobs could be lost, and consumers would face higher prices. Denied access to low-cost, labor-intensive processes in Mexico, California would be increasingly vulnerable to Japanese and European competition and less able to serve as a hub for world trade and production.

Conclusion

In the long run, a rollback of Mexico's economic reform is not likely to prevail. The process of decentralization in Mexico, nearly a decade old, has gained its own, unstoppable momentum. Individual actors are having ever greater de facto decision-making power, and the Mexican border is likely to continue the process of integration with California one way or another. Any future attempt to recentralize economic policy would create such chaos that a recast of the reform would not be an unlikely or surprising event.

But even the short-run demise of the Mexican reform would have extraordinary costs for both California and Mexico. By scaring off trade, investment, and savings, stop-and-go policies would prevent the process of integration from realizing its full potential on either side of the border. Ups and downs along the way could well sour U.S. investments in Mexico, diminishing the pace, but not the fact, of integration along the border.

De facto integration is a reality for Mexico and California that will not go away, a fact of life with which both regions will have to contend in the decades to come. Barring a dramatic regional economic collapse (in both nations), California and Mexico are likely to experience a deeper and ever more important process of integration, regardless of what happens in Mexico City. Whether this process is smooth and mutually reinforcing or fraught with difficulties, however, will depend heavily on decisions made in the U.S. and Mexican capitals. A critical step toward realizing the first scenario is the formalization of free trade and, thus, the consolidation of Mexico's economic reform.

CHAPTER 4

The Connection at Its Source

Changing Socioeconomic Conditions and Migration Patterns

AGUSTÍN ESCOBAR LATAPÍ

SOCIAL AND ECONOMIC conditions in Mexico have an important impact on the flows of people, goods, and capital that make up the California-Mexico Connection. These flows, in turn, have a major influence on California and a feedback effect on Mexico. The result is a complex set of interrelationships that have become increasingly entrenched and self-reinforcing.

From a social and demographic point of view, the most important feature of the California-Mexico Connection is migration and its impact on the work force and the population's general well-being. Gradually, the nature of this migration has changed. Labor flows have been joined by family reunification, educational and health-related mobility, and cross-border network maintenance. Additionally, the surge of migration of the late 1970s and the 1980s has produced much vaster migration networks than before, tapping the large demographic reserves in Mexico's main metropolitan areas as well as those in rural, poor states.[1] Mexico's economic crisis not only pushed more people to migrate, it also changed their assessments of Mexico's future and together with U.S. immigration reform produced a shift towards more permanent migration patterns.[2]

Also, although the economic policies of the Mexican government are meant to increase the long-term viability of the economy, they contribute to an increase both in migration and length of stay. The drop in minimum and real wages in Mexico is a factor that may help skilled workers decide to go north. Trade liberalization has marginalized large sectors of Mexico's domestic industry from the economy's partial recovery, and imports dumped in Mexico have damaged farmers and small employers, further destabilizing employment and promoting migration. The demise of Mexico's long-standing subsidy structure and inflationary financing of urbanization has impinged on the quality of life of urban Mexicans.

As a result, Mexican popular sectors now face an international opportunity structure: jobs, family, social environment, and relevant social services are geographically dispersed. The movement of people from one place to another reinforces social relations spanning the border and serves as a channel for cross-border influences. Migrants do not disconnect themselves from their hometown when they first leave it, nor do they forget California when they return to Mexico: migration forges links that long outlive individuals.

Since social conditions in the two regions will probably retain their marked unevenness, Mexican migration to California is likely to increase, barring a major recession. This deepening migratory link is reshaping social and economic conditions on both sides of the border. In California, migration helps to define the character and work conditions in agriculture, services, and manufacturing activities, and has an important impact on the socioeconomic profile of Latinos. In Mexico, migration has become a key element in the livelihood of a growing number of settlements. While in the early 1960s migration and remittances were clearly concentrated in a few states in Mexico, after 1980 it became relevant to "popular sectors" throughout the country, including Mexico City and Guadalajara.

Socioeconomic Developments in Mexico

The evolving character of Mexican migration to California is closely related to socioeconomic developments in Mexico. Mexico's social structure in the early 1990s is the outcome of a period of growth and development stretching from 1940 to approximately 1980 and a subsequent period of crisis and adjustment. The changes that took place during these two periods have recast the life chances of most Mexicans and the migratory component of the California-Mexico Connection.

Urbanization and the Emergence of New Social Classes

The period of rapid economic growth from 1940 to 1980 is often referred to as "the Mexican Miracle," during which Mexico underwent a rapid transformation of its occupational and sectoral employment structures. The proportion of the economically active population (EAP) employed in agriculture dropped from 65 percent in 1940 to 28.9 percent in 1980. Although pockets of subsistence agriculture persisted, wage labor became prominent in the countryside, and commercial crops replaced maize and beans. Many of Mexico's workers entered manufacturing, whose share of the EAP increased from 17.9 percent in 1950 to 27.5 percent in 1979. Even more workers moved to the tertiary sector (commerce and the services), which grew from 23.7 percent to 43.2 percent of EAP. Within this period, modern services such as health care and finance expanded still more rapidly, both in the government and in the private sector.

Mexico also experienced a rapid transformation of the kinds of work being performed. As its occupational structure became more diversified, overall growth in nonmanual employment and increasing salarization[3] were accompanied by consistent drops in self-, family, and domestic employment. Mexico's occupational structure moved directly from an agrarian-based profile into a "tertiarization" stage, skipping the classic "secondarization" (or industrial) stage undergone by Great Britain and other countries. The main components of this shift were an expansion in government employment; an expansion of modern services in the private sector and the modernization of some traditional services; and, least of all, the growth of urban "informal" occupations, mostly personal or repair-related.

Largely as a result of urbanization and occupational modernization, social mobility during this period was among the highest in Latin America and just under that of the United States during the first half of the twentieth century.[4] Middle-income groups (percentiles 20 to 89) made the greatest gains in their share of total income, which increased from 45.5 percent in 1950 to 60 percent in 1977.[5] Inequality remained high, however, as peasants and casually employed urban workers lowered their participation in total income. The share of income received by the poorest 10 percent of the population decreased from 2.4 percent of Mexico's gross national product in 1957 to only 1.1 percent in 1977. This meant that the number of those living in poverty, while proportionately less important in 1977 than in 1957, remained at around 30 million.[6]

Mexico's sectoral and occupational transformation provided the basis for the creation of two new social categories: the new working class and the new middle class.[7] The new working class enjoyed stable jobs and growing fringe benefits. The new middle class included a significant number of upwardly mobile individuals, who had access to middle or higher levels of education, developed their business talents during the postwar boom, or entered the government at the onset of its expansion. Teachers, health workers, and office workers accounted for most of the growth of nonmanual employment in government.

The new working class emerged as a result of the expansion of modern industry, improving real wages, and the interaction of government policy with urbanization. After 1945, real industrial wages improved more or less systematically until they reached a brief all-time peak in 1976, enabling a growing number of working-class households to subsist on a single industrial wage.[8] In addition, these workers derived benefits from subsidized staples, public transport, electricity, and water rates, and they enjoyed increasing health and pension protection from the Mexican Social Security Institute (IMSS), which was created in 1943 and expanded its coverage to about one-half of the waged work force in 1975.[9] A small number of workers also took advantage of housing provisions secured in the contracts of the largest and most powerful unions, which after 1972 were nominally extended to all stable workers with the creation of Instituto del Fondo Nacional para la Vivienda de los Trabajadores (INFONAVIT). This agency, however, has never provided more than 7 percent of the new housing stock and has been biased toward higher-income manual workers and, since 1983, nonmanual employees.

Despite the importance of the new working class during this period, it failed to consolidate its economic or political position. Its members made up a fairly small portion of the waged labor force, and they were either secluded in small towns, where they exercised significant local power but could not influence larger categories of workers, or merged with other urban workers in shanty towns and barrios, becoming part of the "urban-popular sector." In addition, union-based sectionalism prevented members of the new working class from exercising political leadership over the working class as a whole, and dependence on the state and state-coopted union leaders for improved pay and working conditions severely limited their economic options. This dependence made them all the more vulnerable after 1982, when antiunion government policies slashed their standard of living and left them politically marginalized, as happened in the oil, steel, sugar, electricity, automobile, paper, and other unions.

From the point of view of changes in the composition of Mexican society, the emergence of the new middle class was more significant. In just thirty years, upwardly mobile Mexicans—especially professionals—achieved a standard of living comparable to that of developed countries and a privileged position in the urban-social hierarchy.[10] Unlike the new working class, the new middle class was socially distinctive and called on old bourgeois values to assert itself. Its members lived in good neighborhoods, married amongst themselves, were nationalistic but strongly influenced by foreign culture, mistrusted the government but did business with it, provided their children with distinctive private education, were the mainstay of the expansion of consumer-oriented industry, and traveled abroad.

The growth of the new middle class reflected the changes in Mexico's occupational structure. Until 1975, nonmanual workers improved their incomes in real terms and distanced themselves from manual workers. Although the government was again the sponsor of this trend, the modernization of industry and service firms was partly responsible. The complexity of the tasks carried out by established firms grew: sales and personnel departments were opened, finances and tax counseling became professional activities, lawyers and business graduates were increasingly demanded by growth in economic activities and property transactions, and there was room for new medical specializations. The rapidly expanding construction sector also professionalized at the top, although at the manual end it kept its old trade character and has never been formalized.

The new middle class also benefited much more than the new working class from social expenditures by the Mexican government. Middle-class Mexicans bought formal housing in well-urbanized neighborhoods, enjoyed the subsidies for most staple foods, fuel, water, and electricity, took advantage of real zero-cost credit, and often showed remarkable expertise in the use of social security institutions, where their know-how and connections gave them the best attention possible.

Like the new working class, however, the new middle class was largely dependent on the state to provide jobs and to set salary levels. Public-sector employees were recruited through *camarillas*, groups of professionals loyal to a political patron, and these groups moved within the Mexican political and technical apparatus depending on the fortunes of their patron, not their professional or technical competence or specialization.[11] Even for middle-class employees in the private sector, the sheer weight of the government in the economy had a determining influence on employment patterns.[12]

The growth of Mexico's new social classes lasted only as long as the Mexican Miracle, which began to falter in the 1970s. Lagging industrial growth, declining public-sector salaries, and adjustment policies adopted by the government combined to weaken the new working and middle classes. Anti-inflation measures taken after 1975 caused the real incomes of nonmanual dependent workers to drop rapidly. By the end of the 1970s, the incomes of clerical workers had become almost equal to those of skilled manual workers, and in some cases had dropped below them.[13] Faced with narrowing job opportunities, fewer Mexicans enrolled in professional studies, and growing numbers of nonmanual and manual workers turned to self-employment.[14] With the passage of the golden age of government expansion, bureaucrats also suffered, although generous public spending, fringe benefits, and social expenditure still amounted to a significant part of their total income. Even private-sector professionals, who were not yet feeling a downturn, found their markets becoming progressively saturated.

Until 1975, international migration largely tapped the same source as internal migration, that is, the rural, impoverished areas in Mexico, but particularly those with the oldest migration histories. Therefore, the cities with larger international migrant populations were those, like Guadalajara, that were at the center of regions with long migration histories. Up to 1975, cities attracted internal migrants arriving directly from rural areas and those with international experience. Mexico's "brain drain" in the 1960s and early 1970s consisted mostly of skilled manual workers (plumbers, carpenters), not professionals. The "new" middle class had no incentive to migrate, except under conditions of extreme financial insecurity, as in 1976. In many ways, demand had expanded faster than the supply of nonmanual labor, so that often employees, professionals, and managers who had experienced significant lifetime social mobility could not aspire to similar occupations in the U.S. But it was approximately then that stagnation in the growth of the new classes and the cities' incapacity to keep pace with growing demand started to change people's outlooks.

Crisis and Adjustment

The deterioration of Mexico's urban occupational structure and income distribution in the 1970s reached crisis proportions during the 1980s. Faced with falling oil prices, soaring interest rates, and the drying up of foreign credit, Mexico's economy went into a tailspin in late 1981 and 1982. For the next eight years, Mexico would suffer its worst economic crisis since the Revolution (1910–21).

The most dramatic index of the crisis and adjustment of the 1980s is the evolution of wage levels. The minimum wage lost 60 percent of its purchasing power between 1982 and 1991, and real average *maquiladora* and industrial wages fell 25 and 35 percent, respectively, between 1982 and 1986. Although *maquiladora* and manufacturing wages rose slightly in 1987, all wages continued to fall after that year up to 1990.[15]

Income trends among nonmanual workers differed according to their insertion in the public or private sectors. In 1990 public-sector employees (teachers, bureaucrats, health providers) earned less than half their 1980 salary, but their situation improved slightly afterwards, following major labor protests. Employees, managers, and higher-ranking executives in large-scale private enterprises lost between 10 and 30 percent of their purchasing power between 1982 and 1987, but their pay levels had, by 1991, improved in real terms over those of 1982.[16]

One of the most striking results of Mexico's economic crisis was an "equalization through impoverishment" up to 1984.[17] Although income inequality diminished across the board, the number of Mexicans living in poverty is estimated to have soared from 32.1 million in 1980 to 41.3 million in 1987.[18] These figures reflect the modern sector's inability to generate employment, and the diminishing share of wages in gross domestic product, which decreased from 36.7 per cent in 1981–82 to 26.8 per cent in 1987–88.[19] The Economic Commission on Latin America and the Caribbean[20] estimates that the number of informally employed in Mexico grew by 80 percent from 1980 to 1987. In Guadalajara, the self-employed accounted for over 19 percent of the total work force in 1990. Throughout urban and rural Mexico, there are more workers per household now than in 1982, largely as a result of women entering informal service occupations and often working unpaid in small family workshops.[21]

In addition to suffering lower wages, Mexicans found their standard of living curtailed by a dramatic decline in government expenditures. Social spending dropped in real terms as well as relative to total spending, and investment in social infrastructure and regional development fell calamitously.[22] As cities became less able to fund and manage growth, the transit from illegal, unserviced land occupations to legal, serviced barrios came to a standstill, and overcrowding became more severe.[23] Additionally, Mexicans faced lower subsidies in the price of all staples, and real rises in interest rates and land, water, and electricity rates.

Surprisingly, health indicators in Mexico did not follow the same downward trajectory as living standards. Credit should probably be given to the Mexican government for emphasizing basic health care. As Fernando Torres-Gil discusses in this volume, Mexico's key health service institutions are the Instituto Mexicano del Seguro Social and the Secretaría de Salud. The first provides health care for stable workers and their families, as well as to some small farmers, and the second is an "open coverage" institution. Although major efforts at reorganizing the health sector in order to reach dispersed, poor areas were neither efficient at improving services nor welcome by the central health agencies,[24] emphasis on primary care seems to have worked at least in urban areas, where coverage is reasonably good. In Guadalajara, over 50 percent of mothers and 74 percent of patients requiring other kinds of hospital treatment relied on IMSS and Secretaría de Salud clinics and hospitals from 1988 to 1990.[25] Professionals made particularly heavy use of these resources, perhaps indicating their lessened ability to pay for private care.[26]

Because of increasing poverty and the serious financial pressures placed on government institutions since 1982, however, health indicators in Mexico have not maintained the pace of improvement of the 1970s. Poverty and malnutrition-related deaths have risen among children, and the gap between rural and urban mortality levels has increased.[27] Both affiliates and doctors complain of lack of equipment and crowding in hospitals and clinics.

Mexico's Social Profile in the 1990s

Mexico entered the 1990s substantially changed by events in the previous decade. Just as the period of rapid growth from 1940 to 1980 created "new" working and middle classes, the crisis of the 1980s has modified Mexico's occupational and hierarchical structure. These changes have important implications for Mexican immigration to California.

The only dynamic source of growth in the formal-modern sector during the 1980s was the *maquiladora* industry, which expanded from 100,000 workers in 1980 to just under 500,000 in 1990.[28] In addition to growing rapidly, the *maquiladoras* experienced qualitative changes that made them more similar to the rest of Mexican industry. For one, the profile of *maquiladora* workers changed significantly. Instead of relying primarily on women and secondary family earners, the *maquiladoras* began to hire increasing numbers of men. In 1987, for example, women accounted for over 40 percent of the workers employed by Ford and General Motors in their *maquiladora* plants manufacturing cars or components.[29] This shift reflects a lack of jobs and falling wages in the modern sector, excessive demand for young women workers in some cities, and the broadening scope of *maquiladora* production, which now encompasses many nontraditional products.[30] In addition, *maquiladora* wages, which were far lower than those of other industries, approached "normal" levels because others dropped faster, suggesting that *maquiladora* jobs are as much of a deterrent to migration as any other kind of industrial employment in Mexico.

The shrinking of the formal-modern sector was accompanied by a dramatic increase in the informal economy. Almost all of the urban-popular sectors, whether formally employed or not, perform informal money-earning activities of one type or another and are much more occupationally unstable than ten years ago. The informal working class, organized in households lacking any stable, protected jobs, has mushroomed; because industrial wages have been pushed down systematically, the income of self-employed workers in repair or manufacturing shops can equal two or three industrial wages, prompting a further exodus of skilled workers from the modern sector. Moreover, the character of work and employment in general has shifted towards informality, even in the so-called formal sector.

The collapse of the formal sector has not only affected manual workers. Young professionals are finding it increasingly difficult to get jobs and, if they do, must accept extremely low entry-level salaries and unstable working conditions. Independent professionals and small businesses face a still-depressed market, and credit is hard to obtain. Meanwhile, large firms are having trouble filling high-paying positions in international marketing, water and energy management, and communications. The shift in emphasis to business, administration, and computing curricula within universities has not been sufficiently swift, further slowing enrollment.

Agriculture is also changing quickly. Extremely poor rural areas, which were completely neglected from 1982 to 1988, are now being incorporated into the Solidaridad program[31] and receive very small loans to grow maize. More prosperous commercial agricultural regions are being required for the first time to demonstrate a good payment history before receiving loans. Although implementation varies with the political sensitivity of the region, these policy changes are aimed at retaining poor peasants on their land while at the same time stimulating productivity on the part of prosperous small farmers and agro-entrepreneurs.[32]

Perhaps one of the most significant impacts of the Mexican crisis has been a shift in the geographical locus of economic and demographic growth. Mexico City, which had long been the country's economic and political center, was severely hit by the crisis. Government withdrawal from the economy and the lack of private investment to take up the slack meant that the labor market stagnated at all levels. This situation was compounded by the 1985 earthquake, which produced the largest out-migration of Mexico City residents in recent history.[33]

Residents of Guadalajara, Monterrey, and smaller cities in central and northern Mexico felt threatened by the sudden influx of migrants from Mexico City. Pejoratively referred to as *chilangos*, these migrants were stereotyped in two ways: first, as dark-skinned, thick-lipped, black-haired, dirty, uneducated people of Indian ancestry who contrasted with the North and West's typically white, semieducated population; and, second, as hyperactive, overconfident professionals who despised "little townspeople." The two stereotypes depict social categories that were moving out of the Federal District—unskilled workers and middle-class professionals—and indicate a more general phenomenon: Mexico City was deflecting recent rural migrants and the population it had once attracted from the rest of the country.

Although Mexico City's situation has improved since 1988, it seems unlikely that it will regain its status as the center of economic growth. Instead, medium-sized cities in the center, West, and along the northern border, whose "flexible" patterns of employment[34] better survived the crisis of the 1980s, are likely to continue as Mexico's fastest-growing regions. In an externally driven economy, firms are likely to be attracted to smaller, more easily manageable urban places, where they can exercise local influence and better access foreign markets. Medium-sized cities will therefore play a prominent role in the definition of Mexico's post-1980s opportunity structure.[35]

Mexico's International Opportunity Structure

At the nadir of the Mexican crisis of the 1980s, the only good news one heard in popular neighborhoods in Guadalajara had to do with "El Norte," which usually meant California. Whether people talked about opening a small business, making an improvement to their house, or taking a vacation, the United States was usually a part of the story. For the first time, it seemed that success in metropolitan Mexico depended not on "making it" there, but on having California connections or going there oneself. Although villages and small towns had fallen prey to this feeling before, urban areas had been able to offer sufficient opportunities throughout the period of the Mexican Miracle. With the onset of the crisis, however, even large cities were unable to deliver jobs, services, and continuous improvement in the quality of life. This loss of faith marked a turning point in popular urban Mexicans' relationship with the U.S.: the internationalization of their opportunity structure.

Access to U.S. remittances, together with an intensification of local paid work, was one of the key elements allowing these households to survive the 1980s. International migration became a significant source of income for the popular urban sector and thousands of rural settlements. González de la Rocha's follow-up of 100 poor households in Guadalajara revealed that over a quarter of them received dollar remittances systematically at one point or another from 1982 through 1987. A 1990 estimate by Banco de México put yearly remittances at over 2 billion dollars; the figure could be as high as 3 billion if savings brought back by the migrants were accounted for. Unlike income derived from tourism, trade, or financial services, these resources enter the economy through lower-middle- or working-class households, thus having a far more redistributive, and socially pacifying, effect than any other foreign currency income.

Faced with drastic cuts in government spending on education and diminishing returns from this education in Mexico, Mexicans are also migrating to California to gain schooling of different levels and types. In our survey of 3,000 Guadalajara households, 4 percent of the household heads interviewed stated that one or more members had traveled to the United States (roughly four out of ten to the Los Angeles metropolitan area) to study, not work. Although this is a small percentage, it translates into 32,000 households and 58,000 individuals traveling over one thousand miles, from one city alone, mostly to California. This signals both a change in the type of migration (education migration can be thought of as an investment, part of a long-term strategy aimed at improving one's occupational standing in the point of destination) and a change in where these families believe their better chances lie.

The social impact of these changes in migratory patterns is clear: Mexico's working- and middle-class families now face an international opportunity structure, more so if one or more of their members obtain legal residence in California. The size of the migration flow, the diversity of sending communities, the Mexican crisis, and IRCA have worked together to produce a vast network in which people, information, and cultural influences move back and forth with increasing ease.

The Changing Profile of Mexican Immigrants

At the end of the boom, international migration circuits were already well established in thousands of Mexican towns and villages. The crisis of the 1980s enhanced the attraction of migration to the United States for large-city dwellers and the residents of poor states who previously would have moved to Mexico City or other large cities. More Mexicans began to migrate from a wider variety of geographical areas and a broader spectrum of social classes.

There are many recent examples of the change in migration patterns and in Mexican attitudes toward migration. In Jalostotitlán, Jalisco, a *municipio* with a migration history going back to the turn of the century, the number of international migrants began to rise in 1984, most likely in response to the crisis.[36] In a village in Colima that has produced record yields of rice using the best available technologies, farmers who had ceased to migrate began doing so again after large rice imports depressed the market. In Tlacuitapa, rates of emigration to the United States were found to have increased substantially for adult males from 1976 to 1988.[37]

Studies of workers in Guadalajara confirm these migratory trends. Twenty-eight percent of household heads interviewed in 1990 had immediate kin living in the U.S., and a further 32.2 percent had other relatives there. Additionally, labor-market surveys conducted by the author in 1982 and 1989 show that the proportion of manual workers stating they would like to migrate to the United States rose systematically, as did the percentage of those with migration experience who said they would like to go back.

According to Cornelius,[38] casual-labor markets in California include increasing proportions of Mexicans whose last residence in Mexico was a major city. As a result of dim prospects for improved living standards and social mobility even in urban areas, extensive migration networks have formed between large Mexican cities and California.

There is also evidence that the socioeconomic profile of Mexican immigrants is becoming increasingly polarized. Recent U.S. nationwide surveys noticed a drop in the average schooling of recently arrived Mexican immigrants.[39] "Border watch" research techniques have indicated, however, that in the late 1980s California attracted better-educated undocumented migrants—especially women—than did other border states.[40] At the same time, migratory flows have expanded to include lower-middle-class professionals, who face unfavorable employment and business opportunities in Mexico. These migrants include teachers, engineers, architects, and others who may eventually insert themselves into nonmanual occupations in California but who do not weigh heavily in the aggregate.

Mexican Households and Migrants in the 1990s

The impact of migration on California's labor markets and society depends heavily on the character of future Mexican migrants. This character, in turn, is contingent on future Mexican conditions and, specifically, the perceptions of individual Mexican workers and their families of their long-term chances on both sides of the border.

As the focus of growth in the Mexican economy moves from the metropolitan cities towards smaller cities previously based on agriculture or the services, Mexican households tend to become more homogeneous throughout the country. The tendency is for households in smaller cities to increase their share of low-paid manufacturing employment—especially among better-educated young workers—and for households in Mexico City, Guadalajara, and Monterrey to depend less on manufacturing employment and more on local service jobs and income from members working in the United States.

In the present context, working-class households need to maximize their earning potential by increasing the number of their working members, much as they did during the 1980s.[41] Households with fewer than three workers headed by a dependent manual worker live in unmistakable poverty, and U.S. remittances are a welcome element of survival for some. "Successful" working-class households are headed by a middle-aged independent service or manufacturing worker (a mechanic, the owner of a small manufacturing workshop) and include an income-generating housewife and at least one working teenager or young adult, either in Mexico or the U.S. These households depend for their success on the stage of their domestic cycle, the education and skills of their members, and a clearly defined division of labor. Not many working-class households under the present wage, employment, and urban service conditions can be "successful" in these terms. Lower-middle-class families also need multiple jobs and multiple workers: teachers, nurses, and office workers perform morning and afternoon jobs or do informal vending or manufacturing in their off hours. Although these families may not depend for survival on their migrants' remittances, they are unable to finance their stay in the U.S. or their search for a good job there. Significantly, too, they are unable to finance their children's higher education, fundamentally frustrating their hopes and expectations. As if this were not enough, the curricula in public universities are unlikely to help their children's chances: the gap in the orientation, academic level, content, and social-relational aspects of public and private education has widened enormously during the last ten years. Middle-class households doing well are mostly those headed by professionals in finance, trade, and computing or telecommunication fields who have managed well during the present liberalization of trade and investment.

Given the strong information and social networks spanning the connection, the international opportunity structure depicted previously will be important for "successful" and "unsuccessful" Mexicans alike.[42] Unsuccessful working-class and peasant households will continue to depend on members working in California in unskilled occupations to survive; unsuccessful middle-class Mexicans, their opportunities for professional employment thwarted at home, may opt for urban service jobs in California as a stepping-stone to nonmanual U.S. employment. Both groups, in their search for immediate alleviation to their problems, are likely to accept unskilled low-paying jobs and seek legal residence in the United States. It is this kind of migrant that Cornelius reports is increasing in "street corner" labor markets,[43] where migrants with few local connections in the U.S. and short-term cash needs take whatever jobs come their way. Although middle-class migrants in this category are more likely to pursue higher education and thus to prepare themselves to enter nonmanual positions, their short-term impact will also be to add to the supply of low-skilled labor and depress wages.

"Successful" members of the working and middle classes are also likely to spend time in California—for financial, social, labor, or educational reasons—but their migration will have a significantly different impact. Because their experience in Mexico is encouraging, they are unlikely to take the worst jobs, nor will they undergo a lengthy period of extreme poverty in order to attain residence. Their favorable prospects in Mexico will place a lower limit on their U.S. wage levels; they are less likely to glut low-skilled labor markets and claim significant welfare benefits, and they can be expected to return to Mexico eventually.

The Impact of Mexican Social Conditions on California

The outcome of the 1980s has been a much vaster, more diversified, and permanent movement of people of—mostly—lower socioeconomic status toward California. As other chapters will show, this has changed the employment structure and wage levels of several California industries. This chapter will only discuss the present and likely future impact of Mexican migration on California Latinos.

Most studies seem to indicate that Mexican immigrants do not affect the opportunities open to non-Hispanic whites.[44] But national studies show that this migration does have an impact on the wage levels and periods of unemployment of blacks and Hispanics.[45] It is reasonable to assume that increased migration and the California recession worsened this impact throughout the 1980s, since the sheer volume and composition of this migration altered the character and profile of the Latino population. Persons of Mexican origin doubled in number between 1970 and 1980, and Latinos are now more likely to be foreign-born than native. Moreover, there have been adverse effects on the life and job chances of California Latinos. As several other chapters in this volume show, Latinos tend to be concentrated at the bottom of the occupational ladder. They also tend to live in the largest urban centers, which have become the main magnet for recent migrants.[46] As a result of their persistent low scores on educational and occupational mobility, even second- or third-generation Latinos are vulnerable to job competition from new immigrants. Chapa shows that California Mexican-origin Hispanics improve their education and occupation status substantially from the first to the second generation, but then stagnate. Latino women are most at risk, since their most common occupations (domestic and personal services, unskilled manufacturing) are easy to enter; female and family migration are likely to weaken their position further. California often shows the highest Latino unemployment levels of all the southern-border states,[47] but chances of higher incomes and a much more active labor market maintain California as the main magnet for Mexican migrants. This attraction includes better chances of social mobility through education. Chapa's analysis shows that among California professional males, Mexican Americans and Anglos earn indistinguishable amounts, while there is a large gap between the incomes of low-schooling groups.[48] In other words, the rewards of schooling are greater for California Hispanics than for other groups, since it not only provides them with better incomes, but also with an opportunity to exit segregated or discriminated positions.[49] This implies that it is not discrimination in the professions that discourages Mexican Americans from higher levels of education, but rather the *obstacles* to such attainment. While there could be a "culture of poverty" forming among California Latinos that could be barring their entry to—and their performance in—higher education, the presence of newly arrived Mexicans is likely to have worsened competition in the labor market and decreased the chances of some Latinos for higher education by increasing their households' need for additional incomes.

Two unknown quantities will shape the impact of further migration on California Latinos. First, the extent to which the flow is made up of "successful" or "unsuccessful" migrants will alter their impact on the labor market, and consequently on the work and pay conditions of California Latinos. Second, the public-civic and private-familial strategies of California Latinos will influence the extent to which they will suffer from such competition. Those achieving positions in the professions are unlikely to suffer. Those staying in the lower manual strata will almost certainly be caught in low-pay, dead-end corners of the labor market.

The California-Mexico Connection in the Near Future

Whatever the course of events in the near future, popular-sector Mexicans will remain alert to opportunities and conditions in California. The frequency with which they migrate and the character of this migration, however, will vary greatly depending on California's continuing demand for labor and social conditions on both sides.

Mexico's medium-term future depends partly on the impact of the future conditions of trade with the United States. If an agreement is signed, but it fails to generate new employment in Mexico or results in the widespread closure of Mexican firms, the number of "unsuccessful" middle- and working-class households is likely to expand, heightening pressures on California's low-skilled labor market. If, on the other hand, such an agreement succeeds in promoting economic growth, this would change the outlook of Mexican workers, and migrants would tend toward the "successful" type, whose impact on California would be more beneficial in terms of their dispersal across the labor market; their entering higher-skill, more specialized occupations; and their lower demand for health and other social services.

But the success of future trade relations with the U.S. and other countries is not sufficient for Mexico to reconstruct a viable society, one in which individuals perceive their potential livelihood as satisfying. It is fundamentally up to Mexico's society and polity to adapt itself to new economic opportunities in ways that promote further growth in Mexico, to upgrade and modernize its training and university programs, and to facilitate increased productivity and industrial development. Macroeconomic policies, which up to now have worked, will not suffice in the near future. It is necessary to restore long-term confidence in the economy among aliens and nationals, and to visualize and take advantage of Mexico's actual and potential strengths.

Although almost any further intensification of U.S.-Mexico trade relations is likely to foster further growth of *maquiladora*-type employment (mostly unskilled or semiskilled, high-turnover manual work), only domestic restructuring—and domestic investment in university and industrial modernization—is capable of producing a middle class that contributes significantly to Mexico's success in the 1990s and beyond, one with consumption capacities corresponding to their productive capacity. Although in almost any event Mexico is likely to be further integrated into the U.S. production structure, only internal planning and new economic strategies will strengthen the links between Mexico's growing foreign sector and the rest of the economy, which have remained extremely weak throughout the *maquiladora* boom. Additionally, although almost any trade agreement will promote the growth of funds for IMSS health clinics and ensure some form of pension program for older workers, only a global restructuring of Mexico's policies of welfare and urban growth can significantly improve the quality of life in Mexico's "medium" cities, currently starved of social and service infrastructure. Lastly, a policy to manage the privatization of *ejido* land and the resulting demographic instability is needed. Otherwise, both Mexico's and California's tight urban development budgets might suffer.

Unquestionably, the future of the California-Mexico Connection in terms of migration and the profile of Mexican or Hispanic workers on both sides of the border depends on the prosperity or decline of both entities. California will benefit from a Free Trade Agreement that benefits Mexico substantially, and it is important to nurture this understanding to forestall an agreement that could result in a worsening of social conditions in Mexico. But even a favorable FTA can do little to restructure Mexican society. This remains a Mexican task, and an urgent one, if Mexico is to retain any significant capacity for self-organization and increase its long-term viability for Mexicans.

CHAPTER 5

Exporting Conflict

Transboundary Consequences of Mexican Politics

DENISE DRESSER

IN THE OPENING CHAPTER of Paul Bowles's novel *The Sheltering Sky*, Kit, a seasoned traveler, comments that "the people of each country get more like the people of every other country."[1] Kit is right: in an era of common markets, regional trading blocs, and open borders, integration is such that traditionally self-enclosed societies now share common problems and opportunities. Even domestic politics have become international. Perhaps no two other countries have experienced the impact of interdependence and the transnationalization of national politics as clearly as Mexico and the United States. And nowhere is this phenomenon more visible than in the state of California, where chants of "death to the PRI" resonate just as angrily in the streets of Los Angeles as they do in Mexico City.

As a result of radical transformations in Mexico's political economy, Mexican political battles are being waged in new and unprecedented battlefields: in the U.S. Congress, in the U.S. press, in American public opinion forums, and through organizations that for years have sought to organize Mexicans in states such as California. Mexican political leaders—from government and opposition alike—have discovered potential constituencies in the United States. Doing politics across the border has become an important way of doing politics at home.

Mexico's political warfare in California is partly a result of the uniqueness of the 1988 presidential campaign and election. During that year, Mexico witnessed a withering of the electoral clout of the ruling Institutional Revolutionary Party (PRI), impressive returns for the left-wing opposition led by Cuauhtémoc Cárdenas, and an intense feud over the legitimacy of the PRI candidate—and current president—Carlos Salinas de Gortari. Not only did Mexican parties engage in an unprecedented competition for the loyalty of their compatriots, they also began to look towards California in search of electorates to convince and allies to gain. Since 1988 the PRI has been seeking to muster support for President Salinas's economic reforms, while the Party of the Democratic Revolution (PRD) has been attempting to create a favorable climate of opinion for a possible Cárdenas presidency in Mexico. What is so unusual about these combative Mexican politics is that now they are taking place on U.S. soil.

This essay presents two main arguments: (1) Both the PRI and the PRD, for different reasons and with opposite goals, are building constituencies in California in order to shore up support for their respective causes in Mexico; and (2) Mexicans and Mexican Americans in California—particularly in Los Angeles—have become vehicles for PRD and PRI involvement in U.S. politics and policy discussions that affect Mexico. The purpose of this essay is to explore the causes, goals, strategies, and implications for the United States, and California specifically, of Mexico's shift toward "exporting conflict."

The crumbling of the walls between Mexico and California provides a privileged framework for the discussion of internationalized politics and their implications for sovereignty and transboundary political involvement. The overall pattern that binds both regions is one of "cascading interdependence" and decentralization of government-to-government ties.[2] Relations that were once managed government-to-government are being replaced by the lateral level of society-to-society relations. Institutions, organized interests at the national level, and cross-border coalitions are influencing horizontal relations among governments in accordance with specific interests that are often independent of—or even antagonistic to—the national interest as it may be construed by national policymakers.[3] Increasingly the world is witnessing "the decline of the great forms of collective identification and the emergence of fragmented and multiple collective actors."[4]

The evolution of new transnational political, social, and environmental movements, the decreasing scope of government intervention, and the expanded access of citizens everywhere in the world to information and communication technologies has intensified the decentralizing tendencies and transnational links. Leaders and citizens in both regions are becoming increasingly able to discern how the course of events north or south of the border can affect their rights, pocketbooks, and general well-being. This realization, in turn, has led them to promote and participate in various forms of collective action, such as lobbying, public relations campaigns, business ventures, media blitzes, and cultivating alliances with social groups. As a result, the future of California-Mexico relations (and U.S.-Mexico relations generally) will be increasingly determined by the ways in which various groups and elites define their self-, community, and national interests and subsequently pursue those interests across the border.

The Ebbs and Flows of Mexican Politics

In dramatic contrast with previous decades, the Mexican political system appears to be changing at lightning speed. As a result of widespread transformations, Mexico has begun to shed its reputation as the "living museum" of Latin American politics, whose political institutions and practices were well known to all and eminently predictable. Mexico was known for the virtual monopoly of the PRI over political power, regular although rigged elections, fragmented and loyal opposition parties with little electoral support, and a "mixed economy" ruled by a ubiquitous state. In recent years, however, many of the foundations of Mexican politics have been challenged. The financial crisis of 1982 led to unprecedented economic stagnation and decline in a country accustomed to reaping the benefits of the Mexican Miracle. Rapid trade liberalization propelled the country from the labyrinth of solitude into the the supermarket of world integration.[5] Battles waged among advocates of contending recipes to overcome the crisis provoked a rupture within a traditionally cohesive political elite. Popular opposition to the policies of austerity undermined the corporatist grip and welfare machinery of the PRI. The lean years of the de la Madrid administration (1982–88) awakened dormant disaffection among social groups and led to the emergence of numerous politically active grass-roots movements in civil society. And finally, a new kind of opposition embodied in the leadership of Cuauhtémoc Cárdenas took root and quickly blossomed into a full-fledged political movement.

The political impact of this multidimensional process of change was felt with full force in the presidential elections of July 1988. For the first time in Mexico's postrevolutionary history the candidate of the PRI won, even by the official count, with little more than an absolute majority (50.7 percent). For the first time an opposition candidate garnered support from nearly one-third of Mexican voters (30.1 percent). Political analysts and observers alike spoke of "an electoral realignment" and the birth of "a new political geography."[6] The PRI, accustomed to easy and overwhelming victories, discovered much to its chagrin that elections can be won and lost. Salinas's declaration of the "end of the hegemonic party system" seemed to augur the possibility of increased political liberalization.

The PRI's trials and tribulations preceded the economic decline of the 1980s, but the impact of de la Madrid's widespread economic reforms pushed them to center stage. As a result of the economic stabilization and adjustment policies enacted in the mid-1980s, the party became increasingly less able to fulfill its traditional roles as an interest aggregate, policymaker, and legitimator of the political system. Unable to meet the demands of a political clientele accustomed to a flow of material benefits, the party lost representativeness among its bases. Displaced by technocratic teams intent on implementing economic reform, the party was marginalized from decision-making processes. Incapable of guaranteeing mass support via uncontested electoral victories, it had begun to fail as a legitimator of the regime. In the months preceding the July elections, the PRI seemed incapable of making a convincing political offer to old allies or potential newcomers.[7] As a result, in 1988, one out of every four candidates of the official party lost. Support for the PRI fell 20 percent in comparison to previous presidential elections. Cuauhtémoc Cárdenas was declared the official winner in five states and won by an absolute majority in three of them: México, Michoacán, and Morelos. The party's position was further weakened by its diminished representation in Congress, where it was unable to reach the two-thirds majority required to approve a constitutional reform.

The *cardenistas*, on the other hand, reached the zenith of their political power during the turbulent months that followed Salinas's inauguration. Cárdenas's National Democratic Front (FDN) was quick to capitalize on popular discontent with the government's austerity policies and on the PRI's retreat from its welfare commitments. Supported by organizations from the center-left, Cárdenas transformed a national social movement into a political party—the PRD—with a broad base. Building upon the nationalist, left-wing ideology inherited from the era of great reforms carried out by Lázaro Cárdenas, the PRD sought to become the cohesive force behind Mexico's disparate popular movements. PRD activists emphasized the need to return to "the Mexico that was" before the economic adjustment policies; before the end of subsidies; before privatization, advantages to the private sector, and salary reductions. Cárdenas advocated state intervention in the economy, vowed to defend small and medium-sized firms, demanded the immediate suspension of debt payments, and promised to rescue privatized firms that had been sold by a "treacherous regime and its party that defends foreign interests." The PRD found its natural constituency among groups that for the past twenty years had been organizing themselves outside of the PRI's corporatist machine, and among the sectors that since 1982 had borne the brunt of the economic crisis.

The conservative National Action Party (PAN) lost its place as the second electoral force in the country—mainly because the left captured the protest vote—but was able to maintain its appeal as a strong opposition party. The PAN gained solid ground in the Chamber of Deputies, reaffirmed its presence as a potent regional force in the North, strengthened its appeal among Mexico's urban middle classes, and continued to engage in strident criticism of the newly elected government.

Salinas inherited dangerous legacies from his predecessor: a demoralized and divided PRI, a buoyant opposition movement, and a presidential institution tainted by claims of illegitimacy. The surprising strength of *cardenismo* and the rebelliousness of the PAN combined to bring about a potentially explosive mix: an unprecedented coalition between both contenders for the purpose of annulling the results of the election. A united opposition thus defied the PRI machinery, revealed the widespread irregularities of Mexican electoral politics, and questioned the legality and legitimacy of Carlos Salinas de Gortari's rule.

Salinas's response to the intense postelectoral dispute was quick action. Within weeks of taking office, the president proved that he was far more of a political risk-taker than his detractors expected and launched a series of preemptive strikes against the "internal Leviathans of the Mexican state."[8] By arresting the leader of the powerful oil workers' union and forcing the head of the teachers' union into early retirement, Salinas scored points among constituencies opposed to corruption and clientelism. Through the image of a strong and populist president, Salinas sought to mobilize the population and build support for his modernization drive. Salinas was initially perceived as a president "with initiative" waging a war of modernity against the burdensome legacies of the past. Renewed presidentialism thus became a kind of great national palliative, capable of restoring legitimacy and paving the way for real political and economic change.

The president's decision to recognize, in Baja California Norte, the first-ever victory of an opposition party for a state governorship reinforced his image as a political reformer. Under Salinas, the PRI and the opposition engaged in negotiations to amend the electoral law, leading to the approval of the Federal Code of Electoral Institutions and Practices (COFIPE), which in principle allows greater surveillance and participation of the opposition in electoral contests.[9] During the first two and a half years of the Salinas term, the opposition also won the mayors' offices in important cities such as Mérida and San Luis Potosí. A new voter registration list (*padrón*) and a National Committee on Human Rights were created. Pushed and prodded by Salinas, "modernizing" forces within the PRI recognized that in order to survive as a political institution, the PRI had to change.[10] To assure its preeminence in a more competitive and demanding environment, the PRI began to institute gradual changes in the selection process of its candidates, leaders, and administrators. As a PRI leader expressed: "The party finally acknowledged that it was at a crossroads; it either modernized or died."[11]

The government's promotion of political reform, however, has undergone ebbs and flows and appears half-hearted in light of the speed and depth of economic modernization. Salinas has proceeded full speed ahead with privatization, deregulation, and measures—such as the North American Free Trade Agreement (NAFTA)—designed to integrate Mexico into the international economy. But while Mexican *perestroika* seems to be bolting forward, Mexican *glasnost* has lagged behind. The government's will to run clean contests and defend legitimate opposition victories has varied greatly, from one state to another, and from one election to the next.

Salinas recognized the PAN victories in Baja California and Mérida, but elections throughout 1989 and 1990 in PRD strongholds—Michoacán, Guerrero, and the state of México—were marred by violence, repression, and a return to "politics as usual" by the PRI. Elections have been shadowed by problems such as voter brigades and "carousels" voting several times at different booths, irregularities in voter registration lists (living people whose names did not appear and the deceased who kept on voting), false voter registration cards monopolized by groups linked to the ruling party, a self-congratulatory attitude on behalf of the PRI, high levels of abstentionism, and disbelief among observers and participants alike. These events have raised questions regarding the credibility of an administration that explicitly promised to respect the vote and of a PRI avowedly committed to modernizing the rules of the political game.

Salinas's approach to political liberalization has been incremental, gradual, and selective, at best. The Mexican president has been willing to negotiate with the more palatable center-right opposition embodied in the PAN, while simultaneously excluding the less agreeable *cardenista* left. The PAN's antistatist and free-market rhetoric has dovetailed with the economic modernization policies espoused by Salinas and provided common ground for political accord. In return for *panista* support on key legislative modifications—such as the reprivatization of the banks and the new electoral law—Salinas has conceded victories when and where the PAN has been able to defend them through popular mobilization. The maxim appears to be: "Loosen the reins as little as possible, and lose only when forced to."[12]

The Salinas policy towards the PRD has been much less ambiguous and much more confrontational. The PRD lacks the ideological and policy affinities that have allowed a marriage of convenience between the PRI and the PAN. The PRD was born out of an intraparty schism and is led by prominent renegades from the PRI. *Cardenismo* embodies a set of precepts and principles associated with the Mexican welfare state and a model of development that the Salinas team is intent on replacing. Personal and political animosities between *cardenista* leaders and top PRI and government officials run high. Ultimately, Salinas is unwilling to make concessions to a party that continues to question the legitimacy of his government, and demands radical changes that would lead the PRI to commit political suicide.

Meanwhile the opposition has also faltered, partly of its own accord. *Cardenismo*'s transition from a social movement to a political party has been plagued by problems of bureaucratization and political infighting between groups and personalities. Even though the FDN stood out as an unusually successful social movement, its concrete victories as a political party have been limited and partial, especially in relation to the tremendous efforts spent mobilizing the population. The number of electoral defeats since 1988, and the amount of energy spent in winning relatively minor victories, have led many past participants to drop out or to reduce their involvement.[13] In 1988 Cárdenas was able to mobilize thousands of people, but recently doubts have surfaced as to whether, in the future, support for Cárdenas can be effectively translated into support for the PRD, given that the party still lacks a permanent and positive principle of unity beyond a radical rejection of the Salinas regime.

The roots that enabled the *cardenista* movement to grow have been deteriorating due to internal difficulties, but also as a result of deliberate government action. The Salinas government is providing material goods and services to popular groups affiliated with the PRD in an attempt to curb antipathies that could be translated into electoral gains for the opposition. Salinas's poverty-alleviation efforts carried out through the National Solidarity Program (Pronasol) have been targeted at politically disaffected groups and regions that provided the PRD with electoral backing in 1988.[14] As part of Pronasol's tactics, Salinas tours the Mexican countryside, distributes land titles, and inaugurates public works in some of the poorest municipalities—just before elections. Pronasol has allowed the PRI to engage in pork-barrel politics, undertake quick public works, deliver goods, buy activists, and inspire hope among the poorest of the poor in areas where the government and the party's image had deteriorated. Through Pronasol, the PRI is building upon a presidentialist and providentialist culture and reinforcing old formulas of state patronage in return for legitimizing votes.

These events have put a damper on the optimistic mood awakened by the 1988 presidential election and Salinas's initial statements in favor of political opening. If anything, recent trends—accompanied by tepid and mincing reforms—indicate that the margins for greater liberalization have become very narrow indeed. During the first three years of the Salinas presidency, Mexico witnessed the renaissance of presidentialism, and worrying signs of greater centralized and discretionary control. Salinas seems to have distanced himself from the political reform process that he pledged when he took office and has relegated proposals of political reform to his ineffectual lieutenants in Congress. The PRD, weakened by divergent tendencies, struggles between compromise and confrontation, rupture or engagement with the regime, restoration of the Republic or the reform of *salinismo*. The PAN's alliance with the government has led to serious divisions among leaders who support political negotiations with the powers that be, in exchange for electoral gains, and those who feel that by collaborating with the PRI, the PAN is selling its soul to the devil.[15] Opposition parties appear to be focusing more on interparty issues and squabbles—the denouncement of electoral fraud, the debate on COFIPE, and the selection of their candidates—than on creating a popular base.[16] Despite its modernizing rhetoric, in many regions of the country the PRI seems to have returned to the traditional formulas of patronage, cooptation, and selective repression. Entrenched bosses and "dinosaurs" of the political system continue to dominate the PRI's state and local organizations. Many of them donned modernizing masks simply because they believed that favorable political winds (i.e., those supported by Salinas de Gortari) would blow in their direction. They have adopted the discourse of political modernity but, when put to the test, would probably support the party's old methods—as the turbulent 1991 mid-term elections proved.[17]

These trends, along with the ambiguous response of the Salinas government to electoral challenges, have intensified the contradiction between fast-paced economic reform and slow-paced political liberalization. Apparently Salinas has decided to live with this contradiction. Keeping one eye on the former Soviet Union, the Mexican president has deliberately delayed the process of political reform in order to safeguard the institutionalization of his economic policies. Regarding the relationship between economic and political reform, Salinas has explicitly acknowledged, "They are linked, but we ought to consider the priority that economic reform has, without excluding political reform. We need to consolidate our economic reform. That demands the consensus that makes possible the decisions we have been adopting."[18] Thus, the Salinas recipe could be summed up as vigorous economic restructuring accompanied by gradual and controlled political opening.[19]

The immediate goal of political tinkering appears to be an electoral victory of the PRI in elections throughout the rest of Salinas's term. The long-term goal, however, is to dismantle current political constraints (such as the left-wing opposition) and at the same time construct the bases of consensus that will allow the continuation and deepening of the economic restructuring program. In the political battles still ahead Salinas will wave the banner of economic recovery in an attempt to steal away constituencies from his opponents. The logic is that if the government is getting good economic results, popular discontent will evaporate—so then why pursue more radical political changes, particularly in the electoral front? Salinas's political stalling tactics will be judged by his ability to deliver real growth. If there is growth, as there has been recently in Mexico, then the government can continue to engage in selective political opening and gradualist political reform that will allow the PRI, as Salinas put it, to remain as "the centerpiece of a more competitive party system."[20]

This line of reasoning is also commonly heard in the United States, where Mexico's successes in economic stabilization and restructuring (along with the fears awakened by the near-triumph of a perceived leftist in 1988) dramatically reduced interest in political change in Mexico. The Salinas strategy of economic reform first, political reform second has been strongly supported by what Mexican analyst Lorenzo Meyer calls "the American factor." The Bush administration met Salinas's overtures in search of support for greater economic integration and Mexico's economic model with enthusiasm.[21] By doing so, the U.S. hoped to invest in the success of Mexico's economic reform program in order to assure the political stability of its southern neighbor.

Mexico's Quest for Allies in the U.S.

Among the many novel paths tread by the Salinas administration, the strengthening of ties with the United States is one of the most important. In complete reversal of the Mexican political elite's traditionally defensive and historically suspicious attitude vis-à-vis its North American neighbor, the Salinas team has become a staunch advocate of integration. In a spectacular about-face of 70 years of postrevolutionary history, Mexico is pursuing an active rapprochement with its long-time partner in conflict. Gone is the traditional fear of ending up totally dominated, if not absorbed, by the United States. Gone is the traditional mind-set that asked "whether or not" to collaborate with the U.S., with "not" being the preferred answer. In its place stands a "new nationalist" mentality that asks "under what conditions" Mexico should deal with the United States.[22]

This unprecedented engagement with the the U.S. is part-and-parcel of what has been defined as "the new realism" of Mexico's foreign policy.[23] According to Salinas, Mexico has been forced to redefine its interests in the face of globalization of production, the emergence of commercial blocs, and ideological realignments in the world arena. Mexico's swing from economic insularity to international integration is an inevitable consequence of world events. In this new perspective, Mexico will no longer defend abstract principles such as self-determination or nonintervention in Central America in order to strengthen domestic legitimacy. Rather, Mexico will engage in a global pursuit of its economic goals. The idealism of Mexico's old foreign policy has given way to the pragmatism of Mexico's new economic diplomacy. Mexico will defend and pursue concrete interests, not abstract principles. Whereas in the past, Mexico had no "interests," but only "principles," now the reverse seems true.

In practical terms, this has led to a foreign policy designed to attract investment, assure markets, and obtain financing from the world's great economic centers, especially the United States. Salinas has discarded the age-old view of Mexican sovereignty as synonymous with territorial integrity and proposed a "modern" vision that defines sovereignty as an efficacious insertion in international markets.[24] Mexico's nationalist, independent, and activist foreign policy—which frequently ran counter to U.S. interests—has been placed on the back burner to make room for trilateral negotiations to enact the North American Free Trade Agreement (NAFTA). According to the Salinas government, it makes no sense, on the one hand, to put all of Mexico's eggs in one basket (namely the one that holds foreign financing, business confidence, and U.S. support) and then proceed to kick and quarrel with the owners of the basket.[25] Foremost among the priorities of Salinas's foreign policy is the avoidance of diplomatic conflicts that might sabotage Mexico's shared economic interests with the United States, whose markets and investments are critical to the export-led model of development enacted by de la Madrid and deepened by Salinas.

Mexico's northern exposure is also the result of internal transformations, namely the turbulent 1988 presidential campaign and election. Not only did Mexican political leaders engage in an unprecedented competition for the loyalty of their compatriots; they also began to look towards the United States in search of electorates to convince and allies to gain. Since 1988, the Salinas team has sought to muster support north of the border for a broad array of neoliberal reforms, while members of the opposition have attacked those reforms and attempted to create a favorable climate of opinion for a possible Cárdenas presidency in Mexico. As a result, the new route of Mexican politics runs through New York, Washington, San Francisco, Chicago, and especially Los Angeles.[26] The map of activities of Mexican political parties no longer stops at the border.

Departing from their traditional Washington-centered focus, Mexican lobbying efforts have expanded into previously unexplored territory in search of new partners, markets, and allies. Mexican officials have realized that to obtain massive U.S. investment and political support, it will be necessary to court U.S. business and society at large. As a result, Mexico's diplomatic efforts—by government and opposition alike—have been extended to include agricultural producers, industrialists and financiers, the Mexican-American business community, labor leaders, grass-roots movements, environmentalists, intellectuals, and journalists.

This unprecedented political activism also underscores that for the Mexican government, the recuperation of political legitimacy no longer stops at the border. In a context where Mexico is promoting foreign investment to jump-start growth, the Salinas administration has become extremely sensitive to public opinion in the United States and elsewhere. Ultimately, the Mexican president's economic and political gambles depend on U.S. support from both government and business circles. And from the perspective of sensitive Mexican elites, one *cardenista* busily challenging the PRI's legitimacy, or one congressman worried about Mexico's political stability is one too many.

Key among the Salinas strategies toward the U.S. has been the enactment of a public relations campaign to promote a new Mexican image north of the border. Since July 1988, the Mexican government and the PRI have engaged in a massive campaign designed to revamp the party's negative image and dispel what a foreign correspondent described as Salinas's "original sin"—accusations that his election was the result of electoral fraud.[27] Foreign reporters based in Mexico marvel at their extraordinary access to high-level government officials, and President Salinas himself gives interviews to foreign journalists approximately once every week and a half (a privilege rarely granted to the Mexican press). Between 1988 and 1992, the head of the Office of Social Communication of the Presidency made eighteen trips to newspaper offices in the U.S., and Salinas personally visited the headquarters of the *Wall Street Journal*, *Time*, *Newsweek*, the *Los Angeles Times*, the *Financial Times*, and other key media shapers. Five years ago, the Mexican government had only one press officer in the United States, based in Washington. Currently, there are Mexican press officers in every major city, including Miami, San Diego, San Francisco, New York, Los Angeles, and Houston. PRI leaders have barnstormed the United States, speaking with media managers, policymakers, and influential Mexicanists. Calling themselves "truth squads," high-ranking *priístas* (members of the PRI) constantly visit newspaper editors to dispute what they consider unfair reports from Mexico-based correspondents. In order to boost its standing with U.S. public opinion, the Mexican government has engaged a powerful battery of publicity and advertising firms. Over the past three years, Mexico has taken the U.S. by storm via a broad spectrum of promotional devices that range from "Come. Feel the Warmth of Mexico." to the Mexico Foundation at Harvard. In addition, high-level members of Mexico's Economic Cabinet have crisscrossed the country, promoting Mexico's investment climate and the virtues of North American integration. Salinas has addressed Congress, inaugurated business forums, and delivered lectures at major U.S. universities.

In addition, Mexico is on the verge of upstaging Japan as the foreign government with the most visible lobbying muscle in Washington. Beginning in January 1991, the Salinas team began to assemble an impressive array of reputable lobbying firms for the purpose of influencing Congress's vote on the extension of "fast-track" authority to negotiate NAFTA. In February 1990, Mexico had 27 lobbying contracts registered with the U.S. Department of Justice; by November 1991, the number had grown to 71. The formidable list includes GOP heavy-hitters such as Charles Walker; politically connected Democrats such as Joseph O'Neill (former aide to Senator Lloyd Bentsen); and other powerful companies such as Burson Marstellar, Gold and Liebengood, O'Melveney and Myers, Shearson and Sterling, and Steptoe and Johnson.[28] A Mexican official in Washington, Herman Von Bertrab, heads a staff of eight that is coordinating the pro-NAFTA lobbying drive from an office opened expressly for that purpose. From January 1991 until the approval of fast-track six months later, Mexico covered both Democratic and GOP flanks with a fleet of lobbyists and lawyers who regaled lawmakers with the country's efforts to modernize its economy, environment, and working conditions. Lobbyists disseminated brochures prepared by Mexico's Foreign Commerce Bank describing the growth of the Mexican economy, pamphlets designed by the Ministry of Ecology and Urban Development (SEDUE) listing Salinas's commitments to the environment, and op-eds written by free trade advocates such as Henry Kissinger and Jay Hair, president of the National Wildlife Federation. Ad campaigns began in major newspapers, speeches by Mexican officials were scheduled across the United States, and two weeks before the vote on fast track, visits by Mexican lobbyists to Congress increased to approximately six a day.

In the past, Mexican officials had been reluctant to engage in lobbying in the United States for fear that Mexican "intervention" in politics north of the border might prompt U.S. intervention in Mexican affairs.[29] However, the "historic political reconciliation" trumpeted by presidents Bush and Salinas, as well as the need to secure the signing of a NAFTA, led to an unprecedented explosion of Mexican lobbying. For the first time in its postrevolutionary history, Mexico launched a new policy *towards* the United States *in* the United States.

Along with sophisticated marketing and lobbying techniques, the Mexican government's political strategies in the U.S. include the promotion of a new type of consulate and a new breed of consuls. Mexican consuls in the consulates in the U.S. have become major lobbying machines, and passport-stamping consuls traditionally confined to administrative duties have now been transformed into "mini-Ambassadors," responsible for conveying a better understanding of Mexico.[30] They engage in political debates, promote Mexican interests, lobby in favor of trilateral integration, and strengthen ties with the Mexican and Mexican-American communities in their cities. Dynamic, forceful, and articulate political envoys are now at the helm of offices with a mandate to promote Mexico.

The Cárdenas phenomenon shook the traditional detachment of the Mexican government towards its citizens in the United States. The wave of support for *cardenismo* in major U.S. cities forced Mexican officials to recognize the resentment caused by what the Mexican community perceived as a "lack of attention" from its government. As a candidate, Salinas met with Latino leaders and expressed a desire to achieve a better understanding of the Mexican problem in the United States, but the anti-PRI marches in places such as Los Angeles were the catalyst that led to a new attitude. As José Angel Pescador, the Mexican consul in Los Angeles, explained:

> One of the greatest protest marches against the outcome of the elections took place in Los Angeles. This led to an awakening in Mexican political circles. The Mexican government realized that there are many anti-PRI Mexicans living in California who return periodically to their communities and have influence in Mexico. This recognition took place in the context of a radical reformulation of Mexico's foreign policy. What we want to do now is build bridges with the Mexican community.[31]

Since July 1988 the Mexican government and the PRI have engaged in a massive campaign designed to reconquer lost constituencies and create new ones across the border. The twofold objective is to undermine support for the PRD and Cuauhtémoc Cárdenas, while at the same time restoring the credibility of the PRI among Mexicans, Mexican Americans, and U.S. society at large. To improve the PRI's image with Mexicans in the United States, the party's public relations effort has included the sponsorship of sporting events and cultural events, and the donation of books to public library systems in several border states. In addition, the PRI has sent state governors to California on goodwill tours to win the sympathies of Mexicans and Mexican Americans. Governor Genaro Borrego of Zacatecas and Governor Heladio Ramírez of Oaxaca, for example, visited constituencies in the Golden State to counter Cárdenas's appeal to Michoacán-born Californians.[32]

The Salinas government is also establishing alliances with national political organizations that bring together Latino politicians. The short-term goal of this courtship has been to obtain Latino endorsement of Salinas's policies, while the long-term goal is to create Mexico-supportive constituencies. In the coming years, the United States will witness the election of a growing number of Latino governors and senators. By then, the Mexican government would like to have forged a strong network of allies sympathetic to Mexico's agenda in the United States. The objective of this multifaceted strategy is to build cross-national bridges among groups with common interests in order to influence Washington's attitude toward Mexico. The Mexican government's hope is that a groundswell of support for Mexico at the local level will translate into endorsement of Salinas's policies in the U.S. Congress and Senate.

The strategy of enlisting supporters in the U.S.—in order to influence Washington's stance toward Mexican domestic policy and strengthen positions at home—has also become an important tool of the Mexican opposition. Until recently, lobbying attempts by Mexican opposition parties in the U.S. had always been marginal and sporadic. In 1985, after controversial elections in Chihuahua, the PAN sent representatives to several forums in the U.S. to denounce the Mexican government and its electoral authorities. After accusations of "treason" and "appealing to Uncle Sam's interventionism" from its contenders, the PAN retrenched and refrained from engaging in political promotion. In the early 1980s the Mexican Socialist Party (PMS) made occasional forays into Los Angeles and Washington, but its political efforts were timid and unsystematic. Not until 1988, after the hotly disputed victory of Salinas, did Mexican opposition strategists resurrect the idea of forging alliances in the United States. After the elections Cárdenas toured several U.S. cities to denounce the illegitimacy of the elections, and the PAN's candidate, Manuel Clouthier, condemned "the Salinas fraud" during a trip to California. Since then, political activism in the U.S. has become a key ingredient on the opposition's agenda.[33]

Brigades of PRD officials routinely travel across the United States spreading the gospel of their party. They participate in public forums to forge alliances, promote their programs, and undermine their political foe, the PRI. Prominent *perredistas* (members of the PRD) sponsor political rallies in the U.S., organize press conferences with the media, deliver speeches at universities, and routinely brief congressmen and senators. While the PRI stresses the accomplishments of Salinas's modernization program, the virtues of free trade, and the "successful" reform of the ruling party, the PRD decries the illegitimacy of the Salinas government, sounds apocalyptic warnings against "savage integration" with the United States, and underscores the dark side of the PRI's standard operating procedures.

Opposition leaders have been quick to recognize the influence of Mexican workers who live in the United States and travel back and forth between the two countries, taking back with them not only foreign currency but political ideas as well. The two-way flow of people, money, technology, and ideas across the porous border has suddenly gained strategic importance. The PRD is reaching out to win the hearts and minds—and the financial support—of their compatriots, descendants, and potential allies in the United States.[34]

Mexicans living in the United States, many of whom were driven from their homeland by economic and political problems, have become a natural constituency for Cárdenas. *Cardenismo* encountered fertile ground across the border because it appealed—as in Mexico—to the discontented and disaffected. Mexicans in the U.S. harbor great resentment against a political and economic system in their home country that has been unable (or unwilling) to absorb them into the formal economy or to assure them effective political representation. *Cardenismo* built upon longstanding grievances and alienation, and was able to recover important themes that left-wing political organizers in the U.S. had been proposing for years. Cárdenas's candidacy breathed new life into old causes such as the right of Mexicans to vote abroad by absentee ballot and struck a resonant chord throughout the Southwest. As a result, exiled students and activists from the 1968 antigovernment revolt, grass-roots organizers, human rights advocates, and Chicano activists promptly joined the ranks of the Cárdenas campaign.

The guiding force that has fueled PRD political activism is the Mexican presidential election of 1994. Cárdenas has declared that he will run again, and to that end he and his followers will attempt to woo supporters in the United States and Mexico. The PRD will continue to exert influence in the U.S. with the hope of expanding its constituency, but also in an effort to conduct "boomerang" politics. The PRD's concern for Mexicans in California is a good political card in Mexico, especially given the growing number of Mexicans with relatives working in the United States. At the same time, the PRD has recognized that its activities in California can contribute to altering perceptions in the United States regarding the course of possible political change in Mexico. As the head of International Relations of the party expressed, "In this era of globalization, internal politics are no longer internal. The United States is one of the great voters in Mexico. The United States influences the course of events in Mexico. And we want the United States to accept the possibility of Cuauhtémoc Cárdenas as President of Mexico."[35]

The PRD's message in the United States and California specifically is that in Mexico there are interlocutors other than the government who can articulate a vision of Mexican politics. With this purpose in mind, the PRD will continue to promote a "political socialization" campaign, designed to enlighten the U.S. public about Mexico and open up public debate on both sides of the border regarding the country's future.

According to the *cardenistas*, Mexico's modernization has been conceived in economic terms, and the "archaic features" of the political system are not on Salinas's reform agenda.[36] Mexico's left argues that the economic model Salinas has in mind cannot be implemented without a thorough democratization of the country's politics and society. In order to take root, economic reforms must gain support from the majority of the Mexican people. Salinas's policies will further concentrate wealth and leave broad sectors of the Mexican population out in the cold, and consequently cannot be perpetuated without serious social unrest.[37] By drawing attention to the warts of the Salinas project, Cárdenas hopes to enlist progressive forces in the U.S. in support of an alternative agenda that includes the protection of the human and labor rights of Mexican workers abroad, equitable working conditions for both Mexican and American labor, the enactment of environmental protection laws in both countries, and the inclusion of a social charter in the NAFTA.

Among the prime objectives of the PRD's activism in California is to win the allegiance of the Mexican-American community. Mexicans with the potential to vote in U.S. elections will reach a significant percentage of the U.S. population by the turn of the century.[38] Cárdenas and his apostles have realized that the Latino community can be an important source of financial support, a vehicle for incorporating *cardenista* issues on the bilateral agenda, and a powerful lobby in affecting U.S. policy towards Mexico.[39]

Mexican Politics in California

Mexico's political system has lost its predictable and monolithic character, and Mexico's foreign policy has begun to branch out into unexplored terrain. As a result, political goals and foreign policy objectives are being exported across the border, and both the Mexican government and the opposition are actively pursuing U.S. support for Mexican causes. Although the PRI and the PRD (and to a much lesser extent the PAN) have increasingly made forays into the major cities of the United States, attention has focused mainly on California, and in particular, the greater Los Angeles area. Due to its economic and political importance, and its large concentration of people of Mexican origin—the equivalent in population to a good-sized Mexican state—California has become an obligatory campaign stop.

The 1988 presidential campaign and election marked a major turning point regarding Mexican opposition politics, especially in Los Angeles. As *cardenismo* gained strength in Mexico, it also took root in California. There is a widespread feeling among Mexicans in California that "they think about their country but that their country does not think of them," and that the Mexican government has neglected its responsibilities and obligations toward the millions of its citizens who crossed the northern border in search of opportunities denied to them at home. This widespread anti-government and anti-PRI stance has been reinforced by the mistreatment and abuse that Mexicans immigrants suffer at the hands of Mexican border authorities.

Mexicans in the U.S. are viewed by many Mexicans at home as unworthy citizens who have betrayed their country by leaving it. At the same time, their journey into the American melting pot and "land of opportunity" often does not lead them into a more welcoming society or improve their living standards. Many find themselves second-class citizens in both countries. This hostile environment and brand of "double-marginalization" provided the breeding ground for the Mexican left in 1988. As the head of International Relations of the PRD explained:

> Mexicans in California feel marginalized from their own country. They are economic exiles. But at the same time, they experience an objective marginalization in the United States. When Cuauhtémoc Cárdenas appeared they responded with enthusiasm because they felt that finally someone was taking care of them and paying attention to them. They responded just like people in the Mexican states of Guerrero, Michoacán, and Morelos did. For the Mexicans in Los Angeles, Cuauhtémoc Cárdenas is the President of Mexico. *Cardenismo* in California allowed people to rescue their roots in Mexico and at the same time live their reality in the United States.[40]

Cardenismo built upon the disaffection of many California Mexicans and was able to extend its grasp due to the existence of a previously politicized community. The economic crisis of the 1980s—by forcing groups of professionals to migrate—transformed the profile of the typical Mexican migrant to California. As a result of the depth and scope of the depression, electricians, mechanics, and other people with higher levels of education and even union experience joined the ranks of an expanding immigrant population. Many of these Mexicans exported their organizational experience to places such as San Jose, Los Angeles, Oxnard, and Fresno and thus contributed to the politicization of the Mexican community there, especially in places such as Watsonville and Salinas. Also, Mexicans living in California have traditionally been receptive to those who would fight revolutions in their home country. Cárdenas built upon the legacy left by the Flores Magón brothers, who published insurrectionary pamphlets and raised money and arms in Los Angeles and Berkeley to overthrow dictator Porfirio Díaz in 1910.

Cárdenas also recovered important themes that left-wing political organizers had been proposing for years and linked into an organizing process that was already going on. As Ben Garza, a member of the PRD and a long-time Chicano activist in California, described:

> For 4 or 5 years we had been trying to organize people around the issue of democracy in Mexico. The 1988 election simply brought more people together. Many people of course support Cárdenas, but others joined because of their desire to support democracy in Mexico. They were tired of the PRI and corruption. The coming together of different groups in Mexico into the FDN and later the PRD had enormous impact on the politically "*dormidos*" [asleep] in California.[41]

During the months that preceded the 1988 presidential election, Los Angeles became a hot-bed of *cardenista* support. Mexican and Mexican-American activists engaged in fund-raising and public relations campaigns and even incorporated a controversial resolution into the platform of the California Democratic party urging U.S. intervention to assure "the honesty of the upcoming presidential elections in Mexico."[42] In the summer of 1988, Los Angeles witnessed a flurry of Mexican political activity, including demonstrations in support of political change in Mexico and Cárdenas's whirlwind tours of the state. When Carlos Salinas de Gortari was pronounced the official winner, opposition politics in Los Angeles reached their peak, and the city witnessed a display of support for Cárdenas in the form of mass demonstrations and daily picketing outside the offices of the Mexican consulate to protest fraud and the corruption of the PRI.

Since 1988 the California PRD—as in Mexico—has been struggling to define its identity, organize its disparate constituencies, and define its future course. Initially, Cárdenas supporters organized themselves in independent groups such as Residentes Mexicanos Unidos (United Mexican Residents) and Foro Democrático Mexicano (Mexican Democratic Forum), and in 1989 the PRD established its first *comités de base* (base committees) in several California cities.[43] What began as a social movement bound together by the figure of Cárdenas has gradually become a fledgling statewide organization known as the PRD of California. Backed by national leadership in Mexico City, the party constituted its State Executive Council in May 1991, based on organizational precepts of the PRD in Mexico.[44] Among the PRD's organizational objectives are the following: (1) strengthen and expand the number of base committees and affiliate 5,000 militants to the PRD; (2) build a statewide newspaper and international fax system; (3) build a PRD staff in California that can link up to already existing organizations sympathetic to the PRD; (4) disseminate PRD political literature and establish a presence in the media; (5) engage in massive fund-raising through the creation of a statewide PRD Political Action Committee; (6) create a statewide human rights commission and collaborate with other organizations such as Americas Watch and Amnesty International.[45]

Another goal the PRD has mapped out for California is the promotion of the "right to vote" in Mexican elections. Building upon previous efforts by Mexican organizations in the state, the *perredistas* have launched a campaign to collect signatures among those who support voting rights for Mexicans in the United States. The PRD argues that the Mexican government is denying Mexicans abroad the constitutionally guaranteed right to vote, because Article 9 of the new electoral law, which states that Mexicans can only vote in national territory, contradicts the Mexican Constitution. According to PRD activists, the Mexican Constitution does not establish that living abroad is a condition for negating citizenship and political representation.[46] The PRD contends that the Mexican government has denied the use of absentee ballots because it wants to eliminate at least five million Mexicans who live in the U.S. from the voter registration list and voting booths.

By appealing to legal arguments and taking the issue of voting rights to the floor of the Mexican Congress, the Human Rights Commission of the United Nations, and the Organization of American States, the PRD hopes to pressure the Mexican government into allowing absentee ballots, voting booths at the consulates, or elections via fax in 1994. If the Mexican government does not reverse its position, the PRD will continue to enact strategies such as the promotion of parallel elections by setting up voting booths outside of the Mexican consulates. PRD officials argue that although parallel elections cannot alter official results in Mexico, they nonetheless have symbolic and psychological value. As the president of the State Executive Council of the PRD explained: "If the PRI crushes us in Mexico, through parallel elections we crush it in the United States."[47]

The PRD in California has become a loudspeaker for the Cárdenas position on free trade, particularly regarding the need to expand NAFTA to include the human factor of commerce. Cárdenas has become one of the staunchest critics of NAFTA, and the PRD in California has followed his lead. In February 1991, Cárdenas presented an alternative to NAFTA known as the Continental Initiative on Development and Commerce, which stressed the importance of incorporating issues such as the environment, workers rights, and compensatory investments into the negotiations.[48] During a March 1991 tour of California, Cárdenas publicized his views, met with influential California policymakers, and urged his followers to oppose the Salinas approach to "asymmetrical integration." In the *cardenista* perspective, the Salinas government is marketing free trade strictly as a question of commerce, without admitting its political, social, and economic impact.

In Mexico and California, the PRD is seeking to promote a broad discussion of NAFTA and thus increase its representativeness. The party is disseminating the *cardenista* position in order to establish a coalition among groups opposed to free trade, such as unions, grass-roots organizations, and environmentalists. The PRD, for example, sponsored a visit to Mexico of California unionists linked to the AFL-CIO for the purpose of heightening awareness and promoting solidarity between the labor movements in both countries, and Cárdenas has appealed to Mexican and American workers to call on their governments to do more to protect them. Given their concerns with job loss and worker displacement, California labor groups might emerge as strong and vocal allies of the PRD. As an expert on Chicano politics predicted: "With NAFTA you're going to see a lot of trade unionists talking to Cárdenas. Workers know that immigration laws are going to be directed against them and that the jobs created by Free Trade in Mexico are going to be minimum wage jobs. These issues are on the side of the PRD."[49]

The Mexican left has been able to establish an incipient political organization, but whether Mexican opposition politics in California will flourish is still an open question. Much will depend on the evolution of the PRD in Mexico and whether the party will be able to garner sufficient support in U.S. society. Although the PRD has suffered major setbacks at home, *cardenismo* is still a vital force abroad because support for Cárdenas is larger than the party itself. PRD activists argue that as long as there is a Cárdenas there will be a PRD in California that will not fall apart. This may be true, but if the party wants to behave as one, it will have to institutionalize diffuse admiration for Cárdenas and transform it into concrete political support. The challenge for the PRD in California is to translate widespread endorsement of Cárdenas as a possible future president of

AMERICAN RIVER COLLEGE

Mexico into party militancy. The PRD was able to constitute itself as a political party in California thanks to the existence of organizations that emerged during the Cárdenas candidacy. Now the *perredistas* have to discuss plans and articulate strategies that no longer revolve around a single person. Oftentimes the divisions that have threatened party unity in Mexico repeat themselves in California. The PRD has confused its constituency and succumbed to squabbles generated by power politics and conflicting agendas. The PRD's "rainbow coalition" has incorporated radical groups with a great deal of political baggage whose political strategies and objectives have undermined the credibility of the PRD instead of strengthening it. After the presidential elections of 1988, the *perredistas* squandered precious time denouncing electoral fraud and lost the important momentum provided by popular effervescence, which could have been used to establish a solid statewide organization. The PRD has also mistakenly assumed that its cause—democracy in Mexico—is the cause of all Mexicans in Los Angeles, without realizing that oftentimes, its constituency has concrete and specific local interests. The party has managed to survive as a spokesman for the Mexican opposition in California, but it has yet to live up to its full potential as a political and organizational force.

The PRD, however, is not alone in sensing and pursuing the potential power of California's Mexicans. Its arch-rivals, the PRI and the Mexican government, have also launched an offensive there in an effort to create a presence and to reestablish credibility in the Golden State. Salinas himself inaugurated the California Council of Mexican-American Organizations during a trip to Los Angeles. During the months that preceded the vote on "fast track" in the U.S. Congress, the Mexican consulate in Los Angeles engaged in a massive lobbying effort to diffuse opposition to free trade among California businessmen. The consulate sponsored numerous seminars and conferences on free trade at the Los Angeles Chamber of Commerce, Town Hall, and the World Affairs Council, and provided information on Mexican laws and investment potential.

The message conveyed by the Mexican government's new "economic diplomacy" has found receptive audiences and staunch supporters. After decades of little contact, the Mexican-American and U.S. business community has begun to see Mexican entrepreneurs as potential partners.[50] In a similarly supportive attitude, Mexican-American organizations such as the Mexican American Legal and Education Defense Fund (MALDEF), have become interlocutors of the Salinas government and endorsed the Mexican government's stance regarding free trade.[51]

The Mexican government hopes to establish itself as a political force in the U.S. not only by building support for its positions, but also by undermining those of the *perredista* opposition.[52] The PRI has engaged in a media blitz against opposition leaders who visit California through scathing attacks in the Mexican press, denouncing them as traitors to their country, who are "inviting the U.S. to invade Mexico."[53] Similarly, consular officials in California have responded to PRD demands for absentee ballots with arguments that stress the technical and logistical difficulties involved. When PRD legislators attempted to introduce the issue of voting rights abroad into the Mexican Congress, PRI representatives argued that Mexicans in the U.S. had forgotten about their country, and that if they want to vote they should return to Mexico to do so. PRI officials have declared that the PRI is not against allowing citizens abroad to vote, and that deliberations on the issue "are not conclusive yet."[54] Stalling tactics aside, it appears that in a context of relatively competitive elections, the Mexican government is reluctant to augment the country's electoral registration list with millions of anti-PRI voters based in California. As a PRI organizer in Los Angeles acknowledged: "We *priístas* believe that confidence in the party should be restored in Mexico before elections are opened in the United States and elsewhere."[55] Thus, by pushing the right-to-vote issue to the back burner, the PRI is attempting to eliminate a vehicle for political rallying and contestation in California.

The PRI's efforts to stall PRD advances in the state led to the creation of the Comité de Apoyo a Compatriotas (Support Committee for Compatriots, or CAP) in Los Angeles. Inaugurated after the party's fourteenth assembly in September 1990, the committee's goal is to establish a power base for the PRI in the city through social, political, and cultural activities. The CAP provides free legal counseling, promotes cultural activities, and directs immigrants toward proper institutions and authorities that can attend to their needs. At the same time, the committee engages in active proselytizing and fund-raising for the PRI. Although the CAP is formally independent from the Mexican government, it has established a strong working relationship with the Mexican consulate. As a consular official explained, "It carries out activities that the Consulate cannot engage in without compromising itself politically."[56]

In the same vein, the Mexican Consulate in Los Angeles has extended beyond its traditional administrative duties and is currently engaged in the promotion of Mexican culture, the protection of human rights, and the defense of the Free Trade Agreement.[57] Recent consuls have inaugurated a new style of dealing with the PRD based on negotiation and concert instead of confrontation. José Angel Pescador, for example, continually stressed that he was a representative of the Mexican government, and, as such, his job was to listen to and protect all Mexicans, independent of their party affiliation. This attitude has commanded respect even among Cárdenas's strongest allies. As a member of the Comité Mexicano de Apoyo a Cuauhtémoc Cárdenas (Committee in Support of Cuauhtémoc Cárdenas) described: "Recently a presidential decree in Mexico wanted to impose a (US) $500 deposit for an American car driven into Mexico. We protested, and the Consul paid attention to us. We have a very good impression of Pescador. He became a liaison between us and the Mexican government. He processed all of our protests and contributed to the abolishment of the decree."[58]

The consulate's activities have increasingly focused on the well-being and human rights of Mexican nationals in the United States.[59] Consulates have traditionally engaged in the protection of the rights of Mexican citizens, but their heightened commitment since 1988 undoubtedly stems from the *cardenista* challenge. One of Cárdenas's political banners throughout his California campaign has been the mistreatment and neglect of Mexicans by their own government. By assuming a leading role in the defense of Mexicans abroad via its consulates, the Mexican government hopes to polish its tarnished image and, at the same time, appeal to Cardenas's constituency. As Joe Sánchez, an influential Chicano businessman and ex-president of the Mexican-American Grocer's Association, commented, "Why does the PRI even want an office when they have the Consul?"[60]

Just how successful the Mexican government and the PRI will be at diffusing the *cardenista* movement in California is an open question. The joint activities of the Mexican government have appealed to successful Mexicans and Mexican Americans who have been able to establish a social and economic niche for themselves in California society. But at the grassroots levels, support for Cárdenas still persists. Many of the Salinas government's strategies—such as the accord with United Fruit Workers and the Social Security program—have only benefited a minority of workers. As a PRD activist in northern California underscored: "The actions that the Consulate is carrying out are not enough to affect the daily life of people here, and many Cárdenas supporters continue to view the Consulate with enormous skepticism."[61] It will be difficult to erase generations of resentment against the Mexican government with a few years of consular activities. Although Salinas has gained prestige as a forceful leader, the PRI still lacks moral authority among the majority of Mexicans in California. The party is still viewed as the instrument of a political regime that has harmed the *campesinos*, closed factories, imposed wage freezes, closed public enterprises, and forced people to leave their country. Mexicans in California keep corresponding with their families in Mexico and are aware that living standards have not risen. Even though they applaud the new-found commitment of the Mexican government towards its citizens abroad, a central problem remains unresolved. In the words of a PRD sympathizer, "If things are as good as the PRI says why do people keep crossing the border?"[62] Until Mexico can generate the necessary social, economic, and political conditions to retain its migrant population, in all likelihood Cárdenas will continue to exert influence in California. As a result, Mexico's combative politics will continue to take place in California's streets, and cities such as Los Angeles may increasingly reflect the political clashes and political dynamics that take place south of the border.

Sovereignty as a Bilateral Affair

In recent years Mexico's domestic and international politics have changed in profound ways, affecting constituencies and events beyond the country's borders. Mexico has evolved from a traditionally stagnant polity to a relatively more competitive political system, and from a self-enclosed economy to an international economic player. These transformations have been accompanied by intense disputes between critics and advocates of Mexico's new course, and those disputes have taken place not only in Mexican territory, but also in the United States. As a result of its proximity and large-and-growing Mexican population, California has become the site of a vigorous political warfare between the Mexican government and opposition forces linked to its main contenders, Cuauhtémoc Cárdenas and the PRD.

The future of these developments will ultimately depend on the goals and strategies of government and opposition forces in Mexico. As long as Mexico's leaders continue to harness political change, the politics of confrontation will dominate the country's domestic scenario and its international relations. As long as the Mexican government attempts to remove certain items from the bilateral agenda—such as domestic political reform, workers' rights, and environmental issues—Cárdenas will strive to incorporate them. Each time the PRI seeks to polish its tarnished image in the United States, the PRD will quickly point out the rust on the ruling party's armor. When members of Mexico's Economic Cabinet tour California, *cardenista* policy analysts will retaliate with critical op-ed pieces in California newspapers. When the PRI declares its electoral rebound and the end of the "1988 syndrome," the PRD will begin to organize the next parallel election in Los Angeles. As long as limited political opening, unperturbed relations with the United States, and the wholesale promotion of the Free Trade Agreement continue to occupy the top notches on the Salinas agenda, Cárdenas and the PRD in Los Angeles, as in Mexico City, will remain a thorn in the Mexican government's side.

The battles waged in California as a result of Mexico's 1988 presidential elections continue to be fought today. In their attempts to shore up support, Cárdenas and his party have brandished weapons such as the right of California's Mexicans to vote in Mexican elections through absentee ballots, the need for parallel elections and a *perredista* party, the social and economic implications of the NAFTA, human rights, and the Salinas government's neglect of immigrant workers. The PRI has counter-attacked with roving bands of "truth squads," aggressive newspaper articles criticizing Cuauhtémoc Cárdenas, tours of California by high-ranking officials of Mexico's Economic Cabinet, lobbying efforts to encourage California investment and support for free trade, and a new breed of consuls and consular strategies.

The PRD is using its constituency in California as a loudspeaker to promote *cardenista* causes in Mexico and the United States. On the other hand, the Mexican government and the PRI are attempting to regain credibility and generate support for Salinas's policies north of the border, while undermining the PRD at every turn. As a result of these conflicting agendas, California's political map has become much more complex, and so has its relationship with Mexico. California is now a crucial intersection point between the political struggles taking place in Mexico City and the new relationship that is evolving between Mexico and the United States as a result of free trade. These politics of "exporting conflict" to California have several implications—problems as well as opportunities—for the PRD, the PRI, the Mexican and Mexican-American community in California, California policymakers, and the future of U.S.-Mexican relations.

Mexicans and Mexican Americans in the United States have often been referred to as "a bridge between two worlds."[63] During his visit to California in November 1989, Mexican foreign minister Fernando Solana stressed that vision by suggesting that the Mexican population in California could become an "ideal vehicle" for better communication between Mexico and the United States.[64] Thus, their engagement in Mexican political battles in California could constitute a form of "political education" that might enable Californians to view Mexico with less circumspection and more understanding. One of the transboundary consequences of Mexican politics could be to sensitize public opinion to Mexico. A close-up view of Mexican politics on the streets of Los Angeles could grant Californians a privileged understanding of the political and economic issues at stake in Mexico and why *salinistas* and *cardenistas* are struggling over them. This new understanding could lead, in turn, to the emergence of a receptive and collaborative attitude towards Mexico among California policymakers and the population at large.

PRD lobbying in California underscores that the Mexican government is no longer the only interlocutor in Mexico's relationship with the United States. The PRD's presence as an actor in bilateral affairs could lead to a broader and more enlightened appreciation of Mexico by California policymakers, to a more critical and balanced perspective of the Salinas government, and perhaps to the emergence of cross-border coalitions pushing for democratization.[65] Human rights groups, environmentalists, labor union representatives, and other domestic interest groups have become key players in U.S.-Mexican relations. The impact of these groups has been expressed both through direct contacts with the U.S. and Mexican governments (through lobbying) and their interactions across the border and outside government-to-government channels. During the discussions over the approval of fast-track authority to negotiate NAFTA, these groups were able to introduce several issues, including labor rights, the environment, and Mexico's protracted political reform into the debate on Capitol Hill. Up to now, Salinas's spectacular economic reforms had led officials in the United States to reinforce their support for the PRI and to exclude the issue of Mexico's democratization from the bilateral agenda. Mexican political battles in California and the strengthening of cross-border alliances, however, could resurrect demands for political opening and dislodge Washington's complacency about Mexico's single-party hegemony. By establishing ties with the media and California congressmen, the PRD could publicize the argument that Mexico's economic modernization cannot be implemented without political democratization. Similarly, California *perredistas* could also raise the issue of at what speed, how deeply, and under what conditions should changes such as NAFTA take place.

Californians from all walks of life could benefit from the critical stance the PRD has adopted vis-à-vis the North American Free Trade Agreement. The mere existence of an alternative vision is contributing to public consciousness about the full implications—negative and positive—of an accord that otherwise might be negotiated solely in technical and commercial terms. *Cardenismo's* presence in California is encouraging a much-needed debate about the goals, merits, risks, and long-term noneconomic consequences of Mexico's integration with the United States.

PRD officials have argued that the party's promotion of voting rights is guided by the desire to empower disenfranchised groups that are "citizens of nowhere." According to the *perredistas*, their relationship with Chicano activists who promote Mexican involvement in U.S. politics is collaborative, not competitive. The PRD argues that it encourages Mexicans who are U.S. citizens to vote in U.S. elections, and that its "right-to-vote" campaign is geared towards Mexicans who have not yet acquired citizenship. The PRD states that it is not seeking Mexican or Chicano power but Raza power—so that the party can influence not one country but two—and that one of the PRD's slogans is "Mexicano-Chicano luchando mano a mano" (Mexican-Chicano fighting hand in hand). This stance has provoked contradictory reactions from Mexican-American organizations such as MALDEF and the Southwest Voter Registration Project that have spent years trying to gain acceptance and power in the U.S. political system. Many civil rights leaders in California are concerned that the PRD's drive to focus political attention on Mexico will make the advancement of Mexicans in U.S. society more difficult; Mexicans will focus on the political problems of their home country instead of participating in U.S. elections. Other Chicanos, however, support the PRD's position and have spoken forcefully in favor of "dual citizenship" that would allow them to participate in both U.S. and Mexican elections. Some organizations want Mexicans to remain Mexican so that they can vote south of the border, while others would like them to acquire U.S. citizenship in order to strengthen Chicano positions in U.S. politics. Unless strategies for collaboration and common and particular goals are mapped out, the PRD's activities in California could heighten the divisions within the Mexican-American community instead of empowering it as a whole.

The Mexican government's "economic diplomacy" and consular activism could open a two-way lobbying street for groups with common interests in both countries. Mexican businessmen would be able to forward their interests in California through the consulates, and California businessmen might pursue their goals in Mexico through the same route. In a similar fashion, Mexico's consulates could provide a much needed institutional forum to discuss issues that simultaneously affect Mexico and California, such as immigration, border violence, and the environment. Thus, one of the beneficial impacts of Mexican politics in California would to promote awareness among leaders in both societies that common problems exist on both sides of the border, and consequently, solutions must be found on both sides of the border.

The consensus among PRI and PRD officials in California is that policymakers in the state have responded favorably to Mexican political activities in their domain. This cordial relationship, however, stems largely from the so far limited contact among the three groups. In the future, the construction of foreign parties in California could lead to a host of political and diplomatic problems with which California politicians would be forced to contend. Mexican political support for candidates or causes in the United States—and vice versa—could lead to accusations of interventionism in domestic politics from both sides of the border.[66] In November 1991, for example, the Mexican consul in San Diego was accused of intervening in U.S. politics by supporting the creation of the Hispanic Pro-Human Rights Coalition. This incident indicates the emergence of a trend that will, in all likelihood, determine the future of the California-Mexico relationship. As ties between the two regions grow stronger and encompass more spheres, the boundaries that separate California's state politics from Mexican politics will become increasingly irrelevant.

Los Angeles councilman Mike Hernández has declared that as long as Mexicans keep migrating to California, Mexico's border extends up to the Golden State, and "California is Mexico." The Mexican consulate uses this judgment as a guiding principle that determines its activities in favor of the Mexican population in the state, including extensive lobbying directed towards California officials. The Mexican consul in Los Angeles is referred to in some circles as "the Mexican governor of California," given his political influence in statewide politics. The consul's efforts to reverse Governor Wilson's veto of Proposition 112, which would assign greater funds to adult education for Mexican immigrants, underscore the willingness of Mexican officials to become active participants in state politics.[67]

Mexican involvement in California politics entails significant challenges for the future of the state and for the bilateral relationship. Efforts by Mexican parties to rally their constituencies in support of a U.S. candidate could even determine the outcome of local and statewide elections. Mexico's occasionally violent and confrontational politics might play themselves out in California's cities. If PRI and PRD activism continues, California officials will have to learn to institutionalize political interdependence. They will be forced to devise specific ground rules, delimit spheres of action, negotiate with new and powerful political forces, and incorporate Mexico-bound concerns into their local agendas.

Mexico has become a part of California's domestic battles, creating new coalitions and reinforcing preexistent cleavages. In the future, the growing Mexican presence could possibly alter the power balance between major political contenders. The lobbying wars over free trade in the spring of 1991, for example, pitted the traditional rivals of labor and big business in the state against each other and left many influential allies divided, including environmentalists and farm groups. Mexican lobbying for free trade popularized the trade issue in California and made it a public affair. Different groups voiced their concerns over the trade pact, and ultimately contributed—through representatives and lobbyists in Washington—to pressure the Bush administration into devising a treaty acceptable to all sides. Opponents to fast-track in California and elsewhere in the U.S., along with their Mexican allies, succeeded in influencing the debate.

Although President Bush was able to control the political fissures created by the introduction of Mexico into the U.S. domestic agenda, his wholehearted support of Mexico may have been a double-edged political sword. Towards the end of 1991, Bush's popularity plummeted, largely because of what public opinion perceived as mismanagement of the economy.[68] As a result, opposition to free trade with Mexico became a battle horse for Bush's foes in Congress and elsewhere. Negotiations over free trade opened a golden opportunity for the Democrats to underscore congressional autonomy vis-à-vis the executive branch and/or to raise the profile of the Democratic party. Numerous Democrats declared their ambivalence about free trade and addressed the issue to attack Bush throughout the presidential campaign. After Harris Wofford's unexpected victory in Pennsylvania, populist and protectionist stances gained renewed appeal, and in the future they might be used again as a Democratic party agenda to harness the vote of constituencies who feel negatively affected by integration with Mexico.

The growing Mexican presence in the United States has irreversible and not merely conjunctural implications. For the first time, the politics and economics of a Latin American country occupy a central position of the U.S. domestic agenda. The current debates over the merits of integration with Mexico are distinctly different from the battles waged among U.S. policymakers over Central America in the 1980s. Central American wars were perceived as distant affairs with no specific impact on the U.S. population, and solidarity with one side or the other did not necessarily entail a large degree of commitment. But California's Mexico connection illustrates a degree of interconnection and interdependence with a Third World country that is unprecedented for the United States. Free trade with Mexico will directly affect numerous social and economic structures in California and throughout the U.S., ranging from employment opportunities to cultural identity. The depth of feeling and the diversity of issues and interests that have surfaced in California's relationship with Mexico merely reveal the contours of what has become a more complex relationship to manage.

Not only has Mexico affected California—and United States—politics in unprecedented ways; as a result of growing interdependence, the U.S. has strengthened its voice in Mexican domestic political battles. In the context of free trade negotiations, Mexico's political system was once again placed under U.S. scrutiny and subjected to northern pressures for reform. Democratic representative Robert Torricelli, for example, in October 1991 led a hearing in the Subcommittee on Western Hemisphere Affairs for the purpose of evaluating Mexico's electoral behavior and human rights situation. Although Torricelli voted in favor of fast-track, five months later he declared that given the "absence of democracy in Mexico" he might be forced to reconsider his position and perhaps vote against the agreement.[69] Torricelli's tactical shift illustrates the significant linkages that emerged between Mexican politics and free trade negotiations.

Other political players also adopted a judgmental role of Mexico's politics. The U.S. press, for example, may have influenced the outcome of the 1991 midterm elections—including the downfall of two turbulently elected governors—through influential editorials that called into question President Salinas's commitment to political liberalization.[70] In the future, members of Congress might intensify their collaboration with nongovernmental organizations (NGOs), international organizations, and Mexicans who have called for international observers to supervise Mexican elections.[71] As integration with Mexico proceeds, in all likelihood, the merits and demerits of Mexico's domestic politics will become increasingly important.

The promotion for democracy in Mexico, however, has never been an overriding, permanent concern of U.S. policymakers or the U.S. public. Preoccupation with political change south of the border historically has undergone numerous ebbs and flows.[72] If the past is any indication of the future, democratization will probably take second place to political stability and the pursuit of economic interests in a stable environment under any regime-type that can provide a favorable investment climate. Mexico is on the cutting edge of a new, unconventional security agenda and a new international economic policy being implemented by the U.S. As Delal Baer has argued: "Drugs, immigration and political stability are unconventional security concerns writ large in U.S.-Mexico relations. The U.S. has invested its hopes in the success of Mexico's economic reform program, hoping to stave off the worst of Mexico's social breakdown."[73]

President Salinas's lobbying efforts in California, and in the United States generally, have a political dimension that is closely related to the course of events in Mexico. The political equilibrium—favorable to the PRI—that Salinas has been able to establish is dynamic and fragile, and could easily be upset by economic setbacks and the regrouping of fragmented opposition forces. The PRD may be flailing, but the continuing sympathy for Cuauhtémoc Cárdenas remains a political force with which to be reckoned. In the Salinas perspective, a dynamic market economy operating in conjunction with the United States could help to undermine support for the left and strengthen pro-Salinas forces. Economic growth has become Mexico's containment policy of the 1990s. In order to assure the hegemony of the PRI, the Salinas government must stimulate high growth and investment in the Mexican economy, and this outcome will only come about via a partnership with the United States. Ultimately, by cementing a neoliberal identity, NAFTA might reduce the possibility of shifts in economic policy and their disastrous political consequences.[74] The U.S. is prodding Mexico down the shining path of neoliberal reform to assure Mexico's political stability. Thus, with U.S. support, President Salinas can continue to enact gradualist political reform that will allow the PRI to remain as the centerpiece of a more competitive party system.

This intertwining of foreign and domestic affairs between the two countries underscores that, in an era of cascading interdependence, even the distinction between foreign and domestic issues is becoming increasingly obscure. Both nations are heading towards a large, permanent, and self-perpetuating presence in one another. Political events in Mexico are increasingly shaped by events in the U.S., and vice versa. Both countries are bound by diverse interdependencies and unavoidable interactions that are endemic and likely to endure in the foreseeable future. As a case study, the dynamics of the California-Mexico relationship exemplify ever more numerous, diverse, and salient connections that ignore even the political boundaries between both regions. Transnationalizing patterns have shrunk the distance between California and Mexico and rendered long-standing boundaries between their internal politics even more tenuous. In many areas, the Free Trade Agreement may simply institutionalize a historic process of silent integration. And as Mexican politics in California reveal, in an era of growing economic interdependence, even political sovereignty has become a bilateral affair.

CHAPTER 6

California and Mexico

Facing the Pacific Rim

GABRIEL SZÉKELY

DRAMATIC CHANGES have taken place in the global economy over the last few decades. As neighbors located at the gateway to the Pacific Rim, California and Mexico have the potential to reap significant gains from the emerging international economic order. Success is not guaranteed, however, and will depend on decisions within the two regions and on the future organization of the world economy. If wise policy choices are made by local and national leaders, the California-Mexico Connection may eventually serve as a hub between North America, Latin America, and the Asian Pacific.

This chapter examines the evolving relationship between the California-Mexico Connection and the Pacific Rim. After briefly summarizing the forces reshaping the global economy, the chapter describes the main features of the Pacific Rim and the comparative position of California and Mexico within it. Finally, it suggests alternative scenarios for the organization of the international political economy and assesses the implications for economic relations between California and Mexico and for the global role of the California-Mexico Connection.

Trends in the Global Economy

The end of the cold war has accelerated a series of changes that are affecting the way nations and individual firms go about their business. Now that the Soviet threat has been relegated to the history books, leaders in the industrial countries are working to restructure their economies and to allocate resources in nondefense sectors. In the United States, where defense expenditures have been very high, reducing military contracts will have a major impact upon local economies. Bases and research facilities will close, and thousands of highly skilled personnel and members of the armed forces will require retraining programs if they hope to rejoin the labor market. Adapting to this new reality will be particularly critical in states such as California, where the defense industry now accounts for 8 percent of total output, or $50 billion.[1]

Business executives are also redefining their traditional views about where and how to find new markets. For a growing number of firms, the location of production facilities within specific markets is of strategic importance.[2] In high technology centers such as California, firms from the Asia-Pacific region and from industrial countries are competing with U.S. firms to establish a solid base from which to gain access to U.S. and world markets. These pressures are deepening the globalization of production and marketing.

These changes are related to the multiple challenges facing the multilateral economic system, which has been unable to resolve many important trade and investment issues. According to Lester Thurow, "Institutions and practices that worked in a single polar world do not work in a multipolar world . . . but no country is prepared to make the necessary changes."[3] In the midst of this stalemate, a new system appears to be emerging based on strong regional alliances centered around the major economic powers.

Germany and Japan are poised to play an expanded role in the emerging world order. Already an economic powerhouse, Germany is likely to be strengthened further by the consolidation of Europe in 1992, particularly if sufficient resources and sound policies are applied to economic reform in the Commonwealth of Independent States and eastern Europe. Likewise, Japan has become a leader in manufacturing and finance, exercising tremendous influence over the Asia-Pacific region and playing a dominating role in world financial circles. Japanese bank loans represent $3 trillion of the total pool of international financial assets, which is four times larger than the share held by U.S. banks.[4]

The economic ascendance of Germany and Japan poses the most formidable challenge to the United States since it set out to create the multilateral economic system after World War II. No longer the undisputed leader of this system, the United States is struggling to bolster its position within the world economy. U.S. policymakers view the building of economic alliances in North America, and their possible extension to the rest of the Western Hemisphere, as a critical step in accomplishing this goal.[5]

The rapid changes in the world economy have brought home an alarming message to developing countries: they can no longer take for granted the level of support from industrialized countries that they have grown accustomed to receiving. Many leaders in these countries have come to realize that they must either adapt to the new rules of the game or progressively lose touch with the world economy and suffer a further erosion of their access to scarce resources.

What do these global changes mean for California and Mexico? Despite the difficult adjustments that will accompany declining U.S. defense spending and increased foreign competition, the two regions stand to benefit from greater integration and regionalism. Unlike many developing countries, Mexico enjoys the enviable position of being a desired partner of industrial giants such as the United States and Japan, partly because it shares a border with California.[6] Reflecting its strategic importance, Mexico is being sought after as an economic partner by other Latin American countries. Chile recently signed a free trade agreement with Mexico; Venezuela, Colombia, and Central America are hoping to negotiate similar agreements. Together, California and Mexico possess the factor endowments that are necessary to compete in today's integrated world. And because they are located at the center of the Pacific Rim, they offer access to rapidly growing markets and strategic centers of production. With California's Asian ties and Mexico's policy of building bridges to the south, the California-Mexico Connection may become the focal point of the Pacific economy.

The Pacific Economy

The impact of recent global trends on the California-Mexico Connection cannot be understood outside the context of the Pacific economy. Many of the potential benefits of the new international order for California and Mexico will be related to their pivotal position within this dynamic and changing region.

The countries in the Pacific Rim are at different levels of economic development and characterized by distinct endowments of natural resources and factors of production. It is thus difficult to conceptualize the Pacific Rim as a single region or to make useful comparisons between its component units, which are as diverse as Japan and Central America. In a world of deepening integration and regionalism, however, proximity to the same ocean may be a valid criterion by which to group otherwise disparate nations. The tremendous dynamism displayed by some countries in the Pacific Rim may spread to the rest of the region, assuming sound domestic economic policies and cooperative relations can be maintained.

The market economies of the Pacific Rim can be roughly divided into four parts: North America, the Pacific countries of Latin America, East

TABLE 6.1.
The Economies of the Pacific Rim

North America	*East Asia*
United States	Japan
Canada	South Korea
Mexico	Taiwan
Latin America	Hong Kong
Guatemala	Philippines
El Salvador	Malaysia
Honduras	Thailand
Nicaragua	Singapore
Costa Rica	Indonesia
Panama	China
Colombia	*Australia*
Ecuador	Australia
Peru	New Zealand
Chile	Papua New Guinea
	Fiji
	Micronesia

NOTE: There is an ongoing debate about whether to include within the concept of the Pacific Rim economy those Latin American countries that do not share a border on the Pacific coastline: Argentina, Brazil, Venezuela, and the smaller economies of Bolivia, Uruguay, and Paraguay. Many analysts refer in their discussions to all of Latin America as a region.

Asia, and Australia (Table 6.1). In the last decade, each of these regions has followed a distinct economic trajectory, from extraordinary dynamism in Asia to moderate growth in the United States, Canada, and Australia to crisis and stagnation in Latin America.

Taken as a whole, the relative weight of the Pacific economy has not increased in global terms. In both 1965 and 1989, the gross product of the Pacific Rim represented 52 percent of total production in the world economy. But the U.S. share of this total fell from 63 percent in 1965 to 54 percent in 1989. This change reflects a substantial increase in the participation of Japan; the newly industrializing countries (NICs) of Taiwan, Korea, Hong Kong, and Singapore; and even countries such as Malaysia and Thailand, which have made economic growth a top priority. The participation of Latin American economies in the region's total output, by contrast, has been reduced.

As shown in Table 6.2, the Pacific region's annual economic growth rates averaged, in real terms, 5.8 percent from 1965 to 1980 and 3 percent during the last decade. Such success has been uneven, however, both between and within nations. In particular, the gradual progress achieved by Latin American countries pales in comparison with the performance of the Asian NICs. Korea and Taiwan started a quarter of a century ago from

TABLE 6.2.

Indicators of Socioeconomic Progress in the Pacific Rim, 1965 and 1989

Indicator	Pacific Rim	Japan	United States	California	Mexico	Canada	Korea	Taiwan	Australia
Population[a]									
1965	1,252	98.3	194.3	18.1	43.5	19.7	28.7	12.7	11.4
1989	2,088	124.5	251	29	84.3	26.1	43.3	20.3	16.7
Life expectancy									
1965	NA[b]	68	70	70.6	59.5	69	54.4	NA	71.6
1989	NA	78	76	76.0	69.0	77	70.0	NA	76
Higher education enrollment[c]									
1965	NA	10	32	32.9	4.0	10.6	14.2	NA	15
1989	NA	28	60	62.0	16.0	58.0	36.0	NA	29
Scientists and Engineers[d]									
1987	NA	4,436	3,111	6,540	216	1,449	801	NA	1,625
GDP[e]									
1965	1,115.5	91.1	700.9	75.8	21.6	46.7	3.0	10.0	22.9
1989	8,915.8	2,843.7	4,847.3	619.0	176.7	435.8	171.3	111.5	245.9
Growth rate (%)									
1965–80	5.8	6.5	2.7	3.0	6.5	5.1	9.6	NA	4.0
1980–88	3.0	3.9	3.3	5.0	0.5	3.3	9.9	9.2	3.3
Current account balance[e]									
1980	−40.8	−10.7	1.1	NA	−8.2	−1.0	−5.3	NA	−4.2
1989	−93.6	57.2	−110.0	NA	−5.5	−14.1	5.1	NA	−17.3
Trade balance[e]									
1965	−16.7	.03	6.1	−.13	−0.6	−0.2	−0.4	−0.1	−0.5
1989	−72.0	64.90	−129.8	−31.00	2.2	3.6	0.8	10.9	−3.9
Exports[e]									
1965	57.6	8.5	26.4	3.3	1.1	8.2	0.25	0.5	3.1
1989	1,125.5	275.2	361.9	63.0	33.0	120.7	62.40	60.5	37.0
Growth rate (%)									
1965–80	6.9	11.4	6.4	5.8	7.6	5.4	27.2	NA	5.5
1981–89	4.9	8.0	5.9	6.4	6.0	6.4	15.0	NA	5.8
Manufacturing exports[e]									
1965	24.9	4.8	12.4	2.0	0.2	3.9	0.15	NA	0.5
1989	878.9	250.4	288.8	30.9	23.3	66.9	57.60	NA	2.5

SOURCES: California Department of Commerce, *California Exports: Their Contribution to the Economy* (Sacramento, 1990); International Monetary Fund, *Direction of Trade Statistics* (Washington, D.C., 1990); World Bank, *World Development Report* (Washington, D.C., 1983–90); World Bank, *World Tables* (Washington, D.C., 1990).

[a] In millions [b] Not available [c] Percentage of age group enrolled in higher education [d] Per million population [e] Billions of dollars

a less privileged position than Mexico. Yet today, as a result of economic growth rates that averaged over 9 percent during this period, income per capita in these two Asian nations is between two and two-and-a-half times larger than in Mexico. Likewise, the volume of exports from Korea and Taiwan changed from being a fraction of Mexico's total in 1965 to being almost double Mexico's total in 1989 (Table 6.2). In addition, the Asian NICs have been much more successful in following Japan to become efficient producers of a wide range of manufactured products. Unlike Latin American countries such as Mexico, for example, Korea and Malaysia have developed their own automobiles and have succeeded in penetrating foreign markets.

California and Mexico in the Pacific Economy

California has developed an extraordinarily intense relationship with the Asia-Pacific economies over the last few decades, but its ties with Latin America are mostly limited to Mexico. Meanwhile, Mexico has only recently "discovered" the potential of Asian markets; it has traditionally looked more to Texas than to California as its main economic partner; and it has maintained limited economic association with the rest of Latin America. All this may change, however, following Mexico's decision to integrate its economy more closely with that of the United States. Aware of the potential of a solidified California-Mexico connection, Asian and Latin American firms are seeking access to the California and Mexican markets.

California's Pacific Connection

California's strategic position in the Pacific Rim is a reflection of its economic dynamism and demographic profile. With an economic output of $619 billion in 1989, California has the third largest market economy in the Pacific Rim, surpassed only by Japan and the rest of the United States (Table 6.2). In addition, there are more people living in California than in several Pacific Rim countries, including Canada, Taiwan, and Australia (Table 6.2). A growing number of these people trace their roots to a variety of Pacific nations. According to 1990 census data, 25 percent of the state's population is of Latino (predominantly Mexican) origin, and 10 percent originally comes from the Asian Pacific.

California's ties with Pacific countries were strengthened during the 1980s, when the United States entered a period of rapid economic expansion. The United States is a key trading partner for every country in the

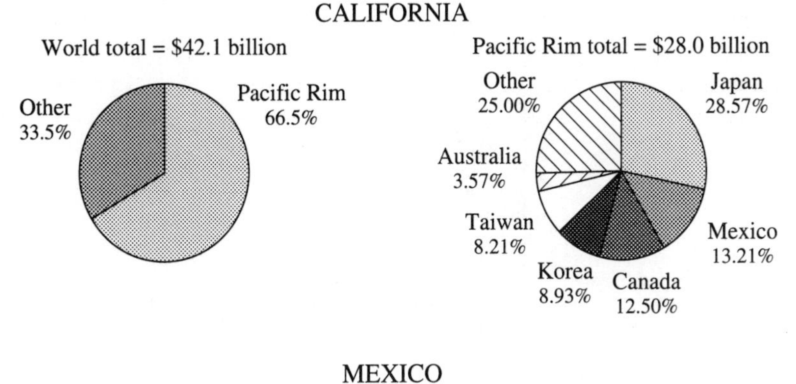

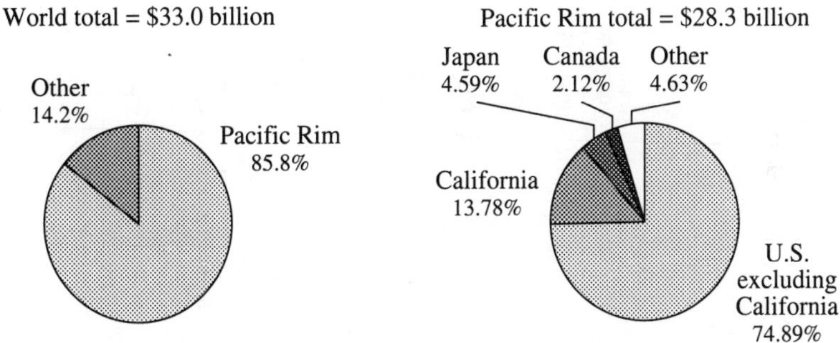

Figure 6.1. Californian and Mexican exports, by destination, 1989. From California Department of Commerce, *California Exports: Their Contribution to the Economy* (Sacramento, 1990); International Monetary Fund, *Direction of Trade Statistics* (Washington, D.C., 1990).

Asia-Pacific region and a preferred location for investment abroad. In response to growing U.S. resentment over the success of Asian exporters, Japan and its neighbors have complemented the accelerated growth of manufactured exports with expanded investments.[7] Japanese exports to the United States increased threefold between 1980 and 1989, when they reached $93 billion. At the same time, the stock of Japanese investment in the United States grew from $8.7 billion in 1982 to $69.7 billion in 1989.[8] Electronic, transportation, and chemical products have been the sectors most favored by Japanese investors.

As shown in Figure 6.1, two-thirds of California's exports in 1989 were sold in Pacific Rim markets ($28 billion). In that same year, 29 percent of export products originating in California went to Japan and 13 percent went to Mexico, nearly equal to Canada's position as California's second

TABLE 6.3.

Foreign Direct Investment in California, 1977 and 1987

	World	Pacific Rim	Japan	Mexico	Canada	Korea	Australia
1977							
Billions of dollars	4.74	1.55	0.56	0.002	0.074	0.00	0.02
Number of affiliates[a]	1,026	495	297	9	115	4	9
Affiliate employment	124,232	46,522	21,670	520	18,683	66	1,800
1987							
Billions of dollars	42.61	17.90	8.10	0.14	6.04	0.49	1.4
Number of affiliates	2,341	1,082	459	44	243	24	25
Affiliate employment[b]	324,200	137,100	68,500	1,000	32,500	2,900	16,000

SOURCE: California Department of Commerce, *Foreign Direct Investment in California* (Sacramento, 1990), pp. A-3, A-5, A-6.

[a] Number of U.S. affiliates with property, plant, and equipment in California [b] Estimate

largest export market. These exports have generated significant employment in California. A recent report by the California World Trade Commission shows that 232,900 jobs in the state are directly related to export industries; 15,000 of these jobs are estimated to result directly from exports to Mexico.[9] Many more jobs have been created to service and supply the export industries. Recent patterns of investment on both sides of the border, primarily within the *maquiladora* sector, account for much of this employment growth, which has taken place not only in manufacturing, but in service industries such as banking, accounting, and law.

Foreign direct investment (FDI) within California also expanded significantly during the 1980s. Table 6.3 shows a tenfold increase of FDI in the state between 1977 and 1987. The share of total FDI originating in Pacific Rim countries increased from 32.7 to 42 percent during this period. Japan alone accounted for 19 percent of total FDI in California, which in turn represented a full one-quarter of the amount of FDI flows from Japan to the U.S. economy up to 1987. Official figures show a more modest role for Mexico, with $140 million invested in California, which in turn accounted for 25 percent of total FDI from Mexico within the U.S. economy. The number of jobs within the California economy that have resulted from these capital flows to the state reached 324,200 in 1987, with Japan, Canada, and Australia together accounting for a little over one-third of this total (117,000 jobs). Most of these jobs are related to the manufacturing and trading activities of the associated firms.[10]

Tourism is another industry in California that benefits from the state's Pacific connection. Figure 6.2 shows that there has been a dramatic rise in the number of international visitors welcomed by the state, from 4 million in 1982 to over 7 million in 1989. More than half of these visitors came from Pacific Rim, with 39 percent of this group coming from Mexico (1.5 million). Canada and Japan followed with 23 and 21 percent, respectively.

Traditionally, the states of Florida and Texas have been the main points of entry for most Latin Americans visiting the United States, as well as for trade flows and financial investments from the region. But increased migration from Latin American countries to California and the success of many Mexican firms in catering to the tastes of Latino consumers has awakened the interest of Latin American exporters in the California market. In turn, a recent report released by Bank of America argues that as Latin American economies start to recover from a decade of stagnation, California businesses are beginning to assess the potential of markets south of the border.[11] Mexico represents the starting point of what many hope will become a strong relationship with Latin America.

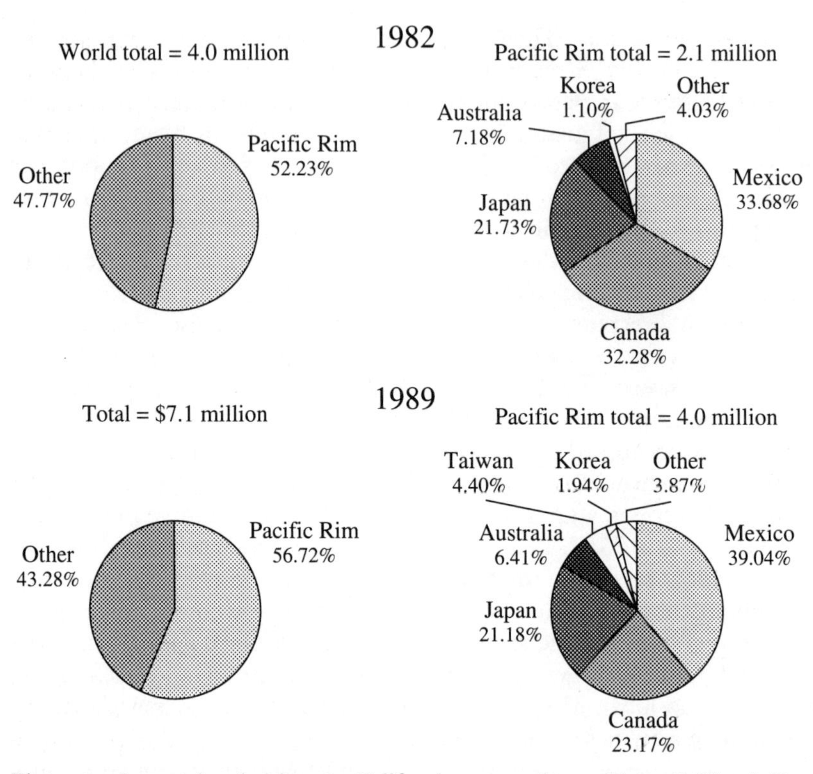

Figure 6.2. International visitors to California, 1982 and 1989. From California Department of Commerce, Sacramento, 1990.

Mexico's Pacific Connection

Mexico also expanded its economic ties with the Asian Pacific economies during the 1980s. This expansion resulted not from economic dynamism but from the complementarities arising from deteriorating economic conditions in Mexico, such as low wages and the falling value of the Mexican peso, and the outward-oriented development strategy pursued by the Mexican government after 1985.

As Luis Rubio and Guillermo Trejo discuss in this volume, exports did not play a significant role in the Mexican economy until the late 1980s, with the exception of oil. The ratio of non-oil exports to gross domestic product (GDP) was a relatively low 4 percent in 1980, before rising to 13 percent in 1989. Even this improvement does not match the performance of countries such as Korea and Taiwan, whose ratios in 1989 were 36 and 54 percent, respectively.

Nonetheless, Mexico's shift toward a more export-oriented economy has deepened its ties with Pacific countries. Today, Pacific markets account for 85 percent of Mexico's total exports. If we focus on trade flows between national economies, Japan is Mexico's second largest trading partner after the United States. If, however, we include the rest of the United States as a separate category, California is in second place as far as Mexico's export markets are concerned ($3.9 billion compared to $1.3 billion worth of Mexican exports to Japan).

As foreign trade has come to play a larger role within the Mexican economy, California's relative significance for Mexico has grown beyond that of most national economies in the Pacific Rim. In 1989, only 4.6 percent of Mexican exports to this region were sold in Japan, and 2.1 percent were sold in the Canadian market, compared to 13.8 percent in neighboring California (Figure 6.1). More importantly, whereas oil continues to represent a significant proportion of Mexican exports to Japan and Canada, manufactured goods account for the lion's share of Mexican sales in the California market.

In the area of investment, Mexico's crisis in the early 1980s lured foreign investors to the border region in ever growing numbers. According to the Mexican government, the number of *maquiladora* plants doing business in Mexico grew from 620 in 1980 to 1,924 in mid-1990.[12] About 40 percent of these plants (763) operate in the state of Baja California, with 499 in Tijuana alone. A large number of *maquiladora* plants (519) are producing goods within the electronics industry, and again a high proportion of them are located in Tijuana.[13] Many of these plants are affiliates of companies on the California side of the border.

Although most of the *maquiladoras* are owned by U.S. corporations, the expansion of Japanese investment is particularly prominent in Baja California, with a fivefold increase in Japanese-owned *maquiladora* plants for a total of 33. Four Korean firms have also begun operations in Baja California, and visits by executives of companies from the Asia-Pacific region who are considering making new investments have become quite frequent. Not surprisingly, most of these investments are concentrated within the electronics industry.

These investments from California and Asia helped the economies of the rapidly industrializing Mexican northern states such as Baja California achieve annual average growth rates of as high as 8 percent during the 1980s. This was an outstanding performance at a time when the rest of the Mexican economy was suffering a deep recession. Many jobs were created in the process, enabling many Mexicans who would otherwise have crossed the border to find jobs in the United States to stay in Baja California.

Mexico's expanded Pacific connection also brought the country important benefits in the financial arena. After Mexico nearly defaulted on its foreign loans during the 1982 debt crisis, U.S. commercial banks took every step to reduce the overexposure of their assets within the ailing Latin American economies. Japanese commercial banks, on the other hand, did not begin to reduce their exposure in the region until the end of the decade. By 1990 the Japanese had cut by about one-third their outstanding loans to Latin America—to $31 billion compared to $28 billion for U.S. banks. In Mexico, Japanese banks reduced their loan position by one-third as well, to $18.9 billion in outstanding loans compared to $15.2 billion for U.S. banks.[14]

At that time, however, Japanese government agencies stepped in to provide much needed capital to the region—especially in support of bold economic reforms. Mexico was the main beneficiary of this policy, but several other Latin American countries also received funds. In recognition of the expanded role played by Japanese private and public financial institutions in the region, the 1991 annual meeting of the Inter-American Development Bank was held in Tokyo.

Although no detailed figures are available on the role of California-based banks in the unfolding drama of Latin America's debt crisis, it is common knowledge that Bank of America and Security Pacific also took high risks in their lending to Mexico and other Latin American countries. When the crisis broke out, these banks could absorb the blow thanks to the booming California economy and the high-growth performance that California's Asian customers continued to enjoy. In the 1990s, as Latin America's economies begin to recover and their financial markets become attractive once again, the challenge is to find new ways to channel capital to the region, building on the painful lessons of the preceding decade.

Alternative Scenarios for the Global Economy

In the last few years, both California and Mexico have deepened their ties with the Pacific economy, particularly with one another and with the rapidly growing Asia-Pacific countries. Although de facto integration between California and Mexico is likely to continue regardless of what happens elsewhere in the world, the extent to which the California-Mexico Connection will become a hub between North America, Latin America, and the Asian Pacific will depend largely on the future organization of the global economy.

Ongoing trends toward greater integration and regionalism yield three scenarios of the world economy that are worth discussing: closed trading blocs, open regionalism, and regional building blocs. As we ponder the advantages and drawbacks of each of these scenarios, it is important to keep in mind that the Asia-Pacific region is at once a competitor and an important market for California and Mexico. This suggests both the need for North America to consolidate its position in the global economy through more formalized integration and the urgency of avoiding measures that would keep third parties away. Restricted access to the North American market would close off opportunities represented by Asian partners.

Closed Trading Blocs

Because of the general progress brought about by the world's multilateral economic system established after World War II, most countries have not invested much time and effort in formalizing the growing integration of their economies. Europe was the exception because its leaders recognized that bringing their markets closer together would help them compete with the United States. As long as multilateral institutions held sway, however, most countries did not worry about the prospect of an emerging "Fortress Europe."

This view changed in the mid-1980s. Just as multilateralism was rapidly eroding, the European Community declared its objective to complete the final stages of economic integration through the creation of a single market by 1992. This announcement evoked fears of a scenario first discussed by Lester Thurow in 1988: a dead GATT and a world of trading blocs at war with one another. These fears were deepened by the hardening of the European position within the Uruguay round of GATT negotiations, especially with regard to the liberalization of agriculture.

Under this scenario, the United States would be likely to erect a number of barriers to curb the participation within its market of both European and Asian investors. A hardened U.S. position toward the rest of the world would reduce the room for negotiation that Mexico enjoys with its neighbor. Mexico would be expected to behave with loyalty toward the United States, in effect limiting the participation within its own market of investors from other regions—including firms from the Pacific Rim. This would represent a great loss for Mexico, especially since Japan has become a critical source of investment and loans. Businesses based in California, especially those with strong ties to Asian firms, would also be hurt under these conditions.

Recent developments in California and the state of Washington illustrate that such a scenario is not merely hypothetical, as resentment of the Japanese continues to grow locally and in the rest of the country. In Los

Angeles, the city council recently reversed its decision to award a contract to Sumitomo Corporation for building trains for the city's new subway system, following complaints by local unions. In Washington, a Japanese businessman was assailed for expressing an interest in bailing the local baseball team out of its financial crisis.

But what investors from outside the North American region are watching with special interest is the outcome of the free trade negotiations. If the agreement includes strict "rules of origin" intended to limit the participation of investors from third countries, particularly from the Far East, these investors will lose their enthusiasm for doing business within this region. A survey of 114 Japanese firms conducted by the Japanese chapter of the Pacific Basin Economic Council in late 1991 revealed that this issue constitutes the top NAFTA-related concern among Japanese executives.[15]

Because Mexican firms have performed so poorly as suppliers to the *maquiladoras*, Mexico stands to lose more than California in the short run. Government officials fear that many businesses may prefer to move their plants north of the border than to meet the requirement of sourcing a greater proportion of the value of their final products within the region. Strict rules of origin and their aggressive implementation would also run counter to the aspirations of Latin American exporters who hope to gain access to markets in California and Mexico. These firms have even fewer resources than their Japanese and other Asian counterparts to purchase a high proportion of their inputs within North America. Thus, were this scenario to materialize, California and Mexico would have greater difficulty attracting trade and investment from both Asia and Latin America.

If, however, rules of origin were sufficiently liberal to allow sufficient time for firms to make the necessary adjustments in finding new local suppliers, both California and Mexico could continue to take advantage of their growing association with businesses from the Pacific Rim. Further, Mexican suppliers might benefit in the long run from a regulation that requires producers seeking to qualify for duty-free status to purchase 60 percent (or more) of the parts and components that they use within North America.

Open Regionalism

In contrast to Europe, the thriving nations of the Asia-Pacific region have until recently made little effort to institutionalize the growing process of integration among their economies. In fact, according to Lawrence Krause, the Asian countries have purposefully pursued a policy of "open regionalism," whereby they have not discriminated against third-party participation in their region's prosperity.[16] Because their economies are so closely linked to North America, particularly to the United States, these countries deplore what they see as a rush on the part of the United States to establish its own trading bloc. Asian leaders would prefer a scenario in which de facto integration, loosely governed by a multilateral trade regime, continues to evolve within different regions of the world. In other words, they support the status quo from which they have benefited so much. In particular, they would like to continue to enjoy a policy of open doors for their investment and trade in the United States, Canada, and Mexico.

Under this scenario, the pace of integration between California and Mexico, as well as between these two economies and the Pacific Rim, would be likely to accelerate. For example, bilateral trade involving California and Mexico grew annually by close to 20 percent from 1988 to 1991, and it has been predicted that if the NAFTA is signed the volume of such trade will expand threefold by the end of the 1990s.[17] This would reinforce the growing interest of investors from Asia and Latin America in the markets of California and Mexico. In such a context, the full potential of the California-Mexico Connection to serve as a hub between North America, Latin America, and the Asia-Pacific region would be more easily realized.

To reap the benefits of this scenario, however, firms in California and Mexico would have to commit much greater resources to cross-border trade and investment. Achieving this goal would not be easy, given the limited contact that exists at present between business firms and the leaders of these two regions. Each has to be convinced that the other offers an opportunity to establish a hub linking all regions of the Pacific Rim.

Regional Building Blocs

A third scenario that lies between the likely confrontation that would result from the establishment of "closed trading blocs" and the loose arrangement associated with "open regionalism" is the negotiation of regional building blocs as a step toward a new multilateral system. In the present context of strengthened integration and regionalism and a worldwide recession, the global economy is likely to be governed by the assumptions discussed in this scenario.

We may witness in the near future a greater formalization of economic integration through several regional agreements whose scope will vary according to the actors involved. In the Americas, this means that NAFTA would eventually expand to make President Bush's Enterprise for the Americas Initiative a reality. In Asia, the determination of Malaysia and its neighbors to establish a free trade area of their own would take hold. Japan itself might consider building on the current efforts of its southern neighbors to establish an Asian trade bloc.

In the early stages, liberalization within these regional blocs would be likely to continue, but between them, trade would be increasingly managed. Thurow points out that the existence of the blocs themselves would not in itself be a cause of concern and could even "be a necessary intermediate step on the way to a truly integrated open world economy."[18] At some point, the Americas and East Asia might consider joining their efforts to liberalize trade further. California and Mexico would be the ideal candidates to promote such a concept, especially if they make the investment of resources that are needed to demonstrate the benefits of an integrated Pacific Rim economy. If successful, this scenario would be a stepping stone to an institutionalized free trade regime at the global level.

Conclusion

A closer and better-managed California-Mexico Connection would strengthen the position of these two neighbors within the global economy. California has strong ties and experience within markets in the Asia-Pacific region, and Mexico is committed to strengthening its role within Latin America. The challenge for the two regions is to help bring about a more closely integrated economy in the Pacific Rim that includes a growing number of Asian and Latin American nations.

The implementation of a NAFTA would offer California and Mexico a test case of how to manage effectively the adjustment required by increased trade liberalization. Both regions would have to adapt to new conditions that favor the production of goods and services by economic agents with a comparative advantage. Mexican firms would have an opportunity to expand production of fruits, vegetables, and a variety of products within the textile and apparel industries—provided that they invest in modernizing existing plants. California businesses would fare quite well in high technology products and services such as banking.

Over the long run, however, reaping the benefits of liberalization requires better regulation of labor markets, more effective responses to environmental concerns, new regional institutions to deal with infrastructure development, and a better-trained labor force. These objectives, in turn, require new political coalitions at both the regional and the national levels. The degree to which California and Mexico can meet these difficult challenges will signal the potential that an expanded Pacific economy holds for the future of the California-Mexico Connection.[19]

PART III

Mexicans in California

CHAPTER 7

Mexicans in Southern California

Societal Enrichment or Wasted Opportunity?

DAVID E. HAYES-BAUTISTA

> In the Editorial (March 15, 1991), it is implied that we must accept continuing waves of new immigrants to our country and that we must learn to live with them, even though our California cities are full to bursting. . . . Obviously, many of our civic problems these days are a direct result from our own Anglo-Saxon, First World culture butting up against the cultures of our Third World immigrants. No other country in the world would subject itself to this cultural upheaval: Why, oh why, do we?
>
> Letter to the editor,
> *Los Angeles Times*, 23 March 1991

> Californians of Anglo descent should be reminded of the fact that our forefathers took this state from Mexico by a force of arms in 1846. It should have been apparent for some time that the descendants of those vanquished Mexicans are retaking California in a peaceful, if not a legal manner, by a force of numbers. A very good friend (who is one of those Mexican descendants) refers to the movement as *reconquista*.
>
> Letter to the editor,
> *Los Angeles Times*, 23 March 1991

The preliminary results from the 1990 census were a shock to some and a source of pride to others. Twenty-six percent of California's population is Latino. These 7.7 million persons, largely of Mexican origin, appear to be filling up the state. In southern California, the Latino representation is even more apparent. Some 3.4 million Latinos live in Los Angeles County alone, where they account for nearly 40 percent of the population. Another 2 million Latinos live and work in the counties of Orange, San Diego, Riverside, and San Bernardino.

And the Latino population will grow. By the year 2000, one in three Californians—about 13 million people—will be Latino.[1] This growth appears to disconcert some of the pre-baby-boom generation, who remember when Latinos were only 5 to 10 percent of the state's population. Judging from their impassioned letters to the editor of the *Los Angeles Times*, they are alarmed by the impression that the state has suddenly become a magnet for Mexican immigrants.

Latino population growth is a given for California. The variable is the state's reactions, on various levels, to this growth. There appear to be two schools of thought on this matter. The well-articulated school says that Mexican immigration is a threat to the state's society, economy, culture, and cohesion. This sentiment is expressed by the first letter to the editor quoted above. The alternative school, expressed by the second letter but rarely heard, does not see Latino population growth as an unmitigated source of social pathology.

The Urban Underclass Approach

"Families without money, skills, opportunities or hope; men without jobs, women without husbands, children without fathers."[2] In these few lines Lisbeth Schorr summarizes nearly 30 years of policy research about the urban underclass and poverty. Bursting into the national consciousness with Harrington's classic book, *The Other America*, the underclass and its accompanying poverty have been discussed and debated at great length.[3] Several key features of the underclass are nearly unanimously agreed upon: high rates of persistent poverty; a high rate of male unemployment; a disproportionate number of males leaving the labor force; a high rate of female-headed households; and a high rate of welfare dependence.[4]

Most lay persons have, no doubt, formed their views of the underclass not from the academic literature but from popular treatments. In his classic work, *The Underclass*, Ken Auletta describes participants in a job training program (designed to remove the underclass from welfare rolls) as fearful, hostile, belligerent, excluded from society, and rejecting commonly accepted values.[5] The underclass, in his view, is comprised of the passive poor, criminals, hustlers, and the psychologically traumatized.

The terms "underclass" and "minority" are often used interchangeably.[6] Latinos are classified as a minority and because they have low levels of income and education are commonly assumed to fit the underclass model. Thus, when Californians see the large and growing Latino population, they often envision nothing but growing social problems and an unending demand for public expenditures.

There is, however, a small but growing body of opinion that the underclass model might not describe the situation of Latinos well. Unfortunately, this opinion has yet to affect public policy to the same degree as the underclass model.

Data will be presented in this paper that support the notion that the underclass model is inappropriate to describe the situation of Latinos in California. Indeed, it will be argued that Latinos are having many positive effects on southern California's economy and society. There are some obstacles, however, to the realization of Latino potential, many of a policy nature. These obstacles will be explored to appreciate why they might result in some negative effects.

The Potentially Beneficial Effects of Mexican Immigration

Rejuvenation and Growth of the Population

Like all other postindustrial societies, the population of the United States is aging. Unlike other advanced economies, however, the United States experienced the baby boom: 75 million persons were born between 1946 and 1964. The aging of this cohort (which shows signs of increased longevity over its parents) will have two effects: (1) to increase the concentration of elderly in society from its current level of 12 percent to around 27 percent by 2030; (2) to reduce the size of the labor force, as the baby-boom generation commences to retire beginning in the year 2000.

Absent any other changes, the future poses a contradiction for public policy: there will be an increasing number of elderly eligible for benefits, but a reduced number of working-age persons to pay for them.[7]

In this regard, the first two noticeable effects that Mexican immigration will have on California are *youth* and *growth*. The population of Mexico is nearly a generation younger than that of Anglo California. Immigrants tend to be young adults and to have high fertility. Thus, not only is the Latino population considerably younger, it is also growing. Hence, in contrast to many other states, California will actually experience growth in the labor force.

California's population is becoming stratified by age and ethnicity, the older generation largely Anglo, the younger largely Latino. This can be seen especially in the case of Los Angeles, where 49.7 percent of all the babies born in 1986 were Latino, and Latino children accounted for more than 62 percent of public school enrollments.

These figures should be seen as a *rejuvenation* of the state's population and labor force at a time when the aging baby-boom generation will become dependent on young workers to fuel the economy. In California as a whole, Anglos will be a minority of the labor force by 2004.[8] Latinos will be the largest single group of workers by that date and will become the absolute majority shortly after 2010. The growing Latino population is bringing about not just a Latinization of the state, but an injection of youth at a critical time.

Strengthened Families

A second effect Mexicans will have on California is a strengthening of the most important social institution: the family. Indeed, it is the strength and functioning of the Latino family that sets Latinos apart from the traditional underclass tendency toward disintegrated, nonfunctional families. There has long been a stereotype of Latinos having strong families, but in the policy world this stereotype is either overlooked or ignored in favor of the underclass model of familial breakdown.

The fact is that Latinos form families at higher rates than anyone else and establish larger households than any other group. According to census data from 1940 to 1980, Latinos consistently have the highest rate of family formation of any group.[9] As shown in Figure 7.1, Latino households in 1980 were twice as likely as their Anglo counterparts and significantly more likely than black or Asian households to be composed of a classic couple with children.

The Latino emphasis on strong families fits within a Latino-Catholic tradition in which the individual is part of a community. Particularly since

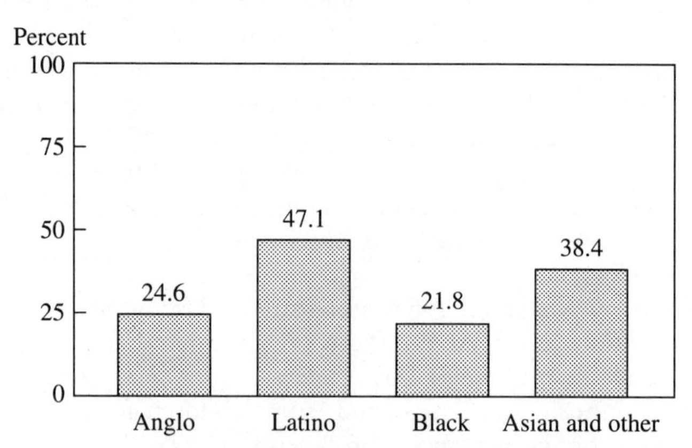

Figure 7.1. California households consisting of couples with children, by ethnicity, 1980. From Employment Development Department, *Socio-Economic Trends in California, 1940–1980* (Sacramento: Health and Welfare Agency, 1986).

Vatican II, the place of community in a person's daily life has been reemphasized. In a survey completed in 1991, the California Identity Project, Latinos were nearly twice as likely (55 percent) as Anglos (28 percent) to feel strongly that older children should take responsibility for their younger brothers and sisters.[10] Similarly, fully 83 percent of Latinos felt that it was important for their family to live nearby, compared to only 44 percent of Anglos. Yet the community is not meant to smother the individual. Instead, a new balance is being offered. Interestingly, and against the stereotype, Latinos tend to exhibit more support than Anglos for individual achievement. The California Identity Project survey found that Latinos were twice as likely (37 percent) as Anglos (18 percent) to agree strongly that a person should make it on his or her own, and not depend on family. And Latinos were about twice as likely (41 percent) as Anglos (22 percent) to agree strongly that once children are eighteen years old, they should take economic responsibility for themselves.

Strong Work Ethic

The throngs of Mexican immigrant day laborers looking for work on the street corners of Los Angeles have been misinterpreted by policymakers. Municipalities such as Costa Mesa and Malibu have outlawed the seeking of work, citing possible public danger from such immigrants (usually male) loitering on street corners.

Overlooked in this policy debate is the fact that, unlike the underclass, Mexican immigrants show every evidence of an extremely strong work ethic. Figure 7.2 shows that in 1980 Latino males age sixteen and over had a higher labor force participation rate (80.6 percent) than any other group, Anglo (76.2 percent), black (66.7 percent), or Asian (74.8 percent).[11] This is a historic trend that can be traced back at least to 1940. Indeed, employment is often a motivation for immigration. In the California Identity Project survey, Mexican immigrants were slightly more likely to be employed (84 percent) than U.S.-born Mexican-origin Latinos (79 percent).

The obverse of labor force participation is labor force desertion, or the syndrome of "discouraged worker." This type of non-participant has given up on the labor force, and no longer even seeks a job if unemployed. Latinos had the lowest rate of labor force desertion of any group from 1940 to 1980. Figure 7.3 shows census data for 1980, when only 19.2 percent of Latinos had left the labor force, compared to 23.1 percent of Anglos, 31.4 percent of blacks, and 24.5 percent of Asians.[12]

This reluctance to leave the labor force has one effect that may be easily misinterpreted: Latinos have a higher unemployment rate (9.2 percent

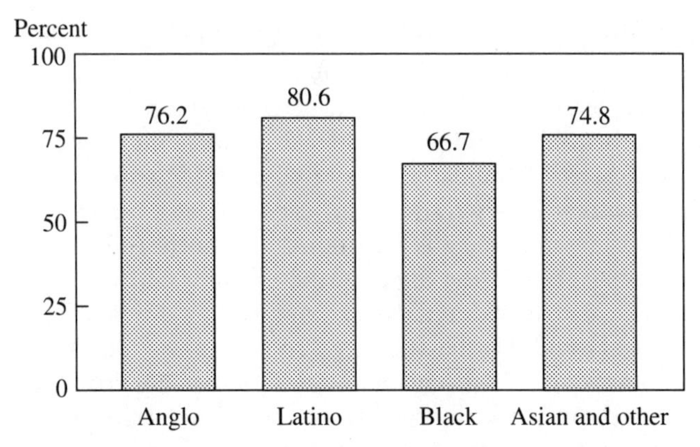

Figure 7.2. California labor force participation of males sixteen and over, by ethnicity, 1980. From Employment Development Department, *Socio-Economic Trends*.

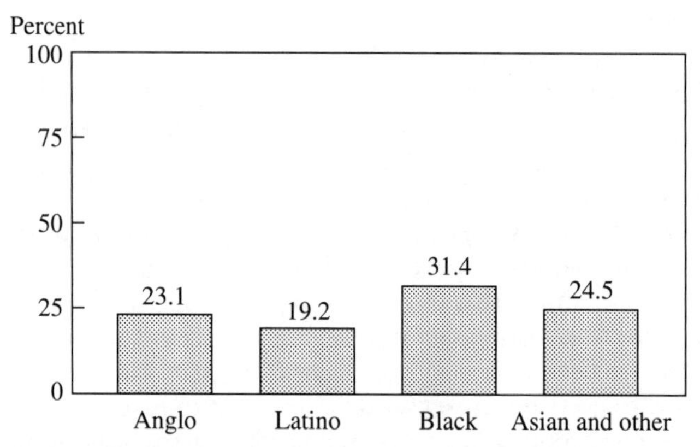

Figure 7.3. California males sixteen and over not in labor force, by ethnicity, 1980. From Employment Development Department, *Socio-Economic Trends*.

in 1980) than Anglos (5.6 percent), although lower than that of blacks (12.0 percent). In part, this is a result of the fact that Latinos seek employment when out of work, rather than deserting the labor force. Thus, paradoxically, Latinos may have a higher rate of both employment and unemployment than other groups. Taken together, these figures show an extremely strong work ethic, not a record of failure. As a result, a third positive effect of the growing Mexican population on southern California will be an increased adherence to the work ethic.

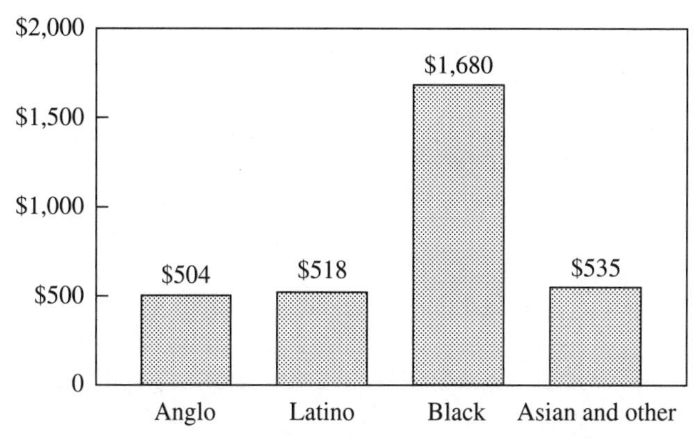

Figure 7.4. Average unearned income of California women aged 20–24, by ethnicity, 1985. From David Hayes-Bautista, Werner Schink, and Jorge Chapa, *The Burden of Support: Young Latinos in an Aging Society* (Stanford, Calif.: Stanford University Press, 1988).

Reduced Dependence on Public Assistance Programs

A commonly expressed assumption is that Mexican immigrants must be swelling welfare rolls due to their low amount of education and income. Data from various sources show that this is not the case. If we consider the case of women aged 20 to 24 in California (the prime "welfare mother" age), Latinas did not receive much more unearned income per capita ($518 per year) than did Anglo women ($504 per year); see Figure 7.4. They received slightly less than Asians ($535) and substantially less than blacks ($1,680).[13]

These figures combine immigrant and U.S.-born Latinas. When the figures are disaggregated, it becomes apparent that the immigrant receives much less ($384 per year) and the U.S.-born much more ($835 per year).

The relative participation of Latinos in public assistance programs is quite low, especially considering the high rates of poverty they endure. A recent study by the Los Angeles Department of Social Services showed that Latinos were consistently underrepresented on the county's Aid to Families with Dependent Children (AFDC) rolls.[14]

Healthy Habits

The underclass is supposed to have a Hobbesian sort of life—nasty, brutish, and short. In the classic picture, the underclass lives fast and hard, and dies young. Poverty and low education are supposedly inextricably entwined with poor health.

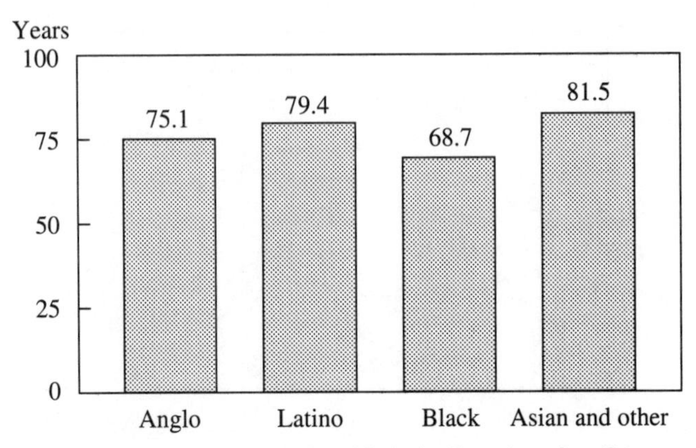

Figure 7.5. Life expectancy at birth in Los Angeles County, by ethnicity, 1986. From Los Angeles County Department of Health Services, Data Collection and Analysis, *Vital Statistics of Los Angeles County* (1989).

Latinos in Los Angeles County, then, present a puzzling picture that health specialists are calling the "Latino epidemiological paradox." In Figure 7.5, we see that Latinos have a life expectancy of 79.4 years at birth, 4.3 years longer than Anglos (75.1) and 10.7 years longer than blacks (68.7).[15] Latinos also have a lower age-adjusted death rate (5.12 per 100,000) than Anglos (7.89) or blacks (11.1).[16] This lower mortality rate for Latinos is consistent with state-level data.[17]

Low-birthweight babies, a high incidence of drug babies, and high infant mortality are hallmarks of the underclass. In all three of these areas, Latinas have consistently better outcomes than Anglos or blacks (Figure 7.6). In spite of having the least education, lowest income, and least access to care (classic risk factors), Latinas in Los Angeles County have a lower incidence of low-birthweight babies (5.32 percent) than either Anglos (5.51 percent) or blacks (13.27 percent).[18]

Preliminary results from an ongoing survey also show that Latino drug babies are born at a rate one-third lower than the Anglo rate and about nine-tenths lower than the black rate.[19] The trend from 1974 to 1986 has been for Latino infant mortality to be consistently about half the Anglo rate and about one-third the black rate (Figure 7.7).[20]

Among the many reasons for these relatively healthy outcomes is the fact that Latinas smoke less, drink less, and use drugs less than their black or Anglo counterparts. This is particularly true for immigrant women, whose incidence of low-birthrate babies and infant mortality is even lower than that of U.S.-born Latinas.[21]

Contrary to popular stereotype, Mexicans in southern California do not constitute a major health risk. There are some health problems that bedevil the Latino community—measles, polio, tuberculosis—but these problems can be rather easily and inexpensively managed. The major threat to Latino health is lack of access. In the California Identity Project, only 39 percent of immigrant females had health insurance, compared with 74 percent of the U.S.-born. Even without good access to health care, Latinos have achieved a respectable health profile. Improved access to care

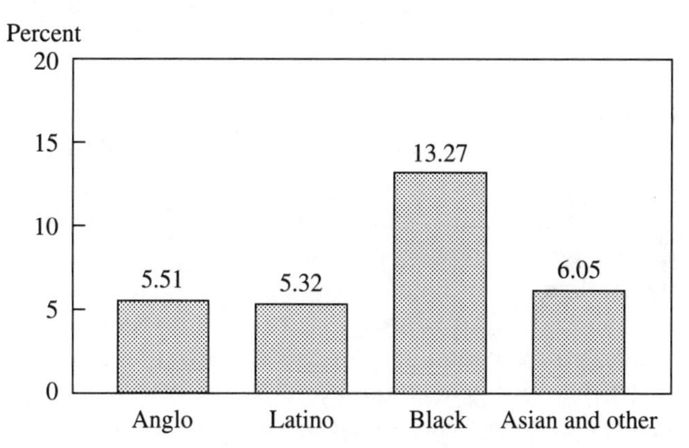

Figure 7.6. Low-birthweight babies in Los Angeles County, by ethnicity, 1986. From Los Angeles County Department of Health Services, *Vital Statistics.*

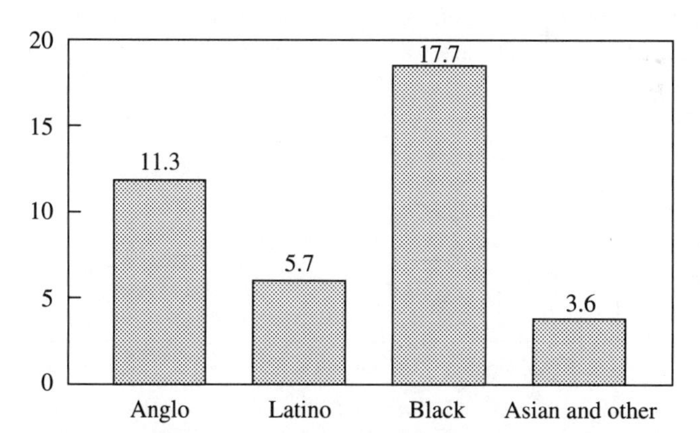

Figure 7.7. Infant mortality per 1,000 live births in Los Angeles County, by ethnicity, 1986. From Los Angeles County Department of Health Services, *Vital Statistics.*

would help bring down the rates of communicable diseases—tuberculosis, measles, HIV/AIDS, polio—and keep the otherwise remarkable Latino health profile strong.

Education and Crime: Not Latino Weaknesses

Two public images held about Mexicans are that they drive down educational levels and worsen crime. A quick glance at some data indicate that these two areas are not the sinkhole of Latino pathology they are so often thought.

Education

In the aggregate, Latinos have lower levels of educational attainment than Anglos or blacks. This has been a historic trend at least since 1940. If one controls for nativity for Latinos, a different picture emerges. The California Identity Project shows a pattern of rapid generational increase in educational attainment. In Figure 7.8, we see the high school graduation figures for first-, second-, and third-generation Latino respondents. True to popular image, very few immigrants graduated from high school—barely 25 percent. By the third generation, however, the high school graduation rate had climbed to 70 percent, not far off the Anglo norm of 80 percent.[22]

At all levels, the third-generation Latino has about three times the rate

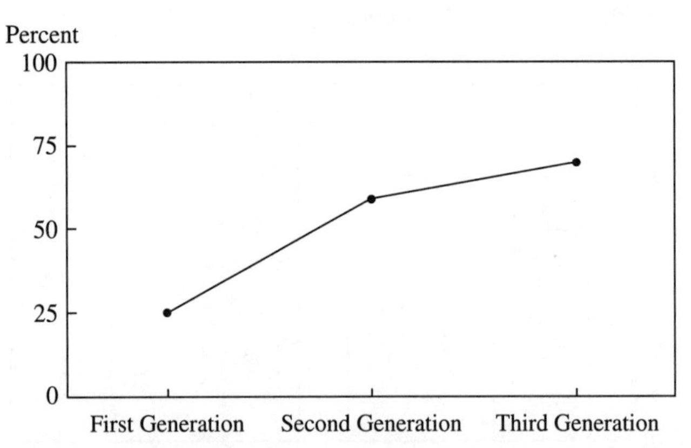

Figure 7.8. Percent of Latinos in California with high school diplomas, by generation, 1990. From Aida Hurtado, David Hayes-Bautista, Robert Valdez, and Anthony Hernández, *Redefining California: Latino Social Engagement in a Multicultural Society* (Los Angeles: UCLA Chicano Studies Research Center, 1992).

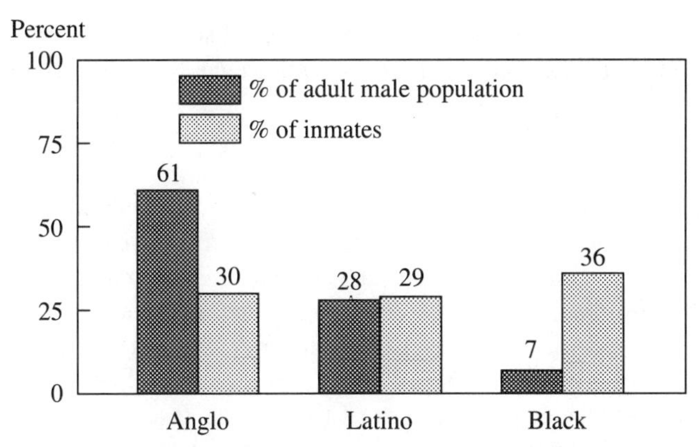

Figure 7.9. Percent of California total adult male population and total prison inmate population, by ethnicity, 1990. From Department of Corrections, 1990, and Current Population Survey, 1990.

of the first generation in high school completion, college attendance, and college graduation. Although the third generation still trails Anglo attainment slightly, the important trend is that the *rate of intergenerational increase is nothing short of phenomenal.*[23] It would seem fair to say that Latino failure to attain higher levels of education is more an artifact of public policy than some innate avoidance of educational experience.

Criminal Justice

Another commonly expressed perception is that Latinos are disproportionately disposed to participate in criminal behavior, especially violent crime. Recently released data from the California Department of Corrections does not square with this perception. When one considers the ethnic breakdown of the inmate population in California prisons, Latinos represented 28 percent of the adult male population in the state and 29 percent of the inmate population, nearly a direct proportional representation. By comparison, Anglos represented 61 percent of this population and 30 percent of the inmates, whereas blacks represented 7 percent of this population and 36 percent of the inmates (Figure 7.9). Judging from these statistics, one cannot say that Latinos are disproportionately criminally disposed.

Possible Positive Changes in Southern California Culture

In a behavioral sense, Mexicans are changing southern California society. But these behaviors are themselves the product of a more qualitative, subtle shift that may become reflected in overall societal values. Although much research remains to be done, several arenas for value changes over the next ten to twenty years can be identified.

Bilingualism

Latino respondents to the California Identity Project survey demonstrate by both behavior and attitudes that the linguistic norm for themselves and their children is bilingualism. Most immigrants (86 percent) understand English, and most (80 percent) speak at least some. Overall, immigrants rated that their level of proficiency was between "some" and "a little," leaving room for improvement. But clearly, there was no rejection of English. Indeed, 82 percent of the sample agreed that everyone in California should know English.

In addition, 95 percent of the respondents felt that Mexicans and other Latinos should know *two* languages and that Latino children should learn to read and write in both Spanish and English. Speaking of the general population (and not just of Latinos), 82 percent felt that any person who knows two languages will be more successful than someone who is monolingual. Respondent behavior is consistent with these desires: over 90 percent read, speak, and/or understand Spanish. Moreover, Latinos would like to share the joys of bilingualism: 72 percent feel that Anglos should learn Spanish. Anglos, on the other hand, were not so receptive to the notion of bilingualism, with only 36 percent professing any desire to learn Spanish.

Bilingualism is both the norm and the desired value. Even third-generation Latinos rate how they speak Spanish as falling somewhere between "very well" and "well." Latinos are quite comfortable being bilingual, and as their numbers grow, it is quite likely that bilingualism will become a regional norm and possible even a value.

Biculturalism

Another norm for Latinos is biculturalism, meaning active involvement in the Anglo-Protestant world *as well as* in the Latino-Catholic one. We can see this clearly in Figure 7.10, which presents cultural engagement over three generations of Latinos in the California Identity Project sample. This scale is a composite of a number of different items that measured, for example, the extent to which one listens to radio in English and in Spanish. As might be expected, the immigrant is more engaged in Latino culture than in Anglo culture, but by the third generation Latinos are equally involved in both.[24] Even those Latinos who are not affiliated with the Catholic Church (and there are both Protestant and Jewish Latinos in the sample) participate actively in the Latino-Catholic cultural discourse.

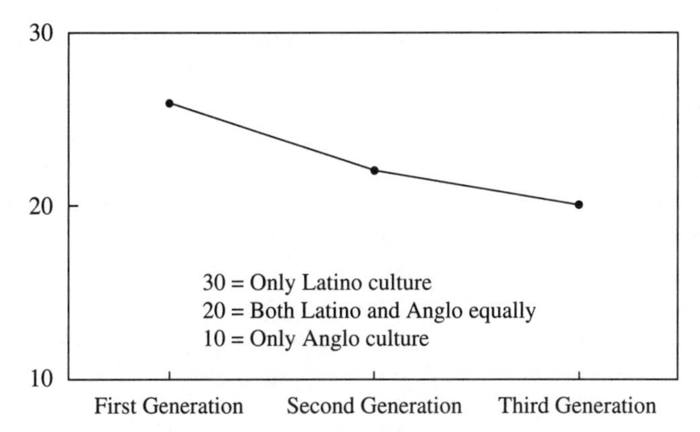

Figure 7.10. Degree of engagement by California Latinos in Latino culture, by generation, 1990. From Hurtado et al., *Redefining California.*

Latinos are very proud to be both Latino and American. Ninety percent of the third-generation respondents described themselves as U.S. citizens, 85 percent as Mexican Americans, 84 percent as U.S. natives, 82 percent as Americans, and 82 percent as Americans of Mexican descent. Thus, there appears to be no "marginal man" situation in which Latinos feel caught between two cultures; in the California Identity Project survey, the prevailing attitude is not "either/or" but "both/and." The future norm, as Latinos form an increasingly large part of the population, will be one of biculturalism.

Obstacles to Full Contribution

The above scenario presents the possible effects of Mexican population growth on southern California society. However, there are alternative scenarios in which these positive contributions might not be made. At least three policy areas may undo any potential positive effect: growth itself, level of employment, and assimilation.

Growth: Burden or Boon?

Population growth has been a constant in California for nearly two centuries. In itself, growth may be viewed as a neutral phenomenon endemic to the state. From 1940 to 1960, when the state grew faster than at any time since the gold rush of 1849, the population expanded by a phenomenal 135.6 percent. From 1970 to 1990, the state actually experienced one of its lowest rates of growth in the century, expanding by only 49.4 percent.[25]

The variable is not growth but society's response. In contrast to earlier decades, there is currently a strong no-growth tendency in the Anglo electorate, which views any further expansion, irrespective of ethnicity, as a burden and danger. This comes at a time when the Latino population is growing and the Anglo population is stagnant.

During the twenty-year period of 135.6-percent growth, when the state's population was around 90 percent Anglo, a sufficiently widespread civic vision of California society allowed the state's basic infrastructure to expand at a rate equal to or ahead of that of population growth. Freeways, water systems, public schools, and universities were all expanding rapidly, with vision and planning for up to twenty years into the future. The public was willing to finance such massive investments; bond issues were routinely passed by wide margins. Clearly, growth itself was not seen as a problem.

By contrast, the period from about 1970 to 1990 may be characterized as one of willful neglect of the state's infrastructure. For very different ideological reasons, the administrations of governors Brown and Deukmejian refused to continue investing in the California vision and allowed public investment to stagnate. Other than prison construction, few major public works were undertaken in almost any area—transportation, education, health, water, or environment. As a result of this lack of investment, population growth began to outpace infrastructure development, despite a significantly slower growth rate.

While Anglo population growth was only 6.6 percent during this period, the Latino rate was 259.5 percent. Thus, the lack of investment began when the Latino population began to expand rapidly. This has yielded a situation in which Latinos are blamed for overcrowded schools, traffic congestion, and water shortages.

Two important features of population growth and public investment are seen: (1) Any population growth, irrespective of ethnicity, would have meant overcrowded schools and overutilized infrastructure simply because the state lost the will to invest in itself in the early 1970s. That population growth did occur, and occurred largely in the Latino population, is an unfortunate coincidence. (2) Given the overwhelming majority of Anglos in the California electorate, any change in the policy of willful noninvestment in the state is a decision that must be made by Anglo voters.

Clearly, there is a lack of a civic vision similar to the one held by much of the state in the 1940–1960 period. If such a vision does not emerge once again, Latino strengths will not be realized, and their potential contribution to the state will be lost.

Vigorous Work, Anemic Returns

Latinos work very hard. Unfortunately, their labor activity is not well utilized by the state's economy and appears to be channeled increasingly into dead-end sectors. The Latino work ethic suffers from three obstacles.

First, there has been very little occupational mobility. While Anglos have changed from a largely blue-collar to a largely white-collar labor force (with a corresponding rise in income), Latinos have experienced virtually no occupational mobility. This is not merely a failure of affirmative action: it should be seen as a tremendous underutilization of an economic asset.

Second, what little economic mobility has occurred has been the result of the heavy unionization of second- and third-generation Latino workers. Whereas the high-wage, good-benefit union job was the pattern for occupational and economic mobility for Anglos in the 1940–60 period, these are precisely the jobs that are being lost in the state. Thus, young Latinos face bleak prospects for matching the upward progress of earlier generations of working-class Californians.

Third, immigration policies actively attempt to discourage and penalize Latino labor force participation. The policies are unsuccessful in that they do not stop immigration. They are quite successful, however, at effectively capping the level of occupational mobility possible for the undocumented segment of the population. There are indications that fear of running afoul of employer sanctions is costing documented immigrants and U.S.-born Latinos job opportunities.

Assimilation

U.S. policy towards "foreign" immigrants is one of unrelenting monoculturalism. It has been assumed that the natural and desirable course of events is for an immigrant group to assimilate as rapidly as possible. By this is meant a shedding of one's earlier identity and culture and the wholesale adoption of the American way of life.

The case of Latinos poses an interesting contradiction for this policy approach. For Latinos, the assimilation process appears to erode the strong qualities that make the Latino population a desirable addition to California. It is the highly assimilated third-generation Latino who is at risk for unemployment, welfare, broken families, poor health, and higher drinking, smoking, and drug use. The question for U.S. cultural policy, then, is this: does the United States want a highly assimilated Latino population that, by so assimilating, begins to approach the underclass? Or is the United States willing to allow a greater amount of cultural and linguistic autonomy, leading to the preservation and strengthening of important behaviors such as labor force participation, low welfare utilization, strong families, and health promotion?

The well-articulated, monocultural perspective would argue the former, that is, that Latinos must and should assimilate by all means possible, irrespective of the consequences. The alternative voice has not yet been widely heard.

In sum, Mexicans may be changing southern California in very positive ways: stronger families, a rigorous work ethic, less government dependency, healthier behaviors. In the long run, these values, undergirded by the Latino-Catholic discourse, may contribute to the balance between the individual and society that will be needed in the more populated and more polluted southern California of the twenty-first century. But current pressures on California's infrastructure, reduced avenues for upward mobility, and the dangers of demanding assimilation threaten to block the full realization of Latino potential. Removal of these obstacles lies primarily in the hands of the largely Anglo electorate, which must decide on its vision of a multicultural California.

CHAPTER 8

Mexican Labor in California's Economy

From Rapid Growth to Likely Stability

GEORGES VERNEZ

OVER THE PAST twenty years, California's history has been marked by a continuous, growing flow of Mexican immigrant laborers. As more and more of them have chosen to remain in California indefinitely, their relative importance in the state's and southern California's economy has increased. Further, they have become the cause of additional growth through family reunification (itself encouraged by U.S. immigration policy), the expansion of immigration communities and networks that reduce the cost of migration to successive waves of migrants, and a fertility rate exceeding that of native women and most other immigrant women.

As a result, California is characterized, more than any other state in the Union, by a large, permanent, self-perpetuating Mexican labor presence. Today, at least one of four new entrants into the California labor force is estimated to be Mexican-born, and nearly one in four workers is of Mexican origin. This relatively large participation of Mexican labor in California's economy is a fairly recent phenomenon. However, it already raises some policy challenges for the state that are likely to intensify with the expected continuation of Mexican labor immigration. The purpose of this chapter is to review the importance of Mexican labor to California's labor market, how its volume and characteristics have changed, and the implications of those changes.

The Changing and Increasing Role of Mexican Labor

Increasing International Immigration into California

For California, there is nothing new about rapid economic and population growth. From 1.5 million residents at the turn of the century, the state's population grew to some 30 million by 1990, averaging an annual

TABLE 8.1.
California Population Growth, 1900–1990, with Breakdown by Birth and Immigration

Decade	Total growth	Percentage of total change: California-born	Other U.S.-born	Foreign-born
1900–1910	60.1	27.2	48.3	24.7
1910–1920	44.1	34.7	49.1	16.2
1920–1930	65.7	29.7	56.3	14.0
1930–1940	21.7	48.1	63.8	−12.0
1940–1950	53.3	37.2	58.3	4.5
1950–1960	48.5	46.6	48.6	4.8
1960–1970	26.9	55.1	35.0	9.9
1970–1980	18.6	56.6	−5.6	49.0
1980–1990	25.7	NA[a]	NA	NA

SOURCE: Kevin F. McCarthy and R. Burciaga Valdez, "California's Demographic Future," in John J. Kirbin and Donald R. Winkler, eds., *California Policy Choices* (Los Angeles: University of California, 1985), Table 3.1; and 1990 U.S. census.
[a] Not available

rate of growth nearly three times the national average (3.5 percent versus 1.4 percent).[1] Even though the state's rate of growth has slowed considerably since 1960, from an average 49 percent to an average 24 percent per decade (Table 8.1), California's growth rate has continued to exceed that of the United States as a whole. In the 1980s, California's population increased by over 25 percent, compared to less than 10 percent for the nation.

What is new for California is the origin of that growth. Until 1960, nearly half of California's population growth was due to migration from other states within the United States (Table 8.1). It was primarily an American phenomenon. The 1960s was a transitional decade, but beginning in 1970, California's population growth became an international phenomenon, with nearly 50 percent of growth due to immigration from outside the United States. The extent of this remarkably rapid shift in the origin of immigration to California is underlined by the fact that, during that decade, net immigration from other parts of the United States stopped. Moreover, for the first time, the state became a net exporter of people to other states of the Union. The 1990 census is expected to show that this pattern continued during the 1980s.

In the last two decades, California has attracted an ever growing proportion of the increasing number of immigrants who have been entering the United States, legally or illegally, since passage of the 1965 Immigration and Nationalization Act, which opened immigration to immigrants from Asia and the Western Hemisphere.[2] During the last decade, over 29 percent of the more than 7.3 million legal immigrants who entered the United States initially settled in California, with many additional immigrants eventually settling in California to be closer to friends and relatives. By 1980, one out of four of the country's 14.1 million foreign-born population were residing in California, compared to only one in six in 1970 (18 percent). Today, an estimated one in five Californians is foreign born, compared to less than one in thirteen twenty years ago.

Among the new immigrants to California, Mexicans constitute the most important group. Mexicans accounted for half of the 1.8 million increase in the number of foreign-born residents in California between 1970 and 1980; Asians accounted for another one-third. Because the fertility rate among the Mexican-born is higher than for the rest of the population, focusing only on the foreign-born population underestimates the growing role that Mexican-origin workers play in the California economy. From 1980 to 1990, the Mexican-origin population contributed 41 percent to the growth of the state's population. Today, it accounts for one of every five new Californians. Higher fertility rates and continued Mexican immigration ensure that the surge of this ethnic population will continue well into the 1990s and the next century—barring a major and sustained recession in California.

What accounts for this phenomenal growth rate in the population of Mexican origin? For one thing, California's economy has been steadily demanding more labor—at nearly three times the national average. California's location is another attraction to immigrants from Mexico and Asia. At the hub of the Pacific Basin and adjacent to Mexico, California is the natural port of entry for the new immigrants. In addition, recent immigrants, like their predecessors from Europe, are drawn to places where their countrymen have settled, and California has a history of immigration from Asia.[3] In addition, for nearly three decades, California was the primary beneficiary of the temporary workers (Bracero) program established in 1942 in response to war-induced labor shortages in the agricultural industry. By the end of the Bracero program in 1964, more than 4.5 million Mexicans had come to work temporarily in the United States (mostly in California), providing the spur and link for the subsequent permanent legal and undocumented Mexican immigration that followed.[4]

Mexican Immigrants in California's Economy

As the number of Mexican immigrants has increased, so has their distribution throughout all sectors of the California economy. The Bracero program of the 1940s did much to foster the image of Mexican labor being primarily linked to agriculture. Although this image persists today, the situation has changed. Certainly, California's agriculture was and continues to be highly dependent on Mexican farmworkers: they constitute 40 percent of the state's agricultural labor force. However, the proportion of Mexican-born immigrants working in agriculture has been halved from one in three to one in six in 1980 (Table 8.2). By 1980, Mexican-born labor was filling a substantial proportion of jobs in all sectors of the California economy. This is particularly true in manufacturing, where the proportion of Mexican-born workers has doubled, increasing from one in six in 1960 to more than one in three in 1980. Figure 8.1 presents the Mexican-born share of total employment by industry. As it shows, the dependence of manufacturing on Mexican labor is higher in Los Angeles County than in the rest of the state, and immigrants are also important to the construction and the service industries.[5]

The distribution of Mexican labor across all sectors of the economy is, however, not reflected in the distribution of Mexican immigrant labor by occupations. Statewide, approximately one in every two workers is employed in a white-collar job, whereas less than one in six Mexican immigrants is so employed.[6] Mexican immigrants are concentrated in low-skilled jobs in even greater proportions today than in earlier times. One in two Mexican immigrants who entered during the 1970–80 decade was an operative or laborer, compared to one in three for the cohort that entered two decades earlier. In 1980, they were three times more likely than other immigrants and natives to be working in the operatives and laborers category (Table 8.2).

Because they are concentrated in lower-skilled occupations, Mexican immigrants as a group command lower wages and have higher unemployment rates than other immigrants and the native-born. In 1980, Mexican-born male immigrants were nearly twice as likely to be unemployed than native and other immigrant males, and their average hourly wages were 70 percent of the average wages of their native counterparts. This has changed very little since 1960, when their wages were 72 percent of their native counterparts' (Table 8.2).

The relative stagnation of the earning power of Mexican immigrants is further documented by James P. Smith.[7] Analyzing changes in male wages from 1940 to 1980, Smith shows that the wage gap for the Mexican-born has deteriorated since 1960, relative both to Anglo men and to U.S.-born men of Mexican origin. Overall for the nation, Mexican-male wages declined from 67 percent of Anglo-male wages in 1960 to 60 percent in 1980. This trend is consistent with the consensus of several studies that increased immigration has its primary effects on the wages of the immigrants themselves.[8] During the same period, wages of U.S.-born Mexican males increased from 71 to 73 percent of Anglo males' wages. These patterns contrast sharply with the trends for black males, who have narrowed

TABLE 8.2.

Comparison of Labor-Force Characteristics of U.S.-Born Workers, Mexican-Born Immigrants, and Other Immigrants, 1960 and 1980

Characteristics	Native		Non-Mexican immigrants	All Mexican-born		Mexican-born cohorts[a]	
	1960	1980	1980	1960	1980	1950–1960	1970–1980
Male	49.1	48.6	45.6	52.5	52.4	49.6	54.2
Age 17–24	10.6	15.1	10.9	10.3	20.4	11.3	27.4
Industry (%)							
Male							
Agriculture	7.7	3.5	1.7	31.1	14.8	20.7	13.0
Manufacturing	30.4	27.2	29.0	13.9	35.3	23.8	37.0
Services		36.8	28.2				
Female							
Agriculture	2.0	1.2	.7	6.7	7.9	5.0	7.6
Manufacturing	22.2	17.6	25.1	30.0	40.1	25.9	50.4
Services	43.7	38.9	41.0	49.6	32.4	46.2	30.7
Occupation (%)							
Male							
White collar	21.6	26.1	29.3	5.9	5.7	6.6	3.8
Operatives/laborers	26.1	21.6	18.8	37.0	41.0	41.5	43.9
Female							
White collar	17.4	24.3	20.3	6.0	6.0	4.3	2.7
Operatives/laborers	17.7	12.2	19.4	35.7	40.0	35.5	51.5
Hourly wages ($)							
Male	2.77	9.45	9.26	1.97	6.75	2.12	5.83
Female	2.50	7.48	7.60	1.95	6.43	1.94	6.02
Employment (%)							
Male	92.6	88.3	88.7	91.9	91.7	92.4	93.0
Female	41.6	58.7	58.7	28.3	47.9	31.1	47.3
Underemployed (%)							
Male	3.8	4.2	4.0	5.6	7.0	6.2	7.4
Female	3.3	3.0	3.7	3.5	5.8	4.2	6.7

SOURCE: Georges Vernez and David Ronfeldt, "The Current Situation in Mexican Immigration," *Science* 251 (8 Mar. 1991): 1191; and author's tabulations from the 1960 and 1980 public use sample of the U.S. Bureau of the Census.

NOTE: Refers to populations aged 25 to 64, unless otherwise noted.

[a] Cohort refers to decade in which these workers entered the United States.

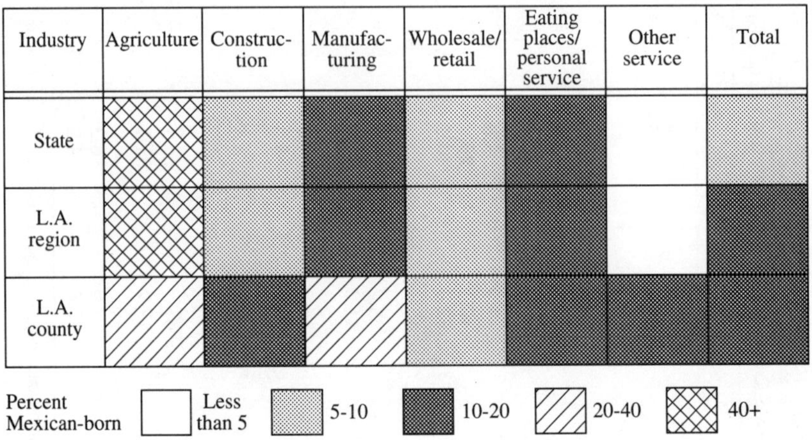

Industry	Agriculture	Construc-tion	Manufac-turing	Wholesale/retail	Eating places/personal service	Other service	Total
State	40+	5-10	10-20	5-10	10-20	Less than 5	5-10
L.A. region	40+	5-10	10-20	5-10	10-20	Less than 5	10-20
L.A. county	20-40	10-20	20-40	5-10	10-20	10-20	10-20

Percent Mexican-born: Less than 5 | 5-10 | 10-20 | 20-40 | 40+

Figure 8.1. Mexican-born share of total employment, by industry. From Kevin McCarthy and R. Burciaga Valdez, *Current and Future Effects of Mexican Immigration in California* (Santa Monica, Calif.: RAND, 1986), Fig. 5.2.

their wage gap relative to Anglo males from 57 percent in 1960 to 73 percent in 1980.[9] In 1980, the earnings of blacks were, on average, similar to those of U.S.-born Mexican workers, whereas only twenty years ago wages of black males lagged behind those of Mexican-origin males by 20 percent.

Mexican-Born Female Labor in the California Economy

Although females have always accounted for nearly one in two immigrants from Mexico, relatively few used to join the labor force; in 1960, less than one in three Mexican-born females were employed (Table 8.2). Over the subsequent two decades the labor-force participation rate of females increased rapidly to over 50 percent. This feminization of the Mexican labor force mirrors the rapid feminization of the U.S. labor force in general, but for Mexican females it has taken place at an even faster rate. Between 1960 and 1980, the labor-force participation rate of Mexican-born women increased by 69 percent, compared to 40 percent for native-born females. The trend towards higher participation rates of Mexican females in the labor force most likely continued into the 1980s.

The sectoral and occupational distribution of female Mexican labor more or less mirrors that of their male counterparts: they are equally concentrated in the manufacturing sector but are somewhat more likely to be working in the service sector than in construction and agriculture. Occupationally, they are concentrated in low-skilled occupations, like their male counterparts (Table 8.2). However, the wage gap between female immigrants and their native counterparts was about half that of males (86 percent versus 70 percent) in 1980. And, whereas the gap has remained relatively constant for men, it has narrowed slightly for women, from 76 percent in 1960 to 86 percent in 1980.

Characteristics of Mexican-Born Labor

Just as Mexican-born labor residing in the United States is highly concentrated in California, it has originated mostly from one region in Mexico, the western Pacific region. This immigrant flow is characterized by the increasing permanence of migrant stays north of the border, the steady educational gap between Mexican-born labor and the U.S.-born population, and the relatively low economic mobility of Mexican-born immigrants in the United States.

Regional Concentration of Origin in Mexico

"The concentration of Mexican migrants in a small proportion of the Mexican national population and in certain Mexican states . . . is the most remarkable but least examined characteristic of Mexican migration."[10] As shown in Table 8.3, three out of four immigrants have come from just 10 of the 32 Mexican states. These states account for one-third of Mexico's

TABLE 8.3.
Undocumented Mexican Immigrants Intercepted at the Border, by Mexican State of Origin, 1984

Main state of origin	Percent of those intercepted at border	State's percent of total population
Baja California	10.2	2.1
Sonora	5.2	2.3
Chihuahua	15.7	3.0
Durango	3.5	1.8
Zacatecas	4.4	1.7
Guanajuato	7.7	4.5
Jalisco	10.0	6.5
Michoacán	11.1	4.3
Guerrero	4.4	3.2
Oaxaca	3.9	3.5
SUBTOTAL	76.1	32.9
Rest of country	23.9	67.1
TOTAL	100.0	100.0

SOURCE: "Encuesta en la frontera norte a trabajadores indocumentados devueltos por las autoritadades de los Estados Unidos de América," Consejo Nacional de Población, México D.F., Dec. 1984, Cuadro 2.7, p. 53; and "Estadística demográfica y económica," Consejo Nacional de Población, México D.F., May 1989, Cuadro 8.

TABLE 8.4.
Distribution of Mexican-Born Population by State of Destination in the United States, 1980

State of residence	Percent of U.S. Mexican-born population	Percent of U.S. total population
California	58.1	10.4
Arizona	3.2	1.2
New Mexico	1.1	0.6
Texas	22.6	6.3
SUBTOTAL	85.0	18.5
Rest of country	15.0	81.5
TOTAL (PERCENT)	100.0	100.0
Number (million)	2.2	226.0

SOURCE: 1980 U.S. census, public use sample file.

population. This concentration on the Mexican side is the mirror image of the concentration of Mexican labor in the United States, where five out of six immigrants reside in the four states along the Mexican border (California, Arizona, New Mexico, Texas); these states accounted for some 20 percent of the U.S. population in the 1980 census (Table 8.4).

The concentration of emigrants from ten Mexican states is all the more remarkable in that it has changed very little over time. Indeed, it increased from 64 percent in 1924 and 1957 to 67 percent in 1977, 76 percent in 1984, and 75 percent in 1987–88.[11] No one has sought to explain why outmigration in Mexico is so concentrated in a few states. Although there are variations in wage disparities and employment opportunities across states and regions of Mexico, they are not in themselves enough to explain this regional pattern.

Three of the ten states, Baja California, Sonora, and Chihuahua, share a border with California, Arizona, New Mexico, or Texas. The other seven are more rural in character and dependent on agriculture. In 1970, 60 percent of their population was classified as rural, compared to 50 percent for the rest of the country. By 1980, that population had been reduced to 50 percent, compared to 40 percent for the rest of the country.[12]

When U.S. agriculture faced a labor shortage at the beginning of World War II, temporary agricultural workers (*braceros*) were recruited in these states. When the Bracero program ended in 1964 and the demand for labor elsewhere in the U.S. and California economy continued to increase, this temporary labor was replaced by an increasingly large flow of illegal immigrants.[13] Over time, self-reinforcing migrant networks were developed between these places of origin in Mexico and their destinations

in the United States.[14] This pattern has been maintained until today and has shown no sign of changing significantly.

Increasing Number of Permanent Stays in the United States

Shaped by experience with the Bracero temporary labor program, the popular image of the Mexican immigrant in the United States remains that of a young male who stays in the United States temporarily, works for a few months to a few years, leaves his family behind, and eventually returns home. This view of Mexican immigration was reaffirmed as recently as 1989 by the Bilateral Commission on the Future of United States–Mexican Relations:

> Leading experts are in agreement that, historically at least, the vast majority of Mexican migrants have been "sojourners," people who spend six to eighteen months in the U.S., and then return to Mexico. Some make the trip more than once. . . . The important point is this: *Their ultimate destination usually lies at the point of origin in Mexico, not somewhere in the United States.*[15]

Although longitudinal information on the mobility of individual migrants is not available, many aggregate indicators contradict this view and support the notion that more and more Mexicans are choosing to remain in the United States indefinitely. Working with 1980 census data, McCarthy and Valdez estimated that of the 1,265,000 Mexican-born immigrants counted in California, 25 percent were "short-term" or "cyclical" immigrants, and 75 percent were permanent immigrants.[16] More than 60 percent of the permanent immigrants were married and resided here with their spouse; three out of four had been in the country for five years or more.

This permanency of Mexican immigration to the United States is further evidenced by the some 2.3 million previously undocumented Mexican immigrants (60 percent of whom reside in California) who applied in 1987 and 1988 for amnesty under the provisions of the Immigration Reform and Control Act of 1986 (IRCA), which required illegal immigrants to have resided permanently in the U.S. since 1982 to be eligible. They constituted 70 percent of all applications for amnesty under that program. This share is 30 percent larger than was originally projected by census and Immigration and Naturalization Service estimates.[17] It confounded experts who expected that the five-year continuous residency requirement would make the bulk of Mexican undocumented "cyclical" labor ineligible for the program. A survey of the legalized population in California indicates that nearly three out of four applicants for legalization (including the Special Agricultural Workers [SAW] program) had been in California for ten or more years; one out of two had at least one family member who already was an American citizen; and four out of five indicated that they intended to apply for citizenship.[18]

Increasing Educational Gap

Level of schooling is a prime determinant of occupational mobility and wages commanded in today's labor marketplace.[19] Given that, one might expect today's Mexican immigrants to be doing much better economically than their predecessors.

Today's Mexican immigrants are better educated than their counterparts of previous years. According to the 1980 census, 63 percent of Mexican immigrants had eight years of schooling or less, compared to 82 percent in 1960; in 1980, 8 percent had two years of college or more, compared to 3 percent in 1960.[20] The average years of schooling of successive cohorts of Mexican immigrants increased by two full years, from 5.5 in 1960 to 7.5 years in 1980. This reflects the increasing access to and upgrading of education in Mexico over the last three decades.

In spite of this steady increase in years of schooling, Mexican immigrants are still behind most other immigrant groups (including Cubans and Central Americans) and native-born Anglos, blacks, and people of Mexican origin.[21] For instance, in 1980, the education deficit between male Mexican immigrants and other male Latino immigrants amounted to 3.5 years; this deficit was even larger relative to blacks and Anglos (4.2 and 5.5 years, respectively).

Not only have disparities in years of schooling between Mexican immigrants and other groups of workers continued to be large, they also have been increasing steadily over time because educational opportunities in the United States have increased even more rapidly than in Mexico. This unfavorable trend is most apparent when examining the schooling deficit of male Mexican immigrant cohorts who entered the country within the last five years preceding the decennial censuses. The ratio of Mexican immigrant cohorts having completed eight years of schooling or less to other immigrants and to the U.S.-born has increased from 1.5 to 3.2, and from 2.5 to 5.1, respectively, between 1960 and 1980 (Table 8.5).

The secular pattern for U.S.-born male labor of Mexican origin contrasts sharply with that of their Mexican-born counterparts. Relative to other groups, the U.S.-born have made steady progress over the past twenty years in average years of schooling. Between 1960 and 1980, their average years of schooling increased from 8.2 to 10.8 years, and their deficit relative to Anglo males decreased by 0.7 years, a 25-percent reduction.[22] Although U.S.-born of Mexican origin have experienced a steady growth

TABLE 8.5

Schooling of U.S. Natives, Mexican-Born Immigrants, and Other Immigrants Aged Eighteen or Older, 1960 and 1980, by Percent of Total Population

		1950–60 cohorts			1970–80 cohorts	
Schooling	Native 1960	Mexican-born	Other immigrants	Native 1980	Mexican-born	Other immigrants
8 years or less	31.7	79.8	52.1	13.0	66.5	20.5
2 years college or more	14.8	3.7	12.9	28.0	7.0	39.5

SOURCE: Author's tabulations from the 1960 and 1980 public use sample of the U.S. Bureau of the Census.

in years of schooling completed, other indicators in educational attainment suggest that they may be falling behind other groups (Anglos and blacks). For Latinos in the United States (62 percent of whom are of Mexican origin), dropout rates continue to be as high today as they were in the late 1960s (about 36 percent), while dropout rates for blacks and Anglos have declined over this period by nearly 50 percent and 25 percent, respectively. [23] This trend may in part be due to the fact that immigrants are included in the figures for Latinos.

Perhaps even more significant, college enrollment rates of Latino high school graduates in the 18–24 age group have declined over the past decade and a half. In the mid-1970s, the estimated enrollment rate of Latinos was higher (at about 34 percent) than that of blacks and Anglos. By the late 1980s, it had fallen to about 29 percent, which is essentially identical to the rate for black high school graduates. In the meantime, enrollment of Anglo high school graduates has increased steadily to over 35 percent.[24]

In addition, Latinos going to college enroll disproportionately in two-year colleges, a tendency that has increased over time. In 1976, 34 percent of Anglos in college were enrolled in two-year colleges, compared to 50 percent of Latinos. By 1986, there had been no change for Anglos, but the percent for Latinos had increased to 55 percent.[25]

Economic Mobility

When Mexican immigrants enter the country they are not only lagging in schooling and thus concentrated in low-skilled and low-wage occupations, they are also young. The population has been getting younger over time. In 1980, one out of four Mexican immigrants who entered in the previous decade was between 17 and 24 years old, an increase from one out of ten for those who entered during the 1950–60 decade (see Table 8.2).

Already at a relative educational and labor market "disadvantage" when they come in, how do Mexican immigrants fare during their working career in the United States? Do their earnings increase relative to other groups; do they decline or stay the same? James P. Smith examined the entry level earnings of successive waves of male Mexican immigrants (between 1955 and 1980) and followed their economic progress over time. His main findings can be summarized in four conclusions.[26]

First, the wage differential between Anglo males and male Mexican immigrants, at time of entry, increased between 1960 and 1980 by nearly 40 percent. Because education is highly correlated with wages, this is consistent with the schooling gap noted above.

Second, the beginning wage differential remains largely constant over the Mexican immigrants' working lives. In other words, they experience little if any relative economic mobility. This pattern appears to hold over successive waves of immigrants.

Third, the longer a male immigrant worked in Mexico before coming to the United States (and, hence, the older he is), the lower his initial U.S. wages are. Again, this relative pattern appears to have held over time.

Finally, the wage differential was significantly smaller for those immigrants who came in as young boys or adolescents to this country, and hence did some or all of their schooling in the United States. Indeed, there is little wage differential with immigrants who had all, or nearly all, of their schooling in the United States. Mexican immigrants who are children or adolescents when they enter the country do better when they enter the labor market than their parents did, although they do not fully close the wage differential. These findings are generally consistent with previous studies that suggest that the economic mobility of immigrants operates primarily intergenerationally.[27] They also confirm the critical role U.S. education plays in the economic mobility of immigrants' children.

Looking Ahead

As Mexican immigration has increased and successive waves of Mexican immigrants are staying here indefinitely, the number of Mexican-born immigrants in the country has increased rapidly, as has the number of native Mexican Americans. The growth of the latter is fueled by a fertility rate among Mexican immigrants 40 percent higher than that of Anglo women.[28] The Mexican-born population in the United States has more than quintupled in the space of two decades, from .8 million to some 4.5 million, and the Mexican-origin population has tripled from 4.5 to some 13 million.[29] Assuming that further concentration of Mexican-born

TABLE 8.6
Mexican-Born and Mexican-Origin Population in California, 1970–1990 (millions)

Year	Total population	Mexican-origin	Mexican-born
1970	20.1	2.0[a]	0.4
1980	23.7	3.7	1.3
1990	29.8	6.1	2.9[b]

SOURCE: U.S. census, 1970, 1980, and 1990.
NOTE: Includes all who answered the question on origin or descent in the 1970, 1980, and 1990 censuses.
[a]Owing to a classification error, this figure may be underestimated by about 200,000.
[b]Extrapolated from the 1988 figure of 4.1 million Mexican-born immigrants estimated from the 1988 Current Population Survey User Tape and assuming that 64 percent of the nation's Mexican-born population now resides in California.

immigrants in California continued throughout the 1980s, we estimate that both the Mexican-born and the Mexican-origin populations in California have doubled in the last decade alone (Table 8.6).

In sum California, and particularly southern California, where nearly four out of five of the state's Mexican immigrants reside, is headed toward a labor market that is increasingly dependent on Mexican-born laborers and their offspring born in the United States.

The Challenge Raised by Immigration of Mexican Labor

California faces difficult policy challenges because of the relatively low level of schooling, low wages, and low economic mobility that characterize an increasingly larger stock of Mexican immigrants (including the 1.3 million previously undocumented Mexican immigrants who are legalizing their status under IRCA). Traditionally, federal and state policies have been to let the first generation of immigrants fend for itself and to leave those immigrants who desire to upgrade their education and/or training to pay their own way. As a result, economic mobility of immigrants in the past has occurred primarily across generations.

There are reasons to believe that this policy may not be a sustainable and/or desirable public policy in the future. First, IRCA's short-term federal support for English-language and civic education has revealed a large latent demand and desire by immigrants to upgrade their English and other skills.[30] Second, their growing number and increased political activism will exercise a growing pressure to attend to this demand. And third, and perhaps most important, how this generation of immigrants fares may affect the speed and the nature of the educational and eventual economic mobility of their children. Since the children of these immigrants will constitute an increasing proportion of the growth in California's labor force, California has much at stake in their future.

To date, the available data indicate that the children of California's (and the nation's) Mexican immigrants are doing better than their parents, although they continue to lag behind native-born Anglos. Still, there are reasons to be concerned that future generations may not make the (relatively) rapid progress that previous, smaller waves of immigrants did. First, as successive waves of immigrants command relatively lower wages at entry, the incidence of poverty among Mexican-born and U.S.-born Latinos of Mexican descent might increase. Second, the schools are finding it difficult to respond to growing educational needs and to language and cultural diversity.[31] Third, federal and state governments are feeling serious budgetary constraints at the same time that intergenerational competition is increasing for public resources to support health care and other social needs. These issues will arise whether or not there is continuing Mexican immigration into California; however, continuing immigration may intensify them.

Declining Mexican Immigration?

Will immigration from Mexico increase, stabilize, or decline over the next decade or two? The answer depends on one's assessment of the trends that are expected to affect the demand for and the supply of Mexican labor, and the potential effects of policy changes.

On the demand side, the demand for labor by the California economy is expected to remain strong. California is well situated on the Pacific Rim to take advantage of growing trade with Asian countries. It also has a tolerant and generally supportive culture concerning immigration and immigrants. Although the California economy (like the national economy) is demanding an increasing proportion of higher skilled and trained labor, demand for low-skill, low-wage occupations is expected to continue to grow, albeit at a lower rate than in the past.

For the near future, Mexican immigrants will not only continue to be attracted by California's continuing demand for labor, but will be drawn by family reunification, particularly the 1.3 million previously undocumented Mexican immigrants who applied for amnesty, most of whom became eligible for naturalization by 1992. Once naturalized, their immediate relatives will qualify for entry into the country outside of specific "aggregate" and "country" quotas.

The only constraining factor that might decrease demand in California for Mexican immigrant labor is the increasing competition with immigrants from other countries, including Asians (their number in the 1980s grew even more rapidly than that of Mexicans) and Central Americans.

On the supply side, conditions that encourage Mexicans to stay in Mexico may be getting somewhat more favorable. The Mexican economy is slowly recovering and enjoying good developmental prospects. Also, the rate of population growth peaked in 1970 at 3.4 percent, declined to 3.2 percent by 1980, and reached an estimated 2.3 percent by 1985.[32] However, the differential in wages and job opportunities between Mexico and the United States will remain large for the foreseeable future, and these long-term favorable trends in Mexico are unlikely to visibly affect propensities to emigrate in the short run (say, five to ten years). Hence, the key to emigration rates may lie less in economic factors (short of a major economic depression in Mexico and/or the United States or other major disruptive events) than in factors particular to the Mexican western region, which traditionally has provided emigrants to the United States; and the rest of Mexico, which to date has not been heavily linked with the emigration network. With respect to the first region, it can be argued that the high rate of outmigration from those states suggests that most of those who wanted to migrate have done or are doing so. Manuel García y Griego has estimated that, for the western region, one out of three new entrants in the labor force went to the United States, and in some states one in two have gone to the United States.[33]

With respect to the rest of Mexico, it can similarly be argued that not having been heavily linked to the migration network throughout the post–World War II history of Mexican immigration, there is no apparent reason for immigration to begin now or in the future. At the very least, it would require a policy-driven or other major economic or political event for that potential to be unleashed, as the Bracero program eventually unleashed the permanent legal and undocumented emigration from the western region of Mexico.

Hence, on the supply side, the conditions seem to be moving in the direction of a stabilization, arguably even a decline, of emigration flows, as the demand for Mexican labor in California can be expected to do the same.

Ultimately, however, the size and composition of Mexican immigration to California will be primarily influenced by policies that have been or are being set at the federal levels: (1) immigration policy as reflected in the Immigration Act of 1990; (2) the zeal with which the United States will enforce IRCA's employer sanctions and other means designed to limit undocumented immigration from Mexico and other parts of the world; and (3) the eventual signing of a North American Free Trade Agreement (NAFTA).

Beginning with 1992, the Immigration Act of 1990 allows for a sizable increase in legal immigration from Mexico through three provisions: an increase of nearly 40 percent (from the current 500,000) in the aggregate number of immigrants who can be admitted annually; an increase in the country ceiling from 20,000 to 26,000; and a set-aside of 55,000 visas for three years, beginning with 1992, for the immediate relatives of the IRCA-legalized population. In addition, the 1990 Immigration Act grants work authorization and relief from deportation to the spouses and unmarried children of aliens who were legalized under IRCA and/or who were residing in the United States legally as of May 1988.

Overall, these provisions will allow for a sizable increase in the number of legal immigrants from Mexico in the early 1990s, with a subsequent decline as the provision for set-aside of visas for the legalized population expires in 1995. Because this increase in legal immigration from Mexico is primarily linked to family reunification and to the legalized population, it is expected to take place at the expense of undocumented immigration instead of leading to an increase in aggregate Mexican immigration. Also, the increase in employment-based admissions (from 58,000 to 140,000 yearly) primarily for professionals and skilled labor (only 10,000 are available for unskilled labor) will encourage more outmigration of skilled labor from Mexico, a process that will begin slowly but may accelerate over time.

To date, efforts to reduce undocumented immigration through increased border interdiction and enforcement of IRCA's employer-sanctions provisions have had only a modest effect, and that effect has been eroding over time.[34] Some of the reasons for the modest effect of employer sanctions include the inadequate allocation of resources for enforcement and the use of widely available and affordable counterfeit documents.[35] Hence, enforcement is not only difficult, it has been at a low level itself. It can be expected that federal budget constraints and pressures to reduce the budget deficit may well continue to put enforcement low on the scale of the nation's priorities.[36]

Finally, much hope is being placed on the prospect that the signing of a NAFTA involving the U.S., Mexico, and Canada would foster more rapid growth of the Mexican economy and eventually lead to a decrease in Mexican immigration, particularly undocumented, to the United States. Critics, however, suggest that the reverse might be true, particularly in the short run, because free trade might disrupt the structure of the economy, "displacing" workers particularly from the agricultural sector. What actually happens will depend greatly on the kind of and speed with which trade barriers are reduced, and on how the jobs eventually created in Mexico by free trade will be distributed among regions and sectors of the economy.

This level of specificity may have to await not only a signed agreement, but also its implementation. Until then, the most that can be said is that the potential for a NAFTA to increase or to reduce immigration in the short and medium run is small.

In conclusion, and on balance, California can expect that aggregate immigration of labor, legal and undocumented, from Mexico will stabilize, if not decline, and that more legal immigration will replace undocumented immigration.

CHAPTER 9

Separating Myth from Reality

The Impact of Mexican Immigration on Health and Human Services

FERNANDO TORRES-GIL

IN THE COMING YEARS, California will face extraordinary pressures to improve health care and social services for all its residents. Public debates and political decisions will revolve around the cost of providing these services and the question of who is considered deserving of public benefits. Senior citizens, pregnant women, AIDS victims, the disabled, and many other constituents will compete for limited public funds.

Foreign immigrants, who lack political representation and may be perceived as unworthy of access to state-funded programs, will be particularly vulnerable to retrenchments in social services. Since the majority of immigrants in California are Mexican, the perception and handling of this issue will affect relations with the state's most important neighbor. Although Mexico has gained prominence on the U.S. policy agenda, immigrant needs and the bilateral effects of health and human services have been explored only superficially. Yet no other issue, with the possible exception of language and education, touches individuals more personally.

A basic premise of this chapter is that the debate regarding the provision of health and human services to immigrants must be redefined. Rather than arguing over the rights of immigrants to public benefits, policymakers should focus on how best to meet their needs. What is the true nature of the health and social status of Mexican immigrants and the Latino community? How does it differ from popular perceptions? What federal and state programs exist to ameliorate the conditions facing immigrants? What are the consequences of not meeting the needs of the immigrant population? Without greater attention to these questions, immigrants may not receive the health care, housing, education, and welfare necessary for them to become productive and acculturated members of society.

The Importance of Meeting the Needs of Mexican Immigrants

High immigration and fertility rates assure that California's Mexican-origin population will continue to grow rapidly. Since Mexicans who come to California are increasingly likely to settle and raise a family, it behooves U.S. residents and policymakers to adjust to their long-term presence.

During the 1980s, Latinos increased their share of California's population by 69.2 percent. According to the 1990 census, nearly one-third of southern California's population and one-fourth of the state's population comprises Latinos. Although precise immigration figures from Mexico and Latin America are unavailable, estimates show that more than half of the people moving to California are from other countries, and Mexico is the largest single source.[1] California and Los Angeles have become the new Ellis Island, replacing New York City as the primary destination of immigrants and refugees.

Although immigrants often have problems adjusting to U.S. society, they represent an industrious, entrepreneurial, and young work force essential to California's economy. The state's nonminority population is aging, and its fertility rates are dropping. By the year 2000, U.S. labor-force growth will be primarily in minorities (20 percent), immigrants (22 percent), and white females (42 percent); white males will comprise only 16 percent of the working population.[2] Faced with these demographic realities, California has a vital stake in what becomes of immigrants and minorities. Meeting their health and human service needs is a necessary step in securing California's economic future.

Contrary to popular perceptions, the overall impact of Mexican immigration on health and human services has been manageable. Latinos are relatively healthy, productive, and persevering. But if they do not receive certain basic services that enable them to integrate successfully into California society, their health and social status may decline. Already, Latinos face chronic school dropout rates, rising crime, and other poverty-related problems that add costs to state programs and foster resentment among other groups. In 1990, one-quarter of the increase in the Medi-Cal budget was attributed to the elderly and children, with most of the youngsters coming from immigrant and minority populations.[3] In that same year, the use of the Aid to Families with Dependent Children (AFDC) program by Latino women was 23 percent higher than that of all other women.[4]

In addition, specific health problems threaten all Californians if basic health and human services are not provided to Mexican immigrants. For example, the spread of communicable diseases such as tuberculosis is a growing problem in California. Of the 3,438 cases of TB reported in the state in 1986, 34 percent were among Latinos. Sixty-five percent of these cases were reported in Los Angeles, San Diego, Orange, and Imperial counties.[5] Restaurants, fast-food outlets, and other retail services are particularly at risk if low-wage workers from Mexico and other countries are not treated for communicable diseases such as hepatitis or have no access to public health programs.

Existing Programs in California and Mexico

Providing public health care, social services, welfare, and other human services is an important government responsibility in the United States and Mexico. Before examining the specific barriers to meeting the health and human service needs of Mexican immigrants, it is helpful to know what these immigrants receive on both sides of the border.

California's Health and Human Service System

California provides a vast array of services and benefits to its residents. The largest and most visible program is the California Medical Assistance Program (Medi-Cal), which entitles recipients to a wide range of health services and is jointly administered and funded by federal and state governments. The state also manages AFDC, the state supplement to the federal Supplemental Security Income Program (SSI/SSP), In-Home Supportive Services (IHSS), Child Welfare Services (CWS), and programs administered through the departments of Developmental Services and Mental Health. Other relevant state programs fall under the jurisdiction of the Department of Housing and Community Development (e.g., the Farm Labor Rehabilitation Loan Program, the Farmworker Housing Grant, and Rural Communities Facilities funds) and the Department of Education. In addition, agencies at the state, county, and local levels provide drug and alcohol abuse rehabilitation, disease control, prenatal and child care, mental health programs, unemployment insurance, job train ing, and food stamps.

Legalized residents and undocumented persons are eligible for some state and federal programs. Limited services are available to persons meeting Medi-Cal eligibility tests: undocumented immigrants (including those under final deportation order), able-bodied aliens between ages 18 and 64 who have been granted amnesty under the Immigration Reform and Control Act (IRCA), and nonimmigrants with a temporary visa who intend to remain in California indefinitely (e.g., students and tourists). In 1986, IRCA and the Omnibus Budget Reconciliation Act expanded Medi-Cal eligibility for aliens.[6] As of 1991, full-scope Medi-Cal benefits were available to lawful permanent residents (or "green card" holders) and persons classified as Permanently Residing Under Color of Law (PRUCOL). The PRUCOL provision allows nonpermanent residents who meet certain program eligibility requirements to receive AFDC, SSI/SSP, Medi-Cal, and unemployment insurance.[7] Finally, undocumented aliens granted amnesty under IRCA have access to full services for children, special services for pregnant women, and emergency services for all eligible aliens under Medi-Cal. They are disqualified, however, from receiving AFDC, food stamps, and nonemergency medical care under Medi-Cal for five years from the date they are granted legal residence.[8]

Some of the funding for immigrant services is provided by the federal government. The State Legalization Impact Assistance Grant (SLIAG) helps defray the cost of state housing services, health and mental health programs, and educational and local services in areas with large numbers of aliens granted amnesty under IRCA. Through fiscal year 1990, California received about $1.1 billion in SLIAG funds. The federal government also aids selected refugee populations through the Refugee Assistance Program, the Refugee Resettlement Program, and the Refugee Cash Assistance Program. In 1990, the U.S. Congress passed the Disadvantaged Minority Health Improvement Act, which created an Office of Minority Health to focus federal efforts on health promotion and prevention, manpower needs, primary health services, and research.[9]

Most of the funding, however, comes from the state of California. Of California's total expenditure of approximately $55 billion in fiscal year 1990–91, more than one-quarter was spent on health and welfare programs.[10] General fund expenditures totaled $6.4 billion for health programs and $6.4 billion for social service programs during that same period. In an effort to reduce these pressures on the state budget, California legislators are pursuing plans to mandate health insurance coverage by employers and to create a "county-state" partnership that would realign funding responsibilities for county health services and community health programs.

Mexico's Health and Human Service System

Mexico outpaces the United States in its public commitment to universal social programs but lags behind in implementation. The Department of Health (Secretaría de Salud, S. Sa.) is charged with providing primary, secondary, and tertiary services on a sliding scale to all Mexican citizens.[11] The middle class, government workers, large firms, union-dominated industries, and communal agricultural communities also have access to the Mexican social security system (Instituto Mexicano de Seguro Social, IMSS). The IMSS provides hospitals, clinics, medical care, and pensions, and offers elective coverage for registered persons who are unemployed, have special circumstances, or fall under special categories.[12] Additional hospitals and clinics are made available to government employees (by the Instituto de Seguridad y Servicios Sociales de los Trabajadores del Estado) and to Mexico City residents (by the Federal District). Emergency services are provided by the Mexican Green Cross (for accident victims), the Mexican Red Cross, and a growing proprietary health-care sector, which includes fee-for-service hospitals.

Although Mexico provides universal health-care coverage for its citizens, the system has serious gaps. The economic crisis of the last two decades has undercut federal funding to public health-care facilities. Physicians employed by IMSS and the Health and Welfare Ministry are opting for private practice or limiting services to patients in large urban areas who can pay. Cross-border use of health-care services occurs frequently because many Mexicans think they will receive better care in the United States or hope to have children born as U.S. citizens.

A recent and novel approach to addressing the cross-border issue of health-care coverage is a 1990 agreement between IMSS and the United Farm Workers of America (UFW), which is expected to benefit approximately 100,000 families. Under this agreement, a Mexican worker in the United States pays a fee through UFW, and IMSS provides services to the worker's family in Mexico in the health-care facilities nearest the family's place of residence. Benefits extend to the spouse, children, parents, or grandchildren of the insured. A similar agreement has been signed with the Federation of United Zacatecaños Clubs, which covers Mexicans born in Zacatecas living in California.[13] To facilitate these agreements, the IMSS is establishing offices in Mexican consulates.

Barriers to Receiving Health and Human Services

Despite federal and state regulations that allow immigrants to receive some public assistance in California, serious barriers remain to their gaining adequate access to health and human services. These barriers threaten the maintenance of relatively healthy behaviors, particularly as Mexicans become acculturated and assimilated into California society.

One obstacle is the sheer challenge of making the system work. As with most states, California has a fragmented network of programs and services along with complex and varied criteria for determining eligibility, making it difficult to utilize the full scope of the programs. For immigrants, this complexity is exacerbated by discrimination, cultural prejudice, and limited bilingual services and personnel.

Another obstacle is a lack of health insurance and an inability to pay for medical care.[14] Although Latinos are relatively healthy and tend to pay for at least part of their health services privately, their access to care is severely limited by inadequate coverage and high levels of poverty. Compared to Puerto Ricans, Cuban Americans, blacks, and white non-Latinos, Mexican Americans are the most likely to be medically uninsured.[15]

The most significant obstacle is heightened competition for shrinking resources. In the context of federal and state deficits, the cost of providing services has become a major political issue. California has slashed funding for emergency medical care, services for children and the medically indigent, and mental health programs. Some public agencies, such as San Diego County and the medical centers at the University of California at Irvine and Los Angeles are threatening to withhold services from undocumented persons and to restrict Medi-Cal coverage unless the state and county provide more funding. Proposals to create a waiting period for new residents seeking welfare services are also gaining support. At the federal level, the SLIAG program faces major cutbacks, with serious implications for California, where about half of the immigrants who have applied for amnesty reside.

Funding cuts are already having a deleterious effect on the Latino population. Reductions in immunization programs and limited outreach efforts have contributed to an increase in preventable childhood diseases such as polio and measles. Drastic cutbacks in trauma systems have significantly limited emergency room access, an important source of care for persons without health insurance. Reductions in mental health programs, especially those serving the Spanish-speaking community, are felt among immigrants who have been traumatized by violence, political repression, or migration.

Historically, taxpayers have been reluctant to expand social programs for disadvantaged groups in times of budget cuts and economic recession, regardless of ethnicity, race, or immigration status. Given the current shortage of state funding for health and human services, competition between young and old, native-born and immigrant, poor and affluent will increase. Political influence will increasingly determine resource allocations and, in that context, immigrants are likely to lose.

The reality is that white non-Latinos, who comprise an increasingly smaller segment of the state's population, will continue to be the overwhelming majority of voters. In 1986, white non-Latinos comprised 61 percent of the state's population but 75 percent of the citizens eligible to vote.[16] More dramatically, of those actually casting ballots in the 1986 general election, 84 percent were white non-Latinos, whereas only 16 percent were minorities. These voters are aging, and their priorities will, by nature, differ from those of a younger, more culturally diverse population. For some time to come, immigrants, refugees, and low-income populations will be at the mercy of an elderly, nonminority electorate.

There are signs that the electorate may respond if the issues are framed properly. The passage of bond measures in recent years to fund education and transportation programs demonstrates the public's willingness to pay higher taxes for clear and compelling social needs. Because the health-care crisis affects the middle class and business as well as the poor, the general public is likely to join the struggle for increased funding of health and social services. Pressure is mounting for universal health coverage at state and federal levels, which would benefit the entire population, including immigrants and undocumented persons ineligible for certain benefits.

In response to the needs of immigrants, advocates and policymakers must be sensitive to the concerns of the electorate, particularly the middle class, as it attempts to adjust to a new California. When the issue is posed solely in terms of providing services to Mexican immigrants, public support from the electorate is lacking. But when the issue is framed as a broader set of challenges to California—and if negative myths about immigrants can be overcome—the electorate may be compelled to support programs that help Mexican immigrants become integrated into the mainstream economy and society.

Separating Myth from Reality

Population growth projections and the health and social problems faced by immigrants generate fears in California that a stratified "Third World state" is imminent. Large immigrant populations in certain metropolitan neighborhoods (e.g., San Francisco's Mission district, the Pico-Union area of Los Angeles, downtown San Diego) conjure up visions of overcrowded, crime-infested ghettos. In turn, these visions create anxiety among the general population that the quality of life in California will decline as the number of immigrants grows.

This scenario need not become reality. California has always attracted large numbers of immigrants and minorities who have, by and large, become part of mainstream society and contributed to economic and social prosperity. Today, as in earlier decades, California must absorb a large influx of new residents, both native-born and immigrant. Meeting this challenge requires the provision of the basic social and human infrastructure of education, health care, and social services to ensure that these new arrivals are able to enhance California's economic growth and contribute to its social stability.

Immigrants, particularly Mexicans, continue to suffer from the misconceived notion that they have serious health and social problems, are highly dependent on public entitlements, and do not cover the cost of these entitlements through taxes or labor. Dispelling these myths is critical to designing effective public policies to meet the health and human service needs of immigrants. Otherwise, the electorate, consisting primarily of populations that do not reflect immigrant and minority communities, may not approve the funding necessary to provide these services, with negative consequences for all Californians.

Health Profile

The general perception of the health status of Mexican immigrants is that they are in very poor health and contribute to serious public health problems. In reality, studies on Latino health care suggest that the health status of Mexican Americans, especially in the Southwest, is quite good given their income and education levels.[17] First-generation Mexican immigrants generally have good health practices, including relatively low rates of smoking, drinking, and drug use. The health of Latino children, measured by pregnancy outcome, prevalence of chronic medical conditions, and birthweight patterns, is also good compared with that of non-Latinos, despite higher poverty rates.[18] As a relatively young and healthy population, Latinos rely on emergency and pregnancy-related services but do not overuse the public health care system.

Nonetheless, Latinos do have some worrisome health problems. Mexican Americans, particularly in the later generations, exhibit high rates of alcoholism and cirrhosis, and violent death among adolescent males and young adults.[19] Immigrants living in poor neighborhoods often lack access to public health clinics and immunization services, and are therefore vulnerable to sexually transmitted and communicable diseases. Border residents face illnesses associated with water and air pollution and hazardous waste dumping, and Mexican farmworkers have above-average accident rates and inadequate access to rural health-care clinics.[20]

Based on this health profile, California policymakers should provide specific services that mitigate negative health behaviors among second- and third-generation Mexican Americans and lessen the public health risk to California society. Targeted programs such as drug abuse counseling, prenatal and maternal programs, immunization campaigns, and sanitary regulation enforcement (e.g., in food services) are likely to be more cost-effective and politically feasible than programs based on the assumption that Mexican immigrants need to receive all of the services available to U.S. citizens.

Human Services Profile

A major public concern regarding Mexican immigrants is that they add to an "underclass" of individuals with high levels of illiteracy, criminal behavior, and welfare dependence. Although most Latinos live in poverty, the Mexican immigrant population is highly diverse and exhibits varying levels of assimilation and acculturation. Generally, the first generation possesses supportive family relationships, communal values (e.g., assisting fellow immigrants to find work), and a strong work ethic. Despite some decline in positive behaviors as Mexicans become assimilated, Mexican immigrants have historically matched the performance of European immigrants in becoming "mainstream" members of society by the third generation.

Another public concern is that Mexican immigrants use welfare programs heavily and contribute to massive public expenditures for social services. Again, the data suggest otherwise. Studies consistently show that Mexican and other immigrant groups use fewer public services, rely more on informal support systems, and are less dependent on welfare income than native families with similar socioeconomic characteristics.[21] Although the IRCA amnesty program may ultimately expand usage of public services by Mexican immigrants, this expansion will be limited in the short term by the five-year prohibition feature and the requirement that immigrants prove they are not "public charges" (i.e., dependent on public cash assistance programs).

The real challenge for California is to help Mexican immigrants retain their positive traditions, such as supportive families and a strong work ethic, as they become integrated into an increasingly competitive economy and society. Involving Mexican parents in the public school systems, expanding mental health and day care in immigrant neighborhoods, and promoting community-based police work may be helpful in achieving this goal. Ultimately, however, the ability of Mexican immigrants to acculturate successfully and to avoid becoming a burden on the health and human service system is contingent upon employment that provides decent wages and employee benefits. The capacity of the California economy to produce such jobs and the willingness of the California electorate to improve the educational system for immigrants and minority populations may have a greater impact on the social conditions of Mexican immigrants and on California society than any social welfare policies.

Policy Directions

How can policymakers and the public respond to the demographic and social changes facing California? What measures should be taken in adjusting to immigration? Although the challenge is great, there are some important, albeit incremental, steps that can move the state in a positive direction.

First, a more precise definition of the needs of Mexican immigrants should be established. California does not have the luxury of assuming that Mexican immigrants, particularly the undocumented, should be entitled to every health and welfare entitlement program that federal and state governments provide. Advocates must identify those services and programs that will enable Mexican immigrants to maintain a healthy status (e.g., preventive medicine, prenatal care) and retain a viable family structure (e.g., day care, after-school recreational activities, drug prevention and education programs).

Second, steps should be taken to ensure that immigrants have access to needed services. Expanding the pool of professionals able to work with Mexican and other immigrants is critical. This goal could be accomplished through a review of the National Health Service Corps, financial assistance to graduate and professional schools in California, and scholarships to encourage students to take an interest in immigrant communities. Serious consideration should also be given to proposals such as that introduced by Assemblyman Richard Polanco (D–Los Angeles) to address the cultural and language barriers facing Spanish-speaking populations in obtaining primary care. Finally, public health outreach programs should be encouraged within immigrant communities, such as mobile vans for screening and vaccination, recruitment of volunteer public health-care workers from immigrant neighborhoods, and special AIDS and drug-abuse projects.

Third, California policymakers should work closely with public and private organizations in Mexico to respond to the health and social needs of Mexican immigrants. The UFW/IMSS project is an example of a creative partnership between Mexico and the United States. It does not involve public funding by the United States or California, and it uniquely recognizes Mexico's responsibility for and commitment to serving the health-care needs of its immigrants. Increased bilateral cooperation is essential to improving the health status of Mexicans before they cross into California. Existing bilateral efforts to develop programs in communicable disease control and environmental sanitation along the border should be expanded to include the creation of health screening stations at border crossings. Although large numbers of undocumented persons would still enter California unscreened, such programs would make an important contribution toward preventing the spread of communicable diseases. In addition, joint efforts should be taken to enhance health and social conditions in Mexico through initiatives such as immunization campaigns, sanitation measures, voluntary family planning programs, maternal and child health care, and vocational training. The Mexican Ministry of Health and Welfare, as well as Mexican and U.S. foundations (e.g., Fundación Mexicana para la Salud and the Kaiser Foundation) should be encouraged to fund these kinds of projects.

Fourth, television stations, newspapers, opinion writers, elected officials, and academics should make an effort to improve public perceptions of Mexican immigrants. While avoiding the temptation to trade negative myths for positive ones, opinion leaders should let the facts speak for themselves. By focusing on California's history of demographic change and the value of immigrants to the California economy, public educators and the media can help dispel the *Bladerunner* scenario of irreconcilable ethnic conflict. Only through a change in public attitudes will appropriate policy responses to the health and human service needs of immigrants have the political and fiscal support they need to be implemented.

A final policy direction concerns the politics of immigration and ethnic diversity. California is facing serious tensions as it adjusts to rapid economic, social, and demographic change. Its ability to respond requires that interest groups representing established minority populations, immigrant and refugee groups, and powerful constituencies (such as business, labor, and environmentalists) develop coalitions focusing on the needs of all people involved rather than narrow, special interests. The health-care crisis facing California and the nation provides an instructive example. Coalitions to promote health-care reform are being forged among private- and public-sector organizations; groups representing the middle class, the unemployed, and the poor; and political leaders from both political parties. In the case of immigrants, the fact that Latino politicians do not necessarily represent undocumented persons or refugees makes advocacy groups such as the National Center for Immigrants' Rights critical to any proimmigrant coalition. An approach based on working partnerships between advocates and elected officials is necessary to address the ethnic diversity of California and meet the health and human service needs of its immigrant population.

Conclusion

Issues of health and human services highlight the complex interaction of immigration, social need, demographics, finances, politics, and policy in Mexico, California, and the United States. The long-range goal of ensuring that immigrants and their descendants have access to such services is sound; but short-term difficulties—paying for programs, liberalizing eligibility, addressing the problems and tensions created by rapid ethnic and demographic change—influence the public response. Serving the needs of immigrants becomes a personal, emotional, and intellectual debate on the appropriateness of large-scale immigration, legal or otherwise, and the provision of services to noncitizens when citizens themselves may lack them.

This paper does not attempt to argue whether or not the United States should allow continued immigration or forcibly close its borders to illegal aliens. It addresses the circumstances facing California and the existing need for some provision of services to prevent greater problems from arising. Policymakers cannot ignore the health and human service needs of immigrants any more than they can ignore the needs of all Californians. The consequences of not providing these services is already apparent in the spread of communicable diseases, crime, overcrowded housing, family strife, and social instability.

California, Mexico, and the United States have much to gain by working together to confront the impact of large-scale immigration. In particular, the citizens of this state have a stake in addressing the basic needs of immigrants. By ensuring that all Californians receive a basic level of health and human services, the state can continue its tradition of national leadership and greatly strengthen its economic and social foundation.

CHAPTER 10

In Search of the American Dream

Obstacles to Latino Educational Achievement

RICHARD ROTHSTEIN

MANY CALIFORNIANS believe that public schools' poor performance blocks the assimilation and mobility of the state's rapidly growing Mexican population. According to the Achievement Council, a well-regarded group focused on improving minority student performance, failure to close the large achievement gap separating minority students from other Californians carries a huge price: (1) our economic system, increasingly dependent upon well-educated workers, will be crippled by the lack of qualified young people; (2) we will continue paying huge downstream costs—more police and prisons, welfare, housing subsidies, and health care—for adults who can't qualify for jobs that will enable them to support themselves and their families; (3) more and more of our citizenry will be unprepared for the privileges and responsibilities of full participation in our democracy; and (4) our society will become increasingly divided, with a well-educated minority, composed primarily of whites and Asians, dominating the upper tiers, while a poorly educated majority, composed primarily of Latinos and blacks, remains at the bottom.

The chorus condemning public schools' failure to educate minority students is joined by California's business leaders. Echoing complaints of the U.S. Department of Labor's report, *Workforce 2000*, the National Alliance of Business claims that 65 percent of Los Angeles's large employers are dissatisfied with entry-level workers' educational preparation.[1] The California Business Roundtable concludes that "until we change the way our schools are structured, . . . we're not going to improve the quality of entry level job skills that we need in the workplace."[2]

This commonplace view implies a "supply-side" understanding of the connection between schools and jobs: if schools increased the supply of well-educated immigrants, California's economy could expand to employ them in higher-wage positions. But supply-side theory represents only a partial truth, ignoring "demand-side" realities. Scarcity of economic opportunity for the majority of Americans below the top tier may reduce the likelihood that school reform can substantially improve Mexican-origin student achievement. An employment market dominated by unskilled, low-wage jobs may discourage minority youth from staying in school and striving for academic success, which they believe will go unrewarded.

In reality, education and employment have a "chicken-and-egg" relationship. California schools that don't educate immigrant students will be a brake on high-wage and high-skill job growth. But student achievement is unlikely to improve significantly without increased job opportunities for educated workers. The challenge for California's schools is to help all minority children make as much progress as possible within the constraints imposed by limited economic opportunity, while equipping the most talented to compete for the highest professional, technical, and managerial roles. Avoiding expectations that academic success will itself open doors to mobility for most Mexican-origin students, schools can nonetheless attempt to deliver better results to California's Mexican-origin community.

The Changing Profile of Public School Students

It has become impossible to ignore the problems of low achievement among California's Mexican-origin students, whose numbers are growing at a breathtaking pace. In the Los Angeles school district, California's largest, 1990 student enrollment was 63 percent Latino,[3] up from 22 percent just twenty years ago.[4] During this period, the white, non-Latino student population declined from 50 percent to 14 percent. The proportion of Latino students in elementary schools, 67 percent,[5] previews even larger Latino majorities in the future. The vast majority of these students are of Mexican origin.

This transformation of California's public school population results in part from changing immigration patterns. Typical Mexican immigrants in California are no longer single male workers. Instead, family migration is increasingly common. The amnesty provisions of the 1986 Immigration Reform and Control Act stimulated newly legalized immigrants to send for spouses and children. Today, nearly 90 percent of all legal Mexican immigrants are admitted under "family reunification" procedures; most others are related to immigrants who enter with "priority skills."[6] Even undocumented Mexican immigration, which has apparently not declined since the 1986 reform, now includes more young women of childbearing age, forced into the labor market by Mexico's economic crisis or no longer content to remain behind while young male family members head north.[7] To the extent that the 1986 law tightened the border at all, the effect was to encourage family migration, since husbands working illegally in the United States could no longer make frequent visits home and be assured of easy reentry to California.

The main reason for a vast increase in the number of Mexican-origin schoolchildren, however, is high fertility rates of Latino women. One-third of the U.S.-born Mexican-origin population is under the age of 14.[8] In Los Angeles County, where Latinos comprise 40 percent of the population, there were an estimated 185,000 live births in 1990, an increase of 15 percent from 1986.[9] These 1990 births will result in over 20,000 more kindergarten enrollments in 1995–96 than there were in 1991–92. Even without expected future immigration, the proportion of U.S.-born, Mexican-origin schoolchildren will continue to grow.

This Mexicanization of California schools is especially dramatic because it has made California's school population increasingly non-English speaking. In Los Angeles, over 200,000 of the public schools' 625,000 students do not speak English well enough to be taught in a mainstream educational program: the district's "limited English proficient" (LEP) enrollment has been increasing by more than 10 percent annually. Statewide, in 1989 there were over half a million LEP Spanish-speaking students in public schools, a 46-percent jump from 1985.[10] Another half million have progressed to receiving English academic instruction.[11]

Obstacles to Improving the Achievement of Mexican-Origin Students

The average achievement of Mexican-origin students falls far short of that of their white, non-Latino counterparts. California schools are not preparing most Mexican-origin students to assume positions of equality and accomplishment in a technologically advanced economy.

The achievement gap starts early. Data for the California Assessment Program (CAP) show that in 1987 Latino third graders had average combined reading and math scores of 500, compared to 614 for non-Latino whites.[12] By eighth grade, the gap was wider: average scores were 414 for Latinos and 567 for whites. Latino high school seniors in California generally perform at a ninth grade level in reading and math—three years behind the average performance of white seniors.

Forty-five percent of Latino youth entering ninth grade in California do not graduate;[13] one-third of these students drop out before the tenth grade.[14] Statewide, the Latino dropout rate is roughly double the rate of non-Latino whites.[15]

Many Latinos who graduate from high school are ill-prepared to go on to college. Latino students do not enroll heavily in college preparatory courses, essential for college admission and success. Only 57 percent of Latino high school sophomores in California take college preparatory math courses, compared to 74 percent of non-Latino whites.[16] Half as many Latino seniors as non-Latino white seniors in California take the college-qualifying Scholastic Aptitude Test (SAT).[17] Those who do have an average verbal/math score of 793; non-Latino whites average 952.[18] Only 10 percent of California's Latino high school seniors actually go on to a four-year college, compared to 21 percent of non-Latino white seniors.[19]

Reforms to improve the educational achievement of Mexican-origin students in California face daunting obstacles—overcrowding, parental illiteracy, a language gap, and the persistence of pedagogical practices that confirm teachers' self-fulfilling low expectations for Mexican-origin students. In the background is the challenge of inspiring minority students and their parents to believe that school makes a difference—in the face of daily evidence that, for many Mexican-origin students, improved education may not bring the economic rewards promised by conventional wisdom.

Overcrowding

Before reforms to improve academic achievement for Mexican-origin students can be successful, California must find classroom space in which to educate them. The Mexican-origin student population is growing so rapidly that public schools cannot cope.

California's student-teacher ratio is higher than any other state's;[20] an average class has 28 students.[21] A reduction from 28 to 25 would not only require hiring nearly 10 percent more teachers, it would mean building 10 percent more schools and classrooms in communities where school buildings are already used to full capacity. With statewide enrollment growing at 200,000 a year, over 7,000 new classrooms (about 370 new elementary schools, at a construction cost of $2.8 billion) are needed annually just to absorb growth with no reduction of overcrowding.[22] There is little vacant land in overcrowded minority communities, turning each attempt to build schools into a confrontation with homeowners, tenants, or businesses targeted for demolition.

Exacerbating the construction backlog in Los Angeles is that, until 1984, federal courts prohibited building new schools in minority communities, since these schools would be de facto segregated. As an alternative to school construction, courts insisted that minority students be bused to suburban white-majority schools. Although this policy has since been abandoned, the pace of new school construction is painfully slow, worsening an already existing backlog. California voters approved school construction bonds totaling only $1.6 billion in 1990, with no approvals in 1991. In 1990, only 3,500 new classroom seats were added in Los Angeles,[23] while nearly 50,000 students, mostly Latino, were bused out of their neighborhoods to distant schools with available space.[24]

Busing is a short-sighted solution to the problems of overcrowding. Beyond the educational disadvantages of putting children on a bus for up to three hours a day, taking them out of their home communities, busing is more expensive than building neighborhood schools. Land and construction costs in Los Angeles for a 1,200-student elementary school are approximately $20 million. Per-pupil bond servicing costs for such a project are less than the $1,400 average annual cost of transporting a student to a suburban school. Even the $100 million expense of a 3,000-student high school is barely greater than the cost of busing excess capacity students—especially since land acquired for schools, unlike buses, appreciates in value.

Faced with inadequate school construction, many California school districts have converted overcrowded schools to "multi-track, year-round" schedules, which enable schools to increase their capacity by 25 percent. By 1990, nearly 600,000 students in California were on year-round schedules, up more than 60 percent in two years.[25] Educators believe that year-round schooling is beneficial, especially for language-minority students not exposed to English during vacations.[26] But year-round schedules make school facilities harder to maintain, and one study suggests that demographically similar minority students do more poorly in Los Angeles's year-round schools than in traditional schools.[27]

Nonetheless, debate about the desirability of year-round schooling misses the point. For most Mexican-origin students, schools that run on a traditional calendar are not an alternative. Their only choice is between year-round schools and lengthy bus rides away from overcrowded neighborhoods. It is the refusal of California's taxpayers and political leaders to finance needed school construction, rather than year-round schooling, that robs many Mexican-origin students of equal educational opportunity.

Limited Parental Involvement in Education Inhibits Student Success

President Bush's first secretary of education, and the nation's first Mexican-American cabinet member, Lauro F. Cavazos, argued that Latino parents need an "attitudinal change. . . . We must have a commitment from Hispanic parents especially, that their children will be educated."

> As Hispanics we have often held others responsible for our failures. I submit that ultimately we are the ones who have failed because success in education is within us. . . . We cannot escape the fact that the single most important

predictor of a child's educational achievement—across all ethnic and racial groups—is parental involvement. . . . Yes, there are other factors: the quality of teaching, school facilities, school budgets, poverty and many others which must be addressed over time. But a parent's concern for his or her child's education is independent of these, and can make all the difference in the world, right now, today.[28]

Although Cavazos's motives for conveying this message were suspect—he was primarily concerned with defending the Bush administration's efforts to improve schools without allocating the necessary resources—he hit upon a dilemma of educational reform. Parental literacy, intellectually supportive childrearing practices, and parental involvement in a child's schoolwork contribute more to a child's academic success than anything the schools can do; yet children who fail in school do not acquire the parental literacy skills that help prevent academic failure in their own children.

Jonathan Kozol summarized the generational consequences of low academic achievement:

Illiteracy does not "breed" illiteracy. But it does set up the preconditions for perpetuation of the lack of reading skills within successive generations. Illiterate parents have no way to give their children preschool preparation which enables them to profit fully from a good school or—the more common case—which will protect those children, by the learning that takes place at home, against the dangers of the worst of schools.[29]

Conventional wisdom, supported by research, accepts that low student achievement among minority youth is related to the low socioeconomic status of their families. For example, one recent study of eighth graders found that 49 percent of those from advantaged families had academic scores in the top 25 percent, whereas only 9.3 percent scored in the bottom quarter. Among disadvantaged students, in contrast, only 8 percent scored in the top group, while 44 percent scored in the bottom.[30] In Los Angeles, there is an inverse relation between a school's average scores on statewide academic tests and the percentage of the school's students having means-tested eligibility for free lunches.[31] Parents of California seniors with average SAT scores of 600 to 649 had average income of $54,000 in 1985, while parents of those with average scores of 350 to 399 had average income of $39,000.[32]

However, the most important socioeconomic indicator of student success is not family income itself but parental education, particularly that of the mother. Better-educated parents can teach their children literacy and cognitive skills, assist them with homework, or help them negotiate educational bureaucracies. In addition, literate parents tend to have higher educational aspirations and expectations for their children. This is why each additional grade of a mother's schooling predicts an extra half-grade of academic achievement for her children.[33] California eighth graders whose parents are college graduates have average CAP reading scores of 277, whereas those whose parents did not graduate from high school average 188.[34]

Similar findings are supported by specific data on Mexican-origin students. One study found a positive correlation between a Mexican-American mother's education level and the likelihood of a child's completing high school and then attending college.[35] Another study found that 40 percent of Mexican-American children whose mothers had eleven to fourteen years of schooling learned to read or write before kindergarten, whereas 22 percent of children whose mothers had seven to ten years of schooling did so.[36] For mothers who had less than seven years of formal education, only 12 percent of their children had preschool literacy.[37]

This research also found a link between education levels and parenting styles. Better-educated Mexican-American mothers read to their preschool children more often. Over 55 percent of children whose mothers read to them more than once a week learned to read or write before kindergarten, compared to fewer than 20 percent of the children whose mothers read to them less frequently. Better-educated mothers also tended to use praise and inquiry (questions and answers) as teaching strategies, whereas less educated mothers were more likely to rely on modeling and imitation.[38]

Because of the importance of parental education, the outlook for improved achievement among Mexican-origin students in California is less promising. Forty-two percent of Latino high school seniors in California have parents without high school degrees, compared to 3 percent of non-Latino white seniors. Fourteen percent of the Latino parents graduated from college, compared to 50 percent of the non-Latino white parents.[39] The California Department of Education estimates that 24 percent of adult Latinos in the state are illiterate.[40]

Mexico's hoped-for recovery from a decade of economic crisis may result in an increase in the average literacy deficit of immigrant parents in California. The average education of Mexican immigrants fell during Mexico's economic expansion of the 1970s. This trend was reversed during the 1980s, when economic crisis led urban and highly skilled Mexicans to flee to the United States.[41] If Mexican growth resumes in the 1990s, immigrant education levels may again decline as more highly educated Mexicans remain to take advantage of opportunities at home. Adult Mexican immigrants to the United States already have the lowest educational levels of all immigrant groups. Only 21 percent of Mexican immigrants over the age of 25 are high school graduates, compared to 67 percent of the U.S. population.[42]

Accounts of Mexican-origin students' low achievement compared to other immigrant (particularly Asian) groups make more sense when we consider the varied literacy levels that immigrant parents and grandparents bring to this country. Sixty-four percent of Mexican immigrants have had eight years of schooling or less; only 3 percent have had sixteen years or more. In contrast, only 13 percent of Korean immigrants and 18 percent of immigrants from the Philippines have had eight years or less; 29 percent of Korean immigrants and 37 percent of immigrants from the Philippines have had sixteen years or more.[43]

As Gordon Berlin and Andrew Sum have observed, "Because of this intergenerational effect of the parent's education on the child's, it is unlikely that we will be able to make a major difference for the child unless we place equal priority on education and academic remediation for the parent. . . . We can help children by helping their mothers."[44] Thus, a serious program to improve Mexican-origin student achievement in California must focus not only on the children's education, but on the literacy deficits of their parents, particularly their mothers.

Yet adult literacy programs in California are seriously underfunded, serving fewer than one million of an estimated seven million functionally illiterate California adults. Most adult education programs are English as a Second Language (ESL) programs for immigrants. Eighty-seven percent of the 870,000 students in California's adult education programs, operated by school districts or community colleges, are enrolled in ESL programs for which there are long waiting lists.[45] Because of a state budget crisis, state law effectively prohibits school districts from increasing the number of adults in basic education programs.

Even if ESL programs were fully funded, they would not be sufficient to prepare parents to give literacy support to their children, nor to inspire their children with a belief in the importance of education. Although ESL instruction is needed to help immigrants assimilate, it can do little to enhance parents' ability to support children's school efforts. Mexican immigrant parents of youngsters in bilingual education programs need improved literacy *in Spanish* before they can contribute to their children's academic progress. And for parents of children learning in English, effective academic parenting requires literacy beyond the basic ESL levels—which is as far as most programs go.

In addition to expanded adult literacy programs, direct support for parental pedagogical skills is also needed. The most critical step is to inculcate in parents a belief in the importance of education, even when they have little education themselves. A few such programs already exist in California, but their coverage is small. A more thorough (and expensive) initiative was being promoted nationally by then Arkansas governor Bill Clinton; it provides preschool educational workbooks with twenty-minute daily lessons to functionally illiterate mothers who are visited each week by paraprofessionals for preparation and review. Such programs have reportedly been successful in improving student achievement in Arkansas, Missouri, and Massachusetts, and should be translated into Spanish and imported to California.[46]

The Language Gap

For half a million Spanish-speaking children, "bilingual education" is the cornerstone of California's curriculum. Though controversial, teaching children in their native language has deep support among educational theorists, school administrators, bilingual teachers, and Latino community groups.

California once required all public school teaching to be in English, but in 1968 the federal Bilingual Education Act (Title VII of the Elementary and Secondary Education Act) denied funding to states with such provisions. Six years later, the U.S. Supreme Court (in *Lau v. Nichols*) upheld a federal civil rights regulation requiring native language instruction. In response, the Los Angeles school board adopted a "Lau" Plan, providing for development of a full bilingual education program for language-minority students. Meanwhile, the California legislature in 1967 and 1980 mandated native language instruction for language-minority children, and the state began requiring schoolteachers to learn minority languages.

Bilingual education has since come under attack in Sacramento and Washington. In 1987, Governor George Deukmejian vetoed an extension of the state's native language instruction requirements. Although federal bilingual legislation remains in effect, 25 percent of federal bilingual funds may now be spent in programs other than native language instruction—for example, "structured immersion" in English, with native language used only for clarification. In February 1991, the U.S. Department of Education's director of bilingual programs announced that the Bush administration would attempt to abolish entirely the limits on expenditures of federal bilingual funds for English immersion programs.[47] These changes have had little practical impact in California, however. Bilingual education, with an emphasis on native language instruction, continues to be the policy of the California Department of Education and of most California school districts, notwithstanding the Deukmejian veto.

Bilingual education was initially intended to prevent language-minority students from falling behind in academic subjects (since these would be taught in children's native languages) while these students were learning English. California educators now advance a more elaborate theory: native language instruction not only keeps students from falling behind, but is itself the best foundation for learning English.

According to linguists James Cummins and Stephen D. Krashen, authors of the "theoretical framework" published by California's State Department of Education, "well-developed speaking, reading, writing, and critical thinking skills in the primary language will lead to academic success in a second language, since language skills transfer to a second language."[48] Literacy in a second language is based on what Cummins calls a "common underlying proficiency" initially developed in the native language.[49] "A general fund of knowledge broadens the range of messages a student can understand and, consequently, makes second language acquisition easier."[50]

These views find support among California educators experienced with youths educated in Mexico and literate in Spanish who arrive in California in late elementary or junior high school. According to California's State Department of Education, these students often "catch up and surpass the record of native speakers of Spanish who have been educated in California's public school system since kindergarten."[51]

As bilingual education evolves in California, educators are becoming convinced that Spanish-speaking students need not make early transitions to mainstream English language instruction. Their approach has been buttressed by a U.S. Department of Education study issued in February 1991. The Ramirez Report undertook a longitudinal assessment of three program types—structured immersion; early-exit bilingual education (in which some instruction is in Spanish, but students are expected to be reclassified to mainstream English by the second grade); and late-exit bilingual education (in which most academic instruction is in Spanish, and students are expected to be reclassified after the sixth grade).[52] Although students in all three programs improved in mathematics, English language, and reading skills, late-exit programs were found to be the most successful.[53] One reason for their relative superiority was that a significantly greater percentage of parents helped their children with homework, presumably because native language instruction was also more understandable to the parents.[54]

However, the failure of many children in bilingual programs to achieve at grade level, even in Spanish, suggests practical problems with implementation. In the case of Mexican-origin children in California, the native language fluency on which bilingual methods build may be limited by immigrant parents' illiteracy. Where children are not read to, even as preschoolers, the relative advantage they might gain by being taught in familiar Spanish rather than in unfamiliar English may not be as great as bilingual theory expects. One critic of bilingual education, Rosalie Porter, summarized the opponents' case:

> Many of our students . . . speak a nonstandard Spanish or a mixture of Spanish and English. We know that the more different the home dialect is from the standard, the greater is the difficulty in using standard Spanish as the language of instruction. To begin instruction, therefore, by doing extensive remedial work in vocabulary and grammar in Spanish before attending to English-language development makes little sense, if the goal is to learn English. In some cases, . . . there may not even be much reinforcement for the Spanish language at home if there are not books or newspapers in Spanish on hand.[55]

Another handicap faced by LEP students is their increasing segregation. No matter how good the classroom program, student readiness to learn English is slowed by the lack of opportunity to play with English-speaking children outside of class. If the language of the playground as well as of the classroom is Spanish, children are unlikely to receive the basic "comprehensible input" needed as a foundation for success in ESL classes. Los Angeles requires its LEP students to spend at least 20 percent of each day in an integrated setting with English-speaking students,[56] but this is often impractical; 87 percent of the 50,000 elementary school students in East Los Angeles are Latino, and two-thirds of these have limited English proficiency.[57]

The greatest obstacle to the successful implementation of bilingual education is the shortage of bilingual teachers in California, a shortage exacerbated by the small number of native Spanish speakers graduating from college and entering the teaching profession. Thirty-three percent of California's public school students are Latino, compared to only 7 percent of its teachers.[58] In Los Angeles, Latinos are 63 percent of students but only 12 percent of teachers.[59] The best source of new teachers is the nineteen-campus California State University, where only 15 percent of entering freshmen and fewer than 9 percent of those receiving bachelor's degrees are Latino.[60]

The language gap between teachers and children in California is growing. In 1990, new bilingual teacher hires were barely half the number needed to stay even with LEP student growth. In Los Angeles, where bilingual teachers are offered a $5,000 annual premium, there were only 2,300 certified Spanish bilingual teachers in 1988–89 for 122,000 Spanish-speaking elementary school students,[61] a student-teacher ratio of 53:1. In the next decade, California will need at least 2,000 new bilingual teachers annually, far more than the 415 state college graduates in 1989 qualified to apply for bilingual credentials.[62]

To compensate for the lack of trained bilingual teachers, many California schools rely on the assistance of paraprofessional aides. Although many of these aides are talented and provide adequate instruction to their Spanish-speaking students, they are not certified teachers and may be unqualified to make nuanced evaluations of student progress or to adapt planned instructional programs to individual student needs. In the worst situations, teaching is done by translation for the three hours daily when an aide is present.

Problems with implementing bilingual education have fueled claims of its critics. California's Department of Education reclassifies an average of only 50,000 LEP students each year (out of a total LEP population of over 700,000) to "fluent-English-proficient."[63] In Los Angeles, fewer than 10 percent of LEP students are reclassified annually, a rate that is actually declining as the bilingual program's implementation spreads throughout the school district.[64] In 1987, the Los Angeles teachers' union voted by a 78-percent margin to oppose bilingual education in favor of a program of intensive English instruction. Some teachers complain that program guidelines prohibit the transition of LEP students testing below grade level in Spanish reading, even though many English-speaking peers, whom they would join in a mainstream program, themselves read below grade level in English. This superficial asymmetry encourages arguments that bilingual education is a politically motivated program designed to isolate Spanish-speaking students in a Mexican nationalist culture.

Proponents of bilingual education and immersion can each cite examples of success. Studies of model bilingual programs—Rockwood Elementary School in Calexico, Eastman Avenue School in Los Angeles, Nestor School in San Diego—show that children at these schools learn English and improve their academic achievement when they start school in their native language and then gradually add English language and content.[65] There are also cases of successful structured English immersion programs—in Paramount and Berkeley, California; Fairfax, Virginia; and El Paso, Texas—each of which was implemented after educators and parents became dissatisfied with the lack of successful transitions by bilingual-program students from Spanish-language to mainstream programs.

For highly motivated students, success is likely in either a bilingual or English immersion program. In the case of Mexican-origin children in

California, a full bilingual program may be the preferred method. But unless bilingual education can be administered by qualified staff, immersion may be a needed alternative.

Destructive Pedagogical Practices

Underlying the success or failure of language training programs is the effectiveness of teachers and their methods. The most important finding of the 1991 Ramirez Report was that teaching skills were poor *in all three* bilingual program types:

> Teachers in all three programs offer a passive learning environment. . . . When students do speak, they typically provide only simple information, recall statements in response to simple discrete close-ended questions. This pattern of teacher/child interaction limits students' opportunities to create and manipulate language freely and their ability to engage in more complex learning.[66]

Systemic pedagogical reform will have as great an impact on the achievement of Mexican-origin students as reforms targeted at minority education. For example, contemporary pedagogical theory emphasizes the use of cooperative learning strategies, in which students are taught to conduct group inquiries or help revise and correct each other's work. Although such strategies are appropriate for all children, some research suggests that Mexican-origin children in particular achieve more in cooperative learning situations.[67]

Another reform of benefit to Mexican-origin students would be decreased use of grade retention (requiring low-achieving students to repeat grades). Grade retention is self-perpetuating: older students kept behind are neither expected nor taught to achieve to the same degree as their younger grade-peers. Schools with high concentrations of Latino students have used retention as a policy more frequently than majority schools; thus, Mexican-origin students are held back more often than non-Mexican-origin white students.[68]

Mexican-origin students would also gain from moves away from homogeneous grouping (separating students into "tracks" based on the school's judgement about how well they are likely to achieve). Though "tracking" is pervasive in U.S. education, it is most destructive in minority communities, where students are more likely to be placed in nonacademic tracks. In the case of Mexican-origin LEP students in California, some educators may confuse English language facility with academic ability. In minority community schools, a larger proportion of students is placed in nonacademic tracks, while often the curriculum in higher academic tracks is also watered down.[69]

Tracking is only one reflection of a broader problem—teachers' low expectations for minority student achievement. Low expectations are self-fulfilling; when adults believe in children's ability, those children will more likely strive for higher achievement—as in *Stand and Deliver*, a feature film based on a Los Angeles teacher's successful efforts to teach calculus to Mexican-origin high school students who were not considered capable by other teachers or school officials.

Because wide attention has been paid to the problem of low teacher expectations of minority children, virtually all teachers in urban school systems now claim that they have high expectations of their students. However, many teachers continue to express low expectations of minority students in subtle ways, formal tracking being only the most blatant. Grade inflation, in which inferior schoolwork is rewarded with a higher than deserved grade, is one. Failure of teachers, in class interaction, to work with a child who gives a wrong answer (rather than moving on to the next student) is another.[70] These practices reinforce low self-expectations which Mexican-origin students bring to school from their homes and communities.

Students Must Be Self-Motivated to Achieve

The factor most strongly associated with high achievement is high aspirations of students themselves.[71] Yet only 36 percent of Latino high school sophomores in California even aspire to go to a four-year college; 50 percent of non-Latino white and 62 percent of black sophomores have college aspirations.[72]

Low parent expectations and student ambition make even the best-designed educational reform programs for Mexican-origin students founder. Business, political, and educational leaders would like immigrant families to believe that academic achievement will evoke a response from society—in high-wage and high-skill jobs for those who excel in school. But to Mexican-origin students and their families, the evidence of limited economic opportunity, even for those who are relatively successful in school, contradicts the message that learning is a path to success.

Some analyses suggest that achievement of Mexican-origin students improves by generation: the children of immigrants do better in school than their parents, and the grandchildren of immigrants do better still. Using 1980 California census data, RAND researchers reported that 62 percent of 16–17 year olds born in Mexico were still in school, compared to 76 percent of 16–17 year olds from the first U.S.-born generation and 86 percent of 16–17 year olds from the next U.S.-born generation.[73] David Hayes-Bautista comes to similar conclusions from 1990 data: 59 percent of the first U.S.-born generation and 70 percent of the next U.S.-born generation of Mexican Americans complete high school.[74]

Yet this evidence is contradicted by other reports that student achievement *declines* with generational distance from Mexico. Teachers and administrators have long noticed that immigrant students often achieve better than their U.S.-born Mexican-origin peers. One analysis of Mexican-origin students in two Los Angeles area high schools found a strong inverse relationship between generational distance from Mexico and grade point averages.[75] A study of Mexican-origin students in Watsonville, California, found that 65 percent of LEP students (presumably either immigrants or their children) graduated from high school in the class of 1985, whereas fewer than half of U.S.-born students did so.[76] And even the RAND researchers noted that their data on increased educational attainment by generation show significant improvement only through high school; college completion rates for grandchildren of Mexican immigrants are not much greater than those of their parents' generation.[77]

A 1991 report concluding that Mexican-origin student achievement improves over the generations was in fact based on more ambiguous statistics. The analysis of current population reports by the American Council on Education claims that "Mexican Americans follow the classic pattern of steady, progressive increase through each generation. . . . Third generation [i.e., children of U.S.-born parents] Mexican Americans completed an average of 11.4 years of school in 1988—substantially more than the 7.4 years completed by first-generation immigrants that year."[78] Yet "first-generation" data are relatively useless for judging educational success, since the data incorporate in their averages low educational attainment of immigrants who arrived as teens or adults and never enrolled in U.S. schools. Of greater value are comparisons of second-generation (children born in the U.S. of Mexican immigrant parents) and third-generation students. If acculturation has a positive effect on educational achievement, we would expect to see dramatic gains. Yet the council's own data show that second-generation Mexican-origin youth complete an average of 10.9 years of school, not much different from the 11.4 years completion rate of third-generation students. And only 64 percent of third-generation Mexican-origin students graduated from high school in 1988, compared to 65 percent of second-generation students.[79]

A 1986 analysis of Latino (mostly Mexican-origin) youth in San Diego also suggests lack of generational progress. The study divided 7,000 high school students into those who spoke English at home (presumably mostly "third generation"); those who spoke Spanish at home, but who were themselves fluent in English (most likely either second-generation or settled immigrants); and those who spoke Spanish at home and were themselves of limited proficiency in English (most likely recent immigrants). Although the high school dropout rate declined from the first to the second generation (from 62 percent to 42 percent), it rose to 53 percent for the third generation.[80]

Bilingual education theory explains stagnating or even declining achievement of Mexican-American students as an expression of alienation from English-language instruction. Attempts to educate these children in English undermine their sense of self-worth and thus their motivation to succeed in school. Many rebel by adopting an oppositional culture, in which school success is rejected as a form of "acting white." Students closer to their Mexican roots are less likely to experience this ambivalence about the culture of schools. Many of the most academically successful Mexican-origin students in the Watsonville study were those who claimed an ethnic identity of "Mexicano" and participated in Mexican-oriented student organizations and events such as the Cinco de Mayo festival.[81]

Yet this "cultural ambivalence" theory does not explain why third-generation students who speak English at home and whose culture is no longer Mexican do not seem to achieve at higher levels than immigrants' children educated in the United States. Improved bilingual education cannot be expected to help third-generation Mexican Americans for whom Spanish is, at best, a second language.

The reality is that oppositional culture can continue into the third generation because, as University of California anthropologist John Ogbu stated, "minority children learn from older members of their community their shared antagonism toward whites and their institutions. . . . Children who have internalized this cultural antagonism may have difficulty performing according to school norms even if they possess the cognitive and language skills of the schools."[82]

Although Ogbu is best known for research on black students, he also studied Mexican immigrants in Stockton, California. He concluded that antagonism toward school does not develop in the immigrant generation because immigrants are not discouraged by discrimination or the limitations to economic opportunity and mobility. They are highly motivated; the act of immigration itself requires optimism, faith, and self-confidence, often transmitted to children. They are also more likely to compare their hardships to impoverished conditions left behind in Mexico, not to conditions of the more privileged U.S. majority.

In the next generation, however, the frame of reference changes. Greater awareness of the limits of economic opportunity offered to minority workers leads, increasingly, to a culture that incorporates cynicism about the value of education. This cynicism is conveyed to minority children, who "form increasingly accurate and stable images of the system of status mobility as they approach adolescence, and these images determine the type of achievement motivation or behavior they tend to manifest."[83] An implicit belief in the futility of education as a path to economic mobility becomes self-fulfilling, as third-generation academic achievement and completion rates stagnate. Ogbu concludes that "the nature of the minorities' interpretations and responses [to their subordination and exploitation] makes them more or less accomplices to their own school success or failure."[84]

According to Ogbu, most parents teach discipline and work habits that are conducive to school success only if the family believes that "success in school leads to rewards in adult life in terms of jobs, income, prestige and the like."[85] But occupational opportunities for youth not bound for college have declined in the last decade, affecting the Mexican-origin community disproportionately—either because of discrimination or because of low educational levels. Based on their observation of older siblings, friends, and other Latino adults, Mexican-origin youth may conclude that the payoff from additional schooling (short of college completion) is relatively small, if it exists at all.

What Mexican-origin students see today is that the mean income of working Mexican-origin males is about 60 percent of non-Latino white male income; a corresponding figure for females is 40 percent.[86] Latino heads of households (25 to 34 years of age) with high school degrees earn an average of $23,500 annually, compared to an average of $28,000 for non-Latino whites.[87] Twenty-seven percent of the Latino population is now in poverty, in contrast to 10 percent of the non-Latino white population.[88]

The rate of Mexican-origin high school completion has inched up—from 39 percent in 1979 to 46 percent in 1988[89]—but economic rewards for high school completion have been declining. In 1986, over half of U.S. high school graduates under age twenty did not have full-time employment, compared to only 30 percent in 1974.[90] In 1987, male high school graduates with one to five years work experience earned 18 percent less than similar graduates in 1979.[91]

A major cause of this decline has been the demise of manufacturing employment and its replacement not by higher skilled "jobs of the future," but by lower-skilled and lower-paid jobs in service and retail. While manufacturing jobs (paying an average weekly wage of $415 in 1989) declined by 7 percent in the 1980s, retail employment (with an average wage of $276) grew by 31 percent, and services (with an average wage of $357) grew by

57 percent.[92] Roughly two-thirds of the decline in wages during the 1980s was due to this shift of employment from higher-paid manufacturing to lower-paid service and retail work.[93]

Mexican-origin high school graduates and dropouts in California, unlike most U.S. minority youth, continue to find substantial employment in the manufacturing sector. But this has not offset an erosion of earnings. Many of California's unionized manufacturing jobs in automotive, aerospace, and other durable goods industries have been replaced by nonunion jobs in light manufacturing, with wages and lack of benefits similar to those of low-wage service and retail sectors. Average pay of Latino males in manufacturing was 72 percent of non-Latino white manufacturing pay in 1979; by 1987 it had fallen to 66 percent.[94] Forty-two percent of employed Latino workers now earn wages below the poverty line, up from 32 percent ten years ago.[95]

In earlier decades, immigrants who increased their schooling but did not complete college found employment in the more heavily unionized craft and manufacturing sectors, where they earned wages and benefits adequate to support families. But with the decline of the manufacturing sector in the late 1980s and 1990s, nothing short of a college degree entitles young people to comparable income. It is difficult for youth from communities where college attendance is not taken for granted to appreciate the value of education when their immediate goal—high school completion—exhibits declining rewards.

There is ample evidence of increasingly high returns from education; the earnings advantage of college graduates over high school graduates increased from 25 percent in 1979 to 57 percent in 1986.[96] But this may not be relevant for most Mexican-origin youth, wondering whether to seek high school success. Increased earnings from education do not show up until students have graduated from a full four-year college. Second- or third-generation Mexican-origin youths who pursue higher education are more likely to attend a two-year community college than a full four-year institution. In 1988, 30 percent of California's Latino high school graduates went on to a two-year community college; only 10 percent attended a four-year college.[97] Yet wages for Latino youths who complete only one to three years of college have been declining. The real median family income of Latino heads of household aged 25–29 with one to three years of college declined from $28,630 in 1979 to $28,172 in 1987.[98] To the extent that the educational attainment of Mexican-origin youth is increasing, these youth are investing in levels of education (completed high school and community college) that are increasingly less valuable.

Improved returns to this investment could result from adoption of apprenticeship programs linking high schools and junior colleges to the high-skill and high-wage industrial workplaces that remain. But in marked contrast to other industrialized nations, such programs are rare in the United States. Only 5 percent of U.S. high school graduates in 1980 were in apprenticeship programs within their first year after high school graduation, compared to 33 to 55 percent in European countries.[99] Apprenticeship opportunities can increase incentives for school achievement by illustrating to young people the connection between academic effort and secure adult roles. Despite enthusiasm for expanded apprenticeship among some policymakers, however, little has been accomplished, in large part because of the scarcity of high-wage and high-skill jobs to which high school and junior college youth could be apprenticed.

In the unlikely event that Mexican-origin college completion rates jump dramatically, even this might not translate into economic security. Although there are shortages of college-educated workers in some scientific, technical, or specialized fields (such as bilingual education), the United States now has a surplus of educated workers. The pool of college graduates will exceed openings in jobs requiring a college education by about 100,000 annually between now and the year 2000. By that time, 7.3 million college graduates will be employed in jobs not requiring a college degree.[100] This surplus of college graduates will likely be reflected in declining compensation for college graduates, except in specific fields with shortages.

Balancing Educational with Economic Reforms

In a democratic society, citizens are enriched by education even if schooling does not produce immediate economic rewards. Yet, for the Mexican-origin community, the intense scrutiny paid to public education may be excessive. Educational attainment of Mexican-origin students is unlikely to make dramatic improvement until these students and their families can believe that realistic educational goals—high school and junior college completion—will be rewarded in the marketplace. For this to happen, political attention needs to be focused not only on public education, but on the nation's industrial, trade, monetary, and fiscal policies, which have created increasingly polarized income distributions and the loss of high-wage manufacturing employment.

Minorities have always made their greatest gains during periods of economic expansion. Though hardship as well as prosperity should be more fairly distributed, experience suggests that efforts to improve minority access in periods of shrinking opportunity are doomed to frustration. Because there is mutual feedback between improved education and better jobs, advocates of Mexican-American advancement in California should continue to press for improving the pace of school construction, greater parental involvement, expanded bilingual education, pedagogical reform, and more efficient school-to-workplace transitions. But for success from these reforms to be realized, economic growth and rising incomes will also be needed.

CHAPTER 11

The Once-and-Future Majority

Latino Politics in Los Angeles

HAROLD BRACKMAN AND STEVEN P. ERIE

THE 1980S APPEARED to be a watershed decade for Latino empowerment in California. In 1980, according to one study, only 3.6 percent of elected public officeholders in the state were Latino. By 1991, however, the percentage had more than doubled, with Latinos accounting for 217 of California's 2,861 elected officeholders. Many observers predict far greater Latino political breakthroughs in the 1990s. The unadjusted 1990 census count shows that 26 percent of the state's nearly 30 million residents are of Latino descent, up from 19 percent in 1980. Projections are that Latinos—almost 80 percent of whom are of Mexican birth or ancestry—will make up a minimum of 30 percent of California's population by the year 2000 and 36 percent by 2020.[1]

In politics, though, demography is not always destiny, at least not in the short run. Despite the impressive recent gains in elective officeholding, Latinos fall far short relative to their population. And despite the efforts of the minority-oriented California Executive Appointment program under both Democratic and Republican governors, Latinos lag in top-level states administrative appointments as well. Hispanic underrepresentation also extends to state and local government payrolls.

With 44 percent of the state's 1990 Hispanic population of 7.7 million, Los Angeles County is the crucial laboratory for Latino empowerment in California. The state's demographic destiny already has arrived in Los Angeles. The 1990 census shows that nearly 40 percent of the city's 3.5 million residents and the county's 8.9 million residents are of Latino origin, up from 28 percent in 1980. Latinos are forecast to be Los Angeles County's predominant ethnic group before century's end and to achieve majority status shortly thereafter.

Los Angeles also serves as the harbinger of Latino empowerment in California. Measured by the number of Latino officeholders, Mexican-

American political influence is far more advanced in the Los Angeles metropolitan area than elsewhere in the state. By 1991 two Latinos were sitting on the Los Angeles City Council, and one each on the school and community college boards. In the wake of a bitter battle over court-ordered redistricting, Gloria Molina was elected to the County Board of Supervisors in early 1991, the first Latino representative on that powerful body in over one hundred years. Since 1980 Los Angeles County's Latino congressional delegation has increased from one to three; its state legislative delegation from four to five. In all, nearly 75 percent of the Latinos in the California legislature and the state's congressional delegation came from the Los Angeles metropolitan area. Starting with the celebrated county redistricting case, political developments in Los Angeles's Latino community in the 1990s promise to have major reverberations in California, the nation, and Mexico.[2]

The importance of the struggle for Latino empowerment resides not only in emergent demographic trends but in perennial American concerns with democratic citizenship and group equality. European immigrant groups a century ago used ethnic politics to advance toward pluralist integration; but Latinos throughout the Southwest were politically excluded by an Anglo majority who treated them as an alien minority of "border immigrants" with no real stake in American society. Now striving to overcome this history, Latinos seek heightened political participation through voting, officeholding, lobbying, and litigating, both as an end in itself and as a means to greater influence over critical policies regarding jobs, education, health care, and immigrant and language rights. Failure to move toward more equitable Latino empowerment may ultimately frustrate the aspirations of non-Latinos as well. All Californians who aspire to a prosperous future as part of the multicultural Pacific Rim share a stake in reversing trends toward a "two-tier society" resting on the unstable foundation of an economically indispensable but politically alienated majority Latino population.[3]

This chapter examines the barriers to Latino empowerment in the city and county of Los Angeles, the chief strategies employed to overcome these obstacles, and the ramifications of Latino empowerment for three major public policy concerns: education, economic development, and intermestic issues such as immigration.[4]

Barriers to Latino Empowerment

The fundamental barrier to Latino empowerment is lack of voting strength. In the June 1990 state primary election, Latinos represented only 15 percent of adult citizens eligible to vote, 10 percent of registered voters, and 7 percent of actual voters. Growing impressively in numbers but lagging in commensurate electoral influence, the state's Latino community is burdened internally by heavy concentrations of undocumented or unnaturalized immigrants, underage or unregistered citizens, and unskilled and undereducated workers—all major depressants to voter participation rates.[5]

Mexico de Afuera (Mexico Outside Mexico): The Political Paradoxes of National Origins

Well over one million of Los Angeles County's 3.5 million Latinos are foreign-born "Mexicans outside Mexico." Roughly half of these Latinos are illegal residents without the option of becoming enfranchised. The other half are legal aliens with the right to naturalize their status and become voting citizens. The federal amnesty program promises to swell the ranks of legal Latino aliens even further. There were almost 1.2 million amnesty applications in California and over 600,000 alone in Los Angeles County, a majority of them by people of Mexican background.[6]

Legal status, however, does not necessarily translate into voting strength. Mexican immigrants have historically had extremely low rates of naturalization, both absolutely and relative to other immigrant groups. In 1982, only 21 percent of California's legally eligible foreign-born Latinos—and only 18 percent of those born in Mexico—had become naturalized citizens, compared to 66 percent of European immigrants.[7]

Mexico's ostensibly parochial and passive civic culture has long been a popular explanation among both Latino and Anglo scholars (though often with very different political agendas) for the low rates of naturalization among foreign-born Latinos in the Southwest, as well as for low registration and voter turnout among Mexican Americans. This "cultural importation" theory has been used to interpret nearly every facet of Latino political behavior from supposed "fatalistic acceptance of authority" to seeming "distrust of police."[8]

Recent studies of the changing profile of Mexican immigrants should revise the conventional wisdom. Although low rates of naturalization persist, most causal analyses now focus on the effects of exposure to American institutions, particularly the public schools and the immigration bureaucracy. Another relevant factor is the pervasive impact of the nearby border. Even though an overwhelming majority of both documented and undocumented Mexican immigrants intends to stay indefinitely in the United States, there remains the prevalent notion that "it is better to remain a first-class Mexican citizen than become a second-class American." The dialectic by which new-country experiences reinforce old-country identities is not unique to border immigrants, but it does seem especially strong among them. Significantly, Canadian immigrants also have relatively low naturalization rates. It is both paradox and portent that the strong Mexican identity of a swelling Latino immigrant population serves as a formidable barrier to "Latinizing" California politics through the creation of new citizens.[9]

It is important to distinguish nonparticipation by Latino immigrants who cannot or will not naturalize from the characteristic political behavior of those who do become citizens. Contrary to the popular stereotype of the apathetic newcomer, in 1988 naturalized Mexican Americans registered nationally at nearly the same 70-percent rate as all U.S. adults. In terms of political party identification, the Field Institute's June 1990 California poll showed a 61-percent to 30-percent Democratic registration advantage among Hispanics, but only a 54-percent to 35-percent Democratic edge in Hispanic party identification. In terms of issue identification, a 1984 survey of California voters showed small differences between foreign- and U.S.-born Latinos; not surprisingly, the immigrants were more in favor of amnesty for the undocumented and of more bilingual programs.[10]

The foreign-born Latino community is divided between a small naturalized minority integrated into the political system and a much larger group of unintegrated noncitizens. Rather than being political laggards compared to the U.S.-born, naturalized foreign-born Latinos show signs of constituting themselves as a potential electoral vanguard. By virtue of weak party allegiances, they still are up for grabs politically. Nationwide, one-third of Mexican-born U.S. citizens express no party preference. (Among Mexican-born noncitizens, the no party preference rate skyrockets to 62 percent.) Both parties could reap rewards through registration drives targeting this growing population.[11]

Sal Si Puedes (Get Out If You Can): Socioeconomic Barriers

Latino politics is distinct not because it is Latino but because Latinos are disproportionately poor. If one adds a distinctive demographic profile—age and residence—to that of economic impoverishment, this formulation has much to recommend it as an explanation for the limited electoral mobilization of Los Angeles's Latinos. The following discussion will explore how key socioeconomic factors—educational attainment, income level, age distribution, and residential patterns—interact to both depress mass participation and heighten class polarization among Latinos.

Education and Income. For over twenty years the high school dropout rate among the majority Latino student population in the Los Angeles Unified School District has hovered around 50 percent, more than twice the Anglo rate and substantially higher than the black rate. The dropout rate among U.S.-born Latinos is 40 percent; among the foreign-born, it reaches 70 percent. Disadvantaged Latino youth are more likely to enter and stay in the labor force than their black counterparts but less likely to move up. The Los Angeles poverty rate increased from 11 percent in 1969 to 16 percent in 1987. There were small increases among blacks and Asians but a massive jump among Latinos—from 17 percent to 26 percent.[12]

At the same time, progress was made by the Latino middle class. In terms of politics this opened the way for Republican party outreach to the more prosperous one-third or more of the Latino electorate. While Reagan's appeal to traditional cultural values—religion, family, and country—had a resonance with Latinos that cut across class lines, the GOP's small-business ideology struck a particularly responsive chord among middle-class Latinos. By the 1984 election, the political rule of thumb was that a family income of $40,000 was the new dividing line in Latino politics. A majority of those above the line voted Republican; a majority below, Democratic. The trend toward class polarization and partisan diversity meant that Latinos in Los Angeles increasingly were having a difficult time working toward common community goals.[13]

Age Distribution. Though there is a gender gap in the Latino community—women are more liberal—this is dwarfed in political significance by a generation gap between a large cohort of uninitiated youth amidst a smaller group of experienced adults. In California there is a ten-year gap between the average age of the Anglo and Latino communities; in metropolitan Los Angeles some 40 percent of Latinos are twenty years of age or under.[14]

These extreme baby-boom demographics contribute to the view among non-Latino powerbrokers that Latinos currently are a politically immature population that does not have to be taken too seriously at the ballot box. In 1980, with the county's Latino population at 28 percent, the Latino share of adults eligible to vote was only 12 percent. Until a demographic coming of age occurs among Latinos, the size of this voting pool will remain limited.

Residential Dispersion. Greater East Los Angeles, spilling over west of the Los Angeles River and then extending eastward into unincorporated county territory, is the core barrio of the metropolis, but even in 1970 it contained only 45 percent of the county's Latino population. With only one-third of East Los Angeles's residents owning their own homes (compared with two-thirds of San Antonio's westside Latino residents), there have been strong pressures for upwardly mobile Latinos to move outward to the suburbs.[15]

More affluent Latinos have moved north and east into the foothill communities of the San Gabriel Valley. Those less well off have moved south and west into Watts and South Central Los Angeles. In the San Fernando Valley, the old City of San Fernando serves as the nucleus of another burgeoning Latino community. In sheer numbers, the Northeast San Fernando Valley soon will rival the East Side's core city barrio. As a result of dispersion, Latinos by the late 1980s constituted more than 30 percent of the population in ten of Los Angeles's fifteen city council districts.[16]

The political consequences of Latino residential dispersion are complex. On the one hand, Latinos in the City of Los Angeles have had difficulty achieving the critical mass in individual districts needed to maximize their representation on the city council. For example, the Seventh District in the San Fernando Valley—63 percent Latino in 1990—seemed the best bet for a third Latino council seat. Yet this was an insufficient electoral advantage in 1989 for a serious Latino challenge to a longtime Anglo incumbent. On the other hand, the suburbanization of affluent Latinos has opened new vistas for GOP strategists such as former county supervisor Pete Schabarum to groom Latino Republicans for suburban city council races.

The Leaders vs. The Led: Strategies for Latino Empowerment

The decade of the 1980s made "the awakening of the sleeping giant of Latino electoral power" a political cliché. Beneath the cliché was the authentic, formidable challenge of mobilizing an until recently politically inactive population. In 1988, Latinos represented only an estimated 15 percent of the county's registered voters but under 10 percent of its actual voters.[17]

Various strategies have been devised to empower Latinos in Los Angeles County. Because they tend to operate exclusively at either the elite or the mass level, however, none of these strategies is sufficient to achieve Latino empowerment. Without strong and effective leaders, grassroots strategies cannot give Latinos their own voice within the power structure. But without a massive mobilization of new citizens and voters, district lines created to achieve population parity could degenerate into "rotten boroughs" in which inactive residents are ignored by imperious politicians. What is needed in the 1990s are new organizations and strategies that more actively link leaders and the led.

Top-Down Strategies

Reapportionment and Redistricting. Largely because of population trends, the decennial census—and concomitant mandates to redraw local, state, and federal legislative boundaries—has become the new pivot of "top-down" Latino empowerment strategies in Los Angeles. Prior to the 1980s, Latinos were the perennial victims of racial gerrymandering. In 1971, when the U.S. Civil Rights Commission concluded that "the Mexican American in California has been gerrymandered out of any real chance to elect his own representatives," East Los Angeles consisted of nine assembly districts, seven state senate districts and six house districts. And Los Angeles County's First Supervisorial District, which included East Los Angeles, had its lines redrawn five times between 1959 and 1981 to dilute Latino voting power.[18]

Notwithstanding this dismal historical record, the 1980s demonstrated the potential efficacy of top-down Latino empowerment strategies—legislative redistricting and voting rights lawsuits—which may be a prerequisite for successful bottom-up grassroots mobilization efforts. The reapportionment/redistricting battles critical to Latinos stretched over the entire decade of the 1980s and were fought in three different arenas.

The first arena was state and federal reapportionment, where the key Latino actor was then-assemblyman Richard Alatorre, who was appointed chairman of the powerful Elections and Reapportionment Committee in 1980 by the new assembly speaker, Willie Brown. A plan by the Southwest Voter Registration and Education Project (SVREP) to create an additional Latino assembly seat in Los Angeles County was blocked by the joint opposition of Democratic incumbents and the assembly black caucus. The new assembly lines ultimately adopted were also supposed to increase Latino representation, but at the expense of Anglo Republicans outside Los Angeles. Ironically, the U.S. House of Representatives reapportionment plan, engineered primarily by Congressman Phil Burton, actually proved more conducive to Latino aspirations, clearing the way for the election of two new Los Angeles–area congressmen: Matthew G. Martinez of Monterey Park and Esteban E. Torres of La Puente.[19]

In the second arena, Los Angeles city council redistricting, the major Latino player at City Hall was again Alatorre, who was elected Fourteenth District councilman in 1985 following the retirement of the scandal-plagued Anglo incumbent. The first Los Angeles Latino councilman since Ed Roybal had moved up to Congress in 1962, Alatorre became head of the council committee responsible for fashioning a second majority Latino district in conformity with a settlement forced on the city by a U.S. Justice Department lawsuit under Title II of the Voting Rights Act. The plan, crafted by the Mexican American Legal Defense and Education Fund (MALDEF) and approved by the council, was at the probable expense of new councilman Mike Woo, the first Asian American ever so elected. Mayor Tom Bradley protected Woo with a veto in 1986, but the deadlock was broken when the death of an Anglo councilman opened the way to Gloria Molina's election in the redrawn but vacant 68-percent Latino First District.[20]

Finally, the dynamics of Los Angeles County redistricting were quite different. The Los Angeles County Board of Supervisors, called by critics "the five uncrowned kings" of local government, controlled an annual budget of over $10 billion. There was no Latino on the board in 1981 or later when the supervisors refused to increase membership to facilitate minority representation and then adopted what was generally viewed as an incumbent protection plan. Possible settlement of the vote-dilution lawsuit brought in 1988 by the Justice Department in conjunction with MALDEF and the American Civil Liberties Union was blocked by First District Supervisor Pete Schabarum. Schabarum announced his retirement in March 1990 but refused to support Sarah Flores, his Latina deputy, in the June primary held to replace him. This election, in which Republican Flores finished first, was thrown out by U.S. District Court Judge David V. Kenyon because existing district lines "fragment[ed] the Hispanic core." Kenyon ultimately accepted a MALDEF-drawn remap creating a new First District with a 71-percent Latino population and 51-percent Latino voter registration majority centering in East Los Angeles. Two liberal Democrats competed in the February 1991 runoff to fill the open seat. Councilwoman Gloria Molina was outspent by State Senator Art Torres, $1.2 million to $500,000, but won because of her superior grassroots get-out-the-vote campaign. It remained to be seen whether Molina's plans to "shake up the board" would succeed in reversing the policies pursued during the 1980s by its three-man conservative majority, including drastic funding cuts in health and welfare programs in the face of the county's highest poverty rates in fifty years.[21]

The early 1990s presented new challenges. Latino leaders looked at the 1991–92 battles to draw new boundaries in the state capitol and City Hall with both hope and trepidation. A positive development was a united-front approach on the part of SVREP, MALDEF, and the National Association of Latino Elected Officials. But there also were perceived dangers in the proliferation of Latino group involvement. In the early 1980s, according to Carlos Navarro, Californios for Fair Representation "had all the marbles. Now because of all the changes in computers nobody does." In 1991 there were conflicts between MALDEF and SVREP, on the one side, and the Institute for Social Justice and Californios for Fair Representation on the other.[22]

The redistricting strategy espoused by MALDEF and SVREP strived to create as many Latino legislative districts as Latino numbers allowed.

Latino leaders urged the creation of fourteen Latino-majority seats statewide: four new congressional districts, three new state senate districts, and seven assembly seats. At the state level, this strategy exacerbated the Democratic party's ethnic faultlines. There is a widespread perception of reapportionment as a "zero-sum game, making cross-ethnic coalitions very difficult." According to Richard Martinez of SVREP, three-cornered ethnic clashes between blacks, Latinos, and Asians were likely to be followed by an intraparty war with "the Waxman-Berman folks [powerful West Side politicians] who are trying to hustle us on Congressional Districts." To avoid this result, some Latino activists seriously considered a marriage of convenience with GOP reapportionment strategists.[23]

At the local level, the MALDEF-SVREP redistricting strategy also meant substituting district for at-large city council and school board elections. However, as the history of the Los Angeles City Council and County Board of Supervisors shows, single-member districts—particularly "overlarge" districts—do not necessarily prevent racial gerrymandering. They can be used as a very effective vote-dilution tool either by dispersing a group's voting strength over many districts or by overconcentrating it within fewer districts. Even without overt racial gerrymandering, vote dilution may result when a fast-growing minority population spreads out over multiple single-member districts.[24]

Locally, Latino support has been growing for an alternative redistricting approach. The so-called "Chicago model" of representation would, if the new supervisor, Molina, prevails, expand the number of county board seats initially to seven and, if Professor Rudy Acuña ever has his way, the number of city councilman seats to as many as fifty. In one stroke, proponents argue, this would diminish zero-sum competition between minorities, reduce election costs by shrinking the size of individual districts, and increase the likelihood of electing Latino candidates. Skeptics warn that this remedy's side-effects—aggravating the political and economic fragmentation already plaguing the East Side—might be worse than the disease.[25]

Personalismo and Politics: Grooming Latino Leaders. The positive impact of redistricting and reapportionment will be severely limited unless there are Latino leaders capable of exercising effective leadership. This requires that internecine factional warfare be overcome, that broader avenues of candidate recruitment be opened, and that the challenge of adequate funding be met for high-priced campaigns and high-quality leadership development.

East Los Angeles political infighting sometimes is likened to the intrigues of Machiavelli's Florence. Perhaps a better analogy is the fragmented politics under medieval France's turbulent monarchy. In Los Angeles the feudal suzerain—who "reigns but does not rule"—is recently retired Congressman Ed Roybal. There are two heirs apparent, congressmen Martinez and Torres, waiting in the wings in Washington. In the state and local provinces (where the real power lies), there is a powerful baron, Assembly Speaker Willie Brown, aligned with two ambitious dukes, Councilman Richard Alatorre and State Senator Art Torres (leaders of the so-called East Side "PRI machine")—whose retainers include Assemblyman Richard Polanco and school board member Larry González. The PRI machine frequently clashes with community activists—Supervisor Molina (with longstanding ties to Roybal), insurgent candidate Steve Rodriguez, and barrio attorney Antonio Rodriguez—who claim a grassroots mandate to speak for the commoners. Some of the insurgents first developed their populist commitments as part of the radical nationalist (La Raza Unida) and leftist (CASA-HGT) movements of the 1970s. The 1980s featured internecine warfare between these two unstable leadership factions.[26]

The unhealthy consequences of East Side leadership factionalism are often exaggerated. On the positive side, the competitive wars indicate that the Latino political trade still is relatively open. For one thing, compared to West Side Anglo political operators, East Side politicians do not control enough resources to peremptorily scare off all challengers. There is impressive vitality among these still young Latino politicians. In contrast, local black politics until recently has featured aging officeholders so deeply entrenched that younger leadership aspirants were frozen out.[27]

On the negative side, the pattern of East Side candidate recruitment reflects two pervasive political realities about local Latino politics that may inhibit future progress. First, with the exception of a few insurgents, candidates are recruited "top down" in a process of sponsored mobility. This is the *papacito* system, in which contenders are drawn from the ranks of an extended family of blood relations and legislative aides. Even insurgent supervisor Molina sponsored Mike Hernandez, her successor as First District Councilman, in this way.

Second, there is the daunting problem of raising the substantial amounts of campaign money needed for media buys and direct mailings. Gloria Molina would not have been able to defeat the East Side PRI machine in 1982 (assembly) and 1987 (council) had she not managed to raise $600,000 for the two races. Even more expensive are races for supervisor, mayor, and congressman, where the price tag of credibility is $500,000 and up.[28]

Campaign funding is the umbilicus linking the East Side PRI machine to Speaker Brown. Another source of money for the Alatorre/Torres organization are the minority contractors associated with the East Los Angeles Community Union (TELACU). A War on Poverty experiment funded by government and foundations, TELACU was the eighth largest Latino-owned business in the United States by 1984. The high-tech capital-intensive politics pioneered by the West Side's Waxman-Berman forces now has spread across town. Among the Latino practitioners is TELACU alumnus George Pla. In addition to his role in the successful 1982 campaigns of congressmen Martinez and Torres, Pla boasts of having raised among Latinos $300,000 for Jerry Brown in 1978 and $1 million for Jimmy Carter in 1980 "without really trying." Pla's pioneering fundraising efforts have become a permanent part of the East Los Angeles political landscape.[29]

Los Angeles's grassroots Latino activists concerned about too much money in politics are not necessarily hostile to middle-class values and leadership. In fact, they typically complain that their own middle class, unlike middle-class Latinos in San Antonio, lacks "the organic character" needed to generate political leadership responsive to the community's needs. Part of the reason is the "up and out" trajectory of successful Latinos, who as soon as possible depart the East Side and thereby weaken its grassroots leadership. But others see a more general "reversion to the assimilationist and accommodationist attitudes of the Mexican American Generation of the 1950s" on the part of college-educated young people, who are less interested today than their counterparts twenty years ago in politically mobilizing the Latino community. The politicians in the mold of Torres and Alatorre, for example, are accused of ignoring the masses in order to cultivate elite alliances with TELACU and Speaker Brown.[30]

Formal leadership training is one route toward creating a Latino political class. Examples—all, unfortunately, hamstrung by inadequate funding—include the MALDEF training program, NALEO's internship program, the United Way's Kellogg Training Group, and the Sacramento-based Chicano-Latino Youth Leadership Project. Another route of leadership development is informal training through political mentorship and patronage. This approach calls for channeling the young professional class into the public service arena as a way of "opening other doors."[31] According to Harry Pachon of NALEO, the resultant interplay between leaders and the led should unleash a chain reaction: "Once you start getting elected officials in office, minority elected officials, there's a synergy that's built up that brings in the voters. Once people start seeing that one of their own can win, then you get more political participation."[32]

There still may be too few Latino officials, however, to make this synergy happen. Hence the ultimate irony is that the quest for Latino empowerment often becomes a quixotic search for the charismatic individual—an urban Cesar Chavez—who can fill the perceived leadership void. Such a leader could appeal across the divisions among Latinos as well as across those separating them from potential coalitional partners.

Grassroots Mobilization Strategies

Community Organizing. Developing the community's organizational and group lobbying capacity represents one important grassroots mobilization strategy. The United Neighborhoods Organization (UNO), an outgrowth of church-based activism, has played a particularly crucial role in organizing the East Side. Formed in 1976, UNO was modeled on San Antonio's Community Organized for Public Service. It has complex roots both in the old Latino tradition of *mutualistas*, or multipurpose social service organizations, and in Saul Alinsky's approach to community organization.[33]

UNO has been successful and enduring precisely because it has kept its eyes on the grassroots. It never has wavered from organizing around such street-level issues as insurance redlining, absentee slumlords, merchant pricing practices in the barrio, and city street repair and lighting. Parish-based UNO is both cause and effect of the Los Angeles archdiocese's gradual evolution toward social engagement on behalf of Latinos, particularly in terms of giving sanctuary to refugees and sheltering the Latino homeless.[34]

In 1986 UNO was joined by MOELA (Mothers of East LA), an activist community group more willing to challenge entrenched local politicians. MOELA took the political initiative by mobilizing the East Side against construction of a new state prison, organizing demonstrations by as many as 3,000, such as had not been seen on the East Side since the late 1960s. UNO and MOELA ultimately joined to push a new environmental agenda, which included opposition to an East Side gas pipeline and the Vernon toxic waste incinerator. By 1990 their ally, Councilwoman Molina, was sparring with Councilman Alatorre over whether and how the Olvera Street redevelopment project should proceed. For the first time, the assumption that the job-hungry East Side was prodevelopment by automatic reflex was being challenged.[35]

Latino community activists also are increasingly interested in politically joining forces with blacks and Asians under the umbrella of such organizations as the Coalition Against the Prison and the South Central Organizing Committee. They seek to form a common front among racially diverse, working-class communities threatened by economic decline and environmental degradation.[36]

The union movement, which is combatting declining membership by recruiting associate members working for nonunion firms, is another traditional organizational mainstay of the Latino community. Latino service-sector workers are a central target of vigorous union organizing efforts in the Los Angeles area. Innovative union programs directed at Latinos such as the Labor Immigration Assistance Project, jointly sponsored by the AFL-CIO and the County Federation of Labor, are being well received.[37]

Latino professional and business groups embrace a different agenda, which deemphasizes community and working-class issues in favor of the special concerns of upwardly mobile members. Considered "potentially influential" are such groups as the Mexican American Bar Association, the Mexican American Grocers Association, and the Comisión Feminil.[38]

Few community organizations, however, bridge the growing class gap among Latinos. Fewer still bridge the political gap between citizens and noncitizens. Although these groups should make an effort to overcome these shortcomings, part of the solution may be to complement community organizing with other grassroots mobilization strategies such as naturalization and voter registration.

Naturalization Efforts. In Los Angeles County, Latino registered voters—U.S.-native and foreign-born—are outnumbered by unnaturalized *legal* aliens. Naturalization drives are high-risk efforts, however, because of the greater expense involved and the less certain payoff compared to voter registration campaigns. The great mobilization drives of the 1980s—partisan and nonpartisan—were almost exclusively retail rather than wholesale operations, aimed at the uninvolved-but-eligible but not the unnaturalized.

The most effective naturalization efforts have been undertaken by nonpartisan organizations. In conjunction with SVREP, the National Association of Latino Elected Officials (NALEO) has conducted citizenship workshops utilizing a one-step card-signing procedure. Pointing to the doubling in the annual number of Mexican immigrants naturalized between 1984 and 1986, NALEO Executive Director Harry Pachon claims considerable success over the five-year life of his Project Citizenship program.[39]

Yet daunting obstacles to Latino naturalization remain. These include the difficulty of passing Immigration and Naturalization Service citizenship exams; the government's failure to carry through with immigrant education programs designed to meet Stage II amnesty requirements; and the special problems of helping Central American refugees, over 97 percent of whom had their requests for political asylum denied in the 1980s.[40]

Registration Drives. Naturalization must be accompanied by registration if Latinos are to realize their electoral potential. Like naturalization drives, efforts to register eligible Mexican-American voters have been plagued by short-term political considerations. Part of the blame for limited progress toward Latino voter registration must be placed at the doorstep of the political parties, particularly the Democrats. For example, SVREP's Richard Martinez faulted the Feinstein gubernatorial campaign, which still had not opened an office or launched a registration drive on Los Angeles's East Side as late as August 1990, for repeating the error made by the Dukakis campaign in 1988 of "a strategy which focuses on Anglos and gender—virtually ignoring Latinos." Latino critics of the Democratic party's efforts charge the state apparatus with financing local registration efforts "only on the condition that they be run by party operatives from outside the district, while local activists did all the work."[41]

Again, the most effective registration efforts have been nonpartisan. Since switching in 1984 to an "inside California" focus, SVREP has conducted over 400 registration drives in the state, including 100 in Los Angeles County. SVREP's 1986 California registration campaign alone yielded 80,000 new Latino voters. Latino voter registration in the state increased by 25 percent between 1984 and 1989, with the bulk of the gains in Los Angeles County.[42]

In the name of "building political power" rather than merely registering voters, SVREP concentrates on "ascending communities" with the right "generational rhythm" and "indigenous leadership." It typically conducts registration drives in suburban ring communities such as Norwalk with predominantly U.S.-born and upwardly mobile Latino populations. The SVREP strategy precludes much attention to registration in inner city neighborhoods such as Pico Union, which is viewed in terms of "negative community potential" because of the massive influx of impoverished Central American refugees. Latino critics of SVREP charge the organization with "elitism," questioning not so much its professional competence as its breadth of political vision.[43]

Si Se Puede (If It Can Be Done): Coalition Building and Crossover Politics

According to former MALDEF director Vilma Martinez, "political coalitions are the wave of the future." If so, it will be a wave with many eddies and crosscurrents. Will the coalitions be primarily candidate-driven or issue-driven? Will the coalitions be cross-ethnic but within one socioeconomic class, or will they be cross-class? In the City of Los Angeles, will their membership expand beyond the current Bradley biracial coalition? Or will they fracture today's ethnic alignments? If a Latino were to succeed Mayor Bradley in 1993, the victory surely would have to be a triumph of crossover politics by a politician capable of attracting large numbers of non-Latino votes.[44]

Los Angeles in the early 1990s is a congeries of many different ethnic fiefs: the heavily Jewish West Side and Fairfax area; the heavily Anglo Protestant and Catholic West San Fernando Valley; the black (and increasingly Latino) South-Central neighborhoods; the Asian corridor, running along Olympic Boulevard; the Latino communities of Greater East Los Angeles and the Northeast San Fernando Valley. It is within this complex intergroup context that Latinos seek to graduate from their junior partner status in the Bradley years to become full partners in a new cross-ethnic coalition.

A wide spectrum of ethnic coalition outcomes are possible. To borrow William James's distinction, the extremes range from the outcome predicted by "tough-minded" pessimists who foresee twenty-first-century Los Angeles almost in Hobbesian terms as a Third World crucible of intergroup conflicts—the so-called "Bladerunner scenario"—to "tender-minded" optimists who predict a future of multicultural harmony on a prosperous Pacific Rim—the theme of the Los Angeles Festival. Somewhere between these extremes, there are a number of possibilities for coalitions between Latinos and other groups.

Mexicans and Central Americans

Predictions about Latino participation in coalition politics presuppose a Latino *intra*group unity that may have to be achieved rather than assumed. According to Carlos Navarro, "the Latino community [of Los Angeles] is not a community *per se*; it is a community of communities." This can be characterized as a shift from "Mexico de afuera" to "América Latina de afuera." Cubans have been shaped by a unique anti-Castro dynamic. On the other hand, the Central Americans are divided between left-leaning Salvadorans and Guatemalans and right-leaning Nicaraguans.[45]

The crucial split, however, is the ethnic-nationality division between Mexican and non-Mexican. Mexican-American politicians such as Richard Alatorre and Gloria Molina are uncertain about whether and how to meet specifically Central American concerns such as municipal regulation of unlicensed street vendors. Most Mexican-American activists seem to be skeptical about actively aligning with Central Americans who compete with Mexican immigrants for day laborer jobs and are accused of being obsessed with home-country politics.[46]

Latinos and Anglos

The conventional wisdom is that if the liberal black-Jewish coalition of the Bradley years unravels, a new black-Latino coalition will emerge.

This may indeed happen, but only if Latinos choose not to enter into a very different alignment with either the West Side Jewish community or the still predominantly WASP downtown business establishment now at odds over the growth issue. The West Side is strongly antigrowth, while downtown enjoys prodevelopment ties with the East Side PRI.

The Waxman-Berman forces are widely criticized for colonizing the East Side with kept Latino politicians. Dan Garcia, a former Los Angeles police commissioner and founder of the Tri-Ethnic Coalition, grounds this resentment in economic policy differences. He explains that he founded this Latino/black/Asian organization because he "got tired of West Side whites telling the media about minority opinions on growth." Put in coalitional perspective, Garcia's tri-ethnic alignment has a silent but powerful fourth partner—the downtown progrowth Anglo business community.[47]

It will not be easy, however, for many Latino populists to mute their loud protests against the Anglo business elite. In fact, grassroots East Side Latino groups such as MOELA and the Lincoln Heights Preservation Association are more ideologically congruent with the West Side antigrowth movement. This affinity might serve as the building block for a West Side–East Side slow-growth coalition under the joint leadership of Jewish liberals and Latino populists. Despite recent tensions over levels of foreign aid for Israel and domestic assistance for Russian Jews as opposed to Central American refugees, the longstanding good relationship between the Waxman-Berman and Roybal forces provides an historic precedent for building such a new partnership.[48]

A third possibility—a Latino alliance with conservative West Valley Anglos—seems highly unlikely. Anglo valleyites might conceivably vote for a conservative Republican Latino, but it is hard to imagine the same candidate as the choice of the Latino East Side. The candidate of Boyle Heights would probably have to follow the same minimalist strategy as Tom Bradley, the candidate of Watts, did in his early tries for mayor. Bradley's strategy was not to win the West Valley but to get just enough votes there to contain the opposition's Anglo plurality. The logic of "keeping down negatives" among valley Anglos may partly explain why prospective Latino mayoral candidates such as Councilman Alatorre maintained a decidedly low profile in the dispute over placing Police Chief Daryl Gates on leave following the Rodney King beating.[49]

Latinos and Asians

There appears to be a strong basis for collaboration between Latinos and Asians on behalf of an immigrant rights agenda and in opposition to resurgent Anglo nativism. However, the prospects for a broad-based alliance are more problematic. One obstacle is the cavernous socioeconomic gap between so-called Asian model minorities and disadvantaged Latinos. Another is the difficulty posed by Asian ethnocultural diversity.

Latinos who believe that the gaps can be bridged tend to fall into two camps with rival approaches to the growth issue. One camp favors building a grassroots Latino-Asian coalition around the issue of neighborhood preservation. For example, Veronica Gutierrez, aide to former Councilwoman Molina, whose district included much of Chinatown, recognizes the "potential for an Asian-Latino alliance with Latinos supplying the votes and Asians the money." Gutierrez's model is the populist, slow-growth Latino-Asian Coalition to Improve Our Neighborhood (LACTION), with which Molina had worked closely. LACTION connections helped Chinatown activist Sharon Lowe make the runoff to succeed Molina in the First Council District by finishing second to Mike Hernandez in the June 1991 municipal primary.[50]

The other camp puts its priority on forging an elite alliance between the Asian business community and progrowth Latino politicians such as Councilman Alatorre. Strong interethnic prodevelopment ties dating back to when Lincoln Heights was still part of the Fourteenth Councilmanic District helped preserve Alatorre's reputation in the Asian community even after he attempted to redistrict Mike Woo's seat out from underneath him in 1986. His enduring close relations with Chinese developers are part of the reason for the strong anti-Alatorre sentiment voiced by the leadership of Mothers of East LA and the Lincoln Heights Preservation Association, which also would like to promote Latino/Asian political cooperation, but around a slow-growth agenda.[51]

It is not beyond the realm of possibility that the 1993 Los Angeles mayoral race will see Alatorre angling for Asian Pacific votes on a progrowth platform while candidate Woo counters with an appeal to slow-growth Latinos. Such are the ironies of minority coalitional politics in Los Angeles.

Latinos and Blacks

At the leadership level, brown-black ties are quite strong. According to aide Robin Kramer, "Among Councilman Alatorre's best friends in life are Willie Brown and Maxine Waters. They are friends, not just political friends." SVREP's Antonio Gonzalez expresses the general admiration of many Latino leaders for the achievements of Los Angeles's black politicians: "They are on the inside. . . . That's because they've been good coalition partners, they've paid their dues, turned out their vote, cut their deals, and they're in."[52]

A continuing alliance between local Latino and black politicians is a strong possibility. Faced with a declining population base as well as the possible retirement of their remarkably successful mayor, Los Angeles's black political leaders will need the shot in the arm that heightened Latino support could give their biracial coalition. Latino politicians also see the attractions of an alliance with blacks, a group still making up 18 percent of the city's voters. It remains to be seen, however, whether black politicians after twenty years of unprecedented prominence in City Hall will be able to reconcile themselves to playing a supporting role behind an Alatorre or Molina.

Class logic might dictate that disadvantaged Latinos and blacks should make common cause. At the mass level, however, job competition between the groups has generated serious friction on both sides that escalated further in the wake of the Los Angeles riots of April 1992. Among blacks, employer sanctions remain highly popular. Latino opinion erupts in anger over the supposed black stranglehold on public-sector jobs in transitional neighborhoods such as Compton and Watts, where Latinos are moving in large numbers. Black preferment on the county payroll is another source of Latino discontent.[53]

City council redistricting in 1992 is considered another political time bomb just waiting to go off. Any increase in the number of Latino-held seats beyond the current two almost certainly will come at the expense of the three seats held by blacks. From a Latino perspective, new district lines might look like a way to achieve more equitable representation. From a black perspective, however, the same new Latino districts perhaps unfairly swell the influence of a heavily noncitizen, nonvoting population.

The closer one moves to the Latino grassroots, the more problematic the brown/black relationship becomes. Juana Gutierrez of MOELA joined black groups opposing the Vernon incinerator project, but her organization is bitter towards black assemblyman Cecil Green of Norwalk, who changed his vote and supported an East Side state prison at the behest of Speaker Brown. Attempted damage control by rainbow organizations such as the Black-Latino Roundtable fail to address such underlying structural causes of brown-black conflict as economic and neighborhood competition and ethnopolitical succession.[54]

Coalition Building in the 1990s

Latino coalition building has been a problematic enterprise in Los Angeles since the 1950s. There are fond memories of a "proto-rainbow coalition, primarily Latino and Jewish, once based in Boyle Heights." In the early 1960s, this coalition, which had elected Ed Roybal to the city council, became a historical curiosity when the political action shifted westward to the Tenth City Council District. Tenth District councilman Tom Bradley built his mayoral campaign around a durable coalition with the Jewish West Side. In the 1990s, a younger generation of Latino activists worry that Latinos again could be left at the station as new ethnic alliance patterns emerge. "Latinos have been irrelevant in L.A. politics for so long," Professor Jorge Garcia laments, "that it's going to be difficult to get other people to see us as viable coalition partners. . . . Sure, we can be part of the 'rainbow coalition,' but when are any Latino issues ever raised?"[55]

The exact ethnic coalition patterns that crystallize in Los Angeles in the 1990s will largely be a function of two factors: the interplay of the personal ambitions of politicians such as Gloria Molina, Richard Alatorre, Mike Woo, Maxine Waters, Zev Yaroslavsky, and Howard Berman; and the impersonal deals affecting minority empowerment struck by group actors such as MALDEF, SVREP, the National Association for the Advancement of Colored People (NAACP), and the Democratic and Republican parties. Similar to the experience of Irish Americans a century ago or African Americans more recently, Latino anxieties about this process are perhaps the inevitable result when a group moves over the course of a single generation from the politics of exclusion (pre-Voting Rights Act) to the politics of separatism (the era of the Brown Berets and the La Raza Unida party), to the politics of multiethnic, multiracial coalition building. Viewed positively, such anxieties are a price worth paying for the gains—greater and lesser—that will come to Latinos from heightened participation in the give-and-take of pluralist democracy.

Public Policy and Latino Empowerment

Progress toward Latino empowerment is certain to have an impact on both the broad contours and the specific results of public policy. The probable effects include intensified support for family- and child-centered social policies, specifically those involving educational spending; a realignment of the economic development or growth debate, with the center of gravity possibly shifting away from progrowth and antigrowth extremes toward a new centrist position; and greater political attention paid to the intermestic issues that shape the California-Mexico Connection.

Public Education

A serious barrier to Latino empowerment is not directly a matter of voting strength or electoral structure. It involves what President Bush called "the crisis in Hispanic education" and what the American Council on Education in 1991 characterized as the "gross underrepresentation [of Latinos] at every rung of the educational ladder." According to Armando Navarro of the Institute for Social Justice, "We have a massive crisis now in education, and for us as Latinos, it's a super-crisis . . . with devastating implications for the future." The dimensions of this crisis include high dropout rates, adult illiteracy, declining test scores, and Latino underrepresentation in higher education.[56]

Education as a Latino empowerment issue is invariably part of a broader grassroots political-economic agenda with the implicit premise that minority education is too important to be left to Anglo educators. From this perspective, the educational deficit is a *political* problem compounded if not created by biased policies in the areas of "ability grouping" and "tracking," student suspension, and teacher recruitment and training. Positive educational reform is sought as a political consciousness-raising instrument to teach Latinos—long indoctrinated into unquestioning obedience—about "how government really works," including "the social services that are available at different levels."[57]

Variations on this politically oriented Latino educational agenda include proposals to use revitalized PTAs as vehicles for grassroots mobilization; arguments that quality schools, including parochial schools such as Cathedral High, can serve as incubators for community leaders; and strategies to make the crusade for greater educational opportunity into a catalyst for the formation of wider rainbow coalitions. This emphasis on education's political payoff is complemented by the Tri-Ethnic Coalition's emphasis on Latino educational progress as a motor of future economic growth for the Pacific Rim.[58]

Specific reform proposals for improving Latino education include early childhood education, school-based social services, bilingual education, retention programs, parental involvement, and adult education. In particular, bilingual and adult education have direct empowerment ramifications.

Responding to MALDEF's lawsuit, in 1988 the Los Angeles Unified School District adopted the Master Plan for Bilingual Education, designed to benefit the 59 percent of its students either lacking English proficiency or only recently fluent in the language. Implementation of the bilingual plan, however, has been hampered by a shortage of instructional dollars and bilingual teachers. This issue remains a potent political common denominator for Latino leaders "who are still very much 'on board' for bilingual education, and that goes for Republicans as well as Democrats."[59]

Latino leaders also have fought a battle over State Legalization Impact

Assistance Grants (SLIAGs), which were promised under the 1986 Immigration Reform and Control Act (IRCA). The impending deadline for amnesty applicants to meet the language-and-civics requirements mandated by IRCA gave heightened urgency to controversies in both Washington and Sacramento over the appropriation and earmarking of up to $4 billion in SLIAG funds. In the view of business-oriented Latino leaders like Dan Garcia, such educational outreach programs are vital to the economic as well as civic health of the region and the state.[60]

Economic Development

The conventional wisdom is that the growth issue is the great faultline that will dominate the future of Los Angeles politics. Growth issues—particularly redevelopment—do indeed powerfully shape the contours of Latino politics. But there also is an intricate web of divisions on this issue within the Latino community.

Progrowth. A strong prodevelopment axis still exists on the East Side. Its origins are traced to the bonds forged between organized labor and the Latino lower-middle class. "The Latino community will be prodevelopment," says Frank del Olmo of the *Los Angeles Times*, "as long as there is the perception that growth provides unionized jobs." MOELA activist Juana Gutierrez criticizes the Latino developers behind TELACU and their political champion, Councilman Alatorre (she calls them "bandidos") for promoting development projects that ignore the quality-of-life concerns of working-class Latinos. A third, more sophisticated progrowth force that claims to be sensitive to such concerns is represented by Dan Garcia's Tri-Ethnic Coalition of Latinos, blacks, and Asians. It seeks a greater role for minorities in regional planning, infrastructure development, and transportation issues.[61]

The progrowth axis now extends to the Northeast San Fernando Valley. City of San Fernando mayor Jesse Margarito, a former La Raza Unida radical nationalist, has made his peace with the Anglo business community. In office since 1984, Margarito has deliberately "pursued linkage with the business community" because "progressive human services [require] a viable retail sector and a healthy commercial sector." He particularly favors upscale development projects designed to expand the local tax base.[62]

Working-Class Environmentalism. An antigrowth tendency, which contradicts much conventional wisdom about the automatic progrowth reflex of Latinos, is best represented by Mothers of East LA. MOELA long delayed construction of a new state prison on the East Side and successfully defeated other environmentally suspect projects, including the Lancer toxic incinerator. MOELA has worked closely with the Service Employees International Union and the Justice for Janitors Campaign, demonstrating that working-class politics and environmentalism are no longer necessarily mutually exclusive.[63]

Critics tend to dismiss MOELA as the narrow product of neighborhood particularism—the Not In My Back Yard syndrome. This criticism is belied, however by MOELA's success in forging broader ethnic and geographic alliances with other grassroots groups, such as LACTION and the South Central Organizing Committee (SCOC). Professor Rudy Acuña and other sympathizers attribute the failure to date to forge an even more inclusive Anglo-Latino environmental coalition to a default on the part of West Side liberals rather than an unwillingness on the part of East Side activists.[64]

Community Preservationism. Preservationism attempts to maintain the character and stabilize the population of Latino neighborhoods by imposing local priorities on urban redevelopment projects. Composed primarily of working-class renters, the United Neighbors of Temple Beaudry successfully lobbied the city's powerful Community Redevelopment Agency (CRA) and the corporate developers of the Central City West Project to more than double (to 2,000) the number of units of affordable replacement housing allocated for this ambitious attempt to create a "self-contained urban village." As with MOELA, Councilwoman Molina's office was instrumental in helping local residents intervene in the redevelopment process.[65]

More typical of this movement is the homeowner-dominated Lincoln Heights Preservation Association (LHPA). The association organized in the early 1980s to oppose a CRA finding that the area had "minimal historical significance" and preserve its wood-frame Victorian houses against inappropriate rehabilitation by stucco contractors. The association has opposed as too disruptive plans to route the new light-rail transit system into Lincoln Heights. LHPA also has worked positively with the local chamber of commerce to lure young Latino professionals back into the neighborhood.[66]

Viewed in a broader historical context, the evolution of Latino attitudes toward economic development suggests convergence toward a middle ground characterized as either moderately progrowth or moderately slow-growth. For example, Latino elected officials sensitive to the budgetary bottom line and inner-city preservationists concerned about restoring the economic viability of older neighborhoods both are susceptible to sophisticated arguments for "quality of life"-oriented development.

Intermestic Issues

Power ultimately does follow numbers, but rarely in a linear way. The parallelogram of ethnic forces in Los Angeles is leading not exactly to a "Latinized" politics but toward a multicultural hybrid that may be as exotic as the cuisine at one Los Angeles Mexican/Chinese/soul food restaurant. What will be the implications of Los Angeles's exotic new political menu for the California-Mexico Connection and for intermestic issues that transcend the border? In answering this question, we argue that Latino empowerment is already making a positive contribution toward the multicultural Pacific Rim future.

Like New York, Los Angeles already has a foreign policy of its own, reflected in city council debates and resolutions on issues ranging from Tiananmen Square to Soviet Jewry to South Africa to El Salvador. Non-Mexican Latinos are, of course, passionately involved in Central American issues, but Latinos with Mexican roots also have ties that bind. The controversial proposal by a Mexican political party to give nationals living abroad an extraterritorial absentee ballot lays bare community ambivalences about national allegiances. Less controversial are the cooperative efforts between the Mexican government and the "Mexican diaspora" currently institutionalized in the Hispanic Commission (Comisión Mixta de Enlace) and the Directorate General of Mexican Communities Abroad. These efforts have led to a collaborative immigrant education project involving the Mexican Instituto Nacional de Educación para Adultos and the One-Stop Immigration and Educational Center.[67]

So-called intermestic issues can complicate intergroup relations. In the case of Latino-Jewish relations, for example, controversies as far afield as the Soviet Union, the Middle East, and Central America caused shock waves in southern California severe enough for leaders of the two communities recently to hold a regional summit in Anaheim to reconcile their differences. But if Los Angeles does, indeed, elect a Latino mayor in the 1990s, he or she is almost certain to accentuate—as did San Antonio's Henry Cisneros—the positive side of the California-Mexico relationship, already institutionalized in sister city and other collaborative programs.

More important than such symbolic outreach are the ways in which greater Latino empowerment might mitigate the political and economic friction that mars the relationship. Immigration and Naturalization Service factory sweeps and employer sanctions against hiring of undocumented aliens have mischievous intermestic consequences, poisoning the immigration debate on both sides of the border. A positive counter-example is the recent success of Latino politicians and organizations in utilizing the leverage of coalition politics to pressure the NAACP to adopt a resolution calling for the gradual repeal of employer sanctions. This is a portent of how Latino domestic political power may have beneficial intermestic results.[68]

Mexico is at the core of intermestic politics, but there is also a penumbra of broader Latin American concerns, the increasing importance of which is in direct proportion to the continuing refugee influx from Central America. In addition to injecting a new element of complexity into Latino politics, this influx has opened up some surprising possibilities for coalition building. For example, the Indochina Resource Action Center has actively supported congressional legislation granting Salvadorans extended voluntary departure status. Thus, rainbow coalition building around an immigrant rights agenda may be stimulated by the more diverse Latino community's intermestic concerns with political refugees as well as undocumented workers.

Maturing Latino political leadership can help both Los Angeles and California make the transition toward a more prosperous future as part of the Pacific Rim. One manifestation of widening horizons is the formation of the Tri-Ethnic Coalition with a priority on interethnic collaboration on issues of regional growth. Another is the increasingly sophisticated intermestic thinking on the part of politicians such as State Senator Art Torres, a member of the Commission for the Study of International Migration and Cooperative Economic Development. Torres argues that free trade with Mexico, stimulating economic development, ultimately may be one solution to illegal population flows.[69]

Public opinion polls showing strong Latino support for the Free Trade Agreement coexist with considerable evidence of division in the ranks among Latino political elites, particularly those with roots in the labor union movement such as Congressman Esteban E. Torres, a former union organizer. Typically, however, the opponents combine rather narrow objections to the specifics of the agreement with general support for Latino involvement in promoting international trade. Congressman Torres, for example, has his own Pacific Rim agenda, seeking closer economic ties between Latinos and Japan.[70]

"Latino empowerment" is a new term for an old quest: the attempt by America's diverse peoples to combine pride in a distinctive heritage with participation in a unifying civic culture. De Tocqueville called this the "patriotism of the republic," which "grows by the exercise of civil rights." In an age of declining electoral participation, Latino activists seeking mass mobilization through the ballot box (supported, where necessary, by the intervention of the courts) also are trying to revitalize this venerable American tradition of democratic participation. As David Hayes-Bautista has so convincingly shown, the difference in California today is that the traditional social and political contract is increasingly becoming an interethnic as well as intergenerational compact between Latino and non-Latino populations. Carey McWilliams's characterization a half century ago of Latinos as "a voiceless, expressionless minority" is clearly out of date. If California wants to maintain both civil peace and international goodwill as it moves into a new era in which relations with Mexico will be central, it must make this compact acceptable to the Latinos who are voicing the demand for empowerment.[71]

CHAPTER 12

The Mexican Diaspora in California

Limits and Possibilities for the Mexican Government

CARLOS GONZÁLEZ GUTIÉRREZ

IN RECENT DECADES, millions of Mexicans have settled permanently in the United States while maintaining their communal distinctiveness vis-à-vis the rest of U.S. society. As a modern diaspora in international politics, these Mexicans and their children present a critical set of challenges and opportunities to the Mexican government.[1] Depending on Mexico City's long-term vision, the diaspora can become either a source of embarrassing troubles or a precious resource from which to draw support, both in the domestic and international arena. In particular, the Mexican government's success will depend on its ability to use first-generation Mexicans as a bridge to communicate with the diaspora as a whole.

Inherent Heterogeneity

California is home to the largest concentration of Mexicans in the United States. One of every four Californians is Latino (80 percent of them of Mexican origin), and one of every two babies born in the state since 1980 is of Latino parentage. In Los Angeles, the presence of Latinos is even more striking, accounting for 38 percent of the city and county populations. Moreover, half of the undocumented workers from Mexico entering the United States each year cross at the Tijuana–San Diego border.[2]

Only in the most general sense can one speak of a Mexican community in California. The state's Mexican population is a "complex amalgam of interests, backgrounds and goals" that can be stratified not only in terms of nativity (whether they were born in the United States or Mexico) but also in terms of language, length of residence in the United States, or regional, subethnic, and class origins.[3] In many ways a new immigrant from Oaxaca's "sierra" has as little in common with a third-generation, upper-middle-class Mexican American as he does with the Anglo mainstream population.

One of the most striking within-group differences is the gap in socioeconomic status between those who were born in Mexico and those who were born in the United States. A recent survey conducted by the UCLA Chicano Studies Research Center showed that Mexican immigrants in California had a median annual income of $19,433, whereas native Latinos earned $24,057. Mexican immigrants also have an average of 7.8 years of education, compared to 11.3 years for native Latinos.[4] These findings are reinforced by a report issued by the University of California system, which argues that, generally speaking, U.S.-born Latinos earn 25 percent more and have approximately 25 percent more education than immigrants.[5] In addition, U.S.-born Mexicans are usually proficient in English, whereas Mexican immigrants rely on Spanish as their primary tool for communication.

These variations in socioeconomic profile are accompanied by vastly different levels of political clout. As is noted elsewhere in this volume, most Mexican immigrants do not have the right to vote. Even those who become legal U.S. residents wait an average of fifteen years to naturalize, compared to seven to eight years for Asian and European immigrants. Thus, in contrast to their U.S.-born brethren, Mexican immigrants are unable to pursue their interests through the electoral process.

Because they tend to be poor and disenfranchised, Mexican immigrants are also less likely to exercise political leadership on behalf of the Mexican community. Almost no Latino leader of a national or even regional stature is foreign-born. It has been the native-born population, not the immigrants, who have increased the political power of the community and made visible its purchasing power.[6] The struggle has been led by an emerging Mexican-American middle class that graduated from college and is able to compete successfully in the economic market. Unlike foreign-born immigrants, Mexican-American leaders are aware of the increasing political and economic power of the Latino community in the United States and are willing to exercise it. During the last two decades, Mexican Americans have obtained legislation and court decisions that guarantee their status as a "protected minority" regarding issues such as bilingual education, voting rights, school desegregation, and employment practices.

But perhaps the most important sign of within-group differences has to do with self-perceptions. Mexican Americans tend to set themselves apart from Mexican-born immigrants. As Aída Hurtado and Carlos H. Arce point out, sometimes Mexican Americans emphasize the social, cultural, and historical differences that separate them from recent arrivals, with no negative feelings towards Mexico. "However, at other times they distance themselves from first generation Mexicans as a clear rejection to their country of origin and its people."[7] In either case, people who self-consciously designate themselves "Chicano" or "Mexican American" are often making a conscious effort to identify themselves with a culture that is neither "Anglo" nor "Mexican."

The heterogeneity of the Mexican diaspora raises serious challenges to its influence on both sides of the California-Mexico border. Within-group differences place obstacles in the way of group solidarity. On the one hand, the foreign-born segment of the diaspora, which represents more than half of the state's Mexican-origin population, has few resources and limited opportunities. On the other, the growing economic and political clout of U.S.-born Mexicans in California opens up promising new avenues for influence. In this context, the legalization provisions of the 1986 Immigration Reform and Control Act (IRCA) represented a key turning point because they brought closer together the native and foreign-born segments of the Mexican diaspora.

From Sojourners to Settlers

Although people of Mexican descent have lived in California since before the state's incorporation into the Union, the profile of Mexican immigrants in California has changed in recent years. Traditionally, Mexican undocumented workers were temporary, single migrants who worked on the farms and returned to Mexico after the agricultural cycle was over. This type of migrant was called a "sojourner." Since the late 1970s, however, a growing number of Mexican workers have migrated with spouse and children, headed for urban rather than rural areas, and worked in jobs that are year-round rather than seasonal. This type of migrant has been called a "settler."[8]

The shift from sojourner to settler, which resulted from changing socioeconomic conditions on both sides of the border, has been deepened and accelerated by the legalization provisions of IRCA. Before IRCA was passed in 1986, more than 60 percent of Mexican immigrants in the United States were illegal settlers. In the late 1980s, more than three-quarters enjoyed the benefits of legal residence.[9] In the process, more than one million Mexicans in California have gained the opportunity to become legal U.S. residents and improve their economic and political status.

IRCA allowed two groups of undocumented people to regularize their migratory situation. In the first group were immigrants who earned their right to legal permanent residence by demonstrating their continuous presence in the United States since January 1982. Of all the applicants under this program, 1,230,457, or 70 percent, were Mexican, and 54.4 percent were from California, far more than from any other state. Moreover, applicants were concentrated in the 60-mile circle that constitutes the greater Los Angeles area: 35 percent lived in Los Angeles–Long Beach, 5.1 percent in Anaheim–Santa Ana, and 2.9 percent in Riverside–San Bernardino. Twice as many applicants resided in the Los Angeles–Long Beach area as in Texas, the state with the second highest number of applicants, 17.7 percent of the total.[10]

The second group of legalized immigrants were special agricultural workers (SAWs), who adjusted their status by showing that they had been employed in seasonal agricultural work for a minimum of 90 days between May 1985 and May 1986. Of all the applicants under these provisions, 1,040,268, or 81.5 percent, were Mexican. California accounted for 53 percent of the cases, with 15 percent concentrated in Los Angeles–Long Beach, 4.5 percent in Riverside–San Bernardino, and 4.2 percent in Anaheim–Santa Ana.[11]

By legalizing more than two million Mexicans, IRCA removed the clandestine element from the lives of both sojourners and settlers. In the short run, this translates into the freedom to travel back and forth across the border without running the risk of being detained and deported; access to social benefits such as unemployment compensation; greater chances for successfully moving into urban, nonseasonal jobs; and the possibility of becoming eligible for U.S. citizenship after five years.

More significantly, IRCA broke with what Myron Weiner has called "the illusion of impermanence." According to Weiner, diasporas as well as home and host countries tend to ignore the entrenchment of foreign workers in the host economy, in an effort to deny that they are likely to stay for extended periods. The illusion persists because it is not easy for any of the parties to accept reality. Host societies often resist a more pluralistic cultural environment; foreign workers rarely abandon the dreams of returning home and try to maintain their identity through the infrastructure of community life; and home countries, regardless of the workers' remittances, do not want to lose their nationals forever.[12]

According to Wayne Cornelius, IRCA forced many Mexican immigrants to choose between permanent residence in the United States and permanent residence in Mexico:

> It is probable that over the medium to long run, the 1986 immigration law is likely to anchor the legally migrating population more firmly on the US side of the border. . . . With the option of more economically secure, year round

> residence now open to them, more emigrants from traditional sending communities view migration to the US as a permanent change in their life situation, instead of a short-term income-earning strategy.[13]

Thus, at least for this generation of Mexican migrants, the illusion of impermanence is gone. IRCA has given visibility to a large population of Mexicans who have legal status and are likely to become permanent residents, but who will probably never assimilate completely into mainstream U.S. society. As a result, these "Rodinos" (as they are commonly called in reference to the Simpson Rodino law or IRCA) fall somewhere between undocumented Mexican immigrants and U.S.-born Latinos. They are therefore in a unique position to bridge the gap between the heterogenous elements of the Mexican community in California.

Interests and Obligations of the Mexican Government

Why should the Mexican government, with so few resources and so many domestic problems, feel obligated to address the concerns of a Mexican population that has decided to leave the country and settle permanently in the United States?

The importance of cultivating good relations with the Mexican diaspora is closely related to the need to respond to the growing influence of nongovernmental actors in U.S.-Mexican relations. As bilateral ties become more complex, diversified, and decentralized from Mexico City and Washington, D.C., there is likely to be what Cathryn Thorup calls "the pluralization of contacts" between the two societies.[14] In response to greater diversity in Mexican political life, a wide range of U.S. groups is making contact with political actors in Mexico, both within and outside the government. For domestic and foreign policy reasons, Mexico City has a vested interest in being able to count on the support of as many of these groups as possible.

As an important nongovernmental actor, the Mexican diaspora has the potential to affect the interest of the Mexican government in various ways.[15] For example, the diaspora might attempt to use its ties with Mexico and/or its influence on U.S. policy to shape developments south of the border, either in support of or in opposition to the government. Alternatively, officials in the United States might try to mobilize the diaspora as a pressure tool in relations with Mexico. Or the Mexican government might work with the diaspora to push for desired U.S. policies. In each of these cases, the diaspora has the option of forming alliances with other nongovernmental actors on both sides of the border.

The diaspora's ability to influence U.S. policy in a direction that favors the interests of the Mexican government has already been demonstrated in two key cases. During the long congressional battle that eventually resulted in the 1986 Immigration Reform and Control Act, the Mexican-American community helped block several attempts to pass more restrictive legislation. This opposition was seen by most Chicano organizations as a matter of principle and loyalty to the community's origins, as well as a moral obligation to promote solidarity between Mexican Americans and Mexican nationals residing in the United States.[16] Although IRCA was finally passed with restrictive elements, its long delay (and the inclusion of the amnesty program) reflected, in part, the active stance taken by the Mexican-American community. For various reasons, the Mexican government found the diaspora a natural and valuable ally, which, for several years, successfully boycotted a bill that went against Mexico's interests.

The second, more recent, case is the involvement of Latinos in persuading the U.S. Congress to grant the Bush administration "fast-track" authority to initiate free trade negotiations with Mexico and Canada. Bipartisan delegations of up to 200 Latino leaders traveled several times to Mexico City and Washington D.C. to meet the two presidents and express their support for the proposed agreement. Their efforts gave President Bush a crucial base of support in his attempts to shape public opinion against protectionist interests. Democratic Mexican-American congressmen such as Bill Richardson of New Mexico and "Kika" de la Garza of Texas also lobbied for the agreement, not allowing their party affiliation to interfere with their long-standing friendship with Mexico. With the important exception of some Latino labor leaders, the North American Free Trade Agreement (NAFTA) became a unifying issue for the Latino community, at least in these prenegotiation stages.[17] In the process, the Mexican government once again gained a valuable ally in its efforts to bring U.S. policy in line with its interests.

The Mexican government clearly has a vested interest in maintaining and improving its relations with the Mexican diaspora. Because the target population has many faces, there is no option but to pursue several policies at once, which naturally complicates the task of formulating a coherent strategy toward the diaspora as a whole. Through a combination of traditional and new approaches, however, the Mexican government can build strong, long-lasting ties with the different groups in the Mexican community.

Protecting the Interests of Mexican Immigrants

The most immediate and evident obligation of the Mexican government is to protect the interests of its citizens abroad. Following a universally accepted practice that grants any individual residing in a foreign country the right to receive help from his consulate to ensure his rights under host state laws, the Mexican government has a consular network of forty offices in the United States, ten of which are in California.

The need for an active protection strategy on the part of the Mexican government emerged when thousand of Mexicans remained in the territory that Mexico lost to the United States in the mid-nineteenth century. The rights of these Mexicans were laid out in the Treaty of Guadalupe-Hidalgo, a constant source of conflict between the two countries. Since that time, the flows of migratory workers from Mexico have maintained the need for continuous contacts between the Mexican diaspora and the government of its homeland.

Although consular service is usually a peripheral or neglected aspect of the diplomatic history of any country, a long tradition lies behind the Mexican consulates in California, and in general in the Southwest. During the revolutionary period, the consuls played a crucial role as sources of information on the political activities of opposition leaders who, from exile, plotted against the different groups in power. Later, during the 1930s, the Mexican consulates in California and Texas gained legitimacy and respect from the community by organizing the repatriation movement originated during the Great Depression.[18]

The Mexican government has always made clear that protection is the highest priority in its policies towards "el México de afuera."[19] Mexico's traditional position on immigration has been that, although any state enjoys the sovereign prerogative of controlling its borders, the defense of Mexican immigrants' rights in the United States is a dominant and legitimate concern of their homeland, a goal that Mexico will actively pursue within the limits of international law.[20]

Most consular protection is done silently, both because it serves a community of first-generation Mexicans with little clout in the political system, and also because there is a conscious attempt on the part of the consulate to avoid any unnecessary publicity concerning its protection services. When dealing with local authorities, the trick is to be effective without appearing confrontational, since every hostile encounter jeopardizes the long-term relationship that the consulate needs to cultivate with immigration, police, and civil authorities.

The protection of Mexican immigrants should continue to be an integral part of the Mexican government's strategy vis-à-vis the Mexican diaspora in California. Mexico's long tradition of consular protection has made the defense of human rights of Mexicans living abroad a part of the country's political culture, and the consuls are held accountable for their ability to perform their job on these grounds. Particularly during hard times, the collective frustration of being unable to produce enough jobs for the population is to some extent ameliorated by showing concern for the fate of Mexican immigrants. Moreover, regardless of how ambitious the promotional activities of the Mexican government in California might be, the ties between the Mexican community and the government of its homeland will never get closer if the latter fails to deliver in its commitment to protect the basic interests of its citizens abroad.

Promoting Ties with the Mexican Immigrant Community

A second important area of consular responsibility is to promote the social and cultural bonds that link Mexican immigrants to their homeland. These promotional activities include educational and cultural programs (such as the celebration of a Mexican holiday, the organization of music concerts, school conferences, and teacher exchanges) and consular involvement in community affairs. In the latter area, the consul is responsible for supporting the organizational efforts of the Mexican community and representing the Mexican state whenever necessary. The purpose is to enhance the efforts of Mexicans in the United States to improve their standard of living, and to foster relations with their communities of origin.

One of the most promising new initiatives in community affairs is support for the organization of Mexican immigrants into regional clubs. Regional clubs are an institutional mechanism the community develops to strengthen the social networks upon which massive immigration rests.[21] These clubs often operate around athletic competition or the annual celebration of a patron saint. In Los Angeles, for example, immigrants from certain regions of Oaxaca play basketball every weekend, while immigrants from Michoacán or Jalisco play soccer. These games offer the community a valuable opportunity to socialize and exchange information about mutual concerns such as jobs and housing problems in Los Angeles, or the need to send money to their home towns.[22]

Given the huge Mexican-origin population in the greater Los Angeles area, it makes sense to take advantage of their loyalty to their regions of origin, which is a much stronger link than their attachment to class or type of employment (let alone a political party). Sharing in a community of origin creates in the "paisanos" a reinforced commitment to one another for mutual assistance in a hostile land and strengthens their self-imposed duty to help the communities they left behind.

Although clubs and associations of first-generation Mexican immigrants have always existed, their "boom" in recent years reflects the astounding growth of the immigrant population and the end of "the illusion of impermanence." This growing phenomenon offers the Mexican government a unique opportunity to build strong and lasting ties with the immigrant community in California.

The case of the Federación de Clubes Zacatecanos Unidos (FCZU) illustrates this point. The FCZU is a confederation of several clubs from Zacatecas's *colonia* in Los Angeles that meets once a year with the governor of their state of origin. At each gathering, the clubs present a report of the public works sponsored in their home towns during the previous twelve months and describe projects for the years to come. The governor, in turn, reports to the community on the level of state commitment to the clubs' projects, usually matching every dollar offered by the clubs. These yearly meetings build confidence in the *colonia* and encourage the clubs to continue helping their communities of origin.

The role of the Mexican consulate and the Secretariat of External Relations (specifically the Directorate General of Mexican Communities Abroad) in these ventures is to coordinate efforts by state governments to identify the leaders of each community and cultivate a long-term relationship. During 1990 and 1991, the governors of the states of Zacatecas, Chihuahua, Jalisco, Nayarit, Sinaloa, and Baja California visited Los Angeles (most of them more than once) to meet with their respective *colonias*. Communities of people from Oaxaca, Durango, Michoacán, and Colima are also working to establish relationships with the governments of their home states.[23]

But the role of the Mexican government is not simply to encourage immigrant groups to send their money back to Mexico. Perhaps even more important is to help them improve the quality of their lives in California. To some extent regional clubs and state governments work in that direction by promoting the mobilization of first-generation Mexicans. To work with fellow countrymen for the development of the community of origin creates new incentives to help each other in the solution of common local problems in the United States. This is not enough, however. The Mexican government at the federal level bears a greater responsibility as the only entity capable of providing social services to the Mexico-born portion of the diaspora. The administration of President Salinas has been the first to acknowledge this by formulating programs that aim to reach the masses of Mexican citizens living in the U.S. by helping them to meet their basic needs in areas such as health and education.

Three examples are worth mentioning. In April 1990, Mexico's National System of Social Security, the Instituto Mexicano del Seguro Social (IMSS), began to offer comprehensive health coverage in Mexico to the families of migrant workers living in the United States, based on payment of an annual quota that is considerably lower than U.S. insurance premiums. Cesar Chavez's United Farm Workers of America was the first union to sign, and today the IMSS has opened offices in several key consulates in the United States (Fresno and Los Angeles in California) to handle a growing demand for its services. A second example is the arrangement reached between the Instituto Nacional de Educación para Adultos (INEA), a government agency in charge of adult education in Mexico, and One Stop Immigration and Educational Center (OSIEC), whereby the Mexican government has agreed to sell 150,000 adult educational packages (books and teaching materials) at wholesale prices for use by OSIEC students, most of them Mexican immigrants who need to improve their ability to read and write in Spanish in order to learn English as a second language. A third example is the opening of an office of CONASIDA (the government's agency dedicated to preventing the spread of the AIDS virus in Mexico) at the Mexican consulate in Los Angeles to contribute to the fight against AIDS within the Mexican community in California.

Promoting Ties with the Mexican-American Community

The Mexican government also stands to reap significant benefits from improving its channels of communication with the increasingly powerful Mexican-American community. Sooner or later, Chicanos will reduce the disparity between their numbers and their political power at the federal, state, and local levels. As they consolidate their position on the national political scene, they are likely to concentrate less on ethnic issues (such as bilingual education or immigration) and more on other areas, including Mexico's domestic affairs.[24]

In addition to gaining political influence, Mexican Americans are becoming important economic actors as consumers and entrepreneurs. According to the Census Bureau, nationwide the number of Latino-owned companies nearly doubled from 233,975 in 1982 to 422,373 in 1987 (Los Angeles had the most in the nation with 56,679). Those companies represented 3 percent of all U.S. firms and 1 percent of U.S. sales.[25] In the context of growing integration between Mexico and United States, Latino entrepreneurs could become a valuable source of capital, goods, and markets. They might also be able to serve as a bridge between Mexican business leaders and the U.S. economy at large.

The modern version of the dialogue between the Mexican government and Mexican-American organizations dates back to the beginning of the 1970s, when president Luis Echeverría promoted contacts with leaders from the Southwest. Because there has never been a clearly identifiable pyramid of Chicano leadership, Mexican presidents have tried to meet with leaders of different groups with varying degrees of success. Most of the concrete results of these contacts have been cultural, such as funding of scholarship programs for Chicanos interested in studying in Mexico or the distribution of Mexican books in U.S. libraries and schools.[26]

Since the administration of President Echeverría, Mexican-American leaders have met quite frequently with Mexican presidents. In fact, Mexican-American leader José Angel Gutiérrez, founder of La Raza Unida party, notes that from 1976 to 1986 Chicano leaders had more "face to face meetings with Mexican Presidents, cabinet members, ambassadors and other high ranking government officials than they had with their counterparts in the United States."[27] Through these contacts, both parties have tried to explore areas of mutual interest and reap the benefits of networking and informational exchanges.

The two government agencies primarily involved in the relationship with the Mexican-American community have been the Secretariat of Labor and the Secretariat of External Relations. During the administration of President López Portillo, the Secretariat of Labor was responsible for managing relations with the Hispanic Commission (Comisión Mixta de Enlace), which was formed by several Mexican-American organizations to institutionalize dialogue with the Mexican government.[28] The labor secretariat has also produced studies and official reports regarding the situation of people of Mexican origin in the United States.[29]

The Secretariat of External Relations has had a more permanent relationship with the Mexican-American community through its consulates and the Mexican embassy in Washington. In February 1990, however, the ministry's involvement underwent a qualitative change with the formation of the Directorate General of Mexican Communities Abroad (DGMCA). Created by presidential decree in response to a proposal presented by Mexican-American groups during the campaign of then-candidate Carlos Salinas de Gortari, the DGMCA is responsible for promoting ties with the Mexican diaspora.[30]

The DGMCA represents a promising development in the Mexican government's approach to the diaspora. The agency has three main objectives: to strengthen the links between Mexicans on both sides of the border in six principal fields: business, tourism, culture, education, sports, and health and social welfare; to improve the image of Mexican Americans in Mexico by disseminating information about their struggles and goals; and to promote a better understanding of Mexico's reality among Mexicans in the United States.

In its two years of activities, the DGMCA has been successful in establishing its presence in what can be called the Mexican-American establishment. There is virtually no major event or convention in the community at which a representative of the Mexican government is not present. By now, most Mexican-American leaders know personally the group of consuls and functionaries from the Secretariat of External Relations who are in charge of these programs. In most cases, and as a result of a conscious effort by the last two administrations, the heads of the consular offices of Mexico in the United States are respected figures of the community, active in promoting good relations with Mexican-American leaders who reside within their jurisdictions.

Much more difficult and challenging is the task of reforming the public image of Mexican Americans in Mexico and especially of gaining domestic support for Mexico's policies towards the huge Mexican diaspora. Public perceptions do not change easily, and budgetary constraints are likely to limit forever the capacity of the home country to spend its scarce resources beyond its borders, let alone for the benefit of the foreign-born portion of the diaspora. Consequently, the DGMCA is forced to formulate programs whose survival does not depend on any subsidy by the Mexican government.

Perhaps DGMCA's most important contribution in this regard has been to act as an ombudsman within the Mexican government, helping to make deals between Latino organizations and private and public agencies in Mexico. For instance, the DGMCA was involved in the initial negotiations to "export" the services of the IMSS, INEA, and CONASIDA described in the previous section. Other examples, which more directly affect the Mexican-American population, are exchange programs for Latino students in several Mexican universities and international competitions hosted by the government's athletic agency, the Consejo Nacional del Deporte, which allow teams of the Mexican-American community to play against their Mexican counterparts in a wide range of sports and categories.

A final example involves the Mexican-American business community. Since most Latino companies are small, it is not easy for them to get the attention devoted to big U.S. corporations. The average sales for a Latino-owned enterprise in 1987 were $59,000 nationwide, about one-third the national average.[31] The DGMCA helps these smaller companies by promoting special arrangements. For example, the DGMCA recently convinced the main Mexican chamber of commerce to sign agreements of cooperation with the U.S.-Hispanic Chamber of Commerce to foster trade and joint ventures between people of Mexican origin on both sides of the border. If the North American Free Trade Agreement is passed, Latino business leaders may go further to demand the establishment of trade and investment "quotas" in exchange for their lobbying efforts on behalf of the agreement. Such a proposal is regarded by some observers as the natural next step in the "special treatment" that Mexico has begun to offer the U.S.-born segment of the Mexican diaspora.

Conclusion

The presence of approximately six million people of Mexican origin in California (more than half born in Mexico) in itself is a matter of concern for the Mexican government. Even if the diaspora were not interested in or capable of influencing Sacramento or Washington on behalf of their homeland, the Mexican government would nevertheless need to formulate policy responses to the wide range of issues that arise from the diaspora's role as a nongovernmental actor in U.S.-Mexico relations.

The Mexican government has begun to expand the scope of its relations with the Mexican diaspora in a tacit recognition that there is much to do besides offering the traditional consular services to recent immigrants. In this sense, IRCA has been paradoxically of great help. Because IRCA broke with the illusion of impermanence, it is now clear that millions of Mexicans will not come back to reside permanently in their homeland, regardless of whether they apply for U.S. citizenship. Thus, the need to implement a long-term strategy for this population has become more evident than ever.

Notwithstanding the costs to Mexico of the permanent absence of a large portion of its population, IRCA has created a new milieu in California that is very advantageous for Mexico: more than half of the Mexican diaspora is made up of precisely the kind of people (first-generation immigrants) who are predisposed to strengthen their relations with Mexicans on the other side of the border. To the dismay of the Mexican government, however, this receptive audience will not last long. As the children of this generation of Mexicans are born in the United States (thereby acquiring U.S. citizenship), the U.S.-born members of the Mexican diaspora will again be in the majority, even if immigration from Mexico returns to its pre-IRCA levels. To the extent that second- and third-generation Mexican Americans perceive themselves differently from their immigrant parents, they may not be as receptive to the type of transborder contacts easily cultivated among first-generation Mexicans.

For these reasons, the Mexican government should formulate a long-term strategy to use the generation of Rodinos to build bridges to the Mexican diaspora's future generations. The starting point of such a strategy would be to show them that Mexico is interested in their well-being in California, regardless of whether they are likely to remain in the United States forever. After all, Mexicans in California overwhelmingly hold the least desirable and worst-paying jobs in the economy, lagging behind the income and schooling levels of the Anglo, mainstream population. Such an obvious fact compels the Mexican government to be as interested in improving the standard of living of its nationals in California as it is in developing their communities of origin. Vis-à-vis their homeland, the people of Mexican descent must be seen as legitimate recipients of aid, and not simply as potential donors.

Through its traditional protection services, the development of innovative social service programs, and the strengthening of "community-affairs" activities, Mexico has shown its concern for the welfare of its diaspora. Having in mind a longer term commitment, three main areas of future work should be undertaken: education, business, and community mobilization.

Investing in the education of first-generation Mexicans and their children (the next generation of Mexican Americans) would certainly encourage closer ties between homeland and diaspora. Bilingual education is needed to help the children of Mexican immigrants make the transition into an environment in which English seems to be the only way to get ahead. And California is 12,000 bilingual teachers short, according to the California Association of Bilingual Education. In addition to providing training courses and materials to U.S. instructors (which the Secretariat of Public Education and the DGMCA are already beginning to make available), Mexico could "lend" on a temporary basis bilingual teachers to California schools. Moreover, the consolidation of Mexican cultural institutes like the one created in Los Angeles through the sponsorship of the Secretariat of External Relations could lead to a greater supply of courses and educational services, such as providing transcripts and certificates for studies completed in Mexico.

In spite of its relatively small economic importance, and regardless of the proposed North American Free Trade Agreement, the more organized the diaspora, the stronger the demand for a special relationship with Mexico in the economic arena. As in other ethnic communities in the United States, Mexican-American leaders encourage companies owned by people of Mexican origin to purchase from each other and to support each other. The Mexican government can be of great assistance in this process by supporting a greater exposure of Mexican-American firms and products in Mexico.

On the one hand, Mexico City should facilitate an inevitable trend towards decentralization in the relationship between diaspora and homeland. State governments are in many ways closer to their respective *colonias* thanks to their regional perspective. Immigrants want to participate in the economic development of their communities, and they must feel encouraged to do so by both state and federal governments. Public expenditures at the local level are better invested when coordinated with the money remittances of immigrants. Besides, Mexican nongovernmental actors such as universities and business chambers complement the limited resources of public institutions.

On the other hand, the community mobilization efforts of the Mexican government help recent immigrants gain stature and respectability within the diaspora. Although Mexican-American leaders are interested in promoting solidarity with Mexican immigrants as a matter of coherence, moral obligation, and political convenience (especially in terms of reapportionment and redistricting), nobody will better represent their interests than themselves. By promoting their mobilization in regional clubs, the Mexican government indirectly strengthens their ability to change the environment that surrounds them.

As argued in the introduction, the Mexican diaspora can be either a defiant force or a valuable asset in its relations with the Mexican government. Either way, its size and changing profile will bring it increasing influence on both sides of the border. Although long-term strategies are contrary to the nature of almost any government, there seems to be no alternative if Mexico is to build a mutually beneficial relationship with its diaspora in California.

PART IV

Conclusions

CHAPTER 13

From State to "state"

Managing Mexico's California Connection

CARLOS RICO

CALIFORNIA PLAYS a key role in Mexico-U.S. relations. A significant share of nongovernmental bilateral interactions, which cover practically all the topics considered most significant at the national level, involves actors based in the Golden State. During the 1980s, the combined impact of geographic proximity, wealth, and economic dynamism brought U.S.-Mexican transnational relations, particularly in the southern portion of the state, to a remarkable level. It also steadily increased the significance of the "California connection," not only for Mexican exporters, migrants, or investors, but for Mexican federal authorities as well. This relevance in the wider Mexico-U.S. context, as well as the considerable parallelism between the key components of the federal and the state agendas, is summarized by the frequent references in this volume to California's Mexican connection in which one could easily substitute "California" for "the United States" without fundamentally distorting the authors' meaning.[1]

Direct communication with California-based actors would seem, in the face of the information presented in the preceding essays, not only a good idea but an almost unavoidable necessity for Mexico's federal government. Such communication, however, flies in the face of well-entrenched practices and beliefs that question the propriety and even the advisability of establishing direct ties between political entities of very different legal and political standing. With all the constraints that economic and political realities place on the exercise of its sovereignty, Mexico is an independent state. With all its wealth and dynamism, California isn't. This simple difference has crucial implications for defining the context in which those aspects of public policy affected by "the connection" are framed and managed. California may, for example, have a much larger economic product than Mexico, but Mexican federal authorities control the legal rules of interaction with other international partners—which their California counterparts do only in a limited way. This essay suggests that, far from precluding the possibility of direct communication, the potential for "trading constraints" implicit in these asymmetries may open the possibility for mutually fruitful communication between the Mexican federal government, on the one hand, and California governmental and nongovernmental actors, on the other.

The relevance of direct communication with California-based actors for the Mexican federal government starts with their potential impact on the definition and implementation of federal rules and policies that help shape interactions at this more localized level. There is, however, a second set of reasons that argue in favor of establishing direct lines of communication between Mexican federal authorities and California actors. Many of the key issues of the Mexico-California agenda have dimensions that fall in the sphere of responsibility and authority of state and local governments. Whether or not Mexican federal authorities would prefer otherwise, key aspects of their own public policy agenda are a part of U.S. domestic debates that are frequently played out at the state and even the local levels. Promoting the interests of Mexican communities abroad; protecting the rights of Mexican citizens who may reside permanently or temporarily in the state; developing adequate services for urban communities on the Mexican side of the border, which are now among the largest population centers in the country; adequately regulating natural-resource usage; environmental protection; attracting foreign investors—all these are examples of Mexican public-policy objectives involving state and local spheres of responsibility in California. If Mexican authorities are to affect decisions that will prove increasingly relevant to the success of their policy initiatives, then they must be willing and ready to let their perspective be known in the relevant political arenas. What are the key audiences to be reached? With what policy instruments? Under what basic constraints? These are the issues that will be discussed in this essay, following a brief consideration of the wider context in which any effort on the part of Mexican federal authorities to manage their California connection must be placed.

The Wider Context of the Mexico-California Connection

From the perspective of Mexico City, the California connection is, at the very least, part of three different axes of relations with the United States. First, contacts with state and local actors must be placed within the wider context of the bilateral relation. Second, the fact that a significant share of contacts takes place at the border makes these contacts an important component of interactions in which other states of the Union present similar problems and opportunities. Third, the connection has dimensions that are both specific and statewide. From these three axes emerge the basic dimensions that a Mexico City strategy directed at dealing with the policy challenges present in these different spheres should contemplate: federal / federal dealings, Mexican federal / U.S. border states communication, and Mexican federal / California state and local actors contacts. These three levels of interaction are not alternative options open to Mexican federal actions, but different facets of wider policies, which provide the context of California-specific actions and initiatives and which should be dealt with simultaneously.

Contact with their U.S. federal counterparts has been the preferred option of Mexico City officials for reasons that go beyond the simple search for legal and political symmetry. In most cases the basic issues involved in the California connection are not peculiar to that state but expressions (even if very intense ones) of more general challenges and opportunities. As a result, even within a single issue area, the trade-offs involved in any negotiation frequently involve actors based in states other than California. Also, many historical precedents suggest that federal involvement is crucial if key issues are to be adequately treated.[2] There are, however, some important problems involved in an exclusive reliance on contacts at the federal level. It is not always easy to involve U.S. federal authorities in issues that may not be as high on their policy agendas as they are on the agendas of Mexican federal authorities. The federal/state distribution of responsibilities is quite different on each side of the border for some of the key issues involved in the management of the California connection.[3]

Mexican federal involvement results not only from the more centralized nature of the Mexican political system but also from the simple fact that the majority of bilateral interactions are more important for Mexico and Mexican federal authorities than they are for the United States as a whole or for U.S. federal authorities.[4] On questions perceived as important south of the border, Mexican federal authorities may look for a Washington commitment equal to their own without finding it. This, however, is only one dimension of the "decision-making dilemma." Frequently, in issues of interest to them, California local authorities may look for Mexican counterparts at their own level only to find them heavily constrained not only legally but financially. Jorge Bustamante describes, from a clearly Mexican perspective, one instance of the "dialogue of the deaf" in which local authorities frequently engage as a result:

> Local San Diego authorities tried to pressure local Tijuana authorities to look for a solution, failing to realize all the procedures that must be followed in issues of an international character between both countries. They thought that there was nothing more local than the breaking of a municipal drainage. What they didn't take into account was that the breaking of a municipal drainage just along the international demarcation, producing effects on the other side of the border, automatically becomes a question of international character that goes beyond municipal and even state competence to discuss it or solve it. . . . Municipal authorities in Tijuana correctly considered that the issue went beyond their jurisdiction . . . [and] . . . referred the issue to federal authorities whose answer could not be as opportune as required by the local political situation as a result of the distance between the Northern border and Mexico City. . . . From the Mexican point of view, the environmental perturbation caused by the breaking of the Tijuana drainage should be contemplated in the global context of environmental problems along the whole border, in which in some cases Mexicans are responsible and in others, North Americans are responsible.[5]

In order to solve this dilemma, some voices, particularly on the U.S. side of the border, advocate leaving the management of some of these questions to local authorities in both countries. In their view, the practice of Mexican federalism should more closely resemble that of the United States. The literature on planning urban services in a border setting, for example, abounds with such suggestions, made from both academic and policymaker perspectives.[6] Brian Bilbray, then supervisor of the First District of the county of San Diego and formerly mayor of the city of Imperial Beach, summarizes the rationale for such proposals:

> The cities of Imperial Beach and Tijuana are adjacent, with all the social communication which that implies; so when we have a local issue, I'd like to try to approach the problem like we would a problem between Imperial Beach and Coronado. But when we've tried to do so, we are told, "We really do not have the authority to even discuss the issue with you." Someone who is used to amicable local interchange is shocked by such a response and might end up getting "burned."[7]

For some of the reasons summarized above, however, federal involvement on the Mexican side seems unavoidable. In a mirror image of the situation described in relation to federal involvement on each side of the border, local authority involvement on the U.S. side does not necessarily lead to a symmetric outcome south of the border. The exercise of authority by local and state agencies in the foreign policy sphere involves, in the first instance, complex legal issues. The Mexican Constitution forbids state governments to become involved in international negotiations.

Once again, however, an emphasis on principle and on the legal and political factors constraining the sphere of responsibility and authority of Mexican local and state officials is only one of the elements involved. We are dealing, after all, with relations between nations of widely different levels of development. As a result not only of Mexican centralism but also of this very fact, there are wide differences in the resources available to local authorities on each side of the border in dealing with common challenges. The need for partners who are in a realistic position to make deals constitutes a further reason for Mexican federal involvement in these issues.

Similar observations may be made on arguments in favor of direct state/state relations, sometimes based on the precedent of arrangements worked out, under different institutional and financial constraints, along the northern border of the United States.[8] Some of the issues most relevant to the proposals of local/local communication are in fact common to other states along the border,[9] a parallelism that brings back the question of trade-offs beyond California. As a result, Mexican federal authorities need to place such issues not only in a national context but also among similar questions that may emerge in relations with other border states. Some of the relevant audiences and even the policy instruments available for communications with California actors involve organizations, institutions, and even federal-level instances of communication common to all of them. Mexican federal authorities, in fact, have paid some attention to California not in the context of global policies towards the U.S. but, rather, as a part of their overall policies towards the border. This element should also be included in any attempt to manage the connection.

As stated above, however, California's relevance to and implications for Mexico are also the result of both specific and statewide dimensions. The links between bilateral interactions that take place or have a highly acute expression at the border and those beyond that area are particularly relevant in this connection.[10] It is perhaps exaggerated, in the context of a discussion of Mexico's California connection, to talk of a "San/San" region, extending from San Diego north to San Francisco, but the San Diego / Los Angeles interaction in this regard is certainly not only very real, but crucial in defining the weight of southern California in the bilateral agenda.

The specific and statewide dimensions of the connection also reflect the fact that Mexico-California relations involve topics that go beyond border interactions. The state's connections with Mexican states well beyond Baja California and documented instances of direct communication between local California interests and Mexican federal government agencies have included questions that are not strictly border-related.[11] Such cases of direct communication with California-based local actors in turn constitute relevant examples of the potentially large number of relevant actors that a statewide Mexican strategy aimed at managing the connection would have to reach. The complex network of intergovernmental relations involved and the intergovernmental scope of many of the programs, which, for example, may affect Mexican citizens living in California, and the impact of regulatory activities dealing with equal opportunity in employment, education, and housing, with public utility management in border cities, or even with such activities as Mexican deposits in California banks suggest the potential breadth of any such strategy. A starting point in its formulation should be the consideration of both the most important audiences it must address and the instruments available to reach them.

Key Audiences

The basic dimensions of California's impact on Mexico-U.S. relations—as an influence on federal and/or "whole border" policies and in and by itself—define the basic profile of the audiences that a Mexican federal strategy should strive to reach. The state's representatives in Washington, for example, constitute a key audience in any effort at communicating Mexican perspectives and influencing the making of federal rules and policies, which may, in turn, have an impact on the connection. They are not the only members of Congress who follow and influence "Mexican issues," but they do represent a good example of an attention based not only on personal or wider, national concerns, but also on the concrete interests and priorities of their constituents. Those constituencies must, as a result, also be included in communication efforts.

Executive officials at the state and local levels should constitute a further objective of Mexican communication efforts. This, again, is not restricted to California-specific activities but covers the other two axes of the state's relevance. Its executive, for example, frequently a national-level political figure, is one of four U.S. and six Mexican governors who participate in the annual meetings of the Conference of Border Governors. There is clearly a need to improve communication with this key component of the connection.[12] The increasing role of local authorities in relation to Mexican issues also makes them unavoidable components of a Mexico City strategy of communication with California-based actors. I have already mentioned the precedents of federal/local contacts. Sometimes, the initiative for those contacts has been taken by California local authorities.[13] Contacts with executive agencies, however, should not stop at this level.

Local California authorities also frequently belong to organizations of a state nature, such as the Southern California Association of Governments, or a wider one, such as the Organization of United States Border Cities and Counties, which are significant audiences for Mexican perspectives on some issues. Functionally organized bureaucracies such as school districts and special districts perform single-service functions, frequently in direct contact with federal agencies, which are also often directly relevant to Mexican interests. The Southern California Metropolitan Water District, one of the largest special districts in the U.S., for example, is a key player in water policymaking issues, which may have a direct impact on Mexican border communities. The "issue-networks" involved in the operation of these "single-purpose governments" should also ideally be incorporated in Mexican communication efforts.[14]

Once one assumes that actions by state- and even local-level authorities have an impact on Mexico and California-Mexico relations and should be monitored and, if possible, influenced, it is not hard to take the next step and open the possibility of extending those contacts to a large number of California-based actors. The state court system, for instance, is open to actions such as initiating litigation and presenting amicus curiae briefs in cases filed by other contestants. Members of the state legislature, with whom direct contacts until now have been practically nonexistent, also constitute a clearly relevant audience for Mexican efforts. Congressional appropriations and authorizations are also involved in many of the topics of actual or potential interest to Mexican authorities. As is the case on Capitol Hill, committees and subcommittees, staffs, and so on open several points of access to the lawmaking process through which Mexican concerns may be introduced.

The emphasis on the creation of direct lines of communication with California constituencies, already mentioned in connection to the U.S. Congress, is also relevant in this context. It underlines the wider need to affect the overall political climate in which both governmental and nongovernmental actors act and interact—regardless of the degree to which California's representatives in Washington and Sacramento or state and local officials share their constituents' attitudes and perceptions towards Mexico, the Mexican government, and key issues of interest to both. The relative priority of Mexican issues and issues of concern to Mexico in the agendas of nongovernmental actors, their visibility, and the intensity of feeling they elicit all argue in favor of this dimension's being considered a truly crucial component of the strategy to deal with the California connection.[15] Attentive publics, opinion leaders, and local influentials in general and in specific relation to the issues of interest to Mexico should, then, constitute a key target of Mexican efforts. Identifying them will be a first, urgent, and unavoidable task in this regard. There are, however, other reasons to emphasize relations with nongovernmental actors in the state. Some dimensions of the key issues in the connection are of concern mostly to private actors. Economic promotion efforts, for example, should clearly be directed at them. As Carlos González Gutiérrez describes in this volume, Mexican residents may also be seen not only as potential beneficiaries of contacts developed with California actors, but also as targets of those efforts.

A different kind of California "audience" may in fact be located in Mexico City. The California Office of Representation there should also be considered a potential channel of communication with the Office of the Governor and other relevant actors, both public and private. California is one of four states (Illinois, Louisiana and Texas are the others) with institutional representation in Mexico.[16] There are, however, limits to the potential relevance of the office as an overall channel of communication. From the point of view of the state, activities such as organizing visits of business people or providing information to interested Mexican nongovernmental actors are clearly important. From the perspective of Mexico City, however, these functions and policy objectives are not only considerably limited but also quite different from what would be required in the context of a wider communication effort that the Mexican federal government might consider. They cover only a small fraction of the issues involved in the management of the California connection. This difference in perspective has contributed to a situation in which, as an official of the Secretaría de Relaciones Exteriores's North American Affairs Directorate puts it, the California Office has "practically no contact whatsoever"[17] with the Mexican Foreign Ministry.

Finally, one may count a significant number of binational bodies that may also be seen as audiences of Mexico City's communication efforts. Functional committees and organizations that put in touch some of the most relevant nongovernmental actors on both sides of the border or entities such as the U.S.-Mexico Border Health Association, which have contributed to the creation of channels of informal binational communication; contact between state and local authorities in both countries, such as the Commission of the Californias, created in 1964, through which some degree of state-level dialogue among Baja California, Baja California Sur, and California has been initiated; the Sister Cities International program, which has also established links between communities on both sides of the border (Riverside-Ensenada, San Bernardino–Mexicali, Tijuana–Imperial Beach); the by-now institutionalized conferences of border governors—all represent relevant audiences that may be profitably approached. In fact, the present realities of Mexican federalism may raise the temptation to use these state and local instances of communication as "policy instruments" available to the Mexican federal government. In my view, however, they should not be considered and treated as such but rather as additional audiences, involving in this case both Mexican and Californian actors. The latter should be reached using the several channels of communication open at present.

Available Channels and Instruments of Communication

In the recent past, visits of the Mexican president to California have not only been considerably more frequent than at any other time and served as catalysts of Mexican attention to the connection but have also become significant opportunities to transmit the concerns of Mexican federal authorities to California-based actors. There is, however, a clear need for follow-up activities and more stable contacts. A third-axis strategy (Mexican federal/California state and local actors) such as the one proposed in this essay would involve policy instruments available with the other two. The Mexican embassy in Washington, for instance, would have to actively participate in some of the dimensions involved in contacting California representatives there. The wide (and still untapped) potential of Mexican consulates in the state, however, should provide the backbone of such an exercise. There are other instances of a Mexican federal presence in the state—such as the Banco Nacional de Comercio Exterior and the Secretaría de Turismo offices in Los Angeles—which could and should be incorporated in the wider context. But the consulates represent the more general instances of representation available to the Mexican federal government. As such, they should play a key role not only in establishing and cultivating contacts and direct lines of communication with California's governmental and nongovernmental actors, but also in coordinating the efforts of other Mexican representations within their jurisdiction.

The weight of the California connection for bilateral relations is summarized by California's significant share of Mexican autonomous consular offices. Mexico has 25 general consulates (GCs) and 27 career consulates (CCs) throughout the world, of which 12 GCs and 24 CCs are in the United States. Of these, 3 GCs (Los Angeles, San Diego, and San Francisco), 5 CCs (Calexico, Fresno, Sacramento, San Bernardino, and San Jose), and 2 out of the 3 consular agencies that the Mexican consular service has worldwide (both dependent of the Los Angeles consulate: Oxnard and Santa Ana) are located in the Golden State.[18] Only Texas has a larger Mexican presence in terms of the number of consulates: 4 GCs and 9 CCs.[19] The simple comparison of the number of consulates, however, sharply underestimates the weight of the Mexican offices in California. Here again, a clear concentration in the Los Angeles area emerges when one takes into account the number of personnel in each office and the number of "consular acts" performed by them. In both cases (60 people without taking into account the consular agencies, over 70 if they are included, and 350,000 consular acts), Los Angeles is far ahead of any other Mexican consulate not only in the United States but also worldwide. The most active Texas consulate, for example, performs a number of consular acts quite close to that of the other two Mexican GCs in California but that represents less than one-sixth of those for which the Los Angeles consulate is responsible.[20]

The kinds of activities reflected by these consular acts emphasize the large share of services provided to the Mexican population in the area. Those activities are frequently related to some of the policy objectives discussed earlier in this essay. In Los Angeles alone, for example, more than 3,000 "protection acts" per year put the Mexican consular personnel in touch with federal authorities such as the Immigration and Naturalization Service, county authorities such as sheriffs, and city authorities such as chiefs of police. Protection activities are not restricted to undocumented workers; the possibility, for example, of institutional violence affects Mexican legal residents not only in communities near the border but in other areas as well. Los Angeles, for example, is—to put it mildly—not an exception in this regard, as the Warren Christopher Commission documented in 1991.

Protection-related consular acts, however, only scratch the surface of the kind of California-aimed strategy proposed in these pages. Promotion activities (from Mexico's image to trade and investment), for instance, exist but have a much lower place in the present agenda of Mexican consular activities in California. Documents that try to clarify aspects of Mexican labor law or foreign investment policies, for example, are available in Mexican consulates, but efforts to actively promote a discussion of their contents with some of the key audiences identified above are quite limited. It is also only very recently that consulates are being used to convey Mexican perceptions on wider political or other dimensions of the bilateral relation—activities that until a few years ago were explicitly forbidden to them. Significant change is implied in the instruction that Mexican consular officials now receive, as the director general for consular services in the Secretaría de Relaciones Exteriores puts it, to "open their mouth."[21] The large number of potential audiences previously described, however, clearly suggests the need to step up those efforts, in particular given the large share of the attention of Mexican consular officials presently taken up by politically motivated efforts to improve communications with Mexican residents in the state. It is quite telling of the dominant priorities in the early 1990s, for example, that the Sacramento consulate is a career consulate with a staff of only four people.

Bilateral instances of communication at the federal level, given the intense contacts with relevant state and local actors kept by their U.S. sections, may also be useful in this context. The best example is the work of the International Boundary and Water Commission (IBWC), which has been identified as proof of the "special relationship" between Mexico and the United States.[22] A significant number of the issues involved in the border-management dimension of the connection touch on the sphere of competence of the IBWC. Although its original (1889) mandate was strictly related to boundary issues, it was expanded in 1906 and then in 1944 to cover the management of the Colorado, Bravo (Grande), and Tia Juana rivers. It now deals with not only the problems of boundary mapping but also flood control and quality and sanitary conditions of water resources. The implementation of its decisions often involves state and local authorities on both sides of the border, making it a particularly interesting example not only of the federal/local interface described above but also of its potential as a channel of communication with relevant state and local actors. A critical aspect of the U.S. section's effectiveness in developing its functional domain has been its ability to establish intimate ties with the four border states. Although it implements national interests, it is in fact often viewed as a regional agency and does little to dispel this image—and in fact profits from it. The IBWC-U.S. tries to maintain close links with border-state governments and congressional delegations. It is something of an anomaly at the level of the U.S. Department of State since it has—in its own view—an effective constituency from which it can draw support for its functions and projects. Since the commission must go to Congress for funds with which to initiate new projects, these alliances are a crucial aspect of the domestic politics of the U.S. section.[23]

Even this all-too-brief description of the policy instruments available to the Mexican federal government in managing its California connection suggests that there is considerable space for improvement in this sphere. Attempts on the part of Mexican federal authorities to reach the audiences just described with the policy instruments available to them will face significant problems. The difficulties of transforming those efforts into a coherent strategy, moreover, will certainly be greater than the sum of the particular obstacles. The most important among them will reflect many complex factors, some of them deeply ingrained in the nature of relations between polities as different as Mexico and the United States.

Foreseeable Complexities

Managing the Mexican federal government's California connection will be no easier than dealing with other dimensions of the increasing interface between the political systems and debates of Mexico and the United States, which constitutes the unavoidable result of the "intermesticity" of the bilateral agenda. It will involve, in fact, quite similar challenges. From the Mexican government's perspective, for example, the connection and its management should be seen as both instances and further components of one of the key complexities involved in the management of Mexico–United States relations: the presence of numerous *and* relevant governmental and nongovernmental participants. Several points emerge from such diversity.

First, one must be aware that not only the overall political climate of Mexico-U.S. relations but that of the California connection itself may become hostage to the actions of small, even marginal groups of nongovernmental actors, from border vigilantes to delinquent elements on both sides of the border. Increasing the points of contact between the societies and economies of Mexico and the United States, California in particular, may also increase the number of potential points of tension. Even if the tendency towards conflict is reduced as the result of the increasing familiarity with the issues involved on the part of participants on both sides of the border, the absolute number of instances of conflict may increase. Instances of violence along the border, for example, may not seem numerous when compared to the available data on both documented and undocumented crossings, but they have a high disruptive potential. Elements of racism, which may be involved in reactions by segments of the California population to given instances of the connection, as the San Diego "light up the border" movement clearly suggests, do too. This disruptive potential is increased when federal or state officials are involved in actions such as the unauthorized crossing into Mexican territory by members of the U.S. Border Patrol in September 1991 or the five shootings (three of them fatal) of Mexican citizens by San Diego-based Border Patrol agents recorded during the first six months of 1990.

Second, given financial and other constraints, the multiplicity of participants will force Mexican federal authorities to clearly define their priorities in ways that may allow the relevant communication efforts to focus on actors that play crucial roles in controlling access to the most relevant goals to be pursued. Practically all relevant California actors are in one way or another constrained not only by legal rules but also by the presence and interests of other participants. Some, however, are more constrained than others in general and particularly in reference to the key issues of the Mexico-California agenda. Similar themes are involved in this regard at the level of state and local politics. Dispersion of authority and responsibility, not only between the three levels of local, state, and federal government but even within each one of these spheres, thus represents a significant source of complexity. It also has an impact on issues related to the implementation of federal policy, as shown by the example of the State Legalization Impact Assistance Grants program (SLIAG), incorporated in the Immigration Reform and Control Act of 1986.[24]

The problems that emerge from the presence of numerous governmental and nongovernmental participants are, however, much more than "technical" or "organizational." They are political in the simple sense that, in almost any relevant issue area, the management of the California connection involves domestic "winners" and "losers" in both Mexico and the United States. The connection's differentiated impact constitutes one of the most important dimensions that any Mexican strategy will inevitably have to face. It involves many issue areas. Migration issues and *maquila* activities provide innumerable examples of such a situation, as do transborder interactions, where, as a former supervisor of the county of San Diego put it, "The costs and benefits . . . affect different areas within the region in different ways and to varying degrees."[25] For example, different dimensions of the state's agricultural production may be hurt or benefited as a result of free trade schemes such as the ones presently being negotiated.

A different set of complexities in the management of the California connection (or of Mexico–United States relations for that matter) is related to the constraints placed on policymakers on both sides of the border by the existence of "vast differences in economic development, political systems, demographic patterns, and cultures."[26] The challenges involved in communications between "cultural settings which on each side of the border are marked by contrasting perceptions, predispositions and values"[27] express themselves, for example, in the increasing need to develop a single discourse that may simultaneously satisfy the requirements of the significantly different political debates taking place in each of the two countries. The difficulties that these differences can create for the adequate management of bilateral relations express themselves in many of the concrete issues in which the connection is embodied.[28] This, however, is not the only dimension involved. Differences in legal structure and traditions are also clearly relevant. Putting in contact two very different legal systems is frequently as difficult as addressing audiences whose basic frames of reference are also quite diverse.

The efforts to manage the connection will also have to face several other challenges. There are clear limits to the role that public policy and governmental activities may have in shaping a relation moved more by "markets" than by "politics." The already mentioned differences in the availability of financial resources will have an impact on the priority assigned to different items in the agenda of each side. As a result, the "issue of standards" will continue to complicate dialogue since in spite of all the progress made by cities such as Tijuana in relation to the rest of the country, they will continue to be far behind cities such as San Diego. The difficulties involved in reaching a compromise between each side's sense of fairness and reciprocity on different issues will be multiplied by the simple fact that the responsibilities of Mexican authorities extend to other, much less privileged areas of the country. Finally, there will continue to exist real differences of interest between Mexico City and California-based actors on important issues, no matter how strong an effort is made to contain differences and expand spaces of agreement. For, as a Mexican diplomat reminded us in relation to one of the issues of the Mexico-California agenda, "The best disposition to cooperate is unable to generate a single additional drop of water in addition to that which reaches the international segments of the Bravo [Grande] and the Colorado rivers."[29] In such cases, both sides will have a strong—almost unavoidable—temptation to "raise the issue" to the federal level. This will be a reminder of the most basic facts that shape the connection.

Perspectives

From the Mexico City perspective, the California connection is immersed in a wider web of other "connections": the Washington connection, the border connection, the Pacific Basin connection—even the Mexican domestic politics connection. Intensifying its direct contacts and channels of communication with state- and local-level actors and audiences is, as a result, not the only option open to the Mexican federal government. It could, for example, simply continue to demand the attention of U.S. federal authorities (implicitly asking that *they* be more like *us*) or leave the management of at least some of the issues that conform the Mexico-California agenda in local hands—so that formal symmetry may increase as a result of *us* being more like *them*.

In this essay I have argued that since the drawbacks would exceed the potential benefits in both cases, instead of demanding that either side be more like the other, the alternative seems to be a more active dialogue between different levels of government on either side of the border. Such dialogue would constitute a complement rather than an alternative to activities that might be undertaken along the other axes of the bilateral relation in which the California connection is involved: federal/federal and Mexican federal/U.S. border states interactions. The difficulties involved in such an effort should not be underestimated. But even after the complexities and doubts are fully taken into account,[30] there remain good and concrete reasons for Mexican federal authorities to establish direct contacts and lines of communication with California-based actors.

Given all the nuances and possibilities involved, how realistic is it to expect the Mexican government in the near future to follow such a course of action? Up to now, there have been very limited efforts on the part of the federal authorities to move beyond diplomatic representation centered in Washington—and, for that matter, in the Department of State and at times the White House. Many factors have contributed to such a situation. What seems relevant at this point is that this has been the case not only in relation to the possibilities opened by the concrete workings of U.S. federalism. The Mexican government has not been very proficient at managing relations with Washington either. Only a few of the channels of communication open in the executive branch have been explored, while relations with Congress have been almost nonexistent. This lack of experience may become one of the reasons to be skeptical of the Mexican federal government's commitment and ability to deal with the challenges and opportunities raised by the California connection. Even in the context of a clear decision to have its voice be heard in North American political debate, a credible argument may be made on the need to "take first things first." Let's start, it may be argued, by developing an adequate presence in Washington before establishing contacts with other relevant actors in the U.S. political system.

There are, however, also grounds for optimism. After all, during the first semester of 1991, in the context of Congress's authorization of President Bush to enter into "fast-track" trade negotiations, Mexican federal authorities took a crash course in American politics and proved to be fast learners.[31] They clearly seem to be ready to develop an overall strategy of relations with the U.S., which will involve upgrading their Washington activities and simultaneously exploring the several other points of access to their neighbor's complex society and political system opened by realities such as the everyday practice of U.S. federalism in ways that may be mutually reinforcing. And California, if the arguments presented in these pages make any sense, represents a most attractive case for starting such activities.

CHAPTER 14

Challenges from the South

Enhancing California's Mexico Connection

KATRINA BURGESS AND

ABRAHAM F. LOWENTHAL

CALIFORNIA HAS FOR YEARS been a national trendsetter in economics, politics, demography, and popular culture. The flower children and the Reagan revolution began in California, as have trends in film, music, fashion, and speech. Immigrants from across the country and around the world have flocked to the state, creating a novel mixture of cultures, languages, and mores. Whether California is seen as a society lacking in roots and unsure of its direction or as the land of opportunity and innovation, the very name conjures up an image of rapid change.

California is likely to continue setting trends into the twenty-first century. Ensuring that most of these trends will be positive, however, has become more complicated in an age of crowded spaces, stiffer competition, fewer resources, and a shrinking world. Among the requirements for success will be the management of issues with origins and implications beyond California's borders. As the state's most important neighbor and the country-of-origin for at least six million of its people, Mexico will play a particularly critical role in California's future.

The two-way flow of goods, capital, technology, information, people, and cultural influences between Mexico and California has expanded dramatically since the early 1970s. The number of annual border crossings has increased four-fold, reaching more than sixty million by 1989. Since 1970, California's Mexican-born population has grown by an astounding 700 percent, from 400,000 to 2.9 million. The volume of trade between Mexico and California has nearly tripled since 1985, and the number of *maquiladoras* along the California border has quadrupled in the last decade. Today, the entire region from Cancún to Eureka is more closely intertwined than at any time since Mexico lost control over its rich northernmost territory in 1848.

The links between California and Mexico have changed not only in number and degree but also in kind. Each country is establishing a larger and more permanent presence in the other, primarily through immigration and investment. Under the legalization provisions of the 1986 Immigration Control and Reform Act, over one million Mexicans in California were made eligible for U.S. citizenship, accelerating a trend toward permanent residence north of the border. Economic ties are solidifying as well, as California-owned *maquiladora* plants are upgraded from assembly operations to sophisticated centers of production.

The deepening of interdependence between California and Mexico reflects broader trends in the global economy. Technological advances, particularly in transportation and communications, have made it much easier for capital and labor to cross national frontiers in search of economic opportunity. As firms move through the product cycle, they develop multiple centers of production to combine the low-skill labor and advanced technology they need to survive in an increasingly competitive global marketplace. Entire villages in the developing world are becoming linked through migration to labor markets in the industrialized countries. Trade flows, in turn, are bolstered by intrafirm transactions and the increased purchasing power of less developed communities integrated into migratory networks.

Although Mexico is becoming a key element in shaping California's development, the capacity of policymakers to address Mexico-related issues appears to be diminishing. The new issues raised by interdependence involve a rapidly growing array of actors that often do not fit within traditional jurisdictions. These difficulties are compounded by a fiscal crisis at all levels of government. Following a long period of debt accumulation, inflation, and tax revolt, agencies lack the resources to fund even established infrastructure development and social welfare programs, let alone embark on innovative ventures to meet the demands of increased interdependence.

Mexico's Impact on California

Mexico's proximity and presence has affected almost every facet of life in California. Not only is the state tied to Mexico through trade, investment, and finance, but it has become home to millions of Mexicans and their children. Even quintessentially domestic issues such as education, social services, and housing have an important Mexico dimension.

Mexicans in California

Demographic changes are at the heart of the California-Mexico Connection. One in five Californians is of Mexican descent, compared to fewer than 12 percent in 1970. In Los Angeles city and county, Latinos (mostly of Mexican origin) account for nearly 40 percent of the population; they are expected to become a majority early in the twenty-first century. Today, only Mexico City has more Mexican residents than Los Angeles.

The dramatic increase in California's Mexican-origin population is partly the result of burgeoning immigration. For most of the twentieth century, between half and two-thirds of California's new residents migrated from other parts of the United States. Since 1980, however, the largest single contributor to California's population growth has been foreign immigration. Nearly half of new California residents are recent immigrants, and more than half of the 250,000 foreign immigrants who enter the state legally each year are from Mexico.[1] In addition, at least one million undocumented Mexican immigrants have come to California in the last decade. By 1990, nearly three million foreign-born Mexicans were living in the state, compared to just over one million in 1980.

The other critical factor in explaining the growth of California's Mexican-origin population is the fertility rate of immigrant women, which is estimated to be 40 percent higher than that of Anglos. In 1986, nearly half of all the babies born in Los Angeles were Latino. One in three U.S.-born Mexicans is under fourteen years of age, and approximately 40 percent of all Latinos in metropolitan Los Angeles are twenty years old or younger.

These mutually reinforcing demographic shifts are having a profound impact on the evolution of California's labor force. As the baby-boom generation ages, young minorities will account for the vast majority of labor-force growth. By the turn of the century, one in two new workers in California will be Latino; shortly thereafter, Latinos will become a majority of the state's total labor force. If current trends persist, moreover, most of these workers will live in urban areas and work in low-skill jobs in services, retail, construction, and light manufacturing, contributing to a two-tier economy bifurcated largely along ethnic lines.

Mexican immigration and high fertility rates are also reshaping California's public schools. Statewide, the share of Latino students jumped from 13.6 percent in 1966 to 30.7 percent in 1988. In the Los Angeles Unified School District, Latino (predominantly Mexican) student enrollment in public schools reached 63 percent in 1991. No school system in a major U.S. city has ever experienced such a large influx of students from a single foreign country. The schools of Los Angeles are becoming Mexican.

Many of these students have little or no command of the English language. In 1989, there were over 500,000 limited English proficient (LEP), Spanish-speaking students in California, a 46-percent jump since 1985. In Los Angeles, where LEP enrollment has been increasing by more than

10 percent annually, nearly one in three students is unable to speak English well enough to be placed in a mainstream program.

Demographic shifts are reshaping California's politics as well. Although Latino participation lags far behind its share of the population, Latino voters, activists, and elected officials are beginning to make their voices heard, particularly in Los Angeles. Since 1980, the proportion of Latino elected officials in California has more than doubled, and the Latino congressional delegation from Los Angeles County has increased from one to four. In 1991, Gloria Molina became the first Latino in over one hundred years to serve on the Los Angeles County Board of Supervisors, an extremely powerful body with an annual budget of more than $10 billion.

Increased political clout is being matched by a growing Latino presence in the marketplace. In Los Angeles County, Latino consumers exert a purchasing power of at least $22 billion per year. Major California businesses are responding to this emerging market with specialized stores (e.g., the Tianguis markets created by Vons) and bilingual services (e.g., Spanish-language automated teller machines). Latino entrepreneurs are also gaining influence. Between 1982 and 1987, the number of Latino-owned companies in the United States increased by more than 80 percent, compared to a 14 percent increase for all companies. Nearly one-third of these firms (132,212) were located in California, where they earned receipts of $8.1 billion in 1987.[2]

Finally, the doubling of the state's Mexican-origin population since 1970 is having a subtle impact on society and culture. Californians of all ethnic groups enjoy Mexican cuisine, celebrate Cinco de Mayo, hear Latin beats on the radio, see Mexican crafts in the stores, or have picked up a few Spanish words. Although most aspects of Mexican culture are admittedly still ignored or misunderstood by the majority of non-Mexicans in California, the sheer size of the Latino community means that Mexican values, traditions, and mores are having an increasing influence on the state.

Cross-Border Networks of Goods and Capital

People are not the only link between California and Mexico. In the last twenty years, goods and capital have also been crossing the border with rising frequency. Each year, billions of dollars change hands among farmers, bankers, manufacturers, retailers, investors, and consumers—of both legal and illegal goods—in the two regions.

Mexico is California's sixth largest trading partner, accounting for $9 billion in two-way trade in 1990. Since 1988, California's exports to Mexico have been growing by 25 percent a year, compared to an average annual growth rate of 17 percent for its imports from Mexico. The largest share of trade in both directions is in electronic and nonelectronic equipment and machinery. Some 25 percent of all color televisions sold in the United States are produced in Tijuana alone.[3]

California-Mexico trade relations have deepened through a program of economic liberalization undertaken by the Mexican government since the mid-1980s. In an effort to strengthen its ties to the global marketplace, Mexico joined the General Agreement on Tariffs and Trade, eliminated most import permits, sold off or reorganized more than 700 state-owned enterprises, liberalized its foreign investment regulations, and reprivatized its banking sector. In addition to lowering barriers to California goods, these reforms have attracted the attention of California exporters by generating favorable coverage of Mexico in the U.S. press. All these trade-intensifying measures have been strongly reinforced since 1991 by the concerted moves toward a North American Free Trade Agreement (NAFTA).

Since the 1980s, California has also become the focal point for narcotics trafficking between Mexico and the United States. Centered in Los Angeles, the California drug market looms larger than that of any other state. California's involvement in the drug trade has been exacerbated by a shift in cocaine supply routes and money laundering operations. The massive U.S. interdiction program in the Caribbean during the 1980s pushed South American traffickers away from their traditional routes through southern Florida and toward new routes through Mexico and into southern California. The program also contributed to the emergence of Los Angeles as the money laundering capital of the country. Between 1985 and 1988, the cash surplus in the city's Federal Reserve Bank—widely viewed as the best indicator of money laundering—surged from $166 million to $3.8 billion.[4]

Another deepening link between California and Mexico is investment in the *maquiladora* industry. With the collapse of oil prices and the sharp devaluation of the peso in the early 1980s, Mexican wages plummeted. The combination of low labor costs and proximity to the U.S. market generated a dramatic surge of investment in the *maquiladoras*. By the early 1990s nearly 2,000 plants employed some 500,000 Mexican workers and exported more than $6 billion worth of goods to the United States each year. Forty percent of the *maquiladoras* are located in Baja California, more than 500 in Tijuana alone, and over 300 plants have their home base in San Diego. Most California-owned *maquiladoras* assemble or manufacture electronic equipment, textiles, or paper products. An astounding 80 percent of California imports from Mexico come from the *maquiladoras*; in 1987, plants located in Tijuana exported an estimated $2.1 billion in goods to southern California.[5]

California and Mexico are also increasingly connected through the flow of capital. During the late 1970s and early 1980s, California-based banks such as Security Pacific, Bank of America, First Interstate, and Wells Fargo lent the Mexican government billions of dollars. With the onset of Mexico's economic crisis in 1981, the direction of capital flows shifted, and vast sums left Mexico in the form of interest payments and capital flight. Mexico lost more than $30 billion in flight capital between 1981 and 1986, and private deposits by Mexican citizens in U.S. banks grew each year between 1981 and 1985. In 1986, the total value of Mexican assets in the United States was estimated to be $55 billion, more than Mexico's total commercial bank debt.[6] Although some of these funds were returned to Mexico during the economic recovery of the early 1990s, many wealthy Mexicans continue to hold bank accounts in the United States.

Significant amounts of Mexican flight capital have come to California. According to local banking officials in San Diego, Mexican exiles brought at least $3 billion to the city between 1976 and 1985. In 1986, Mexicans were said to hold a total of $250 million in cash deposits and other liquid instruments just in the La Jolla and Pacific Beach branches of the Bank of America.[7] Much larger sums of money have no doubt been deposited in banks in Los Angeles and San Francisco.

Though Mexico became a net capital exporter during the 1980s, not all funds traveled north. Just as wealthy Mexicans sent their savings abroad, thousands of poor Mexicans weathered the economic crisis with financial help from relatives in California. According to a survey of 100 Guadalajara households, a quarter of the families received dollar remittances regularly between 1982 and 1987. In 1990, the Bank of Mexico estimated yearly remittances at over $2 billion; the figure could be as high as $3 billion if savings brought back to Mexico by migrants are included. These remittances strengthen cross-border ties for thousands of Mexican families.

Benefits of Mexico's Proximity and Presence

The flows of people, goods, and capital that define the California-Mexico Connection have brought important benefits to California. Most of these benefits are related to the changing global environment, which is marked by the growing importance of foreign trade and investment, increased foreign competition, and heightened multicultural interaction.

Facing the International Economy

Located at a crossroads between the dynamic Asia-Pacific region and the huge U.S. market, California has emerged as a center for international commerce, investment, and finance. Since 1967, southern California's share of U.S. trade has more than doubled. According to the U.S. Chamber of Commerce, one in ten jobs in the state was related to foreign trade in the mid-1980s; this figure is expected to increase to one in five by 1995. Foreign direct investment in California, which for the last fifteen years has been the most attractive site for foreign investors in the United States, has increased ten-fold since 1977. California is also home to the second and third largest banking centers in the country (Los Angeles and San Francisco), and foreign banks have established over 150 offices in California in recognition of the state's importance as a world financial center.

Mexico has played an important role in expanding California's participation in the global economy. Mexico is now California's second largest export market, absorbing nearly 14 percent of the state's exports. Sales by California firms to Mexico jumped from $1.9 billion in 1986 to $3.9 billion in 1990 and account for over 100,000 California jobs.[8] Although some of this growth can be explained by a fall in the U.S. dollar, Mexico's shift from fourth to second place among the state's export markets is largely a result of Mexico's economic reforms.

In addition to opening up new markets, these reforms are creating a demand for goods and services in which California has a competitive edge. Recent steps to liberalize Mexico's computer trade, combined with tax incentives for domestic producers, have tripled the size of Mexico's computer market since 1990. With the modification of Mexico's laws governing intellectual property rights, high-tech companies in California have added incentives to establish facilities in Mexico, generating intrafirm transactions across the border. Finally, the Mexican government has created mechanisms whereby foreign investors can have limited participation in the social capital of banks and mutual funds; further opening of Mexico's financial sector is likely to provide opportunities for California's banks.

Mexico is also helping to attract foreign investment to the border region. A growing number of Asian firms are setting up shop in northern Mexico, particularly in Tijuana. The number of Japanese-owned *maquiladoras* has quintupled since 1986, and Japanese firms employ at least 10 percent of the Tijuana work force. Taiwan and South Korea are also establishing a presence in the industry in an attempt to compete more effectively with Japan and make up for their recent loss of special tariff breaks under the U.S. System of Generalized Preferences. To avoid U.S. duties on re-exports, these firms often supply their Mexican plants from California-based subsidiaries, which employ local workers, use local services, and bring trade-related jobs to the state.

Finally, Mexico is contributing to California's emergence as a world financial center. By 1991, five Mexican banks were operating in California, with combined assets of approximately $1.9 billion. Although Mexico's share of foreign bank assets was miniscule compared to that of Japan, it was not far behind the state's second largest foreign banker, France.

Increased Foreign Competition

The explosion of trade and investment opportunities has been accompanied by a less favorable development. Since the 1960s, the United States has experienced increased foreign competition, particularly from Asian countries. Burdened with high labor costs, relatively old capital, a soaring federal debt, and increasingly strict environmental regulations, many U.S. firms have been hard-pressed to survive in a highly competitive environment. The result, according to Paul Ong, has been "the bankruptcy of many firms, the abandonment of less efficient capital, the shift of investments to regions with less costly energy and labor inputs, and the acceleration of the adoption of new technology."[9]

These economic adjustments have meant job displacement for U.S. workers, particularly in blue-collar occupations. At least ten million U.S. workers were uprooted between 1979 and 1985, contributing to a fourfold increase in part-time employment.[10] In California, manufacturing jobs fell from over 18 percent of total jobs in 1979 to just under 15 percent in 1990. The corresponding increase in service employment has contributed to a decline in unionized jobs and a demand for different labor skills.

At least until the 1990s, however, California responded to increased foreign competition more successfully than most regions of the country. During the 1970s, California experienced an increase in blue-collar jobs at twice the national rate and an expansion in manufacturing employment at nearly four times the national rate.[11] Although the state lost ground in traditional industries such as steel, rubber, and automobiles, it continued to enjoy rapid growth in high-tech sectors such as aerospace, communications, and electronics and in labor-intensive industries such as textiles, apparel, and furniture.

Mexico played a critical role in easing California's adjustment to increased foreign competition. One source of relief was the *maquiladora* industry. Investment in the *maquiladoras* enabled California firms to compete in world markets without severing ties with the rest of California's economy. Rather than establishing offshore facilities thousands of miles away, these companies kept their labor-intensive operations close to home, generating demand for inputs and *maquiladora*-related services in California. In San Diego, the *maquiladora* boom of the 1980s contributed to a 34 percent increase in population and an unemployment rate of only 3 percent. Some 200,000 high-skilled jobs related to the *maquiladora* industry were created in California in the second half of the decade. According to the U.S. International Trade Commission, the *maquila* payroll generated between $73 and $95 million each year during the late 1980s for the economy of southern California.[12]

Mexican immigration was even more central to California's competitive edge in manufacturing. According to an Urban Institute study, 53,000 manufacturing jobs and 37,000 jobs related to manufacturing would have been lost in California if no Mexican immigration had taken place between 1970 and 1985.[13] Mexican labor was especially vital to the garment, furniture, electronics, rubber products, and food processing industries. By enabling California to adjust more slowly to increased foreign competition and to maintain its economic dynamism at a time when other parts of the country were already in decline, Mexican immigrant labor served as a buffer against the dislocating changes taking place in the global economy.[14]

Heightened Multicultural Interaction

As people, goods, and capital traverse the globe with growing frequency, California cannot afford to isolate itself culturally from the rest of the world. Both at home and abroad, those who speak only one language or who lack an understanding of other cultures are at a disadvantage. Shopkeepers unaware of tastes in ethnically diverse communities lose customers, just as exporters who do not adapt to local customs often find themselves shut out of foreign markets. Job recruiters from banks and corporations increasingly favor applicants who speak Japanese, German, or Spanish. Schoolteachers and health care professionals without language skills or cultural awareness training become frustrated by an inability to serve their students and clients effectively.

Mexico's presence and proximity may help California adapt to the cultural demands of an ever-shrinking world. The norms of multilingualism and multiculturalism are already widely accepted by the Latino community, which will soon make up one-third of the state's population. Along the border, knowledge of Spanish is recognized as an asset for non-Latinos seeking to profit from the *maquiladora* boom. Although parochial attitudes will no doubt persist in California, they are likely to be counterbalanced by Mexico's strong influence on the state's society and culture.

Challenges to California

The growing links between California and Mexico offer substantial benefits, but they also present difficult challenges. Again, these issues are closely related to broader trends in the global environment. First, the explosion of trade and investment opportunities along the border has generated severe infrastructure and environmental pressures that do not respect national boundaries. Second, economic ties with Mexico have heightened rather than eased the negative impact of foreign competition for some sectors. Third, the influx of poor, undereducated Mexican immigrants without a political voice has contributed to the development of a two-tier society. Finally, rapid demographic change is fueling serious tensions among ethnic groups, especially between Latinos and African Americans. Without effective management, these challenges threaten to undermine the potential benefits of Mexico's proximity and presence.

Pressures on Infrastructure and the Environment

Rapid entrance into the global economy has put serious strains on California's infrastructure and environment. California now ranks fiftieth among all U.S. states in per capita spending on highways, and the Los Angeles area could face gridlock soon if surface transportation systems fail to grow.[15] Despite strict environmental standards, the Los Angeles Basin still has the worst air quality in the nation.

The pressures generated by increased foreign trade and investment are particularly intense along the California-Mexico border. Development in the border region has taken off in the last decade, largely as a result of the *maquiladora* boom. Tijuana has been transformed from a dusty border town of 340,000 in 1970 to a bustling metropolis of over one million people.

Existing customs and airport facilities are insufficient to handle the growing volume of border traffic, which is creating serious bottlenecks and damaging the region's air quality. With a combined population of 3.5 million people, the San Diego–Tijuana region faces severe shortages of housing, water, and sewage treatment facilities. The lack of housing and plumbing is contributing to serious health problems on both sides of the border. Whole sections of Tijuana are without access to sewage lines, and the waste water discharged in these areas runs downhill into the Tia Juana River Valley and then into the Pacific Ocean.

The environmental hazards associated with rapid development are exacerbated by the *maquiladoras* themselves, which generate dangerous amounts of toxic waste. California's Salton Sea contains at least 100 chemicals traceable to factories in Mexico, and the New River, which flows north from the industrial border town of Mexicali, registers high levels of industrial pollutants. Toxins emitted into the air in Tijuana blow into California each night, just as Los Angeles smog heads toward Mexico in the morning.

Despite hazardous-waste regulations that closely parallel those of the United States, the Mexican government lacks adequate resources for enforcement and must rely largely on voluntary compliance. In high-emissions industries manufacturing products such as paint, furniture, and plating, numerous small California companies have been participating in the *maquiladora* program as a way of avoiding the high costs of complying with strict air quality standards north of the border.

Although important steps have been taken to address these problems, including a path-breaking binational accord to build an international sewage treatment plant in San Diego, border infrastructure and environmental protection remains sorely inadequate. Without greater resources for customs and air traffic facilities, housing, waste treatment, and environmental enforcement, the *maquiladora* boom may be suffocated by rising transaction costs and a deteriorating quality of life.

Economic Dislocation

Close ties with Mexico have been favorable to the California economy in the aggregate, but some specific sectors and groups have suffered. In these cases, the difficult process of economic adjustment has been exacerbated rather than eased by Mexico's proximity and presence.

The sector most harmed by increased trade with Mexico is agriculture. California growers have complained bitterly about competition from Mexico, particularly as Mexican agribusiness has expanded into the country's northern states, where the growing season is similar to California's. Mexico supplies 25 percent of all U.S. imports of fruits and vegetables each year, and the value of its exports of fresh tomatoes, broccoli, and cauliflower to the United States is greater than that of all other foreign suppliers combined. California growers, who account for 91 percent of the broccoli and 79 percent of cauliflower produced in the United States, are threatened by Mexico's inroads into these markets.

Other Californians have been hurt by Mexico's *maquiladora* industry. By providing an attractive site for California firms fleeing high labor costs and strict environmental regulations, the *maquiladoras* have been responsible for some job displacement north of the border. For example, the number of employees at the Green Giant processing plant in Watsonville, California, has fallen from 1,200 to 100 since the company's parent firm opened a processing plant in Irapuato, employing 800 Mexican workers at a rate of 50 cents an hour.[16]

Another source of economic dislocation, at least for Latinos, has been Mexican immigration. Mexican immigrants do not typically compete with native U.S. workers for the same jobs, and most workers in California have substantially higher earnings than their counterparts nationwide.[17] But the state's Latinos, whose wages are close to the national average, are concentrated in the same low-skill sectors that attract immigrants. These sectors, which tend to be nonunionized or to operate on a subcontracting basis, are characterized by low wages and rapid turnover. Partly as a result of rapid Mexican immigration, the wage differential between Mexican-born males and Anglo males in California increased from 33 percent in 1960 to 40 percent in 1980. California often has the highest Latino unemployment rate of all the U.S. border states.

Intensification of a Two-Tier Society

The rapid influx of poor, undereducated Mexican immigrants is intensifying a trend toward a two-tier society in California. Faced with occupational, ethnic, and political polarization, significant numbers of Californians may be trapped at the bottom of the socioeconomic ladder.

Contrary to popular belief, Mexican immigrants do not place a disproportionate burden on health care, public welfare, or the criminal justice system in California. In fact, Latinos tend to be healthier, have stronger families, work harder, live longer, and rely more heavily on informal networks than other ethnic groups. In 1980, Latinos had a labor-force participation rate of 80.6 percent, compared to 76.2 percent for Anglos, 74.8 percent for Asians, and 66.7 percent for African Americans. Latinos are consistently underrepresented on Aid for Dependent Children rolls in Los Angeles County and have significantly fewer low-birthweight or drug-addicted babies than other groups. Although Latinos represent 29 percent of the inmates in California prisons, this is almost exactly proportional to their 28-percent share of the adult male population.

As with other immigrant cohorts, however, Mexicans in California do tend to be poor and undereducated. In Los Angeles, Latinos account for two out of every three low-wage workers.[18] Statewide, only 10 percent of Latino workers are in professional, technical, or managerial occupations, compared to nearly 35 percent of Anglo workers. Despite their strong work ethic and high labor-force participation, one in four Latinos lives in poverty, compared to one in ten Anglos.

Mexican immigrants often arrive in California at an educational disadvantage. Although schooling in Mexico is compulsory and free through age fifteen, more than 35 percent of all Mexican adults have not finished primary school, and illiteracy rates are estimated to be about 15 percent in the cities and 30 percent in rural areas.[19] The education levels of Mexican immigrants have improved since the 1960s, but on average they still have 3.5 fewer years of schooling than other Latino immigrants, 4.2 years fewer than African Americans, and 5.5 years fewer than Anglos. Only 21 percent of all Mexican immigrants over 25 are high school graduates, compared to 67 percent of the overall U.S. population.

In the past, immigrant cohorts in the United States have been able to achieve economic and educational assimilation over the generations. Mexicans are no exception. U.S.-born Latinos earn 25 percent more and have 25 percent more education than Mexican immigrants, and high school graduation rates increase from barely 25 percent among Mexican immigrants to between 60 and 70 percent for third-generation Latinos.

As a result of structural factors, however, upward mobility may be severely limited for the next generation of Mexicans in California. California's public schools are floundering in their efforts to accommodate the vast numbers of Mexican-origin children entering the classroom. In addition to facing a serious shortage of trained bilingual staff, educators are paralyzed by a pedagogical debate over how best to provide LEP students with the skills they need to be academically successful. Meanwhile, severe overcrowding in the inner cities is contributing to extremely high student-teacher ratios and forcing school districts to bus record numbers of poor, immigrant students to suburban campuses, which are even less equipped to meet their needs than inner-city schools. These problems are magnified by the tax-cutting initiatives passed by California voters during the 1970s, which contributed to a drop in California's national ranking in terms of spending per student from fifth in 1970 to twenty-ninth in 1989.[20]

Because California's schools lack the personnel, facilities, or financial resources to serve an increasingly diverse student population, they are unlikely to provide Mexican immigrants and their children with the educational tools they need to match the upward progress of previous immigrants. Forty-five percent of Latinos entering ninth grade in California do not graduate, and those who remain in school fall far behind their peers in terms of academic achievement. Only 10 percent of California's Latino high school seniors attend a four-year college, compared to 21 percent of Anglo high school seniors.

These educational barriers are compounded by a second structural obstacle to upward mobility for Latinos. As a result of changes in the state's occupational structure, traditional avenues for economic progress by the working poor are being closed off. The combination of deindustrialization in traditional sectors and reindustrialization in light manufacturing and high technology has reduced the pool of relatively well-paying, unionized jobs open to hard-working but undereducated workers.

Although there is heated debate over the extent to which the "middle" is disappearing from California's occupational structure, the state's labor market appears to be becoming segmented into a primary sector with "good" jobs and a secondary sector with "bad" jobs. This segmentation corresponds to a division between a core sector, in which monopolistic and oligopolistic firms make excess profits, and a competitive sector, in which firms earn only marginal profits.[21] Services and high technology, which are the fastest-growing areas of the California economy, are particularly prone to a division of labor between high-skill/high-wage workers and low-skill/low-wage workers.[22]

Even mid-level jobs may be out of reach for many less privileged workers. Located in offices and stores rather than factories, these jobs tend to require higher levels of education and training. Unless schools and employers can reduce the barriers to educational achievement among the working poor, particularly minorities, the labor-force requirements of the California economy may not be met. Meanwhile, growing numbers of workers in the state will face severely limited chances for bettering their place in society.

The consolidation of a two-tier economy is especially disturbing when juxtaposed to demographic trends in the state. Much of Calfornia's population and labor-force growth will come from minorities, particularly Latinos. Historically, Latinos have relied more heavily than other groups on manufacturing employment as a way out of the barrio. Whereas earlier cohorts of immigrants were able to pass on a better life to their children without having high levels of education, today's low-skilled Mexican immigrants may be trapped in low-paying, dead-end jobs.

Unable to escape poverty through hard work alone—and faced with formidable obstacles to educational achievement—Mexican immigrants and their children are in danger of becoming part of a permanent underclass of the working poor. Without alternative escape routes, the state's youngest and most rapidly growing population is likely to be relegated to the bottom tier of the economy. These young workers will not only be at risk of turning to crime and public welfare to make ends meet, but they will be less able (and willing) to fund the retirement and health needs of California's growing elderly population.

Economic polarization in California is exacerbated by a third structural factor: low Latino political participation. Despite the capture of key positions by Latino leaders in recent years, the Latino community continues to be severely underrepresented at all levels of government. In Los Angeles County, Latinos make up nearly 40 percent of the population but cast only between 5 and 10 percent of the votes. The reasons for Latino political weakness are complex, but a central factor is lack of citizenship. Over 1 million of the 3.5 million Latinos in Los Angeles were born outside the United States. Although roughly half of these are illegal residents without the option of becoming enfranchised, many Mexican immigrants with legalized status do not become U.S. citizens. In 1982, only 18 percent of the state's legally eligible foreign-born Mexicans had become naturalized citizens, compared to 66 percent of European immigrants.

As long as these conditions persist, the development of programs to reverse the trend toward a two-tier society will rest squarely in the hands of California's Anglos, who cast over 75 percent of the votes in general elections and are aging and relatively affluent. Although upward mobility for Latinos would serve long-term Anglo interests, most Anglo voters are unlikely to support programs that are of little direct benefit to themselves. Moreover, in an era of earmarking and user-fees, they will be increasingly able to allocate funds only to those programs that address their immediate concerns. As a result, upward mobility for the state's working poor is not likely to be forthcoming unless Latinos gain a stronger political voice.

Ethnic Tensions

The mushrooming of immigrant populations in California, particularly from Mexico, has led to a breakdown of consensus regarding language, culture, and society. As illustrated by the Light Up the Border campaign in San Diego and the English Only initiative, popular attitudes have not kept pace with the demographic changes that are reshaping California's economic, political, and social landscape.

Some Anglos feel threatened by the "browning" of the state's population. According to a 1986 *Los Angeles Times* poll, only 34 percent of non-Latino whites in California support amnesty for illegal aliens, despite a 63-percent approval rating for affirmative action for minorities.[23] The popular perception is that Mexican immigrants are the cause of many of California's social ills. According to the mayor of Santa Maria, "Any talk about growth management has to be ambiguous unless we point directly at the segments of society most responsible . . . and I refer, of course, to the hordes of illegal aliens who pour across our border with Mexico each and every day."[24] In a similar vein, the mayor of Culver City claimed that illegal immigrants "are going to steal just as much from Culver City as they do from Los Angeles."[25]

Such xenophobic reactions sometimes lead to violent attacks against people of Mexican descent, including cruel expeditions to "hunt" Mexicans and police brutality against Latinos. In addition, they often prevent the adoption of programs to address the real (as opposed to mythical) problems raised by Mexican immigration. Although some communities have taken positive steps such as the creation of public centers for day laborers or the implementation of innovative bilingual education programs, others have attempted either to expel immigrants or to ignore their health, housing, and educational needs.

Another obstacle to multicultural cooperation in California is conflict between ethnic minorities, which ranges from political rivalry to gang warfare. In part, these tensions reflect real conflicts of interest. Day laborers from Mexico and Central America vie for scarce employment in construction or gardening. When lines were drawn in 1986 to create a second majority Latino district in Los Angeles, the city's first Asian councilman nearly lost his seat. Latinos resent the high share of African-American workers in Los Angeles's public sector, while the growing Latino population in poor neighborhoods is eroding the political bases of established African-American politicians.

As with negative Anglo attitudes, however, some of these interethnic tensions are based on false assumptions. For example, African Americans are strongly supportive of employer sanctions against illegal immigrants, despite abundant evidence that Mexican immigrants do not generally compete with African-American workers for the same jobs.[26] More important, the conflicts between ethnic minorities are strongly outweighed by their shared interests, which include multilingual services, programs to assist immigrants and refugees, greater access to health insurance, voter naturalization and registration, investment in education, and neighborhood revitalization. As relatively young, poor, undereducated, and disenfranchised populations, these minorities have more to gain from cooperation than from competition.

California cannot turn back the clock on the economic and demographic changes that are transforming it into a multicultural society. Cutting off the flow of immigrants or mandating the official use of English are not viable options. Barring a complete militarization of the border—which would have dire implications for human rights, commerce, and industry—Mexicans will continue coming to California in search of economic opportunity. Likewise, an English-only law is unlikely to prevent people from conducting social and economic affairs in their native language; its main impact would be to marginalize ethnic minorities further and perpetuate their educational underachievement and low political participation.

California's emergence as a center for international finance, trade, and investment requires a tolerance and understanding of different languages and cultures, as well as a commitment to enabling all ethnic groups to participate fully in society. The ethnic rivalries that have paralyzed schools and neighborhoods—and that set Los Angeles on fire during the 1992 riots—highlight the importance of ensuring that no ethnic group is denied access to economic opportunity and social justice. Moreover, as Latina activist Vilma Martinez has said, political coalitions are the wave of the future in California, if only because no single group will be in the majority by the turn of the century. To survive and prosper in the twenty-first century, Californians will have to accept and learn from multicultural diversity.

Managing California's Mexico Connection

Managing the impact of Mexico's proximity and presence will be essential to confront four broad challenges facing California: economic restructuring, socioeconomic polarization, political stalemate, and interethnic conflict. Meeting these challenges can be facilitated by Mexico's proximity and presence, offering a young and growing labor force, expanding markets and investment opportunities, and a rich cultural heritage. To succeed, however, California needs to reverse the deterioration in its human and physical infrastructure and lower the obstacles to upward mobility for lower-skilled workers. California's leadership must develop appropriate strategies, build alliances, create new funding mechanisms, and establish linkages across diverse issue areas.

Who Is in Charge?

The California-Mexico Connection is a maze of issue areas and overlapping jurisdictions. The relevant cast of characters can be found at the federal, state, and local levels, and in the public and private sectors (see Appendix A). Some of these characters operate in what James Rosenau (in Chapter 1 of this book) calls the "secondary zone" of the connection, the focal points of which are Washington, D.C., Sacramento, and Mexico City. In general, these centers of government affect the connection rather than being affected by it. Although they have jurisdiction over critical issue areas, they are very distant from the connection's day-to-day evolution.

The other characters in the California-Mexico Connection operate in Rosenau's "primary zone," which extends from the borderlands to Los Angeles. These officials, legislators, entrepreneurs, workers, and consumers are intimately involved in California-Mexico affairs. Not only do they make a wide range of decisions, but they live with the consequences of measures taken in both zones of the connection.

Recent developments have heightened the role of actors in the primary zone. Since the 1980s, there has been a devolution of resources and authority away from central governments. Federal and state authorities have drastically reduced spending on programs with local impacts. The largest cuts have been in those areas most affected by Mexico's proximity and presence, particularly health and human services, housing and urban planning, public education, and infrastructure. This shift in financial responsibility has been accompanied by some transfer of authority to local communities. California's 1992 budget, for example, granted the counties jurisdiction over $2.3 billion in state social welfare programs.

The devolution of resources and authority away from central governments has been accelerated by the increased salience of "intermestic" issues. As the world becomes more interdependent, traditional "foreign policy" concerns such as trade, investment, and national security have subnational impacts that often prompt state and local action. At the same time, issues that used to be "domestic" in nature now have international implications. Local tax policies, for example, may affect a foreign company's decision to invest in a community or the size of the monthly check received by an immigrant's family thousands of miles away.

Intermestic issues are particularly prevalent in the California-Mexico Connection and have generated numerous attempts by subnational actors to influence bilateral relations. The state of California has an Office of California-Mexico Affairs, an Office of Trade and Investment in Mexico City, a select committee on California-Mexico Affairs, and a joint legislative committee on Refugee Resettlement, International Migration, and Cooperative Development. Local authorities are promoting trade and investment ties with Mexico through sister-city arrangements and are involved in the arrest and prosecution of Mexican nationals suspected of narcotics trafficking. In San Diego, both the city and the county have offices of binational affairs, which handle issues as diverse as urban management, cultural affairs, environmental protection, political relations, and the provision of vital services.

The combination of scarce governmental resources and the internationalization of local communities is also reshaping the role of nongovernmental actors. Private groups have always pressured government officials and shaped local environments. But the drying up of public monies is prompting them to take greater responsibility for areas previously dominated by the public sector. Business leaders are playing an active role in educational reform and infrastructure development, and nonprofit agencies are providing health and human services, welfare, and low-income housing. In addition, nongovernmental actors are increasingly involved in projects with international impact. Environmental groups have broadened their concerns to include clean air and water south of the border. Unions have been working with their members to improve the living standards of migrant-sending communities in Mexico while vehemently opposing a free trade agreement. Churches are on the front line in the battle over sanctuary for illegal immigrants.

Policy Recommendations

Five main concepts should guide California's efforts to manage its Mexico Connection. First, California should develop a comprehensive plan for infrastructure development and environmental protection along the California-Mexico border. The border region is poised to play a key role in the emerging global economic order. But without adequate customs facilities, airports, housing, plumbing, or water, the region will be unable to maintain its economic dynamism. By combining infrastructure improvements with stricter enforcement of environmental regulations, California's leaders can increase the chances that the border economy will flourish while stemming a further deterioration in the quality of life.

Although public resources for massive infrastructure development are scarce, there are promising possibilities for cross-border coalitions built around public/private partnerships. Given their vital interest in maintaining economic growth in California, entrepreneurs on both sides of the border are likely to contribute resources to a well-conceived plan to bring the region's infrastructure into the twenty-first century. They should also be encouraged (if not compelled) to help fund environmental protection. Four concrete proposals should be considered: building a joint San Diego–Tijuana airport to handle the growing air traffic and link border development more closely to the global marketplace; creating mechanisms to finance border projects, such as a border-development bank or a binational infrastructure bonding authority; developing bilateral organizations to provide housing, health, and human services to border communities; and working with Mexican officials to ensure that firms producing goods in Mexico have strong incentives to share the costs of environmental protection.

Second, California needs a strategy to help its workers adjust to a highly internationalized, service economy. Although access to low-cost Mexican labor on both sides of the border has helped California make the transition more easily than other parts of the country, the changing global environment has nonetheless meant wage declines and job losses for California workers. Without a plan to help these workers adapt to the new economic context, California is likely to underutilize its growing labor force and experience rising social tensions.

Before adopting specific adjustment policies, the state should carefully assess what is really happening to California's occupational structure. Is economic polarization primarily the result of a lack of mid-level jobs, or is it largely the consequence of inadequate training? If it is mainly a lack of jobs, then the state should support efforts to improve the wages and job security of low-skill service workers while providing opportunities for minorities to leapfrog into the higher tier through educational reform. If it is mostly a lack of training, the state should focus its efforts on worker retraining, apprenticeship programs, and adult education. When appropriate, state and local leaders should seek the advice, cooperation, and resources of the private sector, which has a vested interest in a well-trained work force.

Third, California should develop a set of social programs specifically designed for the *working* poor. For growing numbers of Californians, particularly Latinos, poverty is not a result of low labor-force participation, but rather of the limited earning potential of lower-skilled workers. Given economic polarization, this earning potential is not likely to increase in the near future, particularly if the "middle" is really disappearing from California's occupational structure. These workers are likely to experience the greatest economic improvement with programs that complement rather than substitute for regular wages. Of particular benefit would be access to health insurance, child care, and affordable housing. In coordinating and funding such programs, public officials should work closely with community organizations, churches, labor unions, and other nongovernmental actors. Poor people from all ethnic groups would gain, including those who have previously had little incentive to participate in the labor force.

Fourth, political participation in California must be broadened to reflect demographic realities. Economic and social polarization are likely to continue unless ethnic minorities, who have an immediate interest in overcoming polarization, become enfranchised. Because empowerment of minorities is a politically charged issue, the initiative will probably have to come from private organizations or ethnic leaders themselves. Among the measures worth pursuing are naturalization and registration drives, reforms to lower the barriers to voting, leadership training, and expansion of the number of seats on state and local bodies. As ethnic minorities gain a stronger political voice, Anglo politicians are likely to get on board in an effort to direct mobilization in a way that serves their interests.

Fifth, California should more actively promote programs to enhance multicultural awareness and cooperation. Such programs should include diversity training in the workplace, innovative bilingual programs in the public schools, improved teaching about Mexico and other foreign countries, media campaigns, and leadership training to promote coalition-building. Educators, journalists, political activists, artists, and corporate managers from California and Mexico should play a pivotal role in designing and implementing these programs. Although such efforts will not eliminate interethnic tensions, they can reduce harmful misperceptions and provide people with better tools for managing diversity. Moreover, California's competitive edge in the global economy will be deepened if its workers and managers can function effectively in a multicultural environment.

In translating these concepts into policy, California's leadership should be guided by the principles of "entrepreneurial government."[27] Since the public sector lacks the flexibility and resources to manage California's Mexico Connection on its own, it should involve private actors whenever possible in the design, funding, and implementation of its policies. Rather than abdicating responsibility for policy management, public officials should play the role of senior partner. As David Osborne and Ted Gaebler show in a recent study, governments around the country have achieved impressive reforms by serving as a catalyst for public/private partnerships, involving communities directly in the policy process, revising incentive structures to bring private behavior more in line with public goals, and focusing on results rather than inputs or rules.[28]

Conclusion

The border that divides California and Mexico is increasingly less relevant than the economic and demographic changes that are pulling them together. This trend can be expected to continue into the next century, particularly with a North American Free Trade Agreement (NAFTA). Its implications, however, will depend on developments on both sides of the border.

Mexico is currently in a period of prolonged economic and political change. Although the liberalizing reforms undertaken by the Mexican government appear to be restoring economic growth, Mexico faces a formidable task in repairing the damage done by nearly a decade of crisis. The number of Mexicans living in poverty mushroomed from 32.1 million in 1980 to 41.3 million in 1987. Battered by government austerity, Mexico's human and physical infrastructure is in grave disrepair. Sustaining positive growth rates and moderate rates of inflation will be difficult.

Mexico's economic problems are compounded by political instability. After years of one-party rule by the Revolutionary Institutional Party (PRI), growing numbers of Mexicans are demanding a more open and responsive system. In July 1988, opposition parties effectively challenged the PRI in national elections for the first time in over half a century. Since then, Mexican political life has been marked by tense negotiations, accusations of electoral fraud, and occasional violence. Although President Salinas has the support of the majority of the Mexican people, his popularity rests on the promise of economic recovery and masks some erosion of the authoritarian political institutions on which his power is based.

Mexico's economic and political future will have an important impact on flows of goods, capital, and people between Mexico and California. The exchange of goods and services is likely to continue under any scenario, but its rate of growth will be strongly affected by economic trends south of the border. Given favorable conditions, trade can be expected to expand dramatically, particularly with the institutionalization of liberal trade policies under a NAFTA. Moreover, if the benefits of growth are widely distributed in Mexico, California will gain a vast market, since Mexicans spend nearly one-sixth of their income on U.S. goods.[29]

Rates of investment and finance are likely to be similarly correlated with economic developments in Mexico. Stagnation or breakdown would dampen U.S. involvement (although only severe crisis is likely to cause a dramatic retreat), whereas rapid growth promises to accelerate it. Although rising Mexican wages might push some manufacturing firms to invest elsewhere, Mexico's strategic location, relatively skilled work force, and liberalized regulations should encourage further California investment. As lenders and investors in financial services, California banks are also likely to increase their involvement in Mexico in response to economic growth.

The relationship between economic and political trends in Mexico and pressures for migration is less straightforward. A failure to achieve economic growth or a serious destabilization of the political system would both increase the rate and change the composition of Mexican immigration. Although the vast majority of immigrants would continue to be poor, unskilled workers, economic or political breakdown would expand the ranks of higher-skilled immigrants. Favorable economic conditions, on the other hand, would reduce the numbers of middle-class Mexican immigrants but would be unlikely to cause substantial decreases in overall immigration rates, at least in the medium term. With ten-to-one wage differentials between the two regions, poor Mexicans are likely to keep coming to California; in fact, improved economic conditions might provide new migrants with the resources necessary to make the dangerous journey north.

Regardless of what happens in Mexico, the net impact on California of Mexico's proximity and presence will depend largely on developments in California. If conditions in Mexico turn sour, no doubt the resulting strains on California's social fabric, economic prosperity, and political coherence will be enormous. But even if all goes well in Mexico—if rapid growth and equitable development take place, if trade and investment flourish, and if immigration slows—Mexico's impact on California will still be negative, and will certainly be perceived as negative, unless California successfully addresses its main domestic problems: deteriorating infrastructure, declining educational standards, inadequate health care, environmental degradation, and social fragmentation. Since all these problems have an important Mexico dimension, their resolution will require addressing issues that extend beyond California's southern border. The future of America's Golden State will largely be defined by how well it manages its Mexico Connection.

Appendixes

North of the Border

Who Makes What Decisions Where

DAN HIMELSTEIN

BY "OPERATIONALIZING" a modified version of Table 1.1 in James Rosenau's introductory chapter, this appendix attempts to identify the actors within and outside of government who exert significant influence on the policy-making process for issue areas particularly relevant to California-Mexico relations. Although it neither lists every entity or actor that has, or claims to have, responsibility within the California-Mexico Connection, nor accurately measures the complexity, scope, or effectiveness of such governmental and nongovernmental activity, it does provide a "mental map" of who makes what decisions where north of the border.

Table A.1 focuses on the executive branch agency (or agencies in some instances) at the federal (United States), state (California), and local (county and city of Los Angeles) levels that has primary administrative authority for the chosen issue areas. Particularly important departments within primary agencies are noted in parentheses. Also listed are special districts that have been created in California to deliver services not provided directly by the county or the city. Where there is no entry (for both Table A.1 and A.2) that jurisdiction possesses minimal or no statutory authority.

Table A.2 identifies the legislative committees (standing, select, joint) in the United States Congress and the California legislature that play the most consequential roles in considering legislation for the chosen issue areas. Although committees generally make or break legislation at the federal and state level, the small size of the Los Angeles County Board of Supervisors (five members) and the Los Angeles City Council (fifteen members) renders committees primarily symbolic. Thus, Table A.2 does not include specific breakdowns of the legislative branches for the county or city of Los Angeles. It is also important to note that the structure of the California legislature may be substantially altered by Proposition 140, which, in addition to imposing term limitations, calls for draconian cuts in the funding allotted for legislative staff.

Nongovernmental organizations are highlighted in Table A.3, which is intended to be purely illustrative and in no way comprehensive. These groups vary in size, scope, and jurisdiction, but all play influential roles in the policy-making process for one or more of the chosen issue areas. In the interest of clarity, they are listed only once, according to their principal (or very considerable) area of concern.

TABLE A.1

Decision Makers: The Executive Branch

Issue Areas / Governmental Jurisdictions	United States Federal Government	State of California	County of Los Angeles	City of Los Angeles
Agriculture	Department of Agriculture	Food and Agriculture Agency	Department of Agriculture, Commissioner of Weights and Measures	
Border region	Department of State (U.S.-Mexico Border Affairs Coordinator) Department of Justice (Immigration and Naturalization Service) Department of the Treasury (U.S. Customs Service) International Boundary and Water Commission, U.S. Section	Office of California-Mexico Affairs	San Diego County Department of Trans-Border Affairs No similar agency in Los Angeles County	San Diego Office of Binational Affairs No similar agency in City of Los Angeles
Commerce, trade, and investment	Department of Commerce United States Trade Representative	Business, Transportation, and Housing Agency California World Trade Commission, office in Mexico City California Commission for Economic Development		Mayor's Office on Business and Economic Development

TABLE A.1
(*continued*)

Issue Areas / Governmental Jurisdictions	United States Federal Government	State of California	County of Los Angeles	City of Los Angeles
Education	Department of Education	Superintendent of Public Instruction, Department of Education	Superintendent of Schools, Board of Education	Los Angeles Unified School District[a]
Energy	Department of Energy	California Energy Commission Public Utilities Commission	Metropolitan Water District[a]	Department of Water and Power
Environment/natural resources	Environmental Protection Agency Department of the Interior	California Environmental Protection Agency (created 17 July 1991 to assume most of the duties of the Environmental Affairs Agency and the Resources Agency)	South Coast Air Quality Management District[a]	
Foreign policy	Department of State	Office of California-Mexico Affairs		
Health and human services	Department of Health and Human Services	Health and Welfare Agency	Department of Health Services Department of Public Social Services	Transferred to Los Angeles County
Housing and urban planning	Department of Housing and Urban Development	Business, Transportation, and Housing Agency Growth Management Council	Department of Regional Planning Community Development Commission/Housing Authority	Planning Department Community Development Department Community Redevelopment Agency Housing Authority

Immigration	Department of Justice (Immigration and Naturalization Service)			
Justice, law, and narcotics	Department of Justice (Drug Enforcement Administration) Department of the Treasury (U.S. Customs Service) Department of State Department of Defense	Attorney General, Department of Justice Youth and Adult Correctional Agency	District Attorney Sheriff's office	City Attorney Los Angeles Police Department
Labor	Department of Labor	Department of Industrial Relations Agriculture Labor Relations Board		
Transportation and infrastructure	Department of Transportation	Business, Transportation, and Housing Agency	Southern California Rapid Transit District[a] Transportation Commission	Department of Transportation Department of Airports Harbor Department
Voter registration/ census	Department of Commerce (Bureau of the Census)	Secretary of State	Registrar/recorder	City clerk

[a] Special district created to deliver services not provided by city or county government.

TABLE A.2

Decision Makers: The Legislative Branch

Issue Areas / Governmental Jurisdictions	United States Senate: Standing, Select, and Joint Committees	United States House of Representatives: Standing and Select Committees	California Senate: Standing Committees	California Assembly: Standing Committees	California Legislature: Joint and Select Committees
Agriculture	Agriculture, Nutrition, and Forestry	Agriculture	Agriculture and Water Resources	Agriculture	
Border region	Foreign Relations	Foreign Affairs			Joint: Refugee Resettlement, International Migration, and Cooperative Development Assembly Select: California-Mexico Affairs
Commerce, trade, and investment	Finance Banking, Housing, and Urban Affairs Joint: Economic	Ways and Means Banking, Finance, and Urban Affairs Energy and Commerce	Banking, Commerce, and International Trade	Banking, Finance, and Bonded Indebtedness	Joint: State's Economy
Education	Labor and Human Resources	Education and Labor	Education	Education Higher Education	Joint: School Facilities Senate Select: Bilingual Education
Energy	Energy and Natural Resources	Energy and Commerce Interior and Insular Affairs Science, Space, and Technology	Energy and Public Utilities	Utilities and Commerce	Joint: Energy Regulation and the Environment

Environment/natural resources	Environment and Public Works	Interior and Insular Affairs Energy and Commerce Science, Space, and Technology	Natural Resources Toxics and Public Safety Management	Natural Resources Water, Parks, and Wildlife Environmental Safety and Toxic Materials	
Foreign policy	Foreign Relations	Foreign Affairs			Assembly Select: California-Mexico Affairs
Health and human services	Labor and Human Resources Finance	Education and Labor Select: Children, Youth, and Families	Health and Human Services	Health Health Services Insurance	Senate Select: Children and Youth
Housing and urban planning	Banking, Housing, and Urban Affairs	Banking, Finance, and Urban Affairs	Housing and Urban Affairs	Housing and Community Development	Senate Select: Planning for California's Growth
Immigration	Judiciary	Judiciary			Joint: Refugee Resettlement, International Migration, and Cooperative Development
Justice, law, and narcotics	Judiciary Foreign Relations	Judiciary Foreign Affairs Select: Narcotics Abuse and Control	Judiciary	Judiciary	
Labor	Labor and Human Resources	Education and Labor	Industrial Relations	Labor and Employment	
Transportation and infrastructure	Commerce, Science, and Transportation	Public Works and Transportation Science, Space, and Technology	Transportation	Transportation	
Voter registration/census	Governmental Affairs	Post Office and Civil Service	Elections and Reapportionment	Elections, Reapportionment, and Constitutional Amendments	

TABLE A.3

Decision Makers: Nongovernmental Actors, by Issue Area

Agriculture
- California Farm Bureau Federation
- United Farmworkers
- Campesinos Unidos
- American Farmland Trust
- Migrant Farmworkers Rights Project
- Association of Farmworker Opportunity Programs
- Northwest Horticultural Council

Border region
- Border Trade Alliance
- American Friends Service
- Western Maquiladora Trade Association
- Border Ecology Project
- Mexican Association of Private Industrial Parks
- Pan-American Health Organization
- U.S.-Mexico Border Health Association
- Institute for Regional Studies of the Californias
- Centro Cultural de la Raza
- San Diego Museum of Contemporary Art, Dos Ciudades Project

Commerce, trade, and investment
- U.S.-Hispanic Chamber of Commerce
- Mexico-U.S. Business Committee
- U.S.-Mexico Chamber of Commerce, Pacific Chapter
- Latin Business Association
- San Diego Economic Development Corporation
- East Los Angeles Community Union
- California-Mexico Chamber of Commerce
- Otay Chamber of Commerce
- California Manufacturers Association
- Mexican-American Grocers Association

Education
- California Association of Bilingual Education
- English Only
- Mexican-American Opportunity Foundation
- California Teachers' Association
- Task Force on K-12 Education on Mexico
- California School Administrators Association
- California Tomorrow
- American Council on Education
- California Association of Mexican Educators
- United Teachers of Los Angeles
- Achievement Council

Energy
- American Petroleum Institute
- Association of California Energy Officials
- Sierra Club
- Utility Consumers Action Network
- Electric Power Research Institute
- San Diego Gas and Electric, Mexico Projects

Environment and natural resources
- National Resources Defense Council
- Environmental Defense Fund
- National Wildlife Federation
- California Public Interest Research Group
- Coalition for Clean Air
- Association of California Water Agencies
- League of Conservation Voters
- San Diego-Tijuana Environmental Committee of the United Nations Association

Foreign policy
- Council of the Americas
- Center for Strategic and International Studies
- U.S.-Mexico Dialogos
- Los Angeles World Affairs Council
- Inter-American Dialogue
- Latin American Studies Association
- Bilateral Commission on the Future of U.S-Mexico Relations
- Center for United States-Mexico Studies

Health and human services
- National Coalition of Hispanic Health and Human Services Organizations
- Roman Catholic Archdiocese of Los Angeles/Catholic Charities
- National Concilio of America
- East Los Angeles Health Task Force
- Family Planning Centers of Greater Los Angeles
- Community Services Organization
- Chicana Action Service Center
- California Hispanic Commission on Alcohol and Drug Abuse
- Health Access of California
- United Way
- AIDS Project LA
- Asociación Nacional por Personas Mayores
- Alta Med Health Services Corporation

TABLE A.3
(continued)

Housing and urban planning	Labor
The Los Angeles 2000 Partnership	Los Angeles County Federation of Labor, AFL-CIO
Central City Association of Los Angeles	Labor Council for Latin American Advancement
United Neighborhoods Organization	Chicano Advocates for Employment
Legal Aid Foundation of Los Angeles, Eviction Defense Center	East Los Angeles Occupational Center
Fair Housing Congress of Southern California	Amalgamated Clothing and Textiles Workers Union
California Neighborhood Housing Services Foundation	Service Employees International Union
Los Angeles Community Design Center	National Hispanic Media Coalition
Mothers of East Los Angeles	Labor Communities Strategy Institute
Esperanza International	
Immigration	Transportation and infrastructure
One Stop Immigration and Educational Center	Southern California Association of Governments
Federation for American Immigration Reform	California Transit Association
National Network for Immigrant and Refugee Rights	Air Transport Association of America
Center for Immigrant and Refugee Services	Pacific Merchant Shipping Association
Centro de Asuntos Migratorios	San Diego Association of Governments
International Ladies Garment Workers Union	Voter registration/census/politics
Light Up the Border	Southwest Voter Registration and Education Project
Justice, law, and narcotics	National Association of Latino Elected Officials
Mexican-American Legal Defense and Educational Fund	Mexican American Political Association
American Civil Liberties Union	League of United Latin American Citizens
Human Rights Watch/America Watch	Comisión Femenil Mexicana Nacional
Mexican-American Bar Association	Californians for Fair Representation
Community Youth Gang Services Project	Hispanic Leaders Coalition of California
California Rural Legal Assistance	National Council of La Raza
La Raza Lawyers Association	

NOTE: Special thanks to Cathryn Thorup, Geoffrey Bogart, Paul Ganster, and Steve Erie for their helpful and insightful suggestions regarding this table.

The California-Mexico Connection in Tables and Figures

DAN HIMELSTEIN AND
IGNACIO GARCÍA LASCURAÍN

TABLE B.1
California and Mexico: Basic Data, 1989–90

	California	Mexico
Population	29.8 million	81.2 million
Area	158,706 sq. miles	1,174,921 sq. miles
Gross product	$717 billion	$201 billion
Per capita income ($U.S.)	$24,141	$2,383
Life expectancy	76	69
Enrollment in higher education	62%	16%

SOURCE: U.S. Census Bureau; Mexican Census; World Bank

Population Demographics

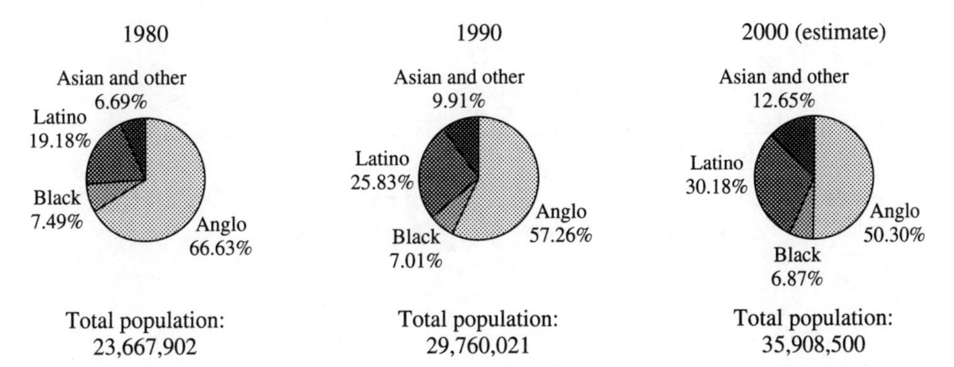

Figure B.1. California population, by ethnicity, 1980–2000. For 1980 and 1990, U.S. Census Bureau; for 2000, Center for Continuing Study of the California Economy.

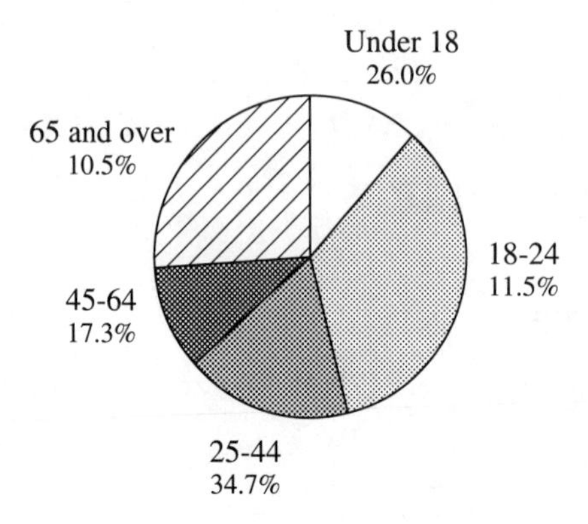

Figure B.2. California population, by age, 1990. U.S. Census Bureau.

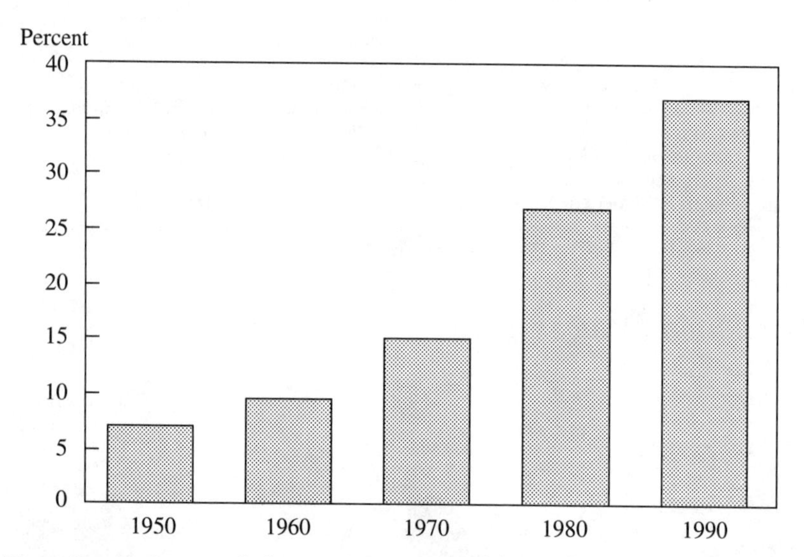

Figure B.3. Latino population as a percentage of the total population of Los Angeles County, 1950–1990. *Los Angeles Times,* 6 May 1991.

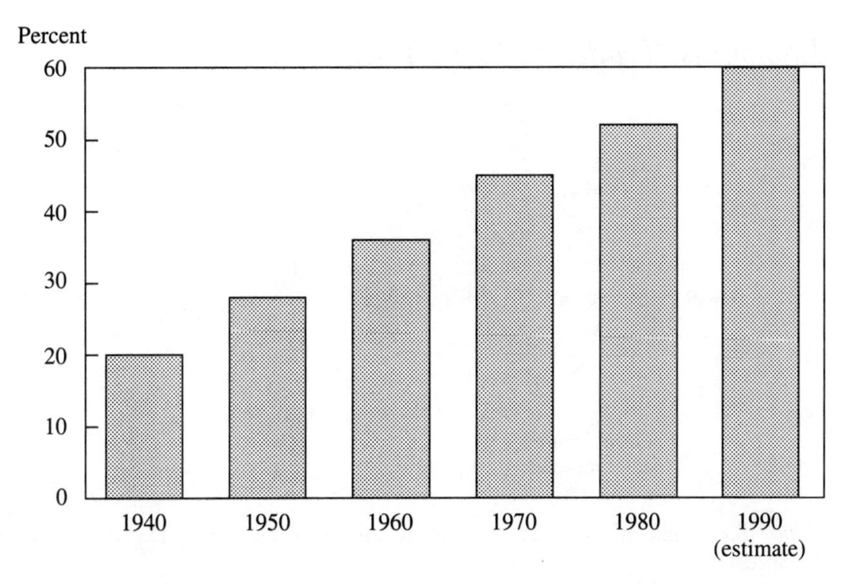

Figure B.4. Urban population as a percentage of the total population of Mexico, 1940–1990. Banamex.

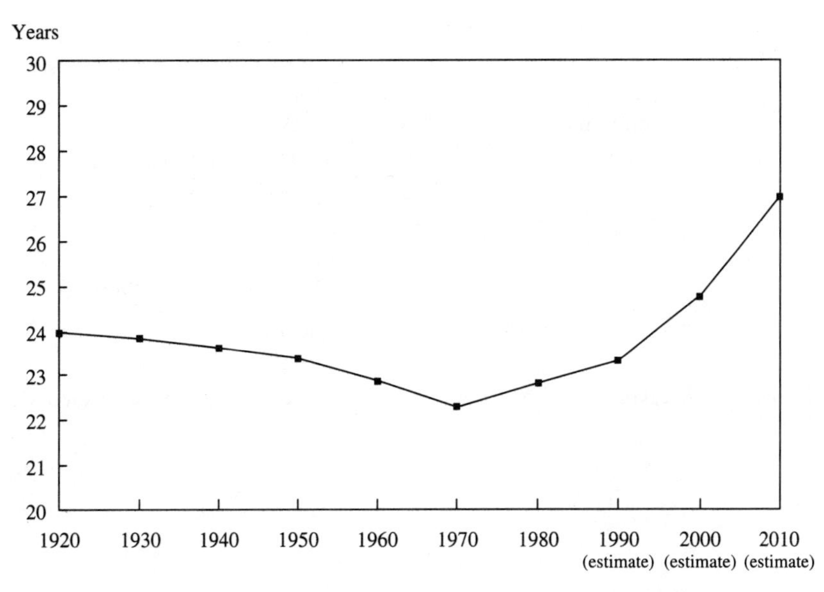

Figure B.5. Average age of the Mexican population, 1920–2010. Banamex.

Economics, Trade, and Investment

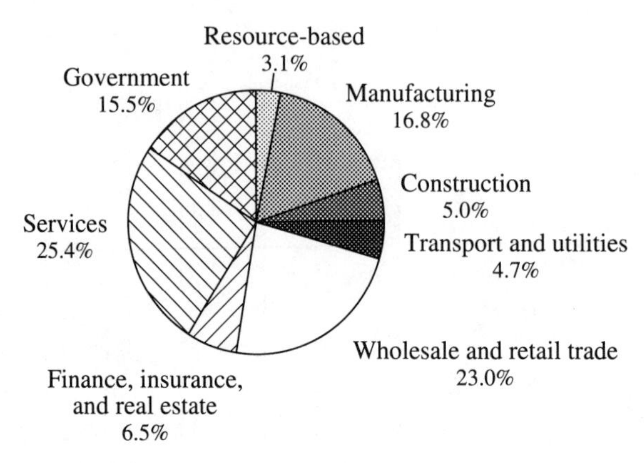

Figure B.6. California employment, by sector, 1989. California Department of Finance.

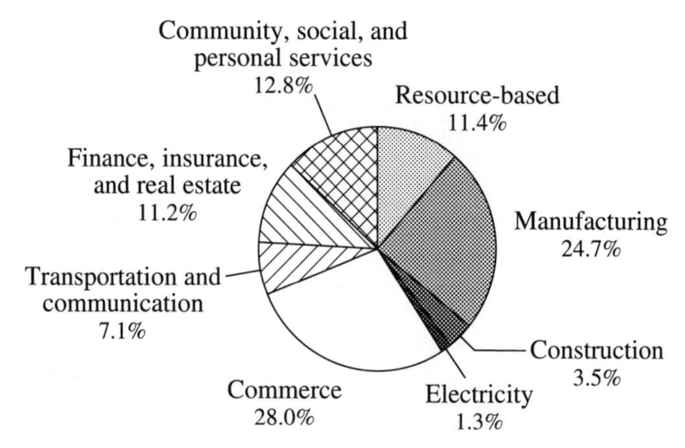

Figure B.7. Breakdown of Mexican gross domestic product, 1989. Banco de México.

TABLE B.2

California's Top Exports to Mexico, 1989 Port Data

	Value (thousands of $U.S.)	Percent of total
Total exports	3,500,000	
Electronic equipment	737,095	21.0
Petroleum refining	332,078	9.5
Transportation equipment	304,647	8.7
Fabricated metals	242,351	7.9
Computer and peripheral equipment	95,904	2.7

SOURCE: California World Trade Commission.

TABLE B.3

California's Top Imports from Mexico, 1989 Port Data

	Value (thousands of $U.S.)	Percent of total
Total imports	3,800,000	
Electronic equipment	1,374,185	36.2
Scientific and control equipment	216,136	5.8
Fabricated metals	197,188	5.1
Foods (processed and prepared)	161,255	4.2
Computer and peripheral equipment	135,439	3.5

SOURCE: California World Trade Commission.

TABLE B.4

Foreign-Owned Financial Institutions in California, 1990

Nation	Number of institutions	Approximate value of combined assets (millions of $U.S.)
Japan	31	104,400
France	7	3,800
Italy	7	3,300
South Korea	9	2,600
Canada	8	2,000
Mexico	5	1,900
Germany	5	1,000
Taiwan	4	885
Hong Kong	4	804
Indonesia	5	777

SOURCE: California State Banking Department.

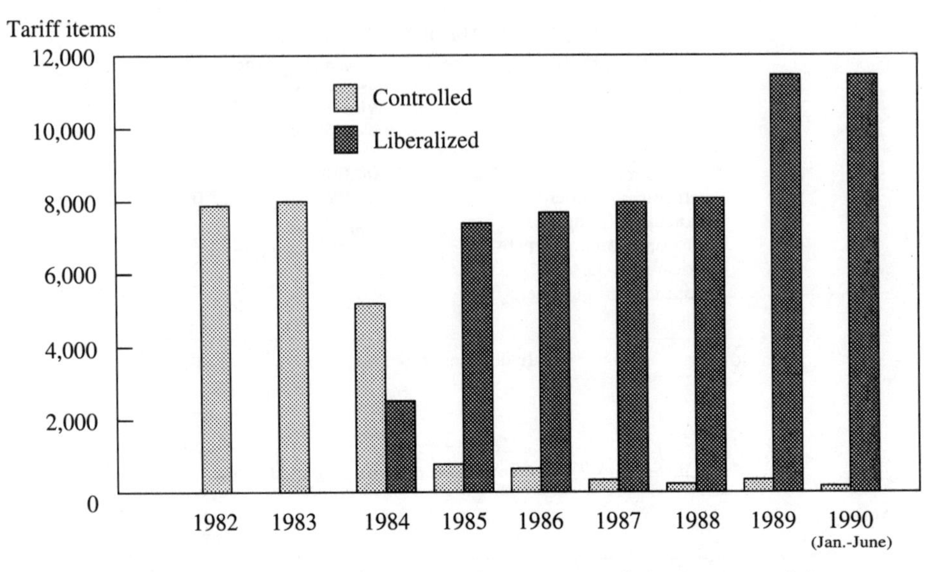

Figure B.8. Liberalization of Mexican import controls, 1982–1990. Salomon Brothers.

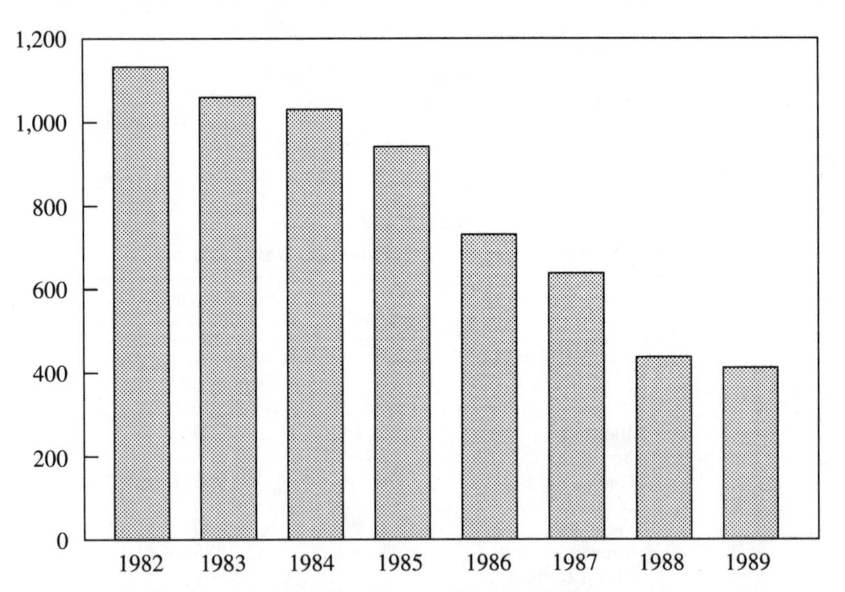

Figure B.9. Number of state-owned enterprises in Mexico, 1982–1989. Salomon Brothers.

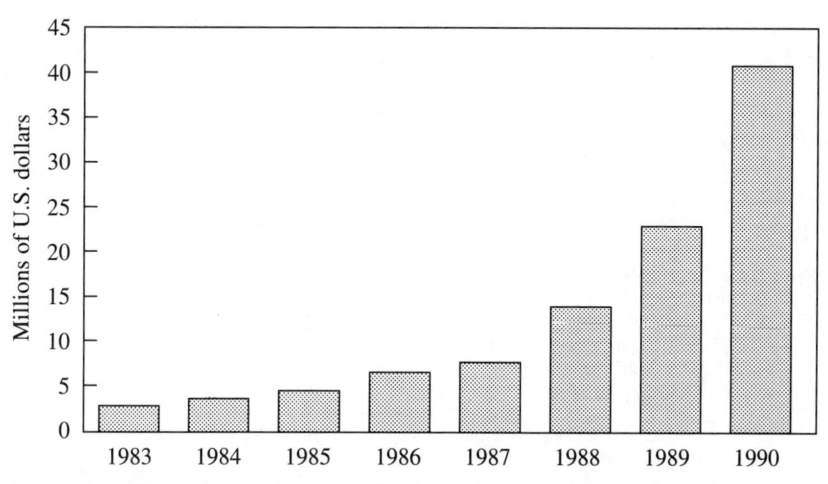

Figure B.10. Increasing market capitalization in Mexico, 1983–1990. Acciones y Valores de México.

Immigration and Naturalization

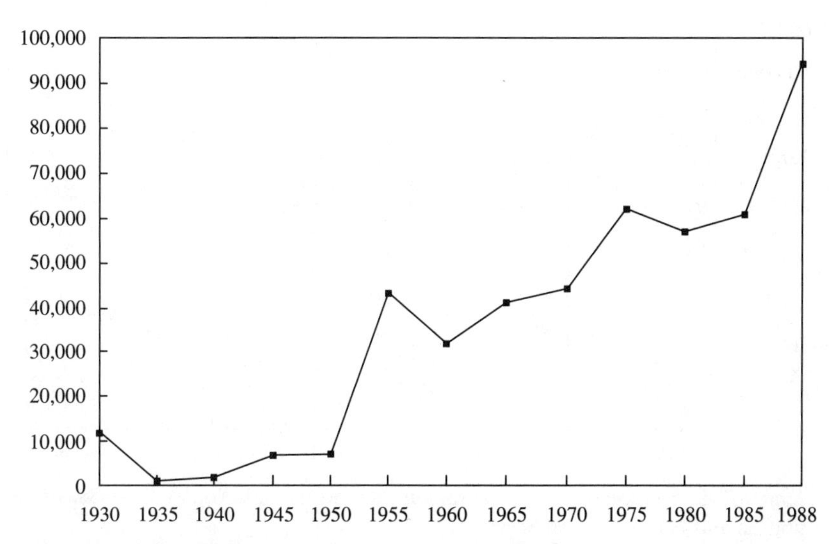

Figure B.11. Legal Mexican immigration to the United States, 1930–1988; Mexican immigrants are defined as resident aliens (i.e., non-U.S. citizens) whose last country of permanent residence was Mexico and who were legally admitted to the United States for permanent residence. U.S. Census Bureau; Immigration and Naturalization Service.

TABLE B.5

Estimates of Undocumented Aliens in the United States by State, 1980

State	Number of undocumented aliens	Percent of total
California	1,024,000	49.75
New York	234,000	11.39
Texas	186,000	9.09
Illinois	135,000	6.59
Florida	80,000	3.90
Arizona, Maryland, New Jersey, Virginia, Washington	150,000	7.29
Other 40 states	—	11.99

SOURCE: U.S. Congress, House Committee on Post Office and Civil Service.

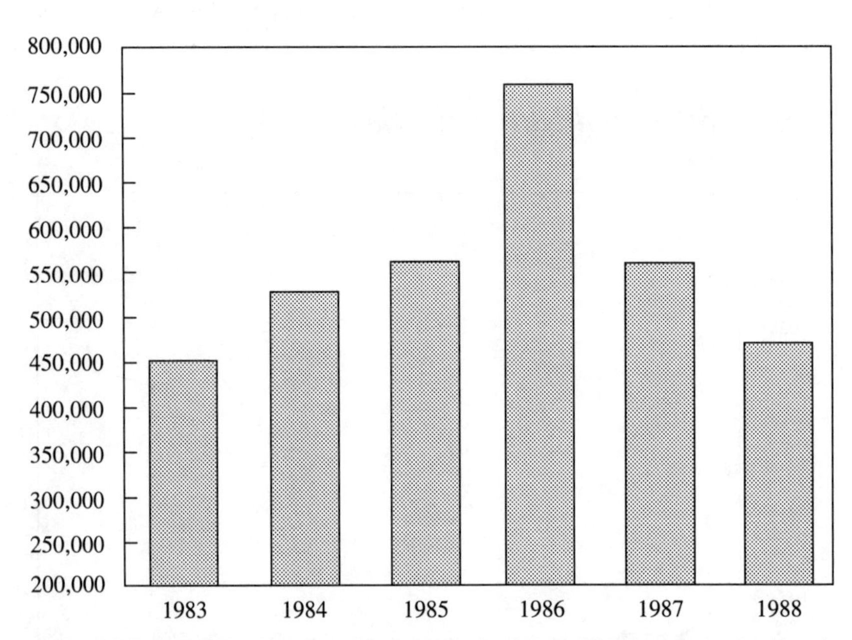

Figure B.12. Number of illegal immigrants seized in California, 1983–1988. Immigration and Naturalization Service.

Political Empowerment and Voter Registration

TABLE B.6
Proportion of Latino Elected Officials in California, 1980 and 1990

	Percent of total elected officials
1980	3.6
1990	7.6 (217 out of 2,861)

SOURCE: *Sacramento Bee*, 31 Mar. 1990.

TABLE B.7
Political Appointments of Latinos in California, 1975–1991

Administration	Percent of total appointments
Governor E. G. Brown, Jr. (1975–83)	8.5 (585 out of 6,866)
Governor G. Deukmejian (1983–91)	6.9 (458 out of 6,643, through June 1989)

SOURCE: Office of the Governor of California.

TABLE B.8
Judicial Appointments of Latinos in California, 1959–1991

Administration	Percent of total appointments
Governor E. G. Brown, Sr. (1959–67)	2.5 (10 out of 400)
Governor R. Reagan (1967–75)	3.3 (16 out of 491)
Governor E. G. Brown, Jr. (1975–83)	10.7 (77 out of 723)
Governor G. Deukmejian (1983–91)	5.1 (49 out of 968, through November 1990)

SOURCE: Office of the Governor of California.

TABLE B.9

Latinos in the June 1990 California Primary Election

	Percent Latino
California's population	26
Vote-eligible adult citizens	15
Registered voters	10
Actual voters	6

SOURCE: U.S. Census Bureau; California secretary of state.

TABLE B.10

Mexico Voter Abstention, 1982 and 1988 Elections

	Vote-eligible, not registered (%)		Registered voters, not voting (%)	
	1982	1988	1982	1988
Mexico total	22.2	36.3	25.2	49.7
Baja California	22.1	41.9	22.2	49.4

SOURCE: *El Cotidiano* 25 (Sept.–Oct. 1988): 12.

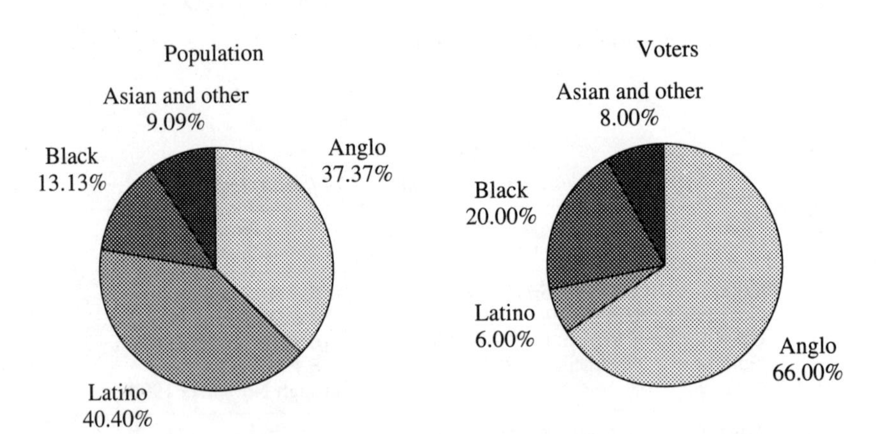

Figure B.13. Voting pattern in 1989 Los Angeles City mayoral election, by ethnicity. Fairbank, Bregman and Maulin.

Education and the Occupational Structure

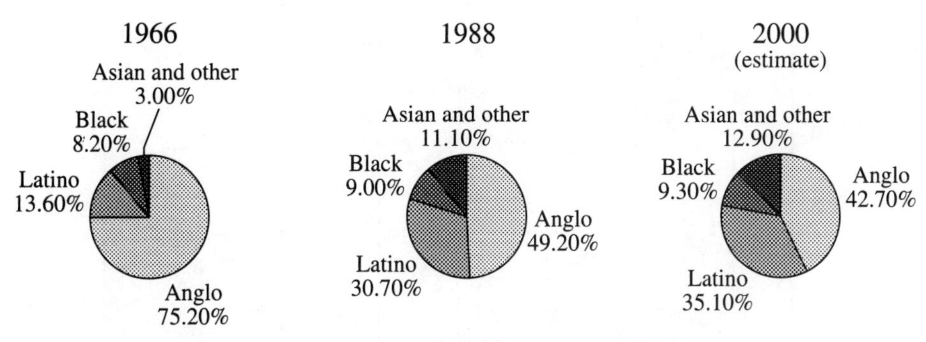

Figure B.14. California public school students, by ethnicity, 1966–2000. *Los Angeles Times,* 7 Sept. 1988.

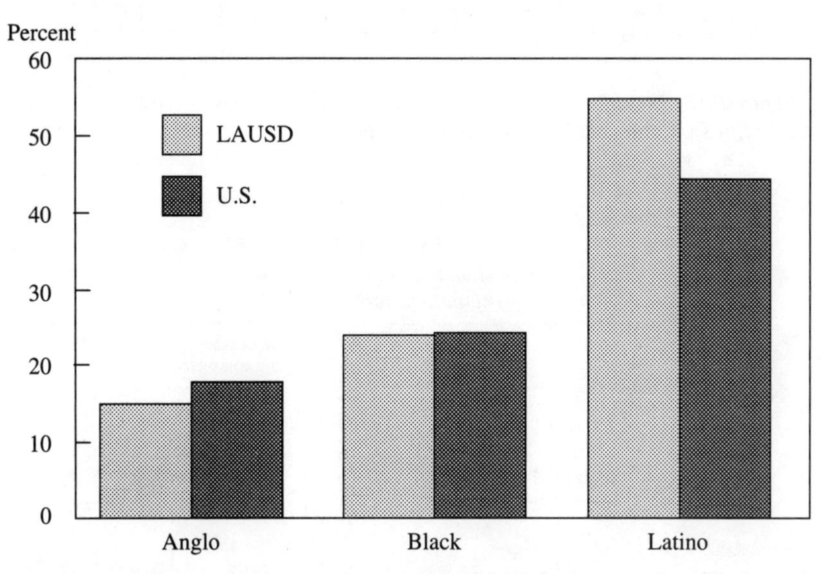

Figure B.15. High school dropout rate, Los Angeles Unified School District (LAUSD) and U.S. average, by ethnicity, 1988–89. LAUSD; American Council on Education.

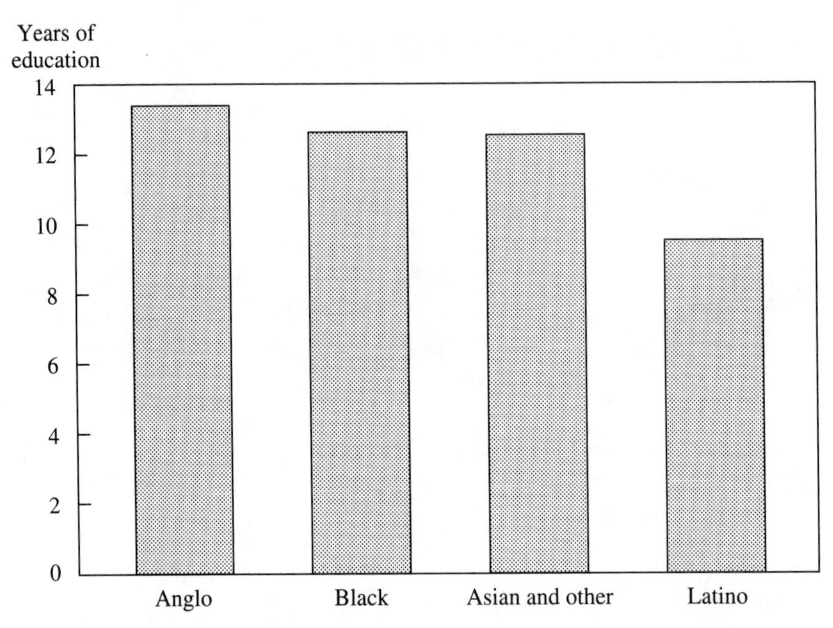

Figure B.16. Average educational levels of Californians age 25 and older, by ethnicity, 1989. California Department of Finance.

TABLE B.11

Educational Level of the Mexican Population, 1978 and 1988

	Average of years of schooling completed
1978	5.1
1988	6.2

SOURCE: Banamex

TABLE B.12
California Occupational Structure by Ethnicity, 1990

	Anglo (%)	Black (%)	Asian and other (%)	Latino (%)	Total employment (%)
Managerial and professional	34.6	23.9	28.4	10.3	27.6
Sales, administration, and technical support	33.8	32.3	38.7	21.9	31.3
Service workers	10.5	16.8	13.9	18.1	13.0
Farm workers	1.6	0.2	0.7	9.5	3.3
Precision and craft workers	10.2	11.7	8.5	13.5	10.9
Operators and laborers	9.2	15.2	9.8	26.7	13.8

SOURCE: Current Population Survey.

Welfare, Health and Human Services, and Housing

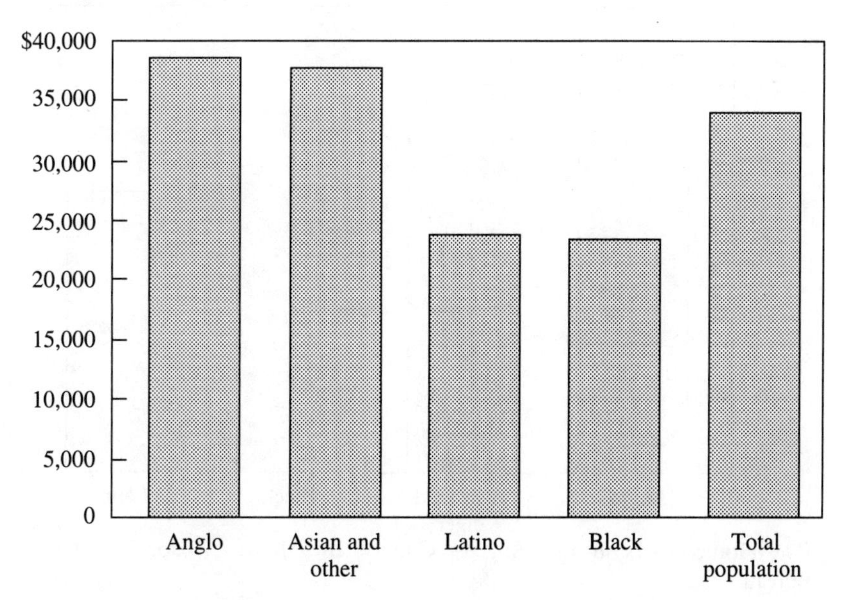

Figure B.17. Median family income in California, by ethnicity, 1988. Current Population Survey.

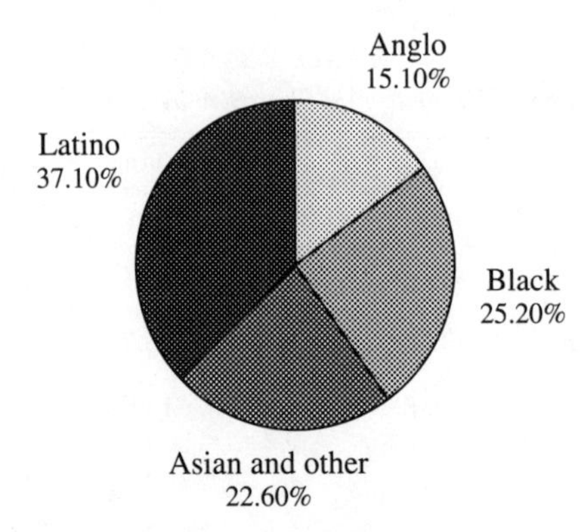

Figure B.18. California adults not covered by health insurance, by ethnicity, 1986. University of California, California Policy Seminar.

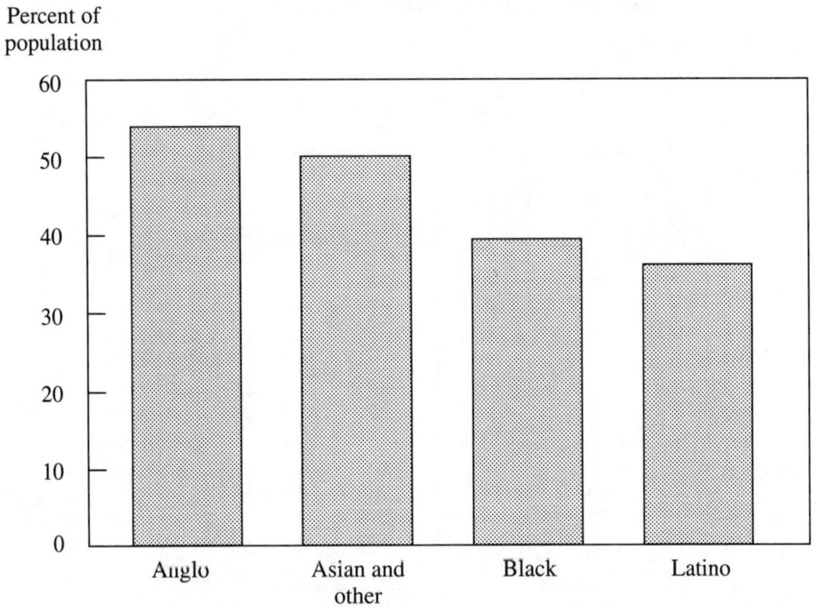

B.19. Homeowners in Los Angeles County, by ethnicity, 1980. U.S. Census Bureau.

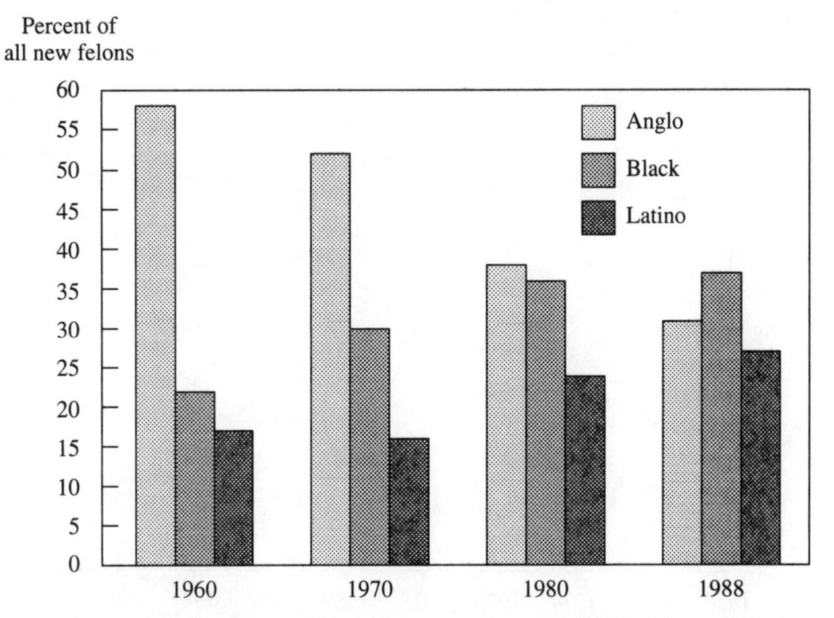

Figure B.20. New felons in California prisons and camps, by ethnicity, 1960–1988. California Department of Corrections.

The Border Regions and the 'Maquiladoras'

TABLE B.13
San Diego–Tijuana "Twin City" Population, 1970–1990

	Tijuana	San Diego	Twin city total
1970	340,583	1,367,200	1,707,783
1980	659,500	1,874,500	2,534,000
1990	1,129,000 (est.)	2,509,900	3,638,900 (est.)

SOURCE: California Department of Finance, Demographic Research Unit; Mexican census and official government projections.

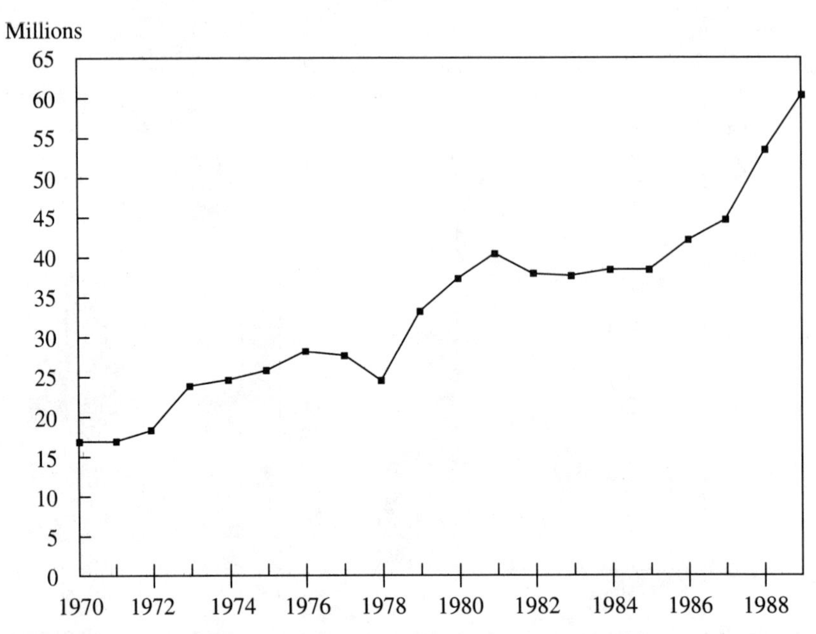

Figure B.21. Annual border crossings into California from Mexico, 1970–1989. San Diego Convention and Visitors Bureau.

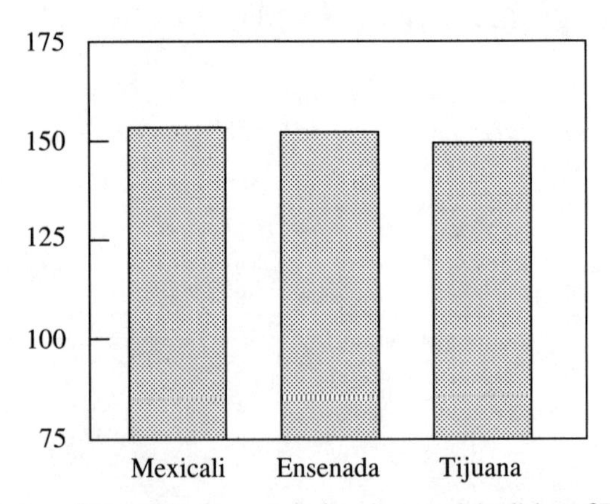

Figure B.22. Index of per capita income in border municipalities of Baja California, 1980; Mexican national average income = 100. James T. Peach, *Demographic and Economic Change in Mexico's Northern Frontier; Evidence from the X Censo General de Poblacíon y Vivienda* (Las Cruces: New Mexico State University, 1984).

TABLE B.14
Distribution of Mexican Maquiladora *Plants by State, 1990*

State	Number of Plants	State	Number of Plants
Baja California	797	Nuevo León	62
Baja California Sur	16	Sonora	116
Chihuahua	354	Tamaulipas	213
Coahuila	109	Other	74

SOURCE: State of California, Office of California-Mexico Affairs.

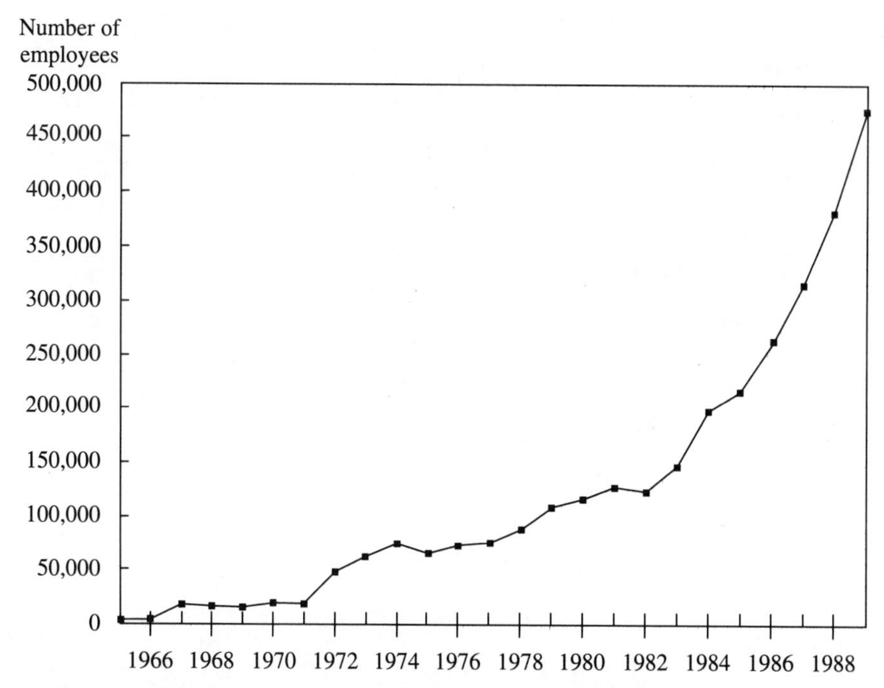

Figure B.23. Mexican *maquila* employees, 1965–1989. Ellwyn R. Stoddard, *Maquila Assembly Plants in Northern Mexico* (El Paso: Texas Western University Press, 1987); David E. Lorey, ed., *United States–Mexico Border Statistics Since 1900* (Los Angeles: UCLA Latin American Center Publications, 1990).

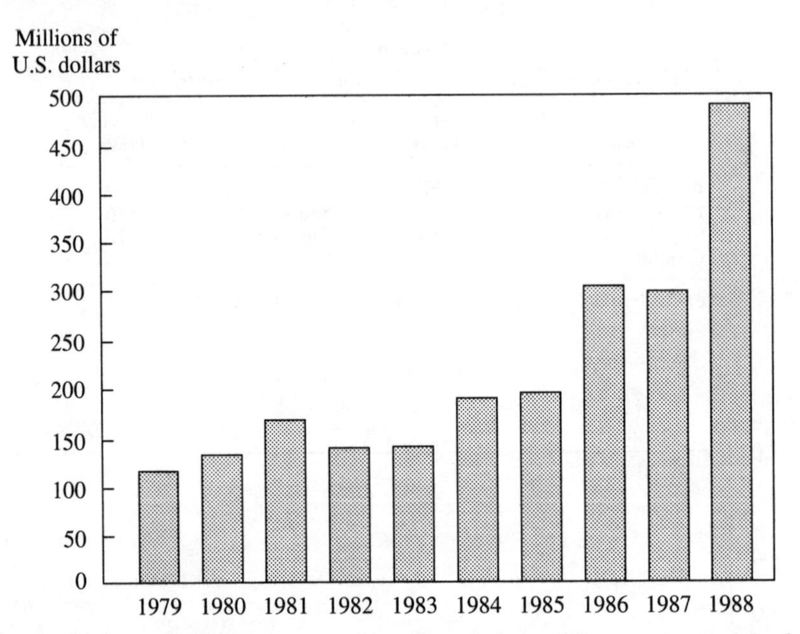

Figure B.24. Value added of Baja California *maquiladora* plants, 1979–1988. Stoddard, *Maquila Assembly Plants.*

Reference Matter

Notes

1. Rosenau: Theorizing About the California-Mexico Overlap

1. Another label that has been used for similar purposes is that of "territorial collectivity." Indeed, the definition of territorial collectivities is in many respects a description of key elements of the California-Mexico Connection and, as such, gives one pause as to the future prospects for the Connection: "Industrial civilizations transform local systems and pose a threat to the existence of their communities. . . . As opposed to the local community which is an integrated group of extended families bound with family or neighborly relationships, the collectivity is made up of atomized nuclear families and lone people. Typical of the collectivity is its fluid composition which makes it impossible to establish permanent and important social ties. Unlike local communities, territorial collectivities do not have a political or institutional expression. . . . Finally, unlike communities, collectivities inhabit an area and not a locality. . . . A locality is something well-known, assimilated, one's own, whereas an area is no one's and alien." B. Jalowiecki, as quoted in Antoni Kuklinski, "Local Development—Experiences and Prospects," in A. Kuklinski, ed., *Globality versus Locality* (Warsaw: University of Warsaw, 1990), p. 219.

2. Both of these interlocal institutions were founded in western Europe in the 1970s.

3. Cf. Ivo D. Duchacek, *The Territorial Dimension of Politics: Within, Among, and Across Nations* (Boulder, Colo.: Westview Press, 1986), chaps. 8–10.

4. One possible exception in this regard could result from a 1990 bill introduced into the California State Assembly that proposed the establishment of the California-Mexico Joint Infrastructure Bonding Authority.

5. See, for example, the papers that emanate from the annual meetings of the U.S.-Mexican Association of Borderland Scholars.

6. Alberto Melucci, "Frontierland: Collective Action Between Actors and Systems," paper presented at the Twelfth World Congress of Sociology, Madrid, 9–13 July 1990), p. 14.

7. For a discussion in which "incoherent structures" are differentiated from structurelessness and conceived as one extreme on a continuum beyond which randomness prevails and structures collapse into formlessness, see James N. Rosenau, *Turbulence in World Politics: A Theory of Change and Continuity* (Princeton: Princeton University Press, 1990), pp. 243–44.

8. Paul Ganster and Alan Sweedler, "The United States–Mexican Border Region: Security and Interdependence," in David Lorey, ed., *United States–Mexico Border Statistics Since 1900* (Los Angeles: UCLA Latin American Center Publications, 1990), p. 426.

9. Ganster and Sweedler, "United States–Mexican Border Region," p. 419.

10. For some general assessments of integration theory, see James A. Caporaso, *Functionalism and Regional Integration: A Logical and Empirical Assessment* (Beverly Hills, Calif.: Sage Publications, 1972); Ernst B. Haas, *The Uniting of Europe* (Stanford, Calif.: Stanford University Press, 1959); Leon Lindberg and Stuart Scheingold, *Europe's Would-Be Polity: Patterns of Change in the European Community* (New York: Prentice-Hall, 1970); David Mitrany, *A Working Peace System* (Chicago: Quadrangle Books, 1945); Charles Pentland, *International Theory and European Integration* (New York: Free Press, 1973).

11. See, for example, Charles Tilly, ed., *The Formation of National States in Western Europe* (Princeton: Princeton University Press, 1975).

12. Especially relevant here is Robert H. Jackson, *Quasi-States, Sovereignty, International Relations and the Third World* (Cambridge, Eng.: Cambridge University Press, 1991).

13. Stuart S. Nagel, "Introduction to Global Policy Studies," *International Political Science Review* 11 (July 1990): 303.

14. Marvin S. Soroos, "A Theoretical Framework for Global Policy Studies," *International Political Science Review* 11 (July 1990): 310.

15. Ibid., p. 309.

16. Ibid., p. 310.

17. Ibid.

18. For elaborate and diverse assessments of regime theory, see Stephen D. Krasner, ed., *International Regimes* (Ithaca, N.Y.: Cornell University Press, 1983). The various contributors to the volume agreed to employ the quoted definition in their essays. It can be found in Krasner's introductory chapter, p. 2.

19. Krasner, *International Regimes*, p. 2.

20. Key entries in the burgeoning literature on world cities include Chadwick F. Alger, "The World Relations of Cities: Closing the Gap Between Social Science Paradigms and Everyday Human Experience," *International Studies Quarterly* 34 (Dec. 1990): 493–518; C. K. Chase-Dunn, "The System of World Cities, 1800–1975," in M. Timberlake, ed., *Urbanization and the World Economy* (Orlando, Fla.: Academic Press, 1985); R. B. Cohen, "The New International Division of Labor, Multinational Corporations and Urban Hierarchy," in M. Dear and A. J. Scott, eds., *Urbanization and Urban Planning in Capitalist Society* (New York: Methuen, 1981); J. R. Feagin and M. P. Smith, eds., *The Capitalist City: Global Restructuring*

and Community Politics (Oxford: Basil Blackwell, 1987); J. Friedman and G. Wolff, "World City Formation: An Agenda for Research and Action," *Journal of Urban and Regional Research* 6, no. 3 (1982): 309–43; and Earl H. Fry, Lee H. Radebaugh, and Panayotis Soldatos, eds., *The New International Cities Era: The Global Activities of North American Municipal Governments* (Provo, Utah: David M. Kennedy Center for International Studies, Brigham Young University, 1989).

21. John Friedman, "The World City Hypothesis," *Development and Change* 17, no. 1 (1986): 74.

22. Ganster and Sweedler, "United States–Mexican Border Region," pp. 430–31.

23. Duchacek, *Territorial Dimension of Politics*, p. 208.

24. Ellwyn R. Stoddard, quoted in Duchacek, *Territorial Dimension of Politics*, p. 266.

25. Ganster and Sweedler, "United States–Mexican Border Region," pp. 423, 424.

26. Duchacek, *Territorial Dimension of Politics*, pp. 260–61.

27. For possible exceptions in this regard, see Duchacek, *Territorial Dimension of Politics*, and Oscar J. Martinez, ed., *Across Boundaries: Transborder Interaction in Comparative Perspective* (El Paso: Texas Western Press, 1986).

28. Rosenau, *Turbulence in World Politics*, chaps. 3–5, 10.

29. Ibid., pp. 305–8.

30. For a probing of how environmental issues have been affected by the advent of turbulence in world politics, see James N. Rosenau, "Environmental Challenges in a Turbulent World," in Ronnie D. Lipschutz and Ken Conca, eds., *The State and Social Power in Global Environmental Politics* (New York: Columbia University Press, 1993), pp. 71–93.

31. Ganster and Sweedler, "United States–Mexican Border Region," p. 437.

32. John D. Negroponte, "U.S.-Mexican Relations: A U.S. Perspective," unpublished paper, 24 Feb. 1990, p. 8.

33. Ganster and Sweedler, "United States–Mexican Border Region," p. 428.

34. See, for example, the dismaying account of one such project in Thomas J. Price, *Standoff at the Border: A Failure of Micro Diplomacy* (El Paso: Texas Western Press, 1989).

35. For a cogent discussion of the diverse organizations and forms of interaction that have recently evolved to cope with the surge in interdependencies that span the U.S.–Mexican border, see Bruce Stokes, "Boom at the Border," *National Journal*, 29 July 1989, pp. 1922–27.

36. Cathryn L. Thorup, "What a Difference a Year Makes: The 'New and Improved' Bilateral Relationship," unpublished paper, p. 4.

37. Ganster and Sweedler, "United States–Mexican Border Region," p. 419.

38. For hints as to the delicacy of the roles played by elites and publics, see John Kincaid, "Rainclouds over Municipal Diplomacy: Dimensions and Possible Sources of Negative Public Opinion," in Fry, Radebaugh, and Soldatos, *New International Cities Era*, pp. 223–49.

39. Ganster and Sweedler, "United States–Mexican Border Region," p. 424.

40. Cathryn L. Thorup, "The Politics of Free Trade and the Dynamics of Cross-Border Coalitions in U.S.-Mexican Relations," *Columbia Journal of World Business* 26 (Summer 1991): 21.
41. Ibid., p. 22.
42. Ganster and Sweedler, "United States–Mexican Border Region," p. 440.

2. *Castañeda: Tolerance and Dedemocratization*

This chapter was written in the spring of 1991 while I was a visting professor at the University of California at Berkeley, whose Center for Latin American Studies I wish to thank for its hospitality and support. The Political and Social Sciences Department at the National Autonomous University of Mexico also deserves a note of thanks for its backing.

1. I am particularly indebted to Carlos Monsiváis for his insights and generosity in sharing with me many of his ideas and sensitivity to these issues. The insights are his; their use and possible abuse are of course mine.
2. Omar Fonseca, *Don Manuel: Historia de un migrante* (Jiquílpan, Michoacán: Desdeldiez, 1986), p. 68.
3. Omar Fonseca and Lilia Morena, *Jaripo, Pueblo de migrantes* (Jiquílpan, Michoacán: Centro de Estudios de la Revolución Mexicana Lázaro Cárdenas, 1984), p. 325.
4. Gustavo López Castro, *La casa divida* (Zamora, Michoacán: El Colegio de Michoacán, 1986), p. 136.
5. *Ibid*., p. 125.
6. *La Jornada*, Mexico City, 17 June 1991.
7. Carlos Monsiváis, "Si existe tal lugar: Los Angeles," *La Jornada—World Media*, 21 June 1991.
8. Jesús Martínez, "The Tigers in the Golden Cage: Binational Culture and Politics in a Popular Song of Mexican Immigrants in the United States," unpublished paper, 1991.
9. In fact, the largest and fastest-growing sects are in states such as Chiapas and Tabasco, largely unlinked to migration. And several of the most important migrant-sending states in Mexico—Guanajuato, Jalisco, and Michoacán—are also the regions with the strongest Catholic past.
10. Ramón "Tianguis" Pérez, *Diary of an Undocumented Immigrant* (Houston: Arte Publico Press, 1991), p. 237.
11. For a detailed analysis of this phenomenon in Los Angeles, see Paul Ong, ed., *The Widening Divide: Income Inequality and Poverty in Los Angeles* (Los Angeles: University of California at Los Angeles, 1989).
12. Mike Davis, *City of Quartz* (New York: Verso Books, 1991), p. 315.
13. Jackie Goldberg, comments at the Third Annual California Studies Conference, California State University, Sacramento, 7 Feb. 1991.
14. Kevin Phillips, *The Politics of Rich and Poor* (New York: Random House, 1990), p. 25.

15. *Los Angeles Times* 1990 exit poll, 6 Nov. 1990; "California is Most Racially Diverse State," *Los Angeles Times*, 13 June 1991.

16. Georges Vernez and David Ronfeldt, "The Current Situation in Mexican Immigration," *Science* 251 (8 Mar. 1991): 1191.

17. "Current Population Survey Voter Supplement File, 1988, Voter Registration, Voter Turnout and Citizenship by Race and Ethnicity."

18. Goldberg, "Comments."

19. Ibid.

20. Thomas Byrne Edsall and Mary D. Edsall, "The Real Subject Is Race," *Atlantic Monthly*, May 1991, p. 84.

21. Vernez and Ronfeldt, "Current Situation," p. 1191.

22. Tomás Hammar, *El derecho de voto de los inmigrantes y la participación electoral* (Instituto Sueco, 1985).

3. Rubio and Trejo: New Economic Ties

1. In 1989, the state of Texas exported $9.8 billion to Mexico, while California sold $3.5 billion. However, California exports to Mexico in 1989 experienced a 27-percent growth rate, compared to the 19.5-percent increase enjoyed by Texas.

2. ITAM, Centro de Análisis e Investigación Económica, *Informe Mensual Sobre la Economía Mexicana* 6, no. 1 (Jan. 1989): 21.

3. *Economic Report of the Governor* (Sacramento: California Department of Finance, 1990); Bank of America, "California, Mexico, and the North American Free Trade Agreement," *Economic and Business Outlook*, Sept.–Oct. 1991.

4. Unless otherwise indicated, the data used in this and the following section are based on *California Statistical Abstract* (Sacramento: California Department of Finance, 1990) and *Economic Report of the Governor*.

5. "Survey on California," *The Economist*, 19 May 1984, p. 5.

6. *81st Annual Report* (Sacramento: California State Banking Department, 1990).

7. These rankings are based on point-of-origin data rather than port data. The latter, which includes all products passing through California's customs districts, puts Mexico fifth in terms of exports and imports. See *Economic Report of the Governor*, p. 24.

8. Bank of America, "California, Mexico, and the North American Free Trade Agreement."

9. This figure is derived from a multiplier developed by the U.S. Department of Commerce, which estimates that every $40,000 of exports translates into one direct or indirect job.

10. Instituto Nacional de Estadística, Geografía e Informática, "Avance de información economica: Industria maquiladora de exportación," Jan. 1991, p. 3; A. L. Carreon, "La industria maquiladora en la franja fronteriza de California," *El Financiero*, 12 Nov. 1990.

11. Bruce Stokes, "Boom at the Border," *National Journal*, 29 July 1989, p. 1924.

12. California State World Trade Commission, *California and the U.S.-Mexico Trade Negotiations* (Sacramento: California State World Trade Commission, 1991), p. 8.

13. California Department of Food and Agriculture, *On the Proposed U.S.-Mexico Free Trade Agreement: Issues for California's Agricultural Sector*, testimony presented to the Assembly Select Committee on California-Mexico Affairs, Sacramento, 24 Oct. 1990, p. 4.

4. *Escobar Latapí: Changing Socioeconomic Conditions and Migration Patterns*

I wish to thank Mercedes González de la Rocha, with whom this project was started, and David Hayes-Bautista, who introduced Mercedes and me to basic aspects of Hispanic life and culture in Los Angeles.

1. Wayne Cornelius, "Los migrantes de la crisis: The Changing Profile of Mexican Migration to the United States," in Mercedes González de la Rocha and Agustín Escobar Latapí, *Social Responses to Mexico's Economic Crisis of the 80's* (La Jolla, Calif.: Center for U.S.-Mexican Studies, UCSD, 1991), pp. 155–94.

2. Georges Vernez and David Ronfeldt, "The Current Situation in Mexican Immigration," *Science* 251 (1991): 1189–93.

3. Brígida García, *Desarrollo económico y absorción de fuerza de trabajo en México* (México D.F.: El Colegio de México, 1988).

4. Peter Blau and Otis D. Duncan, *The American Occupational Structure* (New York: John Wiley, 1967); Agustín Escobar Latapí and Bryan Roberts, "Urban Stratification, the Middle Classes and Economic Change in Mexico," in González de la Rocha and Escobar Latapí, eds., *Social Responses to Mexico's Economic Crisis of the 80's*, pp. 91–114.

5. Jesús Reyes Heroles G. G., "Política económica y desigualdad social: elementos de una estrategia para redistribuir el ingreso en México," in *Igualdad, desigualdad y equidad en España y México* (Madrid: Instituto de Cooperación Económica, 1985), p. 412; Escobar Latapí and Roberts, "Urban Stratification."

6. Carlos Tello, "Combatting Poverty in Mexico," in González de la Rocha and Escobar Latapí, *Social Responses*, pp. 57–66.

7. Escobar Latapí and Roberts, "Urban Stratification."

8. Ibid.

9. Jesús Reyes Heroles G. G., *Política económica y bienestar en México* (México D.F.: Fondo de Cultura Económica, 1983).

10. Ifigenia Martínez de Navarrete, "La distribución del ingreso y el desarrollo económico en México," in *El perfil de México en 1980* (México D.F.: Siglo XXI Editores, 1970).

11. Peter Smith, *Labyrinths of Power: Political Recruitment in Twentieth Century Mexico* (Princeton: Princeton University Press, 1979); Peter S. Cleaves, *Professions and the State: The Mexican Case* (Tucson: University of Arizona Press, 1987).

12. Although less so, a phenomenon similar to *camarillas* was at work in the

private sector, where backgrounds and schools were often more influential than competence in the allocation of professionals.

13. Reyes Heroles, *Política económica y bienestar.*

14. García, *Desarrollo económico.*

15. Fernando Cortés and Rosa María Rubalcava, *Equidad por empobrecimiento y autoexplotación forzada* (México D.F.: El Colegio de México, 1992).

16. Data provided by Intergamma Guadalajara and by Wyatt Consultores, two management compensation consultancy firms.

17. Cortés and Rubalcava, *Equidad por empobrecimiento.* Because of the level of aggregation in their analysis, these authors cannot assess the changes in the distribution of wealth within the highest decile. Indirect evidence strongly suggests the income of the highest 1 percent has risen with unprecedented speed since 1982.

18. Tello, "Combatting Poverty," p. 58.

19. Rolando Cordera Campos and Enrique González Tiburcio, "Crisis and Transition in the Mexican Economy," in González de la Rocha and Escobar Latapí, *Social Responses.*

20. *The Dynamics of Social Deterioration in Latin America and the Caribbean in the 1980's* (San José, C.R.: ECLAC, 1989).

21. Mercedes González de la Rocha, "Economic Crisis, Domestic Reorganisation and Women's Work in Guadalajara, Mexico," *Bulletin of Latin American Research* 7, no. 2 (1988); Brígida García and Orlandina de Oliveira, "Cambios en la presencia femenina en el mercado de trabajo" (México D.F.: El Colegio de México, unpublished paper, 1990); Agustín Escobar Latapí, "The Rise and Fall of an Urban Labour Market: Economic Crisis and the Fate of Small-Scale Workshops in Guadalajara, Mexico," *Bulletin of Latin American Research* 7, no. 2 (1988).

22. Cordera Campos and González Tiburcio, "Crisis and Transition."

23. Alan Gilbert,"Self-Help Housing During Recession: The Mexican Experience," in González de la Rocha and Escobar Latapí, *Social Responses*, pp. 221–42.

24. Miguel Angel González Block, "Economic Crisis and the Decentralization of Health Services in Mexico," in González de la Rocha and Escobar Latapí, *Social Responses,* pp. 67–90.

25. This figure comes from a probabilistic survey of Guadalajara households commissioned by the author to Instituto Nacional de Estadística, Geografía e Informática in 1990. Unless otherwise noted, references to the Guadalajara labor market, migration, and welfare in this city come from one or several of the following sources: a 1982 survey of 1,300 operative-level manufacturing and government workers; a 1985 survey of 100 informal workshop workers; a 1987 survey of 300 Guadalajara and Atotonilco workers, and the above-mentioned survey of 3,000 households and 4,900 households carried out in 1990 in cooperation with INEGI Guadalajara.

26. Author's data, INEGI survey.

27. Ana Langer, José Luis Bobadilla, and Rafael Lozano, "Effects of Mexico's Economic Crisis on the Health of Women and Children," in González de la Rocha and Escobar Latapí, *Social Responses*, pp. 195–220.

28. Since 1988, non-*maquiladora* manufacturing employment is recovering, albeit slowly.

29. Jorge Carrillo, *The Restructuring of the Car Industry in Mexico: Adjustment Policies and Labor Implications*, Texas Papers on Mexico 90-05 (Austin, 1990).

30. J. Brannon, and G. W. Lucker, "Impact of Mexico's Economic Crisis on the Labor Force of the Maquiladora Industry," *Journal of Borderlands Studies* 4, no. 1 (1989).

31. The National Solidarity Program was created in 1988. Although nominally handling less than 2 percent of the federal government's budget, it receives credit for most of the socially significant works and actions carried out by the government in collaboration with local populations, thanks partly to funds generated by the sale of state firms. It is also the entity responsible for the subsidies delivered to poor subsistence farmers and for another program, which reportedly delivers a free kilo of tortillas per day to the poorest three million urban Mexican households.

32. Some of these agro-entrepreneurs and prosperous *ejidatarios* complain that they are being forced to compete with heavily subsidized foreign producers.

33. The Department of the Federal District's budget fell 50 percent in real terms from 1982 to 1986, in spite of the added pressure of reconstruction after the Mexico City earthquake. This was partly the result of reduction in debt service, but available resources were severely reduced, even more so in per capita terms. From Peter Ward, *México: una megaciudad* (Mexico D.F.: Consejo de Cultura, Colección Los Noventa, 1990).

34. These flexible patterns of employment and work are the result both of these towns' local traditions of small-scale, nonunionized, family craft workshops and the arrival of new Japanese and other multinational enterprises, which emphasize worker involvement, productivity, and quality and which require nonmediation of the union in task and job definition. These cities' "ghost" or weak unions yield easily to these demands, and local authorities tolerate many irregularities in order to secure additional sources of local revenue.

35. The dispersion of economic power away from Mexico City has political implications. In the states, Mexico City's preeminence appears as an obstacle to their access to resources proportionate to their levels of growth. In Mexico City itself, the lack of dynamism in the private modern sector and the need to maintain and rebuild PRI support have led to the increase in toleration of, and negotiation with, "informal" vendors and merchants.

36. Mercedes González de la Rocha and Agustín Escobar Latapí, "Impact of IRCA on the Migration Patterns of a Community in Los Altos de Jalisco, Mexico," in Sidney Weintraub and Sergio Díaz Briquets, eds., *Receiving Country Policies and Migration Flows*, Series on Development and International Migration in Mexico, Central America and the Caribbean Basin (Boulder, Colo.: Westview Press, 1991), pp. 205–32.

37. Wayne Cornelius, "Labor Migration to the United States: Development Outcomes and Alternatives in Mexican Sending Communities," final report to the Commission for the Study of International Migration and Cooperative Economic

Development (La Jolla, Calif.: Center for U.S.-Mexican Studies, UCSD, 1990), p. 33.

38. Cornelius, "*Los migrantes de la crisis.*"

39. Frank Bean, Jorge Chapa, Ruth Berg, and Kathy Sowards, "Educational and Sociodemographic Incorporation Among Hispanic Immigrants to the United States," paper delivered at Immigration and Ethnicity: The Integration of America's Newest Immigrants, Urban Institute, June 1991.

40. Jorge Bustamante, "Undocumented Migration from Mexico to the U.S.: Preliminary Findings of the Zapata Canyon Project," in Frank Bean, Barry Edmonston, and Jeffrey S. Passel, *Undocumented Migration to the U.S.: IRCA and the Experience of the 1980s* (Washington, D.C.: Urban Institute/RAND Corporation, 1990), pp. 211–26.

41. González de la Rocha, "Economic Crisis."

42. This simple distinction depends on the differential ability of individuals and households to plan and achieve long-term goals, including social mobility and the fulfillment of aspirations perceived as justly deserved. The distinction, intended to make exposition clear, is also related to the difference between "coping and surviving," which absorb most of the energy of the unsuccessful types, versus "planning" and "strategy implementation," which characterize a substantial part of the actions of the successful types.

43. Cornelius, "Labor Migration."

44. Vernez and Ronfeldt, "Current Situation."

45. *Immigrant Categories and the U.S. Labor Market: Do They Make a Difference?* Urban Institute Project Report, Washington, D.C., May 1991.

46. Whereas 92 percent of Guadalajara inhabitants who migrated to California before 1962 worked in agriculture, this was the sector of employment of only 33 percent of those arriving for the first time after 1972 (author's data, from 1982 survey).

47. Peter L. Reich, *Statistical Abstract of the U.S.–Mexico Borderlands* (Los Angeles: UCLA, 1991).

48. Jorge Chapa, "The Question of Mexican American Assimilation: Socioeconomic Parity or Underclass Formation?" *Public Affairs Comment* 35, no. 1 (Fall 1988): 9.

49. Chapa, "Question of Mexican American Assimilation," p. 12. This analysis refers to 1980. Since the number of Latino professionals is expanding, new research could modify the author's findings because, paradoxically, an increase in their numbers could increase their discrimination, if mechanisms of "embedded solidarity" do not counteract the perception of more Latino professionals as a threat to other groups.

5. Dresser: Exporting Conflict

This research draws upon newspaper articles, journal articles, books, and in-depth interviews conducted from 1988 to 1991 with PRI and PRD officials, political activists, and scholars. Special thanks are due to Pedro Enrique Armendares, David

Brooks, Ben Garza, Ricardo Pascoe Pierce, Ivonne González, Carlos Imaz, David Ayón, Juan Enríquez, and José Angel Pescador for research support. Gratitude is also extended to the participants in the workshop, "California's Mexico Connection," for helpful comments and advice. The usual disclaimers apply.

1. Paul Bowles, *The Sheltering Sky* (New York: Vintage International, 1990), p. 8.

2. See James N. Rosenau, "The State in an Era of Cascading Politics: Wavering Concept, Widening Competence, Withering Colossus, or Weathering Change," *Comparative Political Studies* 21, no. 1 (Apr. 1988).

3. Stephen P. Mumme, "State Influence in Foreign Policy-Making: Water Related Environmental Disputes Along the U.S.-Mexico Border," *Western Political Quarterly* 38, no. 4 (Dec. 1985).

4. Alberto Melucci, "Frontierland: Collective Action Between Actors and Systems," cited by James N. Rosenau, "Coherent Connection or Commonplace Contiguity? Theorizing About the California-Mexico Overlap," this volume.

5. I borrow this idea from Hector Aguilar Camín and Lorenzo Meyer, *A la sombra de la Revolución Mexicana* (México: Cal y Arena, 1989), p. 260.

6. For a sampling of studies that interpret the electoral results of July 1988 as a major political realignment see Juan Molinar and Jeffrey A. Weldon, "Elecciones de 1988 en México: crisis del autoritarismo," in *Revista Mexicana de Sociología*, (México: Universidad Nacional Autónoma de México, 1992); and Edgar J. Butler and Jorge A. Bustamante, eds., *Sucesión Presidencial: The 1988 Presidential Election* (Boulder, Colo.: Westview Press, 1991).

7. The PRI's dilemma is discussed in Luis Rubio, "Es reformable el PRI?" *Cuaderno de Nexos* 28 (Oct. 1990); Jaime Sánchez Susarrey, "PRI: la reforma imposible?" *Vuelta* 160 (Mar. 1990); and John Bailey and Leopoldo Gómez, "The PRI and Political Liberalization," *Columbia Journal of International Affairs* 43, no. 2 (Winter 1990).

8. The term "internal Leviathans" was coined by Federico Reyes Heroles in his influential 1985 article, "Los desconciertos fundamentales de fin de siglo," in *Contrahechuras mexicanas* (México: Joaquin Mortiz, 1987). He was referring to entrenched leaders within some of the country's most powerful and wealthy unions who, over time, had developed interests not always in accordance with those of the executive branch.

9. In December 1989 the Salinas government pushed forward amendments to the electoral law allowing a party that obtains 35 percent of the vote to receive a majority of representatives in the Congress. The reform was intended to shore up the PRI's support within the system and guarantee an automatic majority of support in the Congress in anticipation of opposition challenges in future elections.

10. For a sampling of "modern" *priísta* views see Abraham Talavera, "El tiempo de la modernidad priísta," *Exámen* 3 (Aug. 1989); Agustín Basave Benítez, "El proyecto neopriísta," *El Día*, 8 Sept. 1989.

11. Interview with author, 31 Oct. 1989, Mexico City.

12. Jorge Castañeda, "Urnas cruzadas," *Cuaderno de Nexos* 1 (Sept. 1988): 11.

13. In local elections held in nine states in 1989 the PRD obtained 296,280 votes. In 1988 the FDN had obtained 1,418,837 votes in the same states. Votes for *car-*

denismo decreased from one year to the next by 85.18 percent. Edmundo González Llaca, "PRD: Agonía sin extasis," *Excelsior* 2 (Nov. 1989): 7.

14. For an analysis of the political implications of Pronasol see Denise Dresser, *Neopopulist Solutions to Neoliberal Problems: Mexico's National Solidarity Program*, Current Issue Brief, no. 3 (La Jolla, Calif.: Center for U.S.-Mexican Studies, UCSD, 1991).

15. For an analysis of the PAN's dilemma see Luis Rubio, "¿El PAN: un partido sin brújula?" *La Jornada*, 8 Feb. 1991.

16. See Luis Salazar C., "PRI y PRD: el show del enfrentamiento," *Cuadernos de Nexos* 36 (June 1991); and Soledad Loaeza, "Entre el pluralismo y la fragmentación, *Nexos* 160 (Apr. 1991).

17. As a result of widespread irregularities committed by local *priístas* during mid-term elections in the states of Guanajuato and San Luis, Salinas de Gortari pressured the two newly elected governors to resign their posts and placed one of the interim governorships in the hands of a PAN leader. For an interpretation of these events see Wayne Cornelius, "Victory Snatched from the Jaws of Fraud," *Los Angeles Times*, 27 Aug. 1991.

18. Carlos Salinas de Gortari, cited in Delal Baer, "U.S. Economic Policy and the Unconventional Security Agenda in Mexico," discussion paper, 4 Mar. 1991, p. 15.

19. Castañeda, "Urnas cruzadas," p. 11.

20. Carlos Salinas de Gortari, cited by Wayne Cornelius, "Salinas and the PRI at the Crossroads: Can Mexico Have 'Perestroika' with Democratization?" paper presented to the sixty-fifth Junta Trimestral de Ciemex-Wharton Econometric Forecasting Associates, Monterrey, Mexico, 9 Mar. 1990, p. 9.

21. Lorenzo Meyer, "El límite neoliberal," *Nexos* 163, (July 1991): 34.

22. See David Ronfeldt, "Modern Mexico in the Making," unpublished paper.

23. This argument draws from M. Delal Baer, "The New Globalism and Mexico's Economic Reform," paper presented at the Sixteenth Congress of the Latin American Studies Association, Washington, D.C., 4–6 Apr. 1991.

24. Ibid., p. 7.

25. Jorge Castañeda, "Salinas's International Relations Gamble," *Columbia Journal of International Affairs* 43, no. 2 (Winter 1990).

26. See Carlos Puig, "Nueva York, Los Angeles, Washington, Ottawa, escenarios de la actividad política mexicana," *Proceso* 763 (17 July 1991).

27. The phrase was coined by Larry Rohter, the *New York Times* correspondent who covered the July 1988 presidential election. For an analysis of foreign press coverage from 6 July 1988 to 6 July 1989 see Pedro Enrique Armendares, "México a ojo de corresponsal," *La Jornada*, special supplement, 19 Sept. 1989.

28. "U.S.–Mexico Trade Pact Is Pitting Vast Armies of Capitol Hill Lobbyists Against Each Other," *Wall Street Journal*, 25 Apr. 1991.

29. Before 1988 Mexico had employed lobbying firms for limited and specific projects related mostly to tourism. See Claudia Franco Hijuelos, "El cabildeo en Washington," *Foro Internacional* 111 (Jan.–Mar. 1988).

30. "Mexican Politicians Look North of Border," *New York Times*, 8 Dec. 1989.

31. Interview with author, 19 June 1991, Los Angeles.

32. John Ross, "California Dreamin'," *Mexico Journal*, 11 Dec. 1989.

33. The PAN has been more reticent about undertaking political campaigns in the U.S. because of the loss of credibility its American connection brought the party in the past. Additionally, PAN's low profile abroad is due to its unwillingness to jeopardize the close ties it has established with the Salinas government. In a recent tour, the party's president, Luis H. Alvarez, argued that political change was taking place in Mexico, especially since Salinas recognized the PAN's victories.

34. "Mexican Politicians Look North," *Los Angeles Times*, 10 Nov. 1989.

35. Interview with author, 22 Mar. 1991, Mexico City.

36. "Archaic features" are defined as electoral fraud; the incestuous, corrupt, and undemocratic relationship of the PRI with the Mexican state; authoritarian practices in the union movement and countryside; and control of much of the mass media. See Cuauhtémoc Cárdenas, "Misunderstanding Mexico," *Foreign Policy* 78 (Spring 1990).

37. Ibid., p. 121.

38. See Harold Brackman and Steven P. Erie, "The Once-and-Future Majority: Latino Politics in Los Angeles," this volume.

39. Cárdenas, for example, has urged his followers with political standing to pressure their elected representatives to condemn the PRI for electoral fraud, support democratization in Mexico, and vote against fast-track approval for the NAFTA in Congress.

40. Interview with author, 22 Mar. 1991, Mexico City.

41. Interview with author, 28 June 1991, San Diego.

42. Carlos Ramos, "Oposición mexicana apoya criterio de Demócratas de EU," *La Opinion*, 29 May 1988.

43. The base committees are local cells of the PRD composed of a minimum of ten members. Approximately 15–20 committees have been established throughout California.

44. See "Estructura política del PRD, Estado de California," document prepared for First National Congress of the PRD, 16–20 Nov. 1990, Mexico City. Three members of the PRD of California are members of the National Council of the PRD.

45. "Propuesta de agenda," Party of the Democratic Revolution, First Conference in northern California, 1 Dec. 1990; "The PRD Statewide Democracy Fund-raising Project: The Formation of a Statewide PRD Political Action Committee," unpublished paper.

46. "A Mexican Right to Vote from Abroad: A Key Strategy for Expanding Mexican Democracy," proposal presented to the Statewide Meeting of the PRD, Riverside, California, 16 Mar. 1991.

47. Interview with Ivonne González, president of the State Executive Council, PRD California, 1 July 1991.

48. Cuauhtémoc Cárdenas, "Iniciativa continental de comercio y desarrollo," unpublished paper, 8 Feb. 1991; Cuauhtémoc Cárdenas, "TLC: Una propuesta alternativa," *Nexos* 162 (June 1991).

49. Interview with Rudy Acuña, professor of Chicano studies, California State University, Northridge, 1 June 1991, Los Angeles.

50. Sergio Muñoz, "Mexican Businesses Are Coming," *Los Angeles Times*, 19 Apr. 1991.

51. Arturo Santamaría Gómez, "Chicano lobby, indocumentados y el TLC," *La Jornada*, 12 May 1991.

52. "Cónsules mexicanos en California apoyan al PRI," *La Jornada*, 4 Apr. 1991.

53. For a sample of the attacks made by PRI officials on Mexican critics in the U.S. see Emilio Zebadúa, "Esperando el debate," *La Jornada*, 6 Feb. 1991, and "Aguilar Zínser vs. México," *El Nacional*, 12 Sept. 1991.

54. Luis Morones, aide for international relations to the PRI national president, cited in Ross, "California Dreamin'," p. 26.

55. Interview with Carlos Loaiza, member of the Comité de Apoyo a Compatriotas, 20 June 1991, Los Angeles.

56. Confidential interview, 23 June 1991, Los Angeles.

57. For a description of Mexico's consular activities see Carlos González Gutiérrez, "The Mexican Diaspora in California: Limits and Possibilities for the Mexican Government," this volume.

58. Interview with author, 20 June 1991, Los Angeles.

59. "No más abusos contra indocumentados: Salinas," *La Jornada*, 13 Apr. 1991; "Programa Paisano: notable reducción de violaciones a derechos de indocumentados en la frontera norte," *Gaceta de Solidaridad* 25, no. 15 (Apr. 1991): 14–15.

60. Interview with author, 1 July 1991, Los Angeles.

61. Interview with author, 27 June 1991, San Diego.

62. Interview with author, 1 July 1991, Los Angeles.

63. Frank del Olmo, "They Are a People Living on the Bridge Between Two Worlds," *Southern California's Latino Community*, a series of articles reprinted from the *Los Angeles Times*, 1983, p. 130.

64. "México mejorará relaciones con mexicanos, dice Secretario Fernando Solana," *La Opinion*, 2 Dec. 1989.

65. The potential impact of cross-border coalitions on U.S.-Mexico relations is discussed in Cathryn Thorup, "La democratización y la agenda bilateral," *Nexos* 162 (June 1991); and "The Politics of Free Trade and the Dynamics of Cross-Border Coalitions in U.S.–Mexican Relations," *Columbia Journal of World Business* 26, no. 2 (Summer 1991). Thorup defines "cross-border coalitions" as informal and formal joint activities by nongovernmental groups across national boundaries.

66. See "Acusan al cónsul de México en San Diego de interferir en asuntos políticos de EU," *El Universal*, 15 Nov. 1991.

67. See "Nueva frontera con EU y nuestra seguridad nacional: los tabúes de antaño y las realidades de hogaño," *El Nacional*, 18 Nov. 1991.

68. "La popularidad de Bush en su punto más bajo," *La Jornada*, 27 Nov. 1991.

69. "Representantes de Bush y organizaciones no electorales analizarán las elecciones mexicanas," *El Financiero*, 17 Sept. 1991.

70. See "The Missing Reform in Mexico," *New York Times*, 26 Aug. 1991; and "Salinas's Opportunity," *Wall Street Journal*, 29 Aug. 1991.

71. A prominent Mexican intellectual and contributor to this volume, Jorge Castañeda, has, for example, argued that Congress and international organizations should pressure the United States to condition the signing of a Free Trade Agreement to clean elections, democracy, and the respect for human rights. "Condicionar el TLC a elecciones limpias," *La Jornada*, 27 Oct. 1991.

72. See Lorenzo Meyer's essay, "Mexico: The Exception and the Rule," in Abraham Lowenthal, ed., *Exporting Democracy: The United States and Latin America* (Baltimore: Johns Hopkins University Press, 1991).

73. Delal Baer, "U.S. Economic Policy."

74. Ibid., p. 15.

6. Székely: Facing the Pacific Rim

1. Richard Stevenson, "Slump Catches Up with Once-Booming California," *New York Times*, 24 Feb. 1991.

2. A leading authority on the process of globalization of production is Michael Porter, ed., *Competition in Global Industries* (Boston: Harvard Business School Press, 1986).

3. Lester Thurow, "GATT Is Dead," presentation at the World Economic Forum, Davos, Switzerland, 1988.

4. Frances Rosenbluth and Kim Suyehiro, "Japanese Banks in Mexico: The Role of Government in Private Decisions," paper prepared for the U.S./Japan/Latin America project of the Center for U.S.-Mexican Studies, University of California, San Diego. Of related interest, Takashi Inoguchi and Daniel Okimoto, eds., *The Political Economy of Japan: The Changing International Context* (Stanford, Calif.: Stanford University Press, 1988).

5. White House, Office of the Press Secretary, "Enterprise for the Americas," 27 June 1990.

6. Gabriel Székely, ed., *Manufacturing Across Borders and Oceans: Japan, the United States, and Mexico* (La Jolla, Calif.: Center for U.S.-Mexican Studies, UCSD, 1991).

7. Leading critics include Clyde Prestowitz, *Trading Places: How We Allowed Japan to Take the Lead* (New York: Basic Books, 1988); and James Fallows, "Containing Japan," *Atlantic*, May 1989, pp. 40–54.

8. International Monetary Fund, *Direction of Trade Statistics*, various issues; U.S. Department of Commerce, *Survey of Current Business*, several issues.

9. California World Trade Commission, *California Exports: Their Contribution to the Economy* (Sacramento: California Department of Commerce, 1989), pp. 15, 18.

10. Ibid.

11. Bank of America, "California, Mexico, and the North American Free Trade Agreement," *Economic and Business Outlook*, Sept.–Oct. 1991.

12. Communication with Mexico's National Institute of Geography, Statistics, and Informatics, Sept. 1990.

13. In comparison, a large share of automobile-related *maquiladora* plants (of which there are 157 nationwide) are based in the state of Chihuahua, which shares a border with Texas.

14. Federal Financial Institutions Examination Council, *Country Exposure Lending Survey*, 1990. See also Barbara Stallings and Gabriel Székely, eds., *Japan, the United States, and Latin America: Toward a Trilateral Relationship in the Western Hemisphere?* (Baltimore, Md.: Johns Hopkins University Press; and London: Macmillan, forthcoming).

15. Japan chapter of the Pacific Basin Economic Council, "Results of a Questionnaire on the North American Free Trade Agreement," Jan. 1992 (unpublished draft).

16. Lawrence Krause, "Perspectives on the Main Pacific Economies in the World Economy Context," presentation at Mexico's Ministry of Foreign Affairs, 17 Feb. 1991.

17. Bank of America, "California, Mexico, and the North American Free Trade Agreement," p. 4.

18. Thurow, "GATT Is Dead"; see also David Henderson, *1992: The External Dimension*, Occasional Papers 25 (New York: The Group of Thirty, 1990).

19. Gabriel Székely and Oscar Vera, "What Mexico Brings to the Table: Negotiating Free Trade with the United States," *Columbia Journal of World Business* 26, no. 2 (Summer 1991): 28–37.

7. Hayes-Bautista: Societal Enrichment or Wasted Opportunity?

1. David Hayes-Bautista, Werner Schink, and Jorge Chapa, *The Burden of Support: Young Latinos In an Aging Society* (Stanford, Calif.: Stanford University Press, 1988).

2. Lisbeth Schorr, *Within Our Reach: Breaking the Cycle of Disadvantage* (New York: Doubleday, 1988), p. 15.

3. Michael Harrington, *The Other America: Poverty in the United States* (New York: Macmillan, 1962).

4. William J. Wilson, *The Truly Disadvantaged: The Inner City, the Underclass and Public Policy* (Chicago: University of Chicago, 1987); Charles Murray, *Losing Ground: American Social Policy 1950–1980* (New York: Basic Books, 1984); Schorr, *Within Our Reach.*

5. Ken Auletta, *The Underclass* (New York: Vintage Books, 1982).

6. Wilson, *Truly Disadvantaged*, p. 26.

7. Peter G. Peterson, and Neil Honer, *On Borrowed Time: How the Growth in Entitlement Spending Threatens America's Future* (New York: Touchstone, 1988); Paul C. Light, *Baby Boomers* (New York: W. W. Norton, 1988).

8. Hayes-Bautista, Schink, and Chapa, *Burden of Support.*

9. Employment Development Department, *Socio-Economic Trends in California, 1940–1980* (Sacramento: Health and Welfare Agency, 1986), pp. 18–20.

10. Aida Hurtado, David Hayes-Bautista, Robert Valdez, and Anthony Hernandez, *Redefining California: Latino Social Engagement in a Multicultural Society* (Los Angeles: UCLA Chicano Studies Research Center, 1992).

11. Employment Development Department, *Socio-Economic Trends.*

12. Ibid.

13. Hayes-Bautista, Schink, and Chapa, *Burden of Support*, p. 166.

14. UCLA School of Social Welfare, *GAIN Participant Needs Assessment: A Profile of Recipients of Aid to Families with Dependent Children* (Los Angeles: UCLA School of Social Welfare, 1987).

15. Los Angeles County, *Vital Statistics of Los Angeles County* (Department of Health Services, Data Collection and Analysis, 1989).

16. Ibid., p. 29.

17. Hayes-Bautista, Schink, and Chapa, *Burden of Support*, p. 101.

18. Los Angeles County, *Vital Statistics*, p. 54.

19. Mary Ann Lewis and Maria Hayes-Bautista, *AIDS and Infants Project, Interim Report* (Los Angeles: UCLA School of Nursing, 1991).

20. Los Angeles County, *Vital Statistics*, p. 56.

21. Gerardo Marin, Eliseo Perez-Stable, and Barbara Marin, "Cigarette Smoking Among San Francisco Hispanics: The Role of Acculturation and Gender," *American Journal of Public Health* 79, no. 7 (1989): 196–98; Myrna J. Gilbert, "Alcohol Consumption Patterns in Immigrant and Later Generations," *Hispanic Journal of Behavioral Sciences* 9, no. 3 (1987): 299–314; Mary Booth, Felipe Castro, and Douglas Anglin, "What Do We Know About Hispanic Substance Abuse? A Review of the Literature," in Ronald Glick and Joan Moore, eds., *Drugs in Hispanic Communities* (New Brunswick, N.J.: Rutgers University Press, 1990); R. Williams et al., "Pregnancy Outcomes of Spanish Surnamed Women in California," *American Journal of Public Health*, 1986, pp. 387–91.

22. Hurtado et al., *Redefining California*.

23. Ibid.

24. Ibid.

25. Employment Development Department, *Socio-Economic Trends*.

8. Vernez: Mexican Labor in California's Economy

1. Kevin F. McCarthy and R. Burciaga Valdez, "California's Demographic Future," in John J. Kirlin and Donald R. Winkler, eds., *California Policy Choices* (Los Angeles: University of Southern California Press, 1985), pp. 37–62. The official 1990 census count for California is 29,760,021. The Census Bureau estimates the 1990 census undercounted California's population by 3.7 percent. Hence, the adjusted figure for California is 30,898,000. The undercount for blacks (4.8 percent) and Latinos (5.2 percent) is estimated to be larger than that for Anglos (2.1 percent).

2. Georges Vernez and Kevin F. McCarthy, *Meeting the Economy's Labor Needs Through Immigration: Rationale and Challenges* (Santa Monica, Calif.: RAND, 1990), pp. 4–17, 46, 65.

3. McCarthy and Burciaga Valdez, "California's Demographic Future."

4. E. Galarza, *Merchants of Labor: The Mexican Bracero History* (Charlotte, Va.: McNally & Loftin, 1964), p. 74.

5. Kevin McCarthy and R. Burciaga Valdez, *Current and Future Effects of Mexican Immigration in California* (Santa Monica, Calif.: RAND, 1986), pp. 22, 35–39.

6. Ibid.

7. James P. Smith, *Hispanics and The American Dream: An Analysis of Hispanic*

Male Labor Market Wages, 1940–1980 (Santa Monica, Calif.: RAND, forthcoming).

8. Georges Vernez and David Ronfeldt, "The Current Situation in Mexican Immigration," *Science* 251 (8 Mar. 1991): 1189–93 and Table 1.

9. James P. Smith and Finis R. Welch, *Closing the Gap: Twenty Years of Economic Progress for Blacks* (Santa Monica, Calif.: RAND, 1986).

10. Manuel García y Griego, "The Mexican Labor Supply, 1990–2010," in Wayne A. Cornelius and Jorge A. Bustamante, eds., *Mexican Migration to the United States: Origins, Consequences and Policy Options* (La Jolla, Calif.: Center for U.S.-Mexican Studies, UCSD, 1989), pp. 49–94.

11. García y Griego, "Mexican Labor Supply"; Wayne A. Cornelius, *The Changing Profile of Mexican Labor Migration to California in the 1980s* (La Jolla, Calif.: Center for U.S.-Mexican Studies, UCSD, 1988), Table 4. Cornelius presents a recent survey of 200 undocumented job-seeking migrants who arrived in southern California in 1987 and 1988, which shows a smaller proportion (50 percent) resided in the ten "traditional" states and a greater proportion (22.9 percent) originated from the Mexico City metropolitan area (see Cornelius, *Changing Profile*, Table 5). Whether this finding signals a change in historical trends or simply reflects a sampling bias remains to be seen.

12. Consejo Nacional de Población, *Estadística demográfica y económica* (México D.F., 1989), Cuadros 8, 9, 11.

13. Vernez and Ronfeldt, "Current Situation."

14. Marta Tienda, "Looking to the 1990s: Mexican Immigration in Sociological Perspective," in Cornelius and Bustamante, eds., *Mexican Migration to the United States*, pp. 113–14; Douglas S. Massey and F. Garcia España, "The Social Process of International Migration," *Science* 237 (1987), p. 733.

15. Bilateral Commission on the Future of United States–Mexican Relations, *The Challenge of Interdependence: Mexico and the United States* (Lanham, N.Y.: University Press of America, 1989); emphasis added.

16. McCarthy and Burciaga Valdez, *Current and Future Effects.*

17. Frank D. Bean, Georges Vernez, and Charles B. Keely, *Opening and Closing the Doors: Evaluating Immigration Reform and Control*, Program for Research on Immigration Policy, 1989 Yearbook (Washington, D.C.: Urban Institute Press, 1989), p. 71.

18. Comprehensive Adult Student Assessment System (CASAS), *A Survey of Newly Legalized Persons in California* (San Diego, 1989).

19. Smith and Welch, *Closing the Gap.*

20. Vernez and Ronfeldt, "Current Situation."

21. Smith, *Hispanics.*

22. Ibid.

23. Daniel Koretz, *Trends in the Postsecondary Enrollment of Minorities* (Santa Monica, Calif.: RAND, 1990), pp. 23, 41.

24. Ibid.

25. Ibid.

26. Smith, *Hispanics.*

27. McCarthy and Burciaga Valdez, "California's Demographic Future."

28. Frank D. Bean and Marta Tienda, *The Hispanic Population of the United States* (New York: Russell Sage Foundation, 1987), p. 208.

29. Vernez and Ronfeldt, "Current Situation."

30. CASAS, *Survey of Newly Legalized Persons.*

31. Vernez and McCarthy, *Meeting the Economy's Labor Needs.*

32. Consejo Nacional de Población, *Estadística.*

33. Manuel García y Griego, "Emigration as a Safety Valve for Mexico's Labor Market: A Post-IRCA Approximation," in *Immigration and International Relations: Proceedings of a Conference on the International Effects of the 1986 Immigration Reform and Control Act (IRCA)*, Georges Vernez, ed., Program for Research on Immigration Policy (Santa Monica, Calif.: RAND and the Urban Institute, 1990), pp. 115–34.

34. Keith Crane and Beth J. Asch, *The Effects of Employer Sanctions on the Flow of Illegal Aliens to the United States* (Santa Monica, Calif.: RAND, 1990); Frank D. Bean, Barry Edmonston, and Jeffrey S. Passel, eds., *Undocumented Migration to the United States: IRCA and the Experience of the 1980s* (Washington, D.C.: Urban Institute Press, 1990), p. 97.

35. Smith, *Hispanics*; Elizabeth Rolph and Robyn Abby, *A Window on Immigration Reform: Implementing the Immigration Reform and Control Act in Los Angeles*, Program for Research on Immigration Policy (Santa Monica, Calif.: RAND and the Urban Institute, 1990).

36. Vernez and McCarthy, *Meeting the Economy's Labor Needs.*

9. Torres-Gil: Immigration's Impact on Health and Human Services

1. Legislative Analyst's Office (LAO), "The 1991–92 Budget: Perspectives and Issues," a report from the Legislative Analyst's Office to the Joint Legislative Budget Committee, 1991.

2. Population Reference Bureau, "America in the 21st Century" (Washington, D.C., 1989).

3. LAO, "1991–92 Budget."

4. Ibid.

5. California State Task Force on California-Mexico Relations, "Strengthening California-Mexico Relations," a report prepared and submitted by the California State Task Force on California-Mexico Relations, 1987.

6. Legislative Analyst's Office (LAO), "Analysis of the 1989–90 Budget Bill," report of the Legislative Analyst to the Joint Legislative Budget Committee, 1989.

7. Persons who qualify under PRUCOL are those who are being allowed by the Immigration and Naturalization Service to stay in the country for any number of reasons.

8. There is an exception to this restriction for aliens eligible for SSI/SSP (a program for the aged, blind, or disabled).

9. Wilma Arguelles, "Primary Health Care in the Hispanic Community," a paper presented to Public Administration 501F, University of Southern California, 1991.

10. LAO "1991–92 Budget."

11. Gabriela Quiroz, "The Policy Perspective: Overview of the Mexican Health Care System," a paper presented to Public Administration 501, University of Southern California, 1991.

12. Ibid.

13. Ibid.

14. Ronald Anderson, Aida Giachello, and Lu Ann Aday, "Access of Hispanics to Health Care and Cuts in Services: A State-of-the-Art Overview," *Public Health Reports* 101, no. 3 (May–June 1986): 238–52; Kevin McCarthy and R. Burciaga Valdez, *Current and Future Effects of Mexican Immigration in California* (Santa Monica, Calif.: RAND, 1985); Gallup, "California Hispanics: Health Behaviors, Poor Health Access," a summary report, Mar. 1991.

15. Fernando Trevino, Eugene Moyer, R. Burciaga Valdez, and Christine Stroup-Benham, "Health Insurance Coverage and Utilization of Health Services by Mexican-Americans, Mainland Puerto Ricans, and Cuban-Americans," *Journal of the American Medical Association* 265, no. 2 (9 Jan. 1991): 233–37.

16. Mervin Field, "Falling Turnout—A Nonvoting Majority," *Public Affairs Report*, Mar. 1990.

17. Kyriakos Markides and Jeannine Corei, "The Health of Hispanics in the Southwestern United States: An Epidemiologic Paradox," *Public Health Reports* 101, no. 3 (May–June 1986): 253–70; Fernando Mendoza, Stephanie Ventura, R. Burciaga Valdez, Ricardo Castillo, Laura Saldivar, Katherine Baisden, and Reynaldo Martorell, "Selected Measures of Health Status for Mexican-American, Mainland Puerto Rican, and Cuban-American Children," *Journal of the American Medical Association* 265, no. 2 (9 Jan. 1991): 227–32; "Hispanic Health in the United States," *Journal of the American Medical Association*, 265, no. 2 (9 Jan. 1991): 248–52; Gallup, "California Hispanics."

18. Mendoza et al., "Selected Measures"; Eli Ginzberg, "Access to Health Care for Hispanics," *Journal of the American Medical Association* 265, no. 2 (9 Jan. 1991): 238–41.

19. Ginzberg, "Access to Health Care."

20. David Warner, "Health Issues at the U.S.-Mexico Border," *Journal of the American Medical Association* 265, no. 22 (9 Jan. 1991): 242–47; Ginzberg, "Access to Health Care."

21. Marta Tienda and Leif Jensen, "Immigration and Public Assistance Participation: Dispelling the Myth of Dependency," IRP Discussion Papers (Madison: University of Wisconsin, 1985); California Health and Welfare Agency, "A Survey of Newly Legalized Persons in California," a study prepared by the Comprehensive Adult Student Assessment System (San Diego, 1989).

10. Rothstein: Obstacles to Latino Educational Achievement

I gratefully acknowledge the advice and assistance of this volume's editors, Abraham Lowenthal and Katrina Burgess, who organized a seminar for authors and outside commentators to review early drafts of this book. The seminar comments of Wayne Cornelius, Leo Estrada, Stephen Levy, Emelia McKenna, David Rieff, and Georges Vernez were particularly helpful. Others who helpfully criticized an earlier draft of this chapter include Jan Breidenbach, Cynthia Lim, Patricia Mendoza, and Tim Rutten. I am also indebted to former colleagues at the Independent Analysis Unit of the Los Angeles Board of Education: Roger Rasmussen, Randy Ross, Secundino Garcia, and Charles Schepart. The views expressed in this chapter are solely my own and do not represent the views of the Independent Analysis Unit, the Los Angeles City Board of Education, or the Los Angeles Unified School District.

This chapter was written in winter, 1990–91, and data presented are the most recent available as of that date. Since that time, California's state fiscal crisis, along with a prolonged economic downturn, has exacerbated the problems described. Class sizes are larger, school construction has lagged farther behind, and income declines for high school graduates have accelerated.

1. National Alliance of Business, *National Alliance of Business Work Force Survey* (Washington, D.C., 1990).

2. California Business Roundtable, *Operation Education News* 3, no. 1 (Winter, 1991).

3. Most government statistical reports use the terms "Hispanic" and "non-Hispanic white." We use "Latino" and "non-Latino" as synonyms for them.

4. Los Angeles Unified School District, *Ethnic Survey Report, Fall 1990* (Los Angeles: LAUSD Information Technology Division, 1990), pp. 352–57.

5. Calculated from Los Angeles Unified School District, *Bilingual Program Survey Report 1988–89*, Publication No. 551 (Los Angeles: LAUSD Program Evaluation and Assessment Branch, 1990), p. 14; and Los Angeles Unified School District, *Executive Summary, Ethnic Survey Report, Fall 1990* (Los Angeles: LAUSD Information Technology Division, 1990), pp. 3, 9.

6. Marta Tienda, "Looking to the 1990s: Mexican Immigration in Sociological Perspective," in Wayne Cornelius and Jorge Bustamante, eds., *Mexican Migration to the United States: Origins, Consequences and Policy Options* (La Jolla, Calif.: Center for U.S.-Mexican Studies, UCSD, 1989), p. 119.

7. Wayne A. Cornelius, "From Sojourners to Settlers: The Changing Profile of Mexican Migration to the United States," unpublished paper, 1990, p. 15.

8. Calculation based on Tienda, "Looking to the 1990s," p. 118.

9. Independent Analysis Unit, Los Angeles Unified School District, *Ambassador Facts* (Los Angeles: LAUSD Independent Analysis Unit, 1990).

10. California Department of Education, *Fact Sheet 1990–91: Back to School Information* (Sacramento: California Department of Education Public Relations Office, 1990), p. 45.

11. Calculated from California Department of Education, *Fact Sheet 1990–91*, p. 45; and California Department of Education, *California Education Summit: Meeting the Challenge. The Schools Respond. Background Papers, February 1990* (Sacramento, 1990), p. 67.

12. Kati Haycock and M. Susanna Navarro, *Unfinished Business: Fulfilling Our Children's Promise* (Oakland: Achievement Council, 1988), p. 37.

13. California Department of Education, *Bilingual Education Handbook: Designing Instruction for LEP Students* (Sacramento, 1990), p. 3.

14. Ibid. Also, California Department of Education, *Fact Sheet 1990–91*, p. 13.

15. California Department of Education, *Fact Sheet 1990–91*, p. 13. Other sources used to make these calculations include Julie Johnson, "Hispanic Dropout Rate Is Put at 35%," *New York Times*, 15 Sept. 1989; Los Angeles Unified School District, *Ethnic Survey Report, Fall 1990*; Leonard Britton, "1988–89 District Dropout Statistics," informative presented to Los Angeles Board of Education, 6 Apr. 1990; Deborah J. Carter and Reginald Wilson, *Ninth Annual Status Report on Minorities in Higher Education* (Washington, D.C.: American Council on Education, 1991).

16. California Department of Education, *Opening Doors: California Educational Reform, Annual Report 1989* (Sacramento, 1990), p. 17. For college preparatory science courses, the comparable figures are 44 and 60 percent.

17. Ibid., 29.

18. Ibid., 39. Nationally, Mexican-American average scores are 811, compared to 937 for whites. Lawrence Mishel and David M. Frankel, *The State of Working America*, 1990–91 ed. (Armonk, N.Y.: M. E. Sharpe, 1991), p. 251.

19. Independent Analysis Unit, *Enrollment of LAUSD Seniors in California Public Colleges 1986–1989* (Los Angeles: Los Angeles Unified School District, Los Angeles City Board of Education, Independent Analysis Unit, 1991), pp. 2, 11. These figures, which include only those students who go on to California public colleges (UC and CSU), actually understate the gap. Because of lower average socioeconomic status, it can be assumed that a larger percentage of Hispanic students who go to college go to California public higher education institutions, whereas a larger percentage of white students would attend private colleges.

20. Children Now, *The Right Start for California's Children: The 1990 California Children's Report Card* (Los Angeles, 1990), p. 27.

21. California Department of Education, *Fact Sheet 1990–91*, p. 27. Note that class sizes in many California school districts have increased further as a result of California's state fiscal crisis, which began in 1991.

22. Ibid., p. 26.

23. Independent Analysis Unit, *IAU Reports on the Status of New Construction* (Los Angeles: Independent Analysis Unit, Los Angeles Unified School District, Los Angeles City Board of Education, 1991).

24. Approximately 25,000 students are given no choice and are bused under Los Angeles's "capacity adjustment program" from overcrowded schools to designated receiver schools where space is available. Other programs transport minority students who voluntarily choose to attend integrated schools (such as magnet schools) rather than their home schools. Some proportion of these students would not choose the voluntary integration program if space were available at their home schools.

25. California Department of Education, *Fact Sheet 1990–91*, p. 28.

26. Eighty percent of the difference between advantaged and disadvantaged children in year-to-year retention of learned skills occurs during traditional summer vacations. Gordon Berlin and Andrew Sum, *Toward a More Perfect Union: Basic*

Skills, Poor Families, and Our Economic Future (New York: Ford Foundation, 1988), p. 38. "Disadvantaged students" are those qualifying for federal compensatory education funding.

27. Paul M. Ong et al., *The Widening Divide: Income Inequality and Poverty in Los Angeles* (Los Angeles: Research Group on the Los Angeles Economy, University of California at Los Angeles, Graduate School of Architecture and Urban Planning, 1989).

28. William Snider, "Outcry Follows Cavazos Comments on the Values of Hispanic Parents," *Education Week* 9, no. 30 (18 Apr. 1990); Lauro F. Cavazos, *Address to the LULAC Youth Leadership Convention Banquet, Tucson, Arizona, May 31, 1990* (Washington, D.C.: U.S. Department of Education, Office of the Secretary, 1990); Lauro F. Cavazos, *Remarks to the National Council of La Raza Annual Conference, Washington, D.C., July 17, 1990* (Washington, D.C.: U.S. Department of Education, Office of the Secretary, 1990).

29. Jonathon Kozol, *Illiterate America* (Garden City, N.Y.: Anchor Press/Doubleday, 1985), p. 59.

30. Mishel and Frankel, *State of Working America*, p. 245.

31. Author's calculations.

32. Haycock and Navarro, *Unfinished Business*, p. 39.

33. Berlin and Sum, *Toward a More Perfect Union*, p. 36. The mother's marital status and income level were also important.

34. Haycock and Navarro, *Unfinished Business*, p. 37.

35. George Borjas and Marta Tienda, eds., *Hispanics in the U.S. Economy* (Orlando, Fla.: Academic Press, 1985), pp. 185, 190.

36. L. M. Laosa, "School, Occupation, Culture and Family: The Impact of Parental Schooling on the Parent-Child Relationship," *Journal of Educational Psychology* 74, no. 6 (1982): 805.

37. In neither study did the father's educational level make a difference.

38. Laosa, "School," pp. 794–96.

39. Haycock and Navarro, *Unfinished Business*, p. 22.

40. California Department of Education, *California Education Summit*, p. 56.

41. Cornelius, "From Sojourners to Settlers," p. 25.

42. Alejandro Portes and Ruben G. Rumbaut, *Immigrant America: A Portrait* (Berkeley: University of California Press, 1990), p. 61.

43. George Borjas, *Friends or Strangers* (New York: Basic Books, 1990), p. 53.

44. Berlin and Sum, *Toward a More Perfect Union*, pp. 36–40.

45. Barry Stern, *The California Adult Education System: Background Paper on the Response of the Adult Education Institutions to the Needs of Californians* (Sacramento: California State Department of Education), pp. 51–52.

46. Bill Clinton, "Repairing the Family," *New Perspectives Quarterly* 7, no. 4 (Fall 1990): 12.

47. Peter Schmidt, "Three Types of Bilingual Education Effective, E.D. Study Concludes," *Education Week* 10, no. 22, (20 Feb. 1991). To be lawful, however, these "structured immersion" programs must be specifically designed for language-minority students and taught by ESL specialists. Still prohibited would be pro-

grams placing language-minority students directly into mainstream programs, even where concurrent translation is provided.

48. Los Angeles Unified School District, *The Master Plan for the Education of Limited-English-Proficient Students*, Publication No. GC-120 (Los Angeles: LAUSD Office of Bilingual-ESL Instruction, 1988), p. 8.

49. James Cummins, "The Role of Primary Language Development in Promoting Educational Success for Language Minority Students," in California State Department of Education, Office of Bilingual Bicultural Education, *Schooling and Language Minority Students: A Theoretical Framework* (Los Angeles: California State University, Los Angeles, 1981), p. 23.

50. California Department of Education, *Bilingual Education Handbook*, p. 12.

51. Ibid.

52. Most California programs generally fall between the early-exit and late-exit models, although the Cummins-Krashen theories argue for much later transition to English instruction. Los Angeles's master plan does not go as far, hoping students can make the transition by the third or fourth grades.

53. James Cummins and Michael Genzuk, "Analysis of Final Report: Longitudinal Study of Structured English Immersion Strategy, Early-Exit and Late-Exit Transitional Bilingual Education Programs for Language Minority Children," unpublished paper, 1991. Also, Schmidt, "Three Types."

54. J. David Ramirez, principal investigator, *Briefing Paper, Final Report: Longitudinal Study of Structured English Immersion Strategy, Early-Exit and Late-Exit Transitional Bilingual Education Programs for Language Minority Children* (San Mateo, Calif.: Aguirre International, 1991), p. 6.

55. Rosalie Pedalino Porter, *Forked Tongue, The Politics of Bilingual Education* (New York: Basic Books, 1990), p. 234.

56. Los Angeles Unified School District, *Master Plan*, p. 20.

57. Los Angeles Unified School District, *Ethnic Survey Report, Fall 1990*, p. 33. See also Los Angeles Unified School District, *Limited-English-Proficient Student Enrollment Patterns, District-Region-Division Trends, 1989–90*, Publication No. 536 (Los Angeles: LAUSD Program Evaluation and Assessment Branch, 1990), p. 551.

58. California Department of Education, *Fact Sheet 1990–91*, p. 46.

59. Los Angeles Unified School District, "Executive Summary," *Ethnic Survey Report*, Fall 1990, p. 10.

60. California State University, *Enrollment by Ethnic Group, Fall Term 1989* (Long Beach: California State University, Office of the Chancellor, Division of Analytic Studies, 1990), p. 45 (Table 8). Also, California State University, *1988–89 Statistical Report Number 11: Undergraduate and Graduate Degrees Granted* (Long Beach: California State University, Office of the Chancellor, Division of Analytic Studies, 1990), p. 59 (Table 10).

61. Los Angeles Unified School District, *Bilingual Program Survey Report 1988–89*, p. 20. Actually, not all of these were technically certified by the state. Some had only passed a language fluency exam.

62. Sam Enriquez, "Faculty Can't Fill Bilingual Needs of State," *Los Angeles Times*, 17 Oct. 1990.

63. Robert G. Rumbaut, *Immigrant Students in California Public Schools: A Summary of Current Knowledge* (Baltimore: Johns Hopkins University, Center for Research on Effective Schooling for Disadvantaged Students, 1990), p. 3. See also California Department of Education, *Bilingual Education Handbook*, p. 1.

64. Los Angeles Unified School District, *Bilingual Program Survey Report 1988–89*, p. 13.

65. California Department of Education, *Bilingual Education Handbook*, p. 13. See also Cummins, "Role of Primary Language Development," p. 26.

66. Ramirez, *Briefing Paper*.

67. Neil Fligstein and Roberto M. Fernandez, "Educational Transitions of Whites and Mexican-Americans," in Borjas and Tienda, *Hispanics in the U.S. Economy*, p. 166.

68. Ibid., pp. 187–88. Also Jeannie Oakes, "Tracking: Can Schools Take a Different Route?" in National Education Association, *Getting Untracked*, (Washington, D.C.: National Education Association, 1988), pp. 41–47.

69. Ibid.

70. Haycock and Navarro, *Unfinished Business*, p. 21. Also, Fligstein and Fernandez, "Educational Transitions," p. 163; John U. Ogbu, "Variability in Minority School Performance: A Problem in Search of an Explanation," *Anthropology and Education Quarterly* 18 (1987): 319.

71. Raymond Buriel and Desdemona Cardoza, "Sociocultural Correlates of Achievement Among Three Generations of Mexican American High School Seniors," *American Educational Research Journal* 25, no. 2 (Summer 1988): 177, 185, 187.

72. California Department of Education, *Opening Doors*, p. 16.

73. Kevin F. McCarthy and R. Burciaga Valdez, *Current and Future Effects of Mexican Immigration in California, Executive Summary* (Santa Monica, Calif.: RAND, 1985), p. 59.

74. David E. Hayes-Bautista, "Mexicans in Southern California: Societal Enrichment or Wasted Opportunity?" this volume.

75. J. D. Vigil and J. M. Long, "Unidirectional or Nativist Acculturation—Chicano Paths to School Achievement," *Human Organization* 40, no. 3 (Fall 1981): 273–77.

76. Maria E. Matute-Bianchi, "Ethnic Identities and Patterns of School Success and Failure Among Mexican Descent and Japanese American Students in a California High School: An Ethnographic Analysis," *American Journal of Education* 95, no. 1 (1986): 233–55.

77. McCarthy and Burciaga Valdez, *Current and Future Effects*, p. 57.

78. Carter and Wilson, *Ninth Annual Status Report*, p. 14.

79. Ibid., p. 40 (Table 21).

80. Portes and Rumbaut, *Immigrant America*, p. 193.

81. Matute-Bianchi, "Ethnic Identities."

82. John U. Ogbu, "Research Currents: Cultural-Ecological Influences on Minority School Learning," *Language Arts* 62, no. 8 (Dec. 1985): 866.

83. John U. Ogbu, *Minority Education and Caste: The American System in Cross-Cultural Perspective* (New York: Academic Press, 1978), p. 18, quoting from Robert

A. Levine, *Dreams and Needs: Achievement Motivation in Nigeria* (Chicago: University of Chicago Press, 1967).

84. Ogbu, "Variability," p. 317.

85. Ogbu, *Minority Education*, p. 20.

86. Martin Carnoy, Hugh Daley, and Raul Hinojosa Ojeda, *Latinos in a Changing U.S. Economy: 1939 – 1989* (New York: City University of New York/I.U.P., 1990).

87. Mishel and Frankel, *State of Working America*, p. 198.

88. Ibid., p. 170.

89. Carter and Wilson, *Ninth Annual Status Report*, p. 40 (Table 21).

90. Andrew Sum, Neal Fogg, Robert Taggart, "Withered Dreams: The Decline in the Economic Fortunes of Young, Non-College Educated Male Adults and Their Families," working paper prepared for the William T. Grant Foundation Commission on Family, Work, and Citizenship, 1988, p. 73.

91. Mishel and Frankel, *State of Working America*, p. 98 (Table 3.21).

92. Ibid., p. 104 (Table 3.24).

93. Ibid., p. 69.

94. Carnoy, Daley, and Hinojosa Ojeda, *Latinos*.

95. Mishel and Frankel, *State of Working America*, p. 84.

96. Sum, Fogg, and Taggart, "Withered Dreams," Appendix B (Table B-2).

97. Independent Analysis Unit, "Enrollment of LAUSD Seniors," p. 11 (Table 9).

98. Mishel and Frankel, *State of Working America*, p. 198; data in 1989 dollars.

99. Berlin and Sum, *Toward a More Perfect Union*, p. 23.

100. Jon Sargent, "A Greatly Improved Outlook for College Graduates: A 1988 Update to the Year 2000," *Occupational Outlook Quarterly* (Summer 1988): 2.

11. Brackman and Erie: Latino Politics in Los Angeles

We wish to thank David Ayon, Vanessa Cunningham, Kathy Underwood, Larry Herzog, Jim Ingram, and Jaime Regalado for their helpful comments on an earlier draft. We also wish to acknowledge the financial support of the California Policy Seminar for our research.

1. Frank Clifford, "Barriers to Power for Minorities," *Los Angeles Times*, 7 May 1990; Tony Bizjak, "Majority Rules State's Politics," *Sacramento Bee*, 31 Mar. 1990; Sam Fulwood III, "California Is Most Racially Diverse State," *Los Angeles Times*, 13 June 1991; Dave Lesher and Gebe Martínez, "'90's Forecast as Decade of Increasing Latino Influence," *Los Angeles Times*, 29 June 1991; California Department of Finance, Population Research Unit, "Projected Total Population for California by Race/Ethnicity, July 1, 1970 to July 1, 2020," Report 88 P-4, Sacramento, 1988.

2. This research draws upon in-depth interviews conducted in 1990 and early 1991 with leading Latino politicians, community activists, and scholars in the Los Angeles metropolitan area.

3. Fernando J. Guerra, "Ethnic Officeholders in Los Angeles County," *Sociology and Social Research* 71, no. 2 (Jan. 1987): 93; Louis Freedberg, "Latinos: Building Power from the Ground Up," *California Journal* 18, no. 1 (Jan. 1987): 14; Bizjak,

"Majority Rules"; Richard Simon, "100 Days: Molina Shakes Up Board," *Los Angeles Times*, 16 June 1991.

4. Lawrence H. Fuchs, *The American Kaleidoscope: Race, Ethnicity, and the Civic Culture* (Hanover, N.H.: University Press of New England for Wesleyan University Press, 1990), pp. 239–71. See also Steven P. Erie, *Rainbow's End: Irish-Americans and the Dilemmas of Urban Machine Politics, 1840–1985* (Berkeley: University of California Press, 1988).

5. Field Institute, "A Digest of California's Political Demography," *California Opinion Index*, Aug. 1990, p. 5; Frank Clifford, "Latinos, Asians Gain in Numbers, Not Power," *Los Angeles Times*, 5 Mar. 1991.

6. Frank Sotomayor, "Latinos: Diverse Group Tied by Ethnicity," *Los Angeles Times*, 25 July 1983; Robert Warren and Jeffrey S. Passel, "A Count of the Uncountable: Estimates of Undocumented Aliens in the 1980 United States Census," *Demography* 24, no. 3 (Aug. 1987): 375–84; Los Angeles County Commission on Human Relations, "Racial and Ethnic Population of Los Angeles County: 1989 Estimated," 1989; U.S. Immigration and Naturalization Service, *1989 Statistical Yearbook* (Washington, D.C.: Government Printing Office, 1990), pp. 24–25.

7. John A. Garcia, "Political Integration of Mexican Immigrants: Explorations into the Naturalization Process," *International Migration Review* 17, no. 3 (1981): 608–25; Alejandro Portes and Robert L. Bach, *Latino Journey: Cuban and Mexican Immigrants in the United States* (Berkeley: University of California Press, 1985), pp. 115–18; Martín Sánchez Jankowski, *City Bound: Urban Life and Political Attitudes Among Chicano Youth* (Albuquerque: University of New Mexico Press, 1986), pp. 201, 204; U.S. Bureau of the Census, *Detailed Population Characteristics: California*, PC80-1-D6 (Washington, D.C.: Government Printing Office, 1983), Table 194.

8. William V. d'Antonio and William H. Form, *Influentials in Two Border Cities: A Study in Community* (South Bend, Ind.: Notre Dame University Press, 1965), p. 30; Rodolfo O. de la Garza, "The Politics of Mexican Americans," in *The Chicanos: As We See Ourselves*, ed. Arnulfo D. Trejo (Tucson: University of Arizona Press, 1979), p. 102; Rodolfo O. de la Garza and Arnold Flores, "The Impact of Mexican Immigrants on the Political Behavior of Chicanos," in *Mexican Immigrants and Mexican Americans: An Evolving Relation*, ed. H. L. Browning and Rodolfo O. de la Garza (Austin: University of Texas Press, 1986), pp. 211–19; Ann Craig and Wayne A. Cornelius, "Political Culture in Mexico: Continuities and Revisionist Interpretations," in *The Civic Culture Revisited*, ed. Gabriel Almond and Sidney Verba (Boston: Little, Brown, 1980), pp. 325–93.

9. Thomas J. Mueller and Thomas J. Espenshade, *The Fourth Wave: California's Newest Immigrants* (Washington, D.C.: Urban Institute, 1985), pp. 85, 193; D. S. North, "The Long Gray Welcome: A Study of the American Naturalization Program," *International Migration Review* 23, no. 2 (1987): 311–26; Alejandro Portes and John W. Curtis, "Changing Flags: Naturalization and Its Determinants Among Mexican Immigrants," *International Migration Review* 21, no. 2 (1985): 352; Robert A. Pastor and Jorge G. Castañeda, *Limits to Friendship: The United States and Mexico* (New York: Vintage Books, 1989), p. 309.

10. Louis Freedberg, "Latino Education," *California Journal* 19, no. 8 (Aug. 1988): 326; Jean Merl, "Latinos Lagging on Every School Level, Study Finds," *Los Angeles Times*, 25 Jan. 1991; Paul Ong, "The Widening Divide: Income Inequality and Poverty in Los Angeles" (Los Angeles: UCLA Graduate School of Architecture and Urban Planning, 1989), pp. 16, 85–86, 91.

11. Thomas Weyr, *Hispanic USA: Breaking the Melting Pot* (New York: Harper and Row, 1988), pp. 102–3; Rodolfo F. Acuña, *Occupied America: A History of Chicanos*, 3d ed. (New York: Harper and Row, 1988), p. 384; Kenneth C. Burt, "Competing with the Democrats for the Growing Hispanic Vote," *California Journal* 14, no. 5 (May 1983): 191–92; Richard Simon and Stephanie Chávez, "Upwardly Mobile Latinos Shift Their Political Views," *Los Angeles Times*, 26 Dec. 1987.

12. Bruce E. Cain and D. Roderick Kiewiet, "Minorities in California," California Institute of Technology Symposium, Seaver Institute, 5 Mar. 1986, p. I-10; "Middle Age at 26.1: Hispanics Are Youngest," *Wall Street Journal*, 10 Apr. 1990; "Ethnic Mix Gives California Its Youth," *Wall Street Journal*, 12 July 1990.

13. Ricardo Romo, *East Los Angeles: History of a Barrio* (Austin: University of Texas Press, 1983), pp. 61–88, 163–71; Carlos Navarro and Rodolfo F. Acuña, "In Search of Community: A Comparative Essay on Mexicans in Los Angeles and San Antonio," in *Twentieth-Century Los Angeles: Power, Promotion, and Social Conflict*, ed. Norman M. Klein and Martin J. Schiesl (Claremont, Calif.: Regina Books, 1990), pp. 204, 221; Acuña, *Occupied America*, pp. 284, 319. For recent evidence of a countertrend toward Latino population reconcentration, see Frank Clifford and Anne C. Roark, "Study Finds Racial Lines in LA County Blurring, but They May Return," *Los Angeles Times*, 6 May 1991.

14. Philip García, "Immigration Issues in Urban Ecology: The Case of Los Angeles," in *Urban Ethnicity in the United States: New Immigrants and Old Minorities*, ed. Lionel Maldonado and Joan Moore (Beverly Hills, Calif.: Sage, 1985), pp. 88–89; Ruben Castañeda, "L.A.'s Future as a Latino Capitol," *Los Angeles Herald Examiner*, 24 July 1983; Tom Waldman, "Latinos in the Valley," *California Journal* 20, no. 10 (Oct. 1989): 427–29; Richard Simon, "Representation to Switch for Thousands," *Los Angeles Times*, 6 May 1991.

15. Robert Gnaizda and Mario Obledo, "Latino Vote: The 'Sleeping Giant' Stirs," *Los Angeles Times*, 13 Nov. 1983; Richard Reeves, "The Majority Rules, but Not for Long," *Los Angeles Times*, 27 May 1990.

16. Charles S. Navarro, "California Redistricting and Representation: Los Angeles County's Chicano Community," Ph.D. diss., Claremont Graduate School, 1982; Rodolfo F. Acuña, *A Community Under Siege: A Chronicle of Chicanos East of the LA River* (Los Angeles: Chicano Studies Research Center, UCLA, 1984), p. 249; J. Morgan Kousser, *How to Determine Intent: Lessons from LA*, Social Science Working Paper No. 741 (Pasadena, Calif.: California Institute of Technology, 1991), pp. 15–17, 64–67.

17. Bruce E. Cain, *The Reapportionment Puzzle* (Berkeley: University of California Press, 1984), pp. 81, 92–95, 99–100, 103; Weyr, *Hispanic USA*, pp. 105–7; Carlos Navarro and Richard Santillan, "The Latino Community and California Redistricting in the 1980's: Californios for Fair Representation," in *The Hispanic*

Community and Redistricting, ed. Richard Santillan (Claremont, Calif.: Rose Institute, 1984), pp. 57, 63–64, 68–69.

18. John Schwada, "Richard Alatorre's Risky Switch," *California Journal* 16, no. 12 (Dec. 1985): 524–26; Acuña, *Occupied America*, p. 425; Judy Tachibana, "California's Asians," *California Journal* 17, no. 11 (Nov. 1986): 24–25; Raphael J. Sonenshein, "Biracial Coalition Politics In Los Angeles," in *Racial Politics in American Cities*, ed. Rufus Browning, Dale Marshall, and David H. Tabb (New York: Longman, 1990), pp. 46–47.

19. Sherry Bebitch Jeffe, "Supervisors: Our Powerful 'Little Kings,'" *Los Angeles Times*, 8 Apr. 1990; Kousser, "How to Determine Intent," pp. 2–3, 34–42; Erik Bucy, "Lawsuits Threaten LA Supervisor Fiefdoms," *California Journal* 20, no. 1 (Jan. 1989): 41–43; Richard Simon and Frederick M. Muir, "L.A. County Supervisor Districts Illegal," *Los Angeles Times*, 5 June 1990; Rodolfo F. Acuña, "Now, the Fight for the Spoils," *Los Angeles Times*, 12 Aug. 1990; Tom Waldman, "The Scramble for L.A. County's New Supervisorial Seat," *California Journal* 22, no. 1 (Jan. 1991): 20–24; Hector Tobar, "Key Latino Groups Back Molina in First District," *Los Angeles Times*, 17 Dec. 1990; Jill Stewart and Richard Simon, "First District Foes Target Key Voters," *Los Angeles Times*, 27 Jan. 1991; Richard Simon, "Torres Leads Molina in Fund Raising," *Los Angeles Times*, 14 Feb. 1991; Richard Simon, "Molina Elected to LA Supervisor's Seat," *Los Angeles Times*, 20 Feb. 1991; Simon, "100 Days."

20. Interview with Richard Martinez; David Margolis, "Drawing New Lines," *Jewish Journal*, 5–11 July 1991, p. 13; James A. Barnes, "Minority Mapmaking," *National Journal* 22, no. 14 (7 Apr. 1991): 838; Bill Stall, "Latinos See Majorities in New State and U.S. Districts," *Los Angeles Times*, 10 Mar. 1991; Daniel M. Weintraub, "Minorities Get GOP Support in Remap Battle," *Los Angeles Times*, 26 Aug. 1991; Daniel M. Weintraub, "Latinos Offer Own Plan for Redistricting," *Los Angeles Times*, 6 Sept. 1991.

21. Interviews with Richard Martinez and Professor Leobardo Estrada of UCLA; David R. Ayon, "The Diminishing Returns of the Politics of the Barrio," *Los Angeles Times*, 30 Sept. 1990.

22. Interviews with Rodolfo F. Acuña and Jorge García; Richard Simon, "Molina's First Goal—Expand County Board," *Los Angeles Times*, 21 Feb. 1991; James Rainey, "County Board Expansion Faces a Long, Tough Sell," *Los Angeles Times*, 25 Feb. 1991.

23. Ruben Castañeda, "Latino Unity Stalls in East LA," *California Journal* 18, no. 1 (Jan. 1987): 23–25.

24. A. G. Block, "Montoya's Money Machine," *California Journal* 18, no. 12 (Dec. 1987): 599; Bill Boyarsky, "Running for Supervisor: Cash over Qualifications," *Los Angeles Times*, 27 May 1990; Weyr, *Hispanic USA*, pp. 128–31; Cathleen Decker, "Blacks Face Grim Future in Politics," *Los Angeles Times*, 4 Oct. 1989; Frank Clifford and Dave Lesher, "Young Black Politicians Face New Fears," *Los Angeles Times*, 6 Jan. 1991.

25. Weyr, *Hispanic USA*, p. 129; Navarro and Acuña, "In Search of Community," p. 219; Simon, "Torres Leads Molina."

26. Weyr, *Hispanic USA*, pp. 128–31.

27. Bill Boyarsky, "Crossover Dreams," *Los Angeles Times Magazine*, 22 Nov. 1989, pp. 12, 189; Navarro and Acuña, "In Search of Community," pp. 218–20; interviews with Juana Gutiérrez, David Díaz, and Rodolfo F. Acuña. Also see Mario T. García, *Mexican Americans: Leadership, Ideology, and Identity, 1930–1960* (New Haven, Conn.: Yale University Press, 1989).

28. Interviews with Julie Solis of the Tomás Rivera Center; Henry Lozano, administrative assistant to Congressman Ed Roybal; Ed Avila, deputy mayor of Los Angeles; Yolanda Chávez; and Robin Kramer.

29. Interview with Harry Pachon.

30. Isidro D. Ortiz, "Chicano Urban Politics and the Politics of Reform in the Seventies," *Western Political Quarterly* 37 (1984): 564–70; Joseph D. Sekul, "Communities Organized for Public Service: Citizen Power and Public Policy in San Antonio," in *Latinos and the Political System*, ed. Chris García (South Bend, Ind.: University of Notre Dame Press, 1988), pp. 367–84.

31. Ruben Castañeda, "Community Organizers Bring New Clout to Urban Poor," *California Journal* 19, no. 1 (Jan. 1988): 21–25; interviews with California State University Northridge professors Rodolfo F. Acuña and Carlos Navarro.

32. Castañeda, "Latino Unity Stalls," pp. 23–24; Castañeda, "Community Organizers," pp. 21–25; Rodolfo F. Acuña, "Latinos Fighting for Community, Not Just Property Values," *Los Angeles Times*, 22 Jan. 1990; Boyarsky, "Crossover Dreams," p. 16; "Battle Lines Drawn over Olvera Street," editorial, *Los Angeles Times*, 18 June 1990; interview with Juana Gutierrez of MOELA.

33. Castañeda, "Community Organizers," pp. 21–25; Joel Kotkin, "Fear and Reality in the Los Angeles Melting Pot," *Los Angeles Times Magazine*, 5 Nov. 1989, p. 35; interview with David Diaz of LACTION.

34. Jaime Regalado, "Organized Labor in Los Angeles City Politics: An Assessment of the Bradley Years, 1973–1989," *Urban Affairs Quarterly* 27, no. 1 (Sept. 1991): 87–108; Bob Baker, "Unions Try Bilingual Recruiting," *Los Angeles Times*, 25 Mar. 1991.

35. Interview with Frank del Olmo.

36. National Association of Latino Elected Officials, *The National Latino Immigrant Survey* (Washington, D.C.: NALEO Educational Fund, 1989), pp. 1–5; interview with Professor Harry Pachon of NALEO.

37. Interview with Roberto Bustillo of Clinica Romero; George Ramos and Tracy Wilkinson, "Refugees Pour out Horror Tales as INS Reconsiders Asylum Bids," *Los Angeles Times*, 21 Dec. 1990.

38. Interviews with Yolanda Chávez and with Robin Kramer, chief of staff for Councilman Richard Alatorre. With regard to the GOP, the typical attitude of Latino Democratic leaders combines grudging respect for the Republican Southwest Project, which they credit with an effective "creaming" strategy targeting upscale Latinos, with continuing anger over alleged Republican intimidation of minority voters in Orange County in 1988.

39. Freedberg, "Latinos," p. 17; Valerie Mireles, "Surging Toward a Latino State," *California Journal* 18, no. 1 (Jan. 1987): 21; Lee May, "Latinos Aim for Prog-

ress via Politics," *Los Angeles Times*, 17 July 1987; Ronald Brownstein, "Two States of Progress for Latinos," *Los Angeles Times*, 1 Aug. 1990; interviews with Richard Martinez and Antonio Gonzalez of SVREP.

40. Interviews with Antonio Gonzalez and with Professor Jaime Regalado of California State University, Los Angeles.

41. National Association of Latino Elected Officials, *National Latino Immigration Survey*, pp. 21–22; David Ayon, "Hispanics and Voting Rights Issues in California: A Preliminary Exploration of Research and Evidence," unpublished paper, 1989, p. 29; Cain and Kiewiet, "Minorities in California," pp. I-10, I-33; Field Institute, "A Digest of California's Political Demography," p. 5; Carole Uhlaner, Bruce E. Cain, and D. Roderick Kiewiet, "Political Participation of Ethnic Minorities in the 1980's," *Political Behavior* 11, no. 3 (Sept. 1989): 212, 214–16; Bruce E. Cain and Ken McCue, "The Efficacy of Registration Drives," *Journal of Politics* 47 (1985): 1228–29.

42. Interview with University of California Regent Vilma S. Martinez; Raphael J. Sonenshein, "Continuity and Change in a Biracial Coalition: The 1989 Los Angeles Mayoral Election," paper presented at the Annual Meeting of the Western Political Science Association, Newport Beach, Calif., Mar. 1990, pp. 35–36.

43. Interviews with Carlos Navarro, Roberto Bustillo, Robin Kramer, Yolanda Chávez, and Rodolfo F. Acuña; Juan Gómez Quiñones, *Chicano Politics: Reality and Promise, 1940–1990* (Albuquerque: University of New Mexico Press, 1990), p. 195; Rodolfo O. de la Garza, Nestor Rodríguez, and Harry Pachon, "The Domestic and Foreign Policy Consequences of Mexican and Central American Immigration: Mexican-American Perspectives," in *Immigration and International Relations*, ed. Georges Vernez (Washington, D.C.: Urban Institute, May 1990), pp. 135–47; Jankowski, *City Bound*, p. 210; Hector Tobar, "Panel Urges Districts for Street Vendors," *Los Angeles Times*, 21 Dec. 1990. Cain and Kiewiet's poll data, though, indicate minimal ideological differences between Latinos of Mexican and Central American backgrounds; see "Minorities in California," p. I-10.

44. Interview with Dan Garcia, founder of the Tri-Ethnic Coalition; Mike Davis, *City of Quartz: Excavating the Future in Los Angeles* (New York: Verso Press, 1990), pp. 191–94; Grace Wai-Tse Siao, "Ethnic Coalition Eyes LA Basin's Transportation Issues," *Asian Week*, 16 Nov. 1990, p. 14; Robert Eshman, "Seeking a Common Language: Jews and Hispanics Move Toward the Year 2000," *Jewish Journal*, 31 May/6 June 1991, pp. 8, 10.

45. Interviews with Juana Gutierrez and Veronica Gutierrez, administrative assistant to Supervisor Gloria Molina; Eshman, "Seeking a Common Language," p. 8; Naomi Pfefferman, "Hispanic 'Old Friends,'" *Jewish Journal*, 31 May/6 June 1991, pp. 8, 10.

46. Sonenshein, "Biracial Coalition Politics," p. 43; Frank Clifford, "The Valley: An Urban Evolution," *Los Angeles Times*, 12 Aug. 1990; Jane Fritsch and Paul Feldman, "City Council Acts to Reinstate Gates, Despite Plea from Bradley," *Los Angeles Times*, 6 Apr. 1991; Rodolfo F. Acuña, "Leadership Demeaned by Moral Silence," *Los Angeles Times*, 6 May 1991.

47. Interviews with Veronica Gutierrez and David Diaz; Grace Wai-Tse Siao, "Lowe in Runoff for LA City Council," *Asian Week*, 7 June 1991, pp. 1, 13.

48. Boyarsky, "Crossover Dreams," pp. 12, 18; interviews with Robin Kramer, Juana Gutierrez, and Ray Garcia.

49. Interviews with Robin Kramer and Antonio Gonzalez. See also Charles P. Henry, "Black-Chicano Coalitions: Possibilities and Problems," *Western Journal of Black Studies* 44 (1980): 202–32.

50. Joel Kotkin, "New Interethnic Conflict Replaces an LA History of Biracial Politics," *Los Angeles Times*, 7 Feb. 1990.

51. Melvin Oliver and James Johnson, Jr., "Inter-Ethnic Conflict in an Urban Ghetto: The Case of Blacks and Latinos in Los Angeles," in *Research in Social Movements, Conflicts and Change*, ed. Richard Ratcliff (Greenwich, Conn.: JAI Press, 1984), pp. 57–94; Joseph N. Boyce, "Turf War: Struggle over Hospital in Los Angeles Pits Minority vs. Minority," *Wall Street Journal*, 1 Apr. 1991. Cf. Bruce E. Cain, Elizabeth Gerber, and Byran Jackson, "Blacks, Hispanics, Asians and Anglos: When Do They Coalesce?" unpublished paper, 1990, p. 9, and accompanying tables emphasizing high black "comfort levels" with Latinos. Also see Larry Aubry, "Black-Latino Conflict," *Los Angeles Sentinel*, 15 Mar. 1991, p. A5, and 22 Mar. 1991, p. A6; Frank Clifford, "Tension Among L.A. Minorities Changes the Old Rules of Politics," *Los Angeles Times*, 11 Aug. 1991; interview with Juana Gutierrez.

52. Interviews with Henry Lozano, Jaime Regalado, and Jorge Garcia; Quiñones, *Chicano Politics*, p. 73; Pfefferman, "Hispanic 'Old Friends,'" pp. 8, 10.

53. Robert Suro, "Hispanics in Despair," *New York Times*, 4 Nov. 1990; Merl, "Latinos Lagging"; interview with Armando Navarro.

54. Jean Merl, "New Ways Sought to Boost Latino Education," *Los Angeles Times*, 27 Jan. 1991; Suro, "Hispanics in Despair"; interview with Ed Avila.

55. Merl, "New Ways Sought"; Dick Kirschten, "Spending to Assimilate," *National Journal* 21, no. 35 (2 Sept. 1989): 2146–49; Ed Mandel, "Immigrant Education Funding Passes Hurdle," *San Diego Union*, 29 Jan. 1991; Jerry Gillam, "Wilson to Seek Funds for Immigrant Services," *Los Angeles Times*, 22 Nov. 1991.

56. Interviews with Juana Gutierrez, Frank del Olmo, and Carlos Navarro, and with Armando Navarro of the Institute for Social Justice.

57. Interviews with Frank del Omo, Juana Gutierrez, Veronica Gutierrez, and Dan Garcia.

58. Interview with Jesse Margarito.

59. Interviews with Juana Gutierrez and Jorge Garcia. For reflections on "working class environmentalism," see John R. Logan and Harvey L. Molotch, *Urban Fortunes: The Political Economy of Space* (Berkeley: University of California Press, 1987), pp. 220–23; Clarence Page, "Many Hues Blend with Green," *Los Angeles Times*, 20 Apr. 1990.

60. Interviews with Frank del Omo, Juana Gutierrez, David Diaz, and Rodolfo F. Acuña.

61. Jill Stewart, "Council OK's Huge Central City West Project," *Los Angeles Times*, 30 Jan. 1991; interview with Yolanda Chávez.

62. Interviews with Michael Diaz and Ray Garcia, founders of the Lincoln Heights Preservation Association.

63. Robert Reinhold, "Mexican Politicians Look North of Border," *New York Times*, 8 Dec. 1989. Francisco E. Balderrama, *In Defense of la Raza: The Los Angeles*

Mexican Consulate and the Mexican Community, 1929 to 1936 (Tucson: University of Arizona Press, 1982); Rodolfo O. de la Garza, "U.S. Foreign Policy and the Mexican-American Political Agenda," in *Ethnic Groups and U.S. Foreign Policy*, ed. Mohammed E. Ahari (New York: Greenwood Press, 1987), pp. 101–14.

64. José Angel Gutiérrez, "The Chicano in Mexican–North American Foreign Relations," in *Chicano-Mexican Relations*, ed. Tatcho Mindiola, Jr., and Max Martinez (Houston: Mexican American Studies Program, University of Houston, 1986), pp. 29–32; Rodolfo O. de la Garza, "Chicano-Mexican Relations: A Framework for Research," *Social Science Quarterly* 63, no. 1 (Mar. 1982): 115–30.

65. Rodolfo O. de la Garza, "Mexican Americans as a Political Force in the Borderlands: From Paisanos to Pochos to Potential Allies," in *Changing Boundaries in the Americas*, ed. Lawrence A. Herzog (Boulder, Colo.: Westview Press, 1992), pp. 6–9; Carlos González Gutiérrez, "The Mexican Diaspora in California: The Limits and Possibilities for the Mexican Government," this volume.

66. de la Garza, "Mexican Americans," pp. 10–12; Cathryn L. Thorup, "Democratization as an Issue in U.S.-Mexican Relations," translation of "Mexico-EU: la democratización y la agenda bilateral," *Nexos* 14, no. 162 (June 1991): 57–61.

67. de la Garza, "Mexican Americans," p. 13; Eshman, "Seeking a Common Language," p. 8; Fuchs, *American Kaleidoscope*, p. 356; Sam Fulwood III, "Rights Group Avoids Split with Latino Organizations," *Los Angeles Times*, 6 May 1990; Dick Kirschten, "Hispanics Seek More Recognition with Civil Rights Lobby," *National Journal* 22, no. 22 (19 May 1990): 1210–11; Henry Muller and John F. Stacks, "Interview with Governor Pete Wilson: 'There Is a Limit to What We Can Absorb,'" *Time*, 18 Nov. 1991, pp. 54–63.

68. Rodolfo O. de la Garza, "Chicanos as an Ethnic Lobby: Limits and Possibilities," in *Chicano-Mexican Relations*, p. 39; de la Garza, "Mexican Americans," p. 14; Cecelia Preciado and José Antonio Burciaga, "Prenuptial Jitters for Chicanos," *Los Angeles Times*, 29 Sept. 1991.

69. Cathryn Thorup, "The Politics of Free Trade and the Dynamics of Cross-Border Coalitions in U.S.-Mexican Relations," *Columbia Journal of World Business* 26, no. 2 (Summer 1991): 12–26.

70. Esteban E. Torres, "Our Back Doors Will Need Double Locks," *Los Angeles Times*, 7 June 1991; Leon E. Wynter, "Business and Race: Hispanic Institute Aims to Forge Ties with Japan," *Wall Street Journal*, 5 July 1991; Diego C. Asencio and Art Torres, "A Way to Cut Undocumented Immigration—But It's Not a Quick Cure," *Los Angeles Times*, 29 July 1990; Lawrence A. Herzog, *Where North Meets South: Cities, Space, and Politics on the U.S.-Mexico Border* (Center For Mexican American Studies, University of Texas at Austin, 1990), pp. 50–52, 170, 173.

71. Alexis de Tocqueville, *Democracy in America*, vol. 1, trans. Henry Reeve (New York: Vintage Books, 1945), pp. 251–53; Judith N. Shklar, *American Citizenship: The Quest for Inclusion* (Cambridge, Mass.: Harvard University Press, 1991), pp. 25–62; David E. Hayes-Bautista, Werner O. Schink, and Jorge Chapa, *The Burden of Support: Young Latinos in an Aging Society* (Stanford, Calif.: Stanford University Press, 1988), pp. 31–56; Carey McWilliams, *North from Mexico* (Philadelphia: J. B. Lippincott, 1949), p. 302.

12. González Gutiérrez: The Mexican Diaspora

This article was made possible by the support given me by several members of the Mexican community in Los Angeles, public officials at the Secretariat of External Relations in Mexico City, and the staff of the Consulate General of Mexico in Los Angeles. I want to express my special gratitude to José Angel Pescador for his backing, to Alina Flores Soto for her research assistance, and to Manuel García y Griego, Berenice Rendón, Jorge Mario Rosas, Graciela Orozco, and the authors of this volume for their comments. The observations in this paper are strictly my own and do not necessarily reflect the views of the Mexican government in general or the consulate in particular.

1. Although the term *diaspora* is usually associated with the dispersal of Jews from Israel, it is increasingly used in a more general way to refer to "any population which has migrated from its country of origin and settled in a foreign land, but maintains its continuity as a community." Milton J. Esman, "Diasporas and International Relations," in *Modern Diasporas in International Politics*, ed. Gabriel Sheffer (London: Croom-Helm, 1986), p. 333.

2. The official count of California's residents showed that the overall population of the state was 29,760,021 in 1990, up 23.7 percent from 1980. In Los Angeles County, the population rose 19 percent to 8,863,164. The city rose 17 percent to 3,485,398. *Los Angeles Times*, 11 Mar. 1991.

3. Antonio Ríos Bustamante and Pedro Castillo, *An Illustrated History of Mexican Los Angeles, 1781–1985* (Los Angeles: Chicano Studies Research Center, University of California Press, 1986), pp. 182–88.

4. David E. Hayes-Bautista, "Latino Health Indicators and the Underclass Model: From Paradox to New Policy Models," Ph.D. diss., University of California, Los Angeles, 1990, p. 24.

5. University of California SCR 43 Task Force, *The Challenge: Latinos in a Changing California* (Riverside: UC MEXUS, 1989), p. 19.

6. Juan Gómez Quiñones, *Reality and Promise: 1940–1990* (Albuquerque: University of New Mexico Press, 1990), p. 436.

7. Aída Hurtado and Carlos H. Arce, "Mexicans, Chicanos, Mexican-Americans, or Pochos . . . ¿Qué somos?: The Impact of Language and Nativity on Ethnic Labeling," *Aztlán: A Journal of Chicano Studies*, Spring 1986, p. 108.

8. Leo R. Chávez, "Settlers and Sojourners: The Case of Mexicans in the United States," *Human Organization* 47, no. 2 (1988): 95.

9. Frank D. Bean, Barry Edmonston, and Jeffrey S. Passel, "Undocumented Migration Since IRCA: An Overall Assessment," in *Undocumented Migration to the United States: IRCA and the Experience of the 1980s*, ed. Frank D. Bean, Barry Edmonston, and Jeffrey S. Passel (Washington, D.C.: Urban Institute Press, 1990), p. 260.

10. Immigration and Naturalization Service, *1989 Statical Yearbook of the Immigration and Naturalization Service* (Washington, D.C.: U.S. Department of Justice, 1990), p. xxiv.

11. Ibid., p. xxv.

12. Myron Weiner, "Labor Migrations as Incipient Diasporas," in Sheffer, *Modern Diasporas*, p. 66.

13. Wayne Cornelius, "Impacts of the 1986 Immigration Law on Emigration from Rural Mexican Communities," in Bean, Edmonston, and Passel, *Undocumented Migration*, p. 240.

14. Cathryn L. Thorup, "Más allá del romance bilateral," *Nexos* 146 (Feb. 1990): 59.

15. For a detailed discussion of the ways in which diasporas influence relations between states, see Esman, "Diasporas."

16. David Ayón and Ricardo Anzaldúa, "Latinos and U.S. Policy Toward Latin America" in *Latin America and Caribbean Contemporary Record: 1985–1986*, vol. 5, ed. Abraham Lowenthal (New York: Holmes and Meier, 1987), p. 138.

17. A joint poll made by *Univision* and *La Opinión* showed that 76 percent of Hispanics in the United States considered themselves positively interested in a free trade agreement. See Bill Richardson, "The United States–Mexico Free Trade Agreement: Prospects for Hispanics," *Heritage Lectures* 315 (15 May 1991): 2.

18. The lack of community organizations increased the visibility and importance of the consuls' job at a time when the Mexican *colonia* was battling to survive. In Los Angeles, Consul Rafael de la Colina and his staff routinely denounced discriminatory hiring practices against Mexicans, demanded an end to school segregation, and promoted the celebration of Mexican national holidays in the city. When the county decided to reduce welfare costs by forcing Mexican immigrants to go back to their homeland, de la Colina negotiated with local authorities for assistance with travel expenses for thousands of workers. He also played a leadership role in the founding of several community organizations to enlist the support of the entire *colonia* in providing food, shelter, and clothing to its impoverished members. See Francisco Balderrama, *In Defense of la Raza: The Los Angeles Mexican Consulate and the Mexican Community, 1929 to 1936* (Tucson: University of Arizona Press, 1982), pp. 1–52; Mercedes Carreras de Velazco, *Los mexicanos que devolvió la crisis* (Tlatelolco D.F.: Secretaría de Relaciones Exteriores, 1974), pp. 73–99; and Juan Gómez Quiñones, "Piedras contra la luna: México en Aztlán y Aztlán en México: Chicano-Mexican Relations and the Mexican Consulates, 1900–1920," in *Contemporary Mexico*, ed. James Wilkie, Michael C. Meyer, and Edna Monzón de Wilkie, Papers of the Fourth International Congress of Mexican History (Los Angeles: University of California Press, 1976).

19. Carlos Rico, "The Immigration Reform and Control Act of 1986 and Mexican Perceptions of Bilateral Approaches to Immigration Issues," in Vernez, *Immigration*, p. 50.

20. Jorge A. Chabat, "Algunas reflexiones en torno al papel de los consulados en la actual coyuntura," *Carta de Política Exterior Mexicana*, 7, no. 2 (Apr.–June 1987): 15; Secretaría de Relaciones Exteriores, *Ley Orgánica del Servicio Exterior Mexicano (LOSEM)* (México: Secretaría de Relaciones Exteriores, 1987).

21. Regional clubs are perhaps the most visible components of the social networks upon which massive immigration rests. According to Douglas A. Massey,

these networks consist of "kin and friendship relations that link Mexican sending communities to particular destinations in the United States. As these networks develop and mature, they dramatically reduce the costs of migration, inducing others to enter the migrant work force. Over time, therefore, international migration tends to become a self perpetuating social phenomenon." "The Social Organization of Mexican Migration to the United States," *Annals of the American Academy* 487 (Sept. 1986): 103.

22. The National Latino Immigrant Survey, produced recently by NALEO, showed that approximately 10 percent of legal Latino residents nationwide belong to a club of people from their home country, while 14 percent belong to a sports club. *The National Latino Immigrant Survey* (Washington, D.C.: NALEO Educational Fund, 1989), p. 22.

23. It is important to note that not all states are equally important as sources of Mexican immigrants. The nine top states are Baja California, Chihuahua, Guanajuato, Guerrero, Jalisco, Michoacán, Oaxaca, Sonora, and Zacatecas. See Comisión Sobre el Futuro de la Relaciones México–Estados Unidos, *El desafió de la interdependencia: México–Estados Unidos* (México: Fondo de Cultura Económica, 1988), p. 90; and Jesus Arroyo Alejandre Jesus, "Algunos impactos de la Ley de Control de Inmigración (IRCA) en una región de Jalisco de fuerte inmigración hacia Estados Unidos de Norte America," in Vernez, *Immigration*, p. 149. According to the statistics compiled by the Consulate General of Mexico in Los Angeles based on the number of applications for consular I.D.'s received, the main origins of immigrants to the Los Angeles area are as follows: Jalisco (29 percent), Michoacán (14.25 percent), Zacatecas (9.68 percent), Mexico City (6.51 percent), Guanajuato (4.86 percent), Durango (4.63 percent), Baja California Peninsula (3.86 percent), Chihuahua (3.78 percent), Sinaloa (3.39 percent) and Nayarit (2.53 percent). See Consulado General de México, "Reporte anual de actividades, 1990" (Los Angeles: Consulado General de México, 1991), p. 17.

24. Armando Navarro, "Impacto 2000 and Mexico: el plan de acercamiento" (San Bernardino, Calif.: Institute of Social Justice, 1989), p. 19; Southwest Voter Research Institute, "Latin America Project: A Three Year Hispanic Leadership Initiative," unpublished manuscript, 1988, pp. 8–9.

25. *La Opinión*, 16 May 1991.

26. Jorge A. Bustamante, "Migración indocumentada México–Estados Unidos: hallazgos preliminares del Proyecto Cañón Zapata," in Vernez, *Immigration*, p. 16; Armando Gutierrez, "The Chicano Elite in Chicano-Mexicano Relations," in *Chicano-Mexicano Relations*, ed. Tatcho Mendiola and Max Martinez (Houston: University of Houston Press, 1986), p. 50.

27. Jose Angel Gutierrez, "The Chicano in Mexicano-Norte Americano Foreign Relations" in Mendiola and Martinez, *Chicano-Mexicano Relations*, p. 24.

28. Ibid., p. 22.

29. Manuel Barrera, "Mexican Americans and U.S. Policy Toward Mexico," unpublished manuscript, 1988, p. 43.

30. The discussion that follows is based to a great extent on conversations with the staff of the DGMCA office, headed by Dr. Roger Díaz de Cossío. I would like

to express my gratitude to him and his staff, specially Graciela Orozco, Alfonso Ramón Bagur, and Arturo Unanue.

31. *New York Daily News*, 16 May 1991.

13. *Rico: Managing Mexico's California Connection*

1. A few reminders clearly suggest the extent of that relevance. At the end of the 1980s, for example, California accounted for $8 billion of the $52 billion in Mexico-U.S. trade. Jaime Olivares, "California podría aprovechar muchas ventajas económicas con el Tratado de Libre Comercio," *La Opinión*, 13 May 1991. A considerable proportion of bilateral border interactions takes place in the relatively small but extremely lively stretch of the state's territory that touches on Mexico. From the problems associated with pollution of shared natural resources to instances of racism, which may end up affecting the overall political climate of the relation, the California border raises significant challenges for Mexican foreign policy. The five and a half miles west of the San Ysidro border station, for example, have the most intense concentration of undocumented crossings along the entire border. San Diego–based Border Patrol agents recorded almost 250,000 apprehensions in the first half of the 1990–91 fiscal year, nearing the record levels of the mid-1980s. The patrol, in fact, records more than half of its total detentions along the border, in San Diego. Patrick McDonnell, "A Commanding View of No-Man's Land," *Los Angeles Times*, San Diego County Edition, 7 July 1991. Baja California communities such as Tijuana, in turn, account for the largest number of *maquiladoras* in all of Mexico. *Twin Plant News*, 6, no. 12 (July 1991): 84.

2. In specific reference to the California border, for example, water administration problems have been taken by Mexican authors as examples of how "the commitment of the U.S. federal government may be paralyzed by local interests." Federico Salas, "La resolución de los conflictos en la frontera México–Estados Unidos. El caso de los recursos acuíferos compartidos," in Olga Pellicer, ed., *La política exterior de México: desafíos en los ochentas* (México: Centro de Investigación y Docencia Económicas, 1983), p. 132. The more recent experience of the late 1980s and early 1990s gives further reasons to emphasize the federal dimension. For one, it reminds us of the crucial role that the central authorities of the U.S. political system, and in particular the president, play in setting the overall tone of bilateral relations.

3. On the Mexican side, for example, there is a greater federal involvement in issues such as water and sewer systems, road construction, or the administration of school systems. The more relevant agencies on the Mexican side in relation to policy objectives such as *maquiladora* development are also not local or state agencies but the delegations of the Secretaría de Comercio y Fomento Industrial in Mexicali and Tijuana. Higher federal priority and involvement is clear as well in other issue areas, such as the management of marine resources. Even if both the Department of the Interior and the Department of State are involved in questions related to endangered species and marine mammals, relative levels of priority in the respective federal agendas is reflected in the fact that the Mexican Secretaría de

Pesca has ten times as many employees as the National Marine Fisheries Service. Biliana Cicin-Sain et al., "Conflictual Interdependence: United States-Mexican Relations on Fishery Resources," *Natural Resources Journal* 26, no. 4 (Fall, 1986).

4. The Mexican-American war of the nineteenth century, the 1853 capture of La Paz and Ensenada by William Walker of Central American fame, and what is perceived south of the border as the persistence of initiatives on the part of various Californians to appropriate parts of Baja California in the more recent past have given particular connotations to this area in the Mexican imagination. Issues considered relatively "minor" from the vantage point of the U.S. federal government truly become questions of sovereignty—even the most basic juridical and territorial sovereignty—when looked at from the Mexico City perspective.

5. Jorge Bustamante, "Frontera Norte: Integración Nacional y Política Exterior," paper presented at the Third Coloquio Nacional de Estudios Fronterizos, Mexico City, El Colegio de México, 3–4 Dec. 1984, p. 19.

6. Thus, Kaare Kjos, from the Department of Planning and Land Use of the county of San Diego, argued in the mid-1980s that "just as sewage flows and the winds blow in total disregard of international boundaries, so should our planning efforts transcend the arbitrary line just a little bit to the south." "Trans-Boundary Land-Use Planning: A View from San Diego County," in Lawrence A. Herzog, *Planning the International Border Metropolis: Trans-Boundary Policy Options for the San Diego-Tijuana Region*, Monograph Series 19 (La Jolla, Calif.: Center for U.S-Mexican Studies, UCSD, 1986), pp. 5, 21. A similar point has been made by UCSD professor Lawrence A. Herzog: "Discussions of trans-border land use and planning must transcend national sovereignty because some activities and land uses, such as hospitals and shopping centers, are inherently binational." Herzog, *Planning the International Border Metropolis*, p. 7.

7. Brian Bilbray, "Remarks," in Herzog, *Planning the International Border Metroplis*, p. 97.

8. Canadian provinces and U.S. states, for example, have signed a variety of agreements that, in spite of what some observers consider their dubious legal enforceability, provide the basic ground rules of the relation. In some cases, provincial governments have forced the reopening of negotiations between the federal governments even after treaties had been signed between them. J. Owen Saunders, ed., *Managing Natural Resources in a Federal State* (Toronto: Carswell, 1986), p. 279.

9. See, for example, Jonathan P. West, "Informal Policy Making Along the Arizona–Mexico International Border," *Arizona Review* 27 (2): 1–8. Quoted in Milton Jamail and Scott J. Ullery, *International Water Use Relations Along the Sonoran Desert Borderlands*, (Tucson: University of Arizona Office of Arid Lands Studies, 1979), p. 20.

10. Mexican migration, for instance, raises at least three different sets of issues, each with a different geographical location, in relation to which California plays a key role. First, California constitutes a particularly interesting example of the problems associated with efforts to manage and control the flows themselves, the relevance of which is directly related to the importance of a given area as a point of

crossing. This dimension of the problem is centered on the border area, in spite of enforcement efforts conducted by U.S. immigration authorities throughout the state. Second, the impact on the economic and social life of migrants who do cross the border extends all over the state. The third dimension involves cities and communities where migrants reside, Los Angeles in particular, and revolves around the provision of services and the potential violation of those Mexican residents' rights.

11. "With respect to tuna harvesting on the Pacific coast, in August 1983 the San Pedro–based Fishermen's Cooperative Association (representing the nearshore tuna fleet, composed mainly of older, small vessels) independently concluded an agreement with the Secretaría de Pesca officials in Mexico City for the resumption of tuna harvesting by these U.S. tuna boats in Mexican waters. This agreement was accomplished through very informal channels. A Los Angeles city councilman acted as the liaison between the Mexican officials and the tuna cooperative, with no involvement on the part of U.S. officials." Cicin-Sain et al., "Conflictual Interdependence," p. 791.

12. The elimination in March of 1991 of the Governor's Office of California-Mexico Affairs, which in the previous administration had been located within the governor's cabinet, has not been perceived by Mexican federal authorities as a good omen for the future, a concern reinforced by Governor Wilson's background as a firm critic of Mexico both as mayor of San Diego and as U.S. senator. State officials, on the other hand, are on record as opposing such interpretation of developments in the early 1990s. Francisco Herrera, assistant to governor Pete Wilson for international affairs, for example, has pointed out that the changes introduced in the office—its functions were transferred to the Office of International Affairs, and state officials charged specifically with Mexico were moved to San Diego—reflects the governor's interest in relations with Mexico. Jaime Olivares, "California podría aprovechar muchas ventajas económicas." Some Mexican observers have also noted a "change in the tone of [Wilson's] speeches, showing enthusiasm for the reforms introduced by President Salinas de Gortari." Instituto de Estudios de Estados Unidos, Centro de Investigación y Docencia Económicas, "Perfiles biográficos: los gobernadores electos de California, Florida y Texas y el nuevo asiento demócrata en el Senado," *Estados Unidos, Informe Trimestral* 1, no. 0 (Oct.–Dec. 1990): 36.

13. At the end of May, 1991, for example, San Diego's mayor, Maureen O'Connor, visited Mexico City and had interviews with the highest levels of the Mexican government. Those interviewed went all the way from her counterpart in Mexico City—the "Regente de la Ciudad," Manuel Camacho, appointed by the president—to the head of the Mexican negotiating team for the North American Free Trade Agreement, Herminio Blanco; the undersecretary of foreign relations, Sergio González Gálvez; and the secretario de comunicaciones y transportes, Andrés Caso Lombardo; to President Salinas. The ten-member delegation included representatives of the business and banking sectors, among them a vice-president for general affairs from SANYO of North America, members of her team and of the city council. Both a representative of the U.S. Embassy—then Minister Robert Pastorino—and the Director of the California Office in Mexico, Carlos Valde-

rrama, accompanied Mayor O'Connor during her visit. The wide array of issues in which Mexican/federal–California/local contacts may have a role to play was summarized in topics covered during her visit. Although officially a "trade mission," other issues such as tourism, efforts to change the image of San Diego as a result of the violence that took place on the border with Tijuana during 1990, and in particular the emerging reputation of south San Diego as a "danger zone" for Mexicans were also included in the talks. Very high on O'Connor's agenda was a proposal to build an "international airport on the San Diego–Tijuana border" which would include interconnecting terminals and shared services on both sides of the border. This initiative was based on a proposal to build a new airport approved by the San Diego city council. Selling points included the potential increase in trade in services and economic benefits to the area: "This airport would fully serve the air carrier needs *of the region* for the foreseeable future, and would help further insert San Diego and Baja California in the Pacific Rim economy." City of San Diego, Office of the Mayor, *Setting the Course for Binational Relations in the 90's*; San Diego Trade Mission to Mexico City led by Mayor Maureen O'Connor, 27–29 May 1991; emphasis mine. Differences in perception with Mexican authorities quickly emerged. What for the mayor and her delegation seemed to be technical questions involved much larger issues from the perspective of Mexico City. The sensitive issues went all the way from sovereignty to noise pollution. Mexican authorities initially responded by presenting an alternative proposal based on the example of the Geneva airport, aimed at increasing, with Mexican resources, the Tijuana airport's handling capacity to 20 million passengers, allowing it to serve both cities. A terminal on the San Diego side would be constructed, financed with U.S. resources, where U.S. passengers could document their flights. The de facto integration of transportation services in both communities would be recognized, but the principle of territorial sovereignty would also be respected. Opposition also emerged on the U.S. side of the border.

14. I am using this term in direct reference to Hugh Heclo's "Issue Networks and the Executive Establishment," in Anthony King, ed., *The New American Political System* (Washington, D.C.: American Enterprise Institute for Public Policy Research, 1978).

15. There is, for example, a clear need and much room for activities aimed at modifying the stereotypes of Mexico and Mexicans dominant in the state. Californians may think they "know Mexico" better than other Americans, but their notions are too often limited and based on their contacts with only one group of Mexicans, undocumented workers in their state. An element of rejection may be unavoidable in such a context, less because of racist attitudes than of the sense of otherness resulting from significant differences in cultural values, education, and socio-economic status. Distorted images of Mexico also form an integral part of southern California's popular culture, as attested by the recurrence of "Tia Juana" as metaphor for easy sex, corruption, and general debauchery in both film and literature.

16. The California Office of Trade and Investment was created on 15 February 1989 by then governor George Deukmejian as part of a concerted effort to promote

California trade, independent of parallel activities on the part of the federal government. The Mexico City office is one of five offices of representation the state has around the world—the others are in England, Germany, Hong Kong and Japan. The focus is on export promotion activities, an objective that, according to its director in the early 1990s, Carlos Valderrama, took 85–90 percent of his time. Quoted in Olivares, "California podría aprovechar." Other objectives include the promotion of California technology and capital and the establishment of contacts with Mexican enterprises that may want to invest in California. See, for example, Oficina de Comercio e Inversiones de California en México, "California y la Inversión Extranjera," *El Financiero*, 29 Jan. 1991, p. 41.

17. Interview by the author with Claudia Franco, Director for Political Affairs at the Dirección General de América del Norte, Secretaría de Relaciones Exteriores, 19 July 1991.

18. The third consular agency is located in Tucson, Arizona, where Mexico has neither a general consulate nor a career consulate. Consular agencies are "órganos desconcentrados" of a general consulate.

19. In addition to its general consulates, career consulates, and consular agencies, Mexico has 59 consular sections and 114 honorary consulates, of which 11 are in the United States, but none in California. Information provided by the Dirección General de Asuntos Consulares, Secretaría de Relaciones Exteriores, México. At least in the case of the career consulates, the greater number reflects the length of the Texas border with México.

20. Interview by the author with the Director General del Servicio Consular, Eduardo Ibarrola, Secretaría de Relaciones Exteriores, 19 July 1991.

21. Ibid.

22. Stephen P. Mumme, *Continuity and Change in U.S.-Mexico Land and Water Relations: The Politics of the International Boundary and Water Commission*, Working Paper No. 77 (Woodrow Wilson International Center for Scholars, Latin American Program, 1981), p. 1. A Mexican evaluation along similar lines by a member of the SRE may be found in Marco Antonio Alcázar Avila, "El papel del agua como frontera entre México y los Estados Unidos de Norteamérica," in *Ingeniería Hidráulica en México* 4, no. 1 (Jan.–Apr. 1989). A somewhat more critical account may be found in Jamail and Ullery, *International Water Use Relations.*

23. Mumme, *Continuity and Change*, p. 7.

24. Ultimately enacted as a categorical grant, SLIAG requires not only strict and detailed guidelines, complex regulatory procedures, and communication among federal, state, and local authorities but the coordination of "policy across traditionally separate public health, public assistance, and education organizations at both the state and local levels." Lin C. Liu, *IRCA's State Legalization Impact Assistance Grants (SLIAG): Early Implementation* (Santa Monica, Calif.: RAND Corporation, 1991), p. vi.

25. Brian Bilbray, "Remarks," p. 73.

26. Cornelius "Foreword," in Herzog, *Planning the International Border Metropolis*, p. v.

27. Carlos Graizbord, "Trans-Boundary Land-Use Planning: A Mexican Perspective," in Herzog, *Planning the International Border Metropolis*, p. 14.

28. From the perspective of Mexico City, for example, reining in border violence is important not only in and of itself but also on account of the already mentioned potential impact of specific incidents on the overall political climate of the bilateral relation. There is, however, a significant degree of tension between the practical steps Mexican federal authorities may have to take to control border violence, on the one hand, and the way in which those actions may be explained on either side of the border, on the other. In the early 1990s this issue tended to receive increasing attention on the part of Mexican federal authorities as a result, in good measure, of a series of incidents that took place along the California border. They took a series of measures reflecting their interpretation of the roots of that situation. Three different dimensions of violence in the area were identified by Mexican federal authorities: actions committed by Mexicans against Mexicans in Mexican territory; acts of violence against Mexicans—mostly undocumented migrants—on the other side of the border by non-governmental actors; and "institutional violence" on the part of U.S. authorities against Mexican citizens, again mostly undocumented migrants. Mexican authorities demanded a halt to the last and understood that to combat both delinquent and racially motivated violence, actions would have to be taken on the Mexican side. The result was the creation in 1990 of the Beta Group, a program involving around thirty police officers chosen from federal, local, and state departments, placed directly under the orders of the Mexican undersecretary of the interior, Miguel Limón, and charged with the fight against delinquent elements on the Mexican side involved in border violence. In practice, the Beta Group established direct lines of communication with U.S. authorities such as the Border Patrol. A radio frequency was assigned for that purpose, and there followed a significant exchange of information between police and immigration authorities on each side of the border regarding groups of delinquents who were perceived as being involved in border violence. The kinds of political realities involved in the problems of communication I am trying to illustrate, however, made it necessary for Mexican authorities to play down the collaboration that such an exercise inevitably involves. As a result, when incidents of violence dropped sharply during the following year, Mexican officials had to content themselves with watching as the U.S. Border Patrol claimed the credit. The patrol argued that the positive results reflected a new strategy on their part aimed at channeling potential undocumented migrants towards points where they were more easily controlled by improved lighting in particularly conflictual areas and reinforcing "the fence" with air force surplus landing mats.

29. Marco Antonio Alázar Avila, "El papel del agua como frontera entre México y los Estados Unidos de Norteamérica," *Ingeniería Hidráulica en México* 4, no. 1, (Jan.–Apr. 1989): 22.

30. Doubts may be raised, for example, regarding the economic potential of the state. Reuters dispatch: "California, el estado dorado, pierde su brillo," *El Economista*, 5 July 1991. The possibilities of developing other than *maquiladora* opera-

tions (to achieve, for example, a greater degree of vertical integration of production on the Mexican side of the border) in a relatively isolated setting such as the westernmost end of the Mexican border may also be questioned.

31. See, for example, Todd Eisenstadt, "Cabildeo y relaciones públicas en Estados Unidos," *Este País: Tendencias y Opiniones* 15 (June 1992): 2–21.

14. Burgess and Lowenthal: Enhancing California's Mexico Connection

1. *California Population Statistics* (Palo Alto, Calif.: Center for the Continuing Study of the California Economy, 1988), p. 51.
2. "Number of Latino Firms Increasing Sharply, Study Says," *Los Angeles Times*, 16 May 1991.
3. Bank of America, "California, Mexico, and the North American Free Trade Agreement," *Economic and Business Outlook*, Sept.–Oct. 1991, p. 3.
4. Jonathan Beatty and Richard Hornick, "A Torrent of Dirty Dollars," *Time*, 18 Dec. 1989, p. 55.
5. Larry Rohter, "Bustling Tijuana Lives Down Hooch and Honky Tonk Past," *New York Times*, 2 Aug. 1989.
6. Valdemar de Murguia, *Capital Flight and Economic Crisis: Mexican Post-Devaluation Exiles in a California Community*, Research Report Series 44 (La Jolla: University of California, San Diego, 1986), pp. 6–7.
7. Ibid., p. 24.
8. This jobs figure is derived by a multiplier developed by the U.S. Department of Commerce, which estimates that every $40,000 worth of exports translates into one direct or indirect job.
9. Paul Ong, *The Widening Divide: Income Inequality and Poverty in Los Angeles* (Los Angeles: Research Group on the Los Angeles Economy, 1989), p. 5.
10. Ibid., p. 6.
11. Thomas Muller and Thomas J. Espenshade, *The Fourth Wave: California's Newest Immigrants* (Washington, D.C.: Urban Institute Press, 1985), p. 54.
12. Bruce Stokes, "Boom at the Border," *National Journal*, 29 July 1989, p. 1924.
13. Muller and Espenshade, *Fourth Wave*, pp. 149–50.
14. Wayne Cornelius, "The Persistence of Immigrant-Dominated Firms and Industries in the United States: The Case of California," paper presented at the Second Franco-American Conference on Comparative Migration Studies, Paris, France, 20–23 June 1988.
15. *L.A. 2000: A City for the Future* (Los Angeles: Los Angeles 2000 Committee, 1988), p. 62.
16. Richard Rothstein, "Free Trade Scam," *LA Weekly*, 17–23 May 1991.
17. Muller and Espenshade, *Fourth Wave*, p. 93.
18. Paul Schimek in Ong, *Widening Divide*, p. 38.
19. David Hayes-Bautista, Werner O. Schink, and Jorge Chapa, *The Burden of Support: Young Latinos in an Aging Society* (Stanford, Calif.: Stanford University Press, 1988), p. 113.

20. *Statistical Abstract of the United States* (Washington, D.C.: Bureau of the Census, U.S. Department of Commerce, 1990).

21. Ong, *Widening Divide*, p. 18.

22. *L.A. 2000*, p. 52.

23. Jack Citrin, "Public Opinion in a Changing California," in *The Capacity to Respond: California Political Institutions Face Change*, ed. Terry K. Bradshaw and Charles G. Bell (Berkeley: Institute of Governmental Studies, 1987), p. 57.

24. Miles Corwin, "Caustic Comments: Mayor of Santa Maria Fuels Recall Effort with His Criticism of Latinos and Gays," *Los Angeles Times*, 5 Aug. 1991.

25. Barbarah Koh, "Close the U.S. Border, Mayor Says," *Los Angeles Times*, 28 Mar. 1991.

26. See, for example, Muller and Espenshade, *Fourth Wave*; and McCarthy and Burciaga Valdez, *Current and Future Effects of Mexican Immigration on California* (Santa Monica, Calif.: RAND Corporation, 1985).

27. For a useful review of these principles, see David Osborne, "Government That Means Business," *New York Times Magazine*, 1 Mar. 1992, pp. 20–28.

28. David Osborne and Ted Gaebler, *Reinventing Government: How the Entrepreneurial Spirit Is Transforming the Public Sector* (Reading, Mass.: Addison-Wesley, 1992).

29. Bank of America, "California," p. 4.

Index

In this index "f" after a number indicates a separate reference on the next page, and "ff" indicates separate references on the next two pages. A continuous discussion over two or more pages is indicated by a span of numbers. *Passim* is used for a cluster of references in close but not consecutive sequence.

Library of Congress Cataloging-in-Publication Data

The California-Mexico connection / edited by Abraham F. Lowenthal and Katrina Burgess.
p. cm.
Includes bibliographical references (p.) and index.
ISBN 0-8047-2188-2 (acid-free paper) : — ISBN 0-8047-2187-4 (pbk. : acid-free paper) :
1. Mexican Americans—California. I. Lowenthal, Abraham F.
II. Burgess, Katrina.
F870.M5C35 1993
303.48'2794072—dc20
92-45247 CIP

∞ This book is printed on acid-free paper. It has been typeset in 10/12 Galliard by G&S Typesetters, Inc.

AMERICAN RIVER COLLEGE LIBRARY
4700 College Oak Drive
Sacramento, California 95841